My Brother's Keeper

A Memoir and a Message

By Amitai Etzioni

ROWMAN & LITTLEFIELD PUBLISHERS, INC.
Lanham • Boulder • New York • Oxford

ROWMAN & LITTLEFIELD PUBLISHERS, INC.

Published in the United States of America
by Rowman & Littlefield Publishers, Inc.
A Member of the Rowman & Littlefield Publishing Group
4501 Forbes Blvd., Suite 200, Lanham, Maryland 20706
www.rowmanlittlefield.com

PO Box 317
Oxford
OX2 9RU, UK

Distributed by National Book Network

British Library Cataloguing in Publication Information Available

Library of Congress Cataloging-in-Publication Data

Etzioni, Amitai.
 My brother's keeper : a memoir and a message / by Amitai
Etzioni.
  p. cm.
 Includes bibliographical references and index.
 ISBN 0-7425-2158-3 (hardcover : alk. paper)
 1. Communitarianism. I. Title.
HM758. E895 2003
303.3'72—dc21   2002012981

Printed in the United States of America

♾™ The paper used in this publication meets the minimum requirements of
American National Standard for Information Sciences—Permanence of Paper for
Printed Library Materials, ANSI/NISO Z39.48-1992.

Other Books by Amitai Etzioni

The Monochrome Society (2001)

The Limits of Privacy (1999)

The New Golden Rule:
Community and Morality in a Democratic Society (1996)

The Spirit of Community:
The Reinvention of American Society (1993)

The Moral Dimension:
Toward a New Economics (1988)

Capital Corruption:
The New Attack on American Democracy (1984)

An Immodest Agenda:
Rebuilding America Before the Twenty-First Century (1983)

Genetic Fix:
The Next Technological Revolution (1973)

The Active Society:
A Theory of Societal and Political Processes (1968)

Political Unification:
A Comparative Study of Leaders and Forces (1965)

Modern Organizations (1964)

A Comparative Analysis of Complex Organizations (1961)

For other books and books in other languages see our website:
www.communitariannetwork.org

Never doubt that a small group of thoughtful, committed citizens can change the world; indeed, it's the only thing that ever has!

—Margaret Mead

Contents

Part IV—LAUNCHING THE COMMUNITARIAN PROJECT

Part V—OVERSEAS

Part VI—IMPACT

Part VII—COMING TOGETHER

Figure List

Preface

My Brother's Keeper: A Memoir and a Message

Memoirs are supposed to be candid; so here, with your indulgence, I go. As far back as I can remember, I wanted to make a mark on the world. A big one would be great, but a small improvement was a hell of a lot better than none. What was much less clear, for years on end, was if the word is mightier than the sword. They say that Israelis learn to kill before they learn to make love. I cannot vouch for the validity of this claim. But, growing up in the pioneering Jewish communities that preceded the formation of Israel, I did learn to fire away on a submachine gun long before on a typewriter, and I learned the agonies of war before I discovered the joys of learning. I served as a commando well before I became a student. It was here that I passionately embraced, and ever since offered unto others, my first insight: the abhorrence of violence.

If you are now raising your eyebrows, wondering, "Israel? I thought this guy was Italian?" you are in good company. Numerous people are so sure that I am Italian that they address me in that beautiful tongue, which I regret to say I do not understand one bit. Frank Sinatra invited me to join the *Italian* Anti-Defamation League. I was offered a high post at a Catholic girls college, an invitation that was gently but quickly rescinded once I explained that I was Jewish. In fact, both my first and last names are Hebrew ones, which I acquired growing up in Israel in the 1940s, dropping the names given to me at birth in Germany in 1929, shortly before that country was overtaken by the Nazis. (*Amitai* comes from *Emet*, which means "truth" in Hebrew. The meaning of *Etzioni* is a story whose telling I need to briefly defer.)

Although I was born in Germany, my formative years were spent in the early, idealistic days of the cooperative Jewish settlements, in pre-Israel, Palestine. In those days, the country was quite different from what it has since become; it was strongly imbued with the spirit of community (from which the term *communitarian* arises); most people were dedicated to serving the common good and to erecting a home for Jews escaping Nazi-dominated Europe. It was in that pre-Israel that I first knew the high that one gains when serving a cause greater than self. After a year in a kibbutz, I also acquired both a sense of the virtue of community—and how oppressive it can become when its bonds bundle you too tightly.

And it was in Israel, once the fighting that had engulfed the country from day one had died down (temporarily, I hate to say), that I traded bullets for Buber. Studying with Martin Buber, I was introduced to communitarian philosophy and sociology. He taught me the special importance of not allowing the instruments that we fashion to serve us to take over and become our masters, the way the clay-made golem did. He argued for treating our fellow human beings with full respect rather than as tools to serve our purpose. Soon, I demanded to know, as only a newly minted, fresh freshman might, what it would take to make a society live up to these ideas. (See part I: From Bullets to Buber.)

Upon completing my studies, I acquired my first teaching job, at Columbia University, where I became entangled in what amounts to a subplot of this book: how, in the quest for a better world, to draw on (and contribute to) *both* academic work and social action. Those who attempt this double task, referred to as "public intellectuals," have often been skewered (most recently in a book-length tirade by Richard Posner) precisely for leading a double life, part professor, part public voice, not true to either. I tried to be a pure academic, but time and again, and one more time, I encountered conditions that cried out for my attention; matters I could not merely study—and let be. This urge to mix in is one source of the title of this book.

In the Old Testament, when Cain tells the Lord that he does not know the whereabouts of Abel (whom Cain killed)—asking rhetorically, "Am I my brother's keeper?"—this is viewed as a double sin: slaying a brother and misleading the Lord. However, over the centuries, especially in the recent age of relativism, being one's brother's keeper—rather than denying it—has acquired a negative hue. We are no longer supposed to mind other people's business. It is a notion I came to challenge.

I discovered—what should have been all too obvious from the get go—that ideas have no wings and do not fly on their own. For those ideas I particularly cared for, I had to raise my voice in the public marketplace. Hence, this is not mainly an account of "I have been" and "I have seen," but a story about ideas that I found—and still very much find—of great import and power, and what I learned trying to make ideas fly.

The main issues that I engaged in over forty-five years line up by the decades that framed them. During the rebellious sixties, I was very much part of the critical opposition. As someone who knew war, I cut my teeth on public action in my new homeland, the United States of America, opposing the nuclear arms race and the Vietnam War. (The questions raised at the time regarding what conditions justify striking others—what constitutes a just war—are still very much with us, as we are debating how far to go in preventing terrorist attacks.) On the lighter side, very light indeed, I got a mini-chance to practice what I was preaching: during the student riots at Columbia University in 1968, I joined a line of professors who, fearing violence, separated the jocks who were trying to flush out the left-leaning students who occupied several of the campus buildings. (We were shoved plenty by both sides but the jocks were more polite about it. After one of them planted his elbows deep in my rib cage, he muttered, "Sorry, sir," but he hardly stopped pushing.)

In the midst of teaching, researching, and demonstrating against the nuclear arms race, the FBI popped into my life like a jack-in-the-box. They set such a neat trap that I firmly believe my grandchildren will regale theirs with the story. For me, it was a lesson, as only experience can teach—that safeguarding our rights is more than an abstract classroom exercise in civics.

In the second half of the 1960s a new issue demanded my attention. President Kennedy made man's first trip to the moon (Project Apollo) the major national priority. I raised grave doubts about the merit of this investment compared to others—less technologically rich, but more socially relevant—right down here on earth, in our inner cities and natural environment. It was a very lonely mission. Next to nobody shared my misgivings—at the time.

By the early seventies, a less frenetic decade, during a personal quest, I stumbled upon early bioengineering projects. In vitro fertilization was close at hand (the first in vitro baby, Louise Joy Brown, was born July 25, 1978); there was a lot of discussion of parents going gene shopping and having designer babies with blue eyes, blonde hair, and Einstein's IQ. Some even reinvoked the racist ideas of eugenics to "improve our gene pool." All these developments posed very challenging moral issues. (Granted, I had no inkling of the enormity of the genie that biology was releasing.) The main question I raised is an old one but also one that is still very much with us, as the debate about stem cell research shows: *who is in charge?* Will society have to adapt to whatever scientists brew in their labs—or will our elected officials and community leaders, benefiting from the counsel of ethicists and public moral dialogues, have an effective say in the matter? My modest suggestions to begin to deal with the matter were quite well received. Implementation was and is a rather different matter.

Somewhere in the middle of all this, the same jack-in-the-box popped into my life again. I found myself on Nixon's enemies list.

As the seventies turned into the eighties, as the society, once sharply divided over the Vietnam War, began to heal, I moved from being an outsider, a member of the critical opposition, to the seat of power, Washington D.C., to serve as a senior adviser in the Carter White House. Here, I became so alarmed and enraged by the ill effects of economics on public policy and public morals that I worked long and hard to make a case for a different approach to shoring up the nation's material and social foundations.

Upon leaving the White House, I continued to work on developing an economics that was based on stronger sociological and psychological foundations than the prevailing ones and an economics that was based on higher moral ground than self-interest. A million or more students are taught economics each year, and it influences much of public thinking, biasing it in an amoral way that calls out to be corrected.

My year in the Carter White House was a sort of graduate study in social action: once I saw firsthand the ways political power can checkmate sound ideas, I thought I was reasonably ready to engage in my crowning project. But there was one more lesson in the offing, one that all who make plans, set priorities, and devise strategies too often overlook: there are forces beyond anyone's control. Hit hard by a personal tragedy, which struck without any warning, I was sent reeling for years to come.

As the eighties ended, I was desperately seeking to a change in venue. I jumped at an offer to teach ethics for two years at the Harvard Business School. I admit, to my regret, in the pages that follow that as a teacher of ethics to our brightest and best—the future leaders of American business and society—I failed. At best, I rated a big incomplete. The "B" School, as it is immodestly called by friends and foes, enabled me to launch a new economics (I called it "socio-economics"), drawing on what I learned from Martin Buber and my own studies. It is one of my ideas that has sprouted some wings, but has a long flight ahead of it.

Looking back on these three decades, the ideas I helped forge were on the side of the angels (at least so I still hold) and landed some telling punches. Laboring with others, messages were formulated that mobilized some members of the public to oppose the war in Vietnam, to consider the implications of bioengineering, and so on. However, none of these projects delivered the kind of significant changes in policies, institutions, and hearts that were called for. Finding no ready text for social activists to follow (one reason for these musings), I did learn some from each of my dry and half-wet attempts.

Only when I turned sixty, as the nineties rolled on, did I truly hit my stride. Because my life as a public intellectual turned at this point, a word about motives. There are those who are sure to suggest that all this talk about caring about ideas, and seeking to make them count, is but a thin veneer laid on to cover a naked quest for fame and money. They should read on. Let me just say for now that in the first three decades of my life as an activist professor I gained mainly abuse. It came in droves from those of my colleagues who firmly believed that a professor should stick to his knitting; from conservatives who thought that my opposition to the arms race made me a "pinko" if not a "traitor" (and much worse); from politicians who slammed the door shut; and from a press that was often indifferent. I received enough rejection slips for op-eds I had written that I could have made a doorstop out of them. (See part II: In Opposition.)

All this changed in 1990. The ideas I had been grappling with throughout my life somehow congealed into a coherent whole and—to my utter amazement—sprouted wings. Indeed, they started a social movement or at least a "move-let"! Lest you say, "Sure, sure, and how many mountains have you recently moved?" let me point to 156 publications that referred to the "communitarian movement" that popped up in a limited computer search. Moreover, I have often been dubbed "the founder and the leader" of the movement and, less kindly, its "guru" and "godfather."

I had long asked myself the question, how do societies change in a big way—other than under the prodding of an occupying army? I found only one answer: when a social movement arises. This was true about societies as different as Soviet Russia (under socialism), the United States (under the impact of movements such as the progressive to civil rights ones), and Israel (created by the Zionist movement).

The movement I helped launch has a much greater reach than its esoteric name "communitarian" might make you think. It addresses the same basic challenging *questions* raised by the Christian right, Islamic true believers, and Orthodox Jews—but provides fundamentally different *answers*. These questions concern what is right (and what is wrong); which moral and social values should guide our lives; what we owe our children, parents, neighbors, and the rest of the world; and what we live for (or at least ought to). But instead of answering these questions with simple, by-the-book, rigid answers and seeking to enforce them by some religious authorities or the government, communitarian answers are profoundly democratic. I do not mean by this that a majority of the votes cast determines what is moral, but that our conception of right and wrong are encountered through moral dialogues that are open and inclusive. It is a persuasive morality, not a coercive one. But I am getting ahead of the story.

The apple that hit my forehead, calling attention to the need for a communitarian message, was a finding that numerous Americans, while keen to uphold their right to be tried by a jury of their peers if charged with a crime, were equally keen to wiggle out of the obligation to serve on a jury. They seemed unaware that rights entail a responsibility; that if the peers will not serve, there cannot be a jury of peers. Moreover, that it is indecent to take from the community and not be willing to give anything back.

Once I became aware and deeply concerned about the imbalance between the strong sense of entitlement many Americans had and their meager sense of obligation to the society at large, I saw it reflected in numerous places. For instance, for years on end, the majority of Americans has strongly favored less government (and lower taxes), but has sought more government services of all kinds—from housing to transportation, from defense to education. A member of a TV studio audience captured the "give me" mood well. When he heard about the $500 billion that was needed to bail the country out of the crisis generated by failing savings and loan associations, he shouted: "The taxpayers should not pay for this; the government should." (When I repeated this story in about half of my presentations it was followed by a prolonged silence; people seemed to wonder: why not?)

Seeking a socially effective response, rather than merely lecturing about the importance of responsibilities as the twin of rights, I have drawn on a three-step approach to forming a social movement. You start by *formulating a message*; then you *disseminate*, making sure that it reaches your fellow citizens; and then work with those who see the light to *change* public policies, institutions, and above all the habits of the hearts of one and all. It is easier said than done, I assure you. It took my communitarian colleagues, fellow activists, and me ten years (1990–2000) to cover a good part of the first two phases. Much of the most difficult, third phase largely remains to be carried out. (If your calling leads you in our direction, we are standing by, waiting.)

My account of the communitarian movement to date—its ideas and the ways they were formed, the heads of states that became involved in several countries, the vociferous critics it faces from left and right, both on and off the campus, and its import for the next generation—occupy a good half of this volume. Even those who do not see themselves as potential converts may wish to read a bit more about this worldview. And those interested in social and political action, either as activists or as observers, might find here a worthy tale or two. (Part IV: Launching the Communitarian Project.)

When I speak of being compelled to act, of a *calling,* I realize I am using a big word. Originally, this term had strong religious connotations. It referred to a call to serve the Lord, as the *Oxford English Dictionary* puts it, "the inward feeling or conviction of a divine call." However, the *OED* immediately adds, "the strong impulse to any course of action as the right thing to do." Bingo. If you hear such a call or are even a bit curious about what happens when one heeds it, here follows one account of such a challenged life.

Some people (including a fair number of social scientists) are quick to jump on anyone who says he has a calling. They argue that you are really after self-aggrandizement of some form or another (at least self-satisfaction). As I see it, anyone who is called must be ready to answer the question: what are you called to? One purpose is not as good as the next one. The virtue of all calls must be well examined before they are heeded. I tried to live by this dictum. You may judge how well I lived up to it.

My purpose here, though, is not to add another learned volume on the social science of good intentions or on the ethical deliberations about what amounts to a truly good deed. I merely lay out my personal struggles with these searing questions, hoping that they might aid some others in grappling with them. For now let me merely say that responding to a true calling makes the world around us, and us in it, better than we would be otherwise. This is a story of how one activist professor fumbled, stumbled, tried some more, and gradually—I do believe—learned to better serve ideas that were his calling.

PART ONE

FROM BULLETS TO BUBER

CHAPTER ONE

A Nerd Goes Fighting

To paraphrase Wordsworth: What "curse it was that dawn to be alive; but to be young was very hell."

Being Buffeted

Before I could accomplish anything, I had to liberate myself from all those who thought they owned a piece of me, who sought to control my moves. They included my strong-willed aunt, the Nazis, a high-handed school principal, the British police, and Palestinian Arabs, more or less in that order.

My earliest memory is of being catapulted out of a car in Cologne, Germany, on a very cold day. It was January 1933; I was four years old. The car made a sharp turn and I grabbed a handle that made the door fly open. All I remember is a vague sense of foreboding, like speeding down a hill on a bike that has lost it brakes. The rest of my memory of that ride is of the hushed, scandalized voices in which the story was recounted, first to my aunt and uncle, then to the full assortment of grandparents. My father—it was told—pulled me back into the car at the last moment. But the sense that stayed with me was not one of a last-minute miraculous rescue, but of hurtling into the cold, propelled by some uncontrollable force.

That same year, during which the Nazis took control of my homeland, my grandparents took me for a walk in the woods next to Frankfurt. We had stopped to gape at a forest fire when suddenly two trucks full of young people in brown uniforms, the Hitler Youth, appeared. They jumped off with

Figure 1.1. 1929

great gusto and their commanders filled the air with barked orders. My grand-parents became frantic. We first retreated behind some trees, trying to seem unperturbed. Next, they grabbed me, dragging me between them as they rushed down the hill. They did not explain why they were so panicked, but obviously we'd had a close encounter with some very dark force.

Soon, my father vanished without good-byes. He wiggled his way out of Nazi Germany on the pretext of attending a course in London. My mother summoned him back to attend the funeral of my grandma because that is what a "decent son does." (My mother was full of such strongly felt—and forcefully expressed—notions.) Hours after the funeral, a policeman knocked on our front door. By that time, tens of thousands of Jews had al-ready disappeared into concentration camps. The adults in my home turned grimly pale. There was no time to even pack a small bag or to hug good-bye. Luckily, it turned out that the policeman had come to deliver a modest medal that my father had earned for volunteering to serve as a medic in the German army during World War I. Soon my father was gone again, medal and all. Shortly thereafter, my mother gained permission from the German authorities to visit my father in London for a weekend. My aunt whispered that my mother had no intention of returning to the land of the Nazis. She did not. Thus, without much ado, both my parents left me behind. I had just turned five.

I was left in the care of my aunt and grandparents who were locked in competition as to who was going to more thoroughly improve my manners. There was clearly much work to be done. My main recollection of those days is of several visits by the wrong side of a brush to my lower backside. (The fact that I was a single child, I was repeatedly told, explained why I was so spoiled; it was left rather unclear how I could get myself some siblings.) As there was no one closer to complain to, I cried to heaven that I had been abandoned by those I loved most. But it was not all for naught: the spankings marked the beginning of a lifelong rejection of violence.

My next memory is that of a train station in Italy. A non-Jewish relative had smuggled me out of Germany and left me next to a suitcase, "just to make a phone call." The wailing I did is reported to have been the loudest ever heard in that railway station.

My relative reunited me with my parents in still another place—in Athens, Greece, where my family got stuck trying to make its way to Palestine. The British, who at that time controlled Palestine (as they did countries from India to Ghana), had limited Jewish immigration to the area, in response to Arab demands. While my family was accorded one of the coveted permits allowing immigration to Palestine, there was a mix-up: we were sent a bachelor's permit, and our family permit was sent to some bachelor. The British were in no particular rush to correct the mistake. Thus, we continued to be stuck midway between Germany and Haifa, for a whole year, trying to make ends meet in Athens. Although the Greek authorities did not allow my father to work, he was able to earn a bit by working "off the books" for a shopkeeper. It was not the best of times. Those Greeks who hated Germans treated us as intruders, while those who looked at Germans as allies, shared their view of Jews. My first-grade classmates made no such subtle distinctions. They simply treated me as someone who did not belong, not at all.

Much of the year in Greece is an unpleasant blur, but one warm memory stands out. Four days before Hanukkah, my parents started whispering quite a bit. I could not contain my curiosity and peeked into the kitchen after my bedtime. What I saw just whetted my interest some more. There were several rolls of toilet paper on the small kitchen table; an empty gray shoebox; a piece of glittering paper. My father was working with a pair of scissors; my mother was mixing flour with something else. I could not make heads or tails out of any of this.

On the evening of the first light my parents rolled out a castle they had made, mumbling something about having no money to buy me a real gift. The toilet paper rolls turned into four corner towers; the shoebox—with windows drawn on it—was transformed into the body of the castle. The glittering paper served as water in the moat, which was spanned by a cardboard bridge one could lift by pulling two tiny strings. The whole contraption was covered with sand of different colors attached to it with homemade glue. In the following weeks I played many rounds of war around the castle. My father's chess figures served as the troops. In all the battles the Jews, led by the Maccabim, won against the Romans who were wearing swastikas. I never got a gift I appreciated more.

I spent the year in a Greek school, which meant that I had to learn modern Greek and the rules and mannerisms of a foreign school. By the time I had learned to stand up when the teacher entered, comprehended the difference between omega and beta, and acquired a taste for the greasy food, it was time again to move. The paperwork was finally straightened out; we were permitted to sail for Palestine. A ship took us to Haifa, and I found myself in yet another strange country with another language to learn; Hebrew this time. On our arrival in Haifa in the winter of 1937, my parents were taken in by a friend and I was put into a school.

The kids teased new immigrants like me because we spoke no Hebrew, were dressed in heavy dark European garb, and our names were foreign. Mine was a solid German one: Werner Falk. The principal of the school sent a message to my parents, "You had better teach your son to introduce himself by his Hebrew name." My mother wrote back, "While I know that my son was given a Hebrew name during his Bris, and it is written in the front of the family Bible, I cannot find it among the few things we were able to take with us." (We later found out that I was named "Abraham" at my Bris. It's a name I never missed.) The principal responded, "We had better provide your son with a Hebrew name. I recommend 'Amitai,' which means truth (emet) in Hebrew, and is the name of Jonah's father in the Old Testament." My parents were quite content, but for me it was one more strange thing to get used to. While I had a new first name, I was stuck with my Germanic last name, Falk, which stayed with me until it put me in harm's way.

Living in someone else's home, even a friend's, was less than fortuitous. So, again we moved, this time to a small village, Herzliya Gimmel, which served as a base from which my parents set out with four other families to launch a new community, a cooperative farm, they named Kfar Schmaryahu. It was built on a small hill full of large rocks, bordering on an encampment of Arab Bedouin. My parents were soon busy fulfilling the great Zionist dream of converting members of the Jewish middle class into farmers and expanding the Jewish territory.

As a seven-year-old, I largely missed the greater import of all this. To me, the new place offered a fourth try at the first grade and parents who were not there when I returned to our temporary abode. They stumbled home after sunset, after working long and hard at clearing fields, stringing fences, and paving roads. They were consumed by manual labor for which piano and ballet lessons did not prepare my mother and for which my father's business training did not serve him well. I spent some of the long hours on my own fantasizing about the grand heroic deeds I would soon accomplish. Most of those involved finishing the construction of Kfar Schmaryahu single-handedly, overnight. After that, in my daydreams, my parents stopped dashing away at dawn, returning bushed late.

The high point of the days came during the evenings, when we were called to share a meal prepared by one of the mothers, in turn, for all five pioneering families. The adults did not say much, but when they did, they exchanged horror stories about their escape from Nazi Germany or they teased one another about the difficulties they encountered during the day in the fields. Like "That was quite a scorpion that attacked you" and "No one told me that Zionism meant having to put up with so many mosquitoes." They were like members of one big family. I often played a version of jacks, using gravel, with two other boys, Emmanuel and Yitzhak. That is, when we were not exchanging hidden blows. We had to be discreet; the adults insisted that we be chummy with one another.

After about a year, Kfar Schmaryahu construction advanced to the point that we could move in. My family was assigned a small, boxlike new house on our own little farm in the new settlement. While, technically, ours was not a *moshav* (cooperative village), Kfar Schmaryahu was similar. Farmers had individual lots and it was up to each family to decide what to plant, how hard to work, and what to do with the money it earned. At the same time, purchases of farming equipment, seeds, and fertilizers, as well as marketing of the produce of the individual farms, were carried out collectively through what was called "the co-op." The community also arranged for credit and instructed unseasoned farmers in the ways of the land. For me, the best part of the co-op was spending hours watching chicks hatch in a state-of-the-art incubator owned by the community.

While the co-op hired some experts who freely dispensed their advice, each household had to fend for itself. My father bought two horses, but they were not a match: one was a plodding workhorse, best suited for pulling the fully loaded flatbed we owned. The other was a riding stallion who disdained farm work. It soon caught pneumonia and, despite various administrations by the co-op vet, it expired, to our great sorrow. I particularly missed the horse; his big eyes seemed to be the only warm ones around. And when given half a chance, he would wander over in my direction and park his head on my shoulder.

Our ducks did not fare any better. My mother built a sizable basin for them, with high walls so that the ducks would not escape. We got a dozen ducklings from the co-op, and I looked forward to playing with them. The next day we found them all floating dead in the little pond. It turns out that ducks cannot swim nonstop and need to be able to waddle out of the water for an occasional respite.

We did better with our apple orchard; we learned to graft a sapling on the trunks of uncultivated trees. We also succeeded in growing rows upon rows of potatoes and carrots, but by and large, my parents learned the hard way that farming was not for rank amateurs. I am not sure what weighed heavier on me: the loss of the horse and ducks or my parents' anxieties.

While life in Kfar Schmaryahu had its share of grief, it did serve as early schooling in communitarian thinking. My father took me with him to several co-op meetings, at which the members of our community were engaged in incessant debates about what was the best form of joint living: the high level of communalism of the kibbutz? The each-on-their-own kind, like that practiced in nearby, fully privatized, Herzliya? A higher level of cooperation than Kfar Schmaryahu had, but not as intense as that of kibbutzim of the kind found at Rishpon (a *moshav*), our neighboring community? As with debates about the merit of free enterprise versus the proper role of the government, the question of the right level of commonality was never settled.

Often on Saturday afternoons my father would take me for a walk. He would stop to chat with whomever we ran into, usually about the happenings in our village. (Because all the farmers in our community were German-Jewish immigrants who had a hard time learning Hebrew, the conversations were conducted in German.) People seemed to take to my father. They eagerly chatted with him; some would even come out of their homes to visit as we slowly passed by. Many times the conversations swirled around topic number one: would it be better if we merged all the individual farms into one big one? Who had the right to order the stockpiling of feed for the community? And so on. It was as if I were growing up in a high school of communitarian theory and practice.

Shortly after we moved into our house, my father was elected to be the co-op's executive, a job he did not hold long. My mother confided that this was because he was too much of a visionary. "He is full of marvelous ideas," she complained, "but he is much too candid." It turned out that my father had feared that a war would break out and bought large amounts of animal feed for the co-op, over the objections of the co-op's executive committee. When World War II started and made getting feed very difficult and expensive, my father let it be known, however gently, that he'd been right, which of course implied that most everyone else was wrong. It was not appreciated. A few more such undiplomatic moves, and the co-op elected a new executive. (I do not blame my own tactlessness on my father, but on my not taking heed from his experience.)

The news that my father was in effect sacked found him in his favorite evening spot: sitting next to our large radio, listening to a symphony, reading a book, and smoking a cigarette. I loved to sit on the floor next to him, leaning on his legs, and turning the pages of a book myself. When I complained to him about the endless demands my mother put on me, to clean up, to sit straight, to remain neat, to help with house chores and the farm work, he would smile broadly, pat me on my head, and say very little.

Unemployed and perturbed by Hitler's armies that were closing in on us, already in Egypt, my father left home again in the spring of 1941. This time he left to join the Jewish Brigade, composed of volunteers from the Jewish Yishuv (the Jewish community in Palestine, which preceded and led to Israel's statehood). The Brigade was a Jewish unit formed within the British army.

The result for me was dramatic in an unexpected way: my mother felt—quite correctly—that she could no longer handle me. I was heeding her instructions less and less. Moreover, the principal of the rather authoritarian religious school I attended in nearby Herzliya complained bitterly, "Your son does not dedicate himself to his studies or homework. His handwriting is atrocious. While he might be bright, he is weak in English, geography, and Jewish history. Unless he markedly improves, we have grave doubts about his promotion to the next grade." Shortly thereafter, when I turned thirteen, my mother shipped me to a boarding school, to Ben Shemen. This event turned my life around. Ben Shemen shaped my character, sense of self, and ideals in ways that I would only understand decades later when numerous educators found my peculiar boarding school experience fascinating.

My mother was a disciplinarian by culture; circumstances further hardened her heart. She was evicted from her homeland, but did not benefit from the Zionist ideology that made leaving Germany easier for my father. She was ill prepared for manual labor—her fate in Israel. My father left her to go to the war, saddled her not only with debt, but also with a son, who like many sons of immigrants, rebelled against his parents' values and authority. Her harshness was understandable in retrospect, but I had little of that perspective when it would have counted most.

I do not mean to imply that, by shipping me off to boarding school, my mother did not love me in her own way. We reminisced about the old days when I visited her at her two-room suite in an assisted-living house shortly after her ninety-seventh birthday. My mother said: "You know what Michael Dietrich [her favorite staff member] said to me? 'Tell him Amitai loves him.'" She added dismissively, "I told him 'I *assume* he knows that!'" I responded, "I love you, too, ma," trying to hide that it was not always easy.

Ben Shemen: Virtues and Meanings

A Character-Building Lesson

Ben Shemen was more like a British Eton than an American Boys Town. It occupies its own little village. Its ingenious design calls for each child to have close relations with four adults: a homeroom teacher who serves as the main educator; a "house mother" who is in charge of the dormitories but acts as a sort of mother hen; a youth leader with whom kids hang out after hours during numerous social activities; and a foreman, under whom each child spends two hours a day working in the collective farm. ("Working the earth purifies the soul," was one of Ben Shemen's many mottos.)

The four adults met regularly, usually unbeknownst to the children, to coordinate their guidance of the youngsters toward what Ben Shemen considered the needed direction. Thus, if a child confronted one of the farm's foremen, his house mother would know all about it and would draw on the affection the kid had for her to help him to accept the foreman's authority. And if the child, me in this case, refused to learn the language of the "enemy"—the British who were occupying Palestine—the youth leader would take him for a walk to talk matters out. (In my case it was a young poet, S. Ishar.) When he failed to convince me, the school administration decided, as it often did, that it was better not to coerce me as long as I otherwise kept my nose to the grindstone and behaved.

As a side effect of the school structure, each child was a member of four different peer groups. One was in classrooms with kids of the same age. A second was in the residential houses with kids of divergent ages (which in my case included an older boy by the name of Shimon Peres). The elder boys were expected to foster the communal mores in the younger ones. The third was in youth groups, which met after hours and were coeducational as was the fourth group of those who worked on the farm.

Years later, when I became a sociologist, I understood the extraordinary power peer groups hold over their members, especially when these groups are successfully mobilized to support the values of the institution in which they are formed. The often-used term *peer pressure*, though, seems inappropriate when applied to my life in this boarding school. Ben Shemen's peer groups did not exert pressure; they filled us with a keen desire to follow the group's lead. Thus, when other kids were singing patriotic songs at the top of their lungs, I fervently sought to join in, despite the fact that I cannot carry a tune. And when everyone was making their beds without being reminded, I could hardly leave mine rumpled.

My most important Ben Shemen lesson was as lasting as it was painful. My best excuse was that I was hungry, which is not quite accurate. Merely, our tummies were never quite full. Budget pressures led the boarding school to serve food that might have sufficed for children, but not for the growing bodies of teenagers. Several of us formed a group that occasionally roamed a nearby wood collecting mushrooms, which we sautéed on the sly.

One evening the oldest member of our group suggested that we avail ourselves of a chicken from the communal farm's coop. Five of us invaded it after dark, causing an immense ruckus. We succeeded in cornering a chicken, which the older boy, the son of a farmer, beheaded with a knife he had brought along. He also had no difficulties in removing the innards and the feathers, and soon we had ourselves quite a meal.

How the grown-ups found out, I have no idea, but the response was considerable. Classes were canceled and a school-wide assembly was called. We were charged with violating communal property for a grossly selfish purpose and with slaughtering a chicken with a dull knife. We were made to stand in front of a sea of our peers and elders, who took turns expressing their outrage. Faces around us could not have been sterner, especially those of the younger children. One eighth-grader suggested that we be kicked out summarily. Another favored making us do extra work in the chicken coop for the rest of our stay in Ben Shemen.

I was ready to do most anything to stop the trial, as everybody referred to the assembly: give up a meal each day for the rest of my life; clean the communal toilets (a most despised job) for the balance of the school year; personally ask every remaining chicken for forgiveness.

The jury of our peers was about to send us packing when the teachers convinced them to merely ground us for the rest of the month. The surprisingly light sentence did little to assuage the terror of a community's palpable dismay. Were it not for the much greater drama that soon followed, I probably would still have "chicken killer!" ringing in my ears.

Aside from making me more mindful of respecting the commonweal and animal rights, I was greatly influenced by the event in formulating my thinking about character education. Fashioning experiences, I argued in communitarian writings many years later, are much more formative than lectures about ethics and textbooks.

Israelis Are Reversed Jews

Ben Shemen, most times, did not follow a policy of "just say no." Instead, the staff kept us from the temptations of our newly raging hormones and a few stray cigarettes by keeping us dashing from one engrossing activity to another. We had campfires around which we were told about the strenuous labor of the pioneers who founded the Jewish community in Palestine, the heroism of those who defended us from Arab attacks, and the degrading life of Jews in the Diaspora (i.e., banished from ancient Israel and dispersed all over the world, in exile).

The whole idea of Zionism was summarized for us as an inverted pyramid: Jews were middle class, intellectuals, merchants, and financiers; a heavy middle resting on a narrow base of relatively few Jewish blue-collar workers and even fewer farmers. We Israelis were to set the pyramid upright, by forming a strong base of farmers and workers, and by laboring with the sweat of our brows. *They* relied on others to defend them; *we* would take our fate into our own armed hands. *They* were yellow. *We* were macho.

We were shown cartoons from a Nazi publication. It showed a Jew as a short man, long nose, crooked-legged, holding on to a money bag and puffing on a big cigar while standing—grinning wickedly—on the top of a herd of people. We could not see for the life of us why this was considered offensive or funny. This was what we had been taught, time and again, that Jews were like. (While such views have since greatly moderated, many Israelis in their inner hearts are still contemptuous of Jews in the Diaspora.) I was quite a bit embarrassed by finding in myself some Jewish traits. I was not enamored with working on the farm and loved to read and write.

Much less emphasis was put on another major lesson we acquired from the Jewish communities in the Diaspora. Jews learned over centuries to maintain their own communities and to try not to become entangled in the working of the states in which they survived. Jewish communities had their own inner code, courts, schools, and charities. Our parents did the same in Palestine, building a Jewish community that largely kept itself independent from the British government. Society and state need not be conflated.

Above all, we learned in our civic lessons, the Yishuv (the Jewish community that preceded the formation of Israel) was a place in which commitments to the community took precedence over self-interest and individualistic pursuits. We read stories, sang songs, and heard tales about pioneers who shook with malaria as they drained the swamps, worked long hours clearing boulders from the fields, consumed little, and stood guard at night, all for the common good.

I wondered, "If these lives were so full of sacrifice, why did the pioneers dance the hora in the evenings, compose and sing the songs we recited, and smile broadly in many of their pictures?" My civics teacher explained that while there were, of course, many situations in which individuals did make great sacrifices for the common good, the relationship between the Yishuv and its members was not necessarily one in which the more one gained, the more the other lost—a zero-sum game. Pioneers gained a tremendous inner sense of affirmation from their hard work on behalf of the community. It was a lesson that stuck.

At Ben Shemen one ritual came on the heels of another. One day we were raising and saluting the blue and white flag of a nation yet to be born, followed by a solemn singing of the Hatikvah (national anthem). The next day we were moved by a speech by the local commander of the underground (Hagana), who led us in taking an oath: "Never again will we go like lambs to the slaughter!" Staff and students frequently staged plays extolling the virtues of working the land and fighting for our homeland. Our dancing carried a message all of its own: no pairing off. The most common dance was the communal hora, in which we formed a circle, arms around shoulders, swinging around until we turned dizzy. And still we danced. One high followed another.

A Turnabout

For me, Ben Shemen provided a powerful conversion experience. I entered as a youngster rebelling against my disciplinary mother, the loving weakness of my father, and the religious indoctrination of my school. Upon graduating in 1944, I returned to my parents' home, now comfortable with learning, authority figures, and the expectations of my peers. Above all, I was full of ideals.

On my last day, the principal called me to his office. He smiled broadly first, showing me an unflattering letter I had brought with me from my school in Herzliya. The principal then pointed at my final report card from Ben Shemen. It was dotted with marks of "very good." He added parsimoniously: "You will do us proud." As far as I was concerned, he could have kept talking. When he noted that while I was trying not to show it, I was aglow inside, the principal warned me affectionately: "Just so you do not get too cocky, let me tell you that we figure that you will never become a soccer player or star in any other sport." Education never stopped at Ben Shemen.

I had come to Ben Shemen as the son of parents who, while living in Germany, had abandoned much of their Jewish tradition to become good

Germans. After settling in Palestine, my parents lived in a community of German Jews, who often continued to speak German to one another and whose manners and affectations were quite Germanic. While I rebelled against much of this, I still arrived at Ben Shemen as a little German boy.

I departed from Ben Shemen as a young Israeli, with a sense of purpose that was as strong as it was focused: to join those lining up to fight a war of national liberation against the British occupation and to form a just Jewish society, a new Zion. I could not wait to find a chance to follow in the footsteps of all those hardworking pioneers and courageous warriors who had become part of my inner pantheon. The only thing that seemed uncertain to this fifteen-year-old was how to go about doing it.

A Taste for Action and Service

Illegal Immigration

My Ben Shemen teachers recommended that on graduation I enroll in a good high school, strong in the liberal arts. They seemed to have overlooked that they had convinced us that working with one's hands was vastly superior to intellectual life. ("A pair of boots is worth more than all of Shakespeare" I was taught.) Disregarding my inner misgivings, ashamed of them, I enrolled in a vocational school near Kfar Schmaryahu, to become an electrician. I had returned to live at home, as my father was discharged from military service due to an illness.

Soon after I turned fifteen, there came a day, actually a night, that was more portentous in my life than the day I was taken out of Nazi Germany and the one on which I was brought to the Holy Land. Well after midnight, my father jerked me out of my cot: "*Olim* have arrived!" (We never referred to Jews coming to Palestine as "immigrants" but only as "*olim*," which means those who ascend to a higher place. It is also a term associated with those few who are honored to read from the Torah during Saturday services in the synagogue.) At the time, Jews were trying to escape Europe and find their way to Palestine. The British, who governed Palestine, attempted to stop this flow of refugees by throwing their navy against it and by erecting a chain of police citadels along the beaches—one some 800 yards from my home. The Jewish underground (Hagana) ran the British blockade with small boats loaded with Jews, as has been well chronicled by Leon Uris in his book *Exodus*. That night one such boat was beached nearby, and members of our community, wearing only swimsuits, carried the excited *olim* through the last stretch of the sea, and through the dunes, to hide them in our community.

Figure 1.2.   Illegal immigration at Kfar Shmaryahu

A young Polish Jew ended up in my bed, after my mother served soup, rolls, a leftover casserole, and homemade yogurt. Little was said; the poor guy was too fatigued to speak, but he was sufficiently anxious to keep staring at the door. I sought sleep in our tool shed but was too wound up to doze off.

When the sun rose, members of our community were smuggling the new *olim* from our home and neighboring ones (which were near the beach and hence under close British surveillance) deeper into the country. And—for the first time ever—I was asked to lend a hand, to serve as a lookout.

I stood for hours on top of a small building watching for any signs of the dust British police cars would kick up if they approached. None came, but I felt—for the first time—needed and important. I was helping the cause. A good cause—the best. I was part of a people who were rising against a sinister occupying force that would not let my people come home. This time I was not going to be pushed around; I was going to do the pushing.

The next day, I could not keep my mind on my math homework or the intricacies of Hebrew grammar. For many days that followed, I would suddenly be engulfed by a warm rush, smiling broadly to myself. Finally, I got to do something that would make my Ben Shemen teachers—and peers—proud.

One of the next groups of *olim* arrived one early evening (I noted the day in my diary: November 21, 1945) on our beach. As the *olim* were unloaded, a British destroyer approached. It lowered a boat with armed soldiers who captured a few of the *olim*, the captain of the ship, and several members of our community and arrested them all. Eleven *olim* still on their boat were also dragged away. Shortly thereafter, the Hagana planted a bomb in the British police station overlooking the beach. The explosion shook the windows of my home.

Most of the *olim* succeeded in making it to land and were hidden in Shefayyim, a nearby community. Early the next morning we heard an enormous racket as scores of British police cars, armored vehicles, communication vans, and trucks loaded with British soldiers rumbled by. It sounded as if half the British army was heading our way. Minutes later, the Hagana passed the word that Shefayyim was being surrounded.

The British did not enter Shefayyim, fearing a bloody confrontation in a community full of women and children. Instead, they laid siege to the village and announced that no one would be allowed to enter or leave until the illegal immigrants were turned over, surely to be shipped to detention camps in Cyprus if not back to war-ravaged Europe.

Just as the British finished encircling Shefayyim, Hagana runners mobilized the surrounding Jewish settlements. Soon thousands of Jews rushed to form a huge circle, surrounding the perimeter the British had established around that community. Nobody carried arms; the Hagana's order was to engage in Gandhi-style "passive resistance." People, though, were pushing ever closer to the British line, trying to break it, to mix with the *olim* and thus to thwart their arrest.

The British first responded with blows, using batons and rifle butts. When these did not suffice to quell the crowd, a British officer announced over a bullhorn that his men would shoot anyone who moved closer. A young man from Petach HaTikva pushed forward and was shot dead on the spot. A stunned silence descended on the crowd as his bleeding body was rushed away.

We stopped advancing but no one left the scene; we maintained the outer perimeter. If the British were going to remove the *olim*, they would have to drive over us. The tense standoff lasted most of the day, until the British decided to retreat, midafternoon. Shortly thereafter, they imposed a curfew on all public roads, but it did not prevent us from getting the *olim* out of Shefayyim through back roads and dispersing them among various communities away from the coast.

During these happenings, Emmanuel and Yitzhak (the two youngsters with whom I grew up) and I were dashing about on our bicycles. We served as runners between the Hagana headquarters and the "field commanders," who first served to ensure that there were enough people to encircle the British and who later led the *olim* to safe hiding places. When there were no messages to rush back and forth, we lugged water and freshly baked bread. We were much too busy to be scared even after shots were fired, but not too busy to sense that we were part of something of enormous import and moment. The British were trying to stop Jews escaping post-Nazi Europe; we were helping them to make it. The British were trying to prevent a young nation from being born; we lent a hand at labor. The future of the Jewish people was at stake, and the whole world was watching. We, a bunch of teenagers, were on center stage, only this was not theater; the action was all too real. Most exhilarating, we carried the day: the British armed forces retreated and the *olim* were safe and home!

Before, I did not know what a high was. After, I could not believe one could fly any higher. It was in those history-forming days that I acquired my first taste of action, of being part of a greater whole, of doing good, and the special afterglow of having served. I never could get quite enough of it, although I soon got a mouthful and then some.

Joining the Palmach

As of the middle of 1945 news was coming so fast and furious that it seemed that God had put history on fast-forward. The Yishuv was agitated by a flood of news about the concentration camps and the fate of a million Jewish survivors who were homeless in Europe yet forbidden to immigrate to Palestine. Support swelled for an idea that was previously considered outlandish: push the Brits out of Palestine! The Yishuv community was largely unarmed, counting some 600,000 men, women, and children and facing 100,000 well-armed troops. A direct military confrontation was out of the question. Getting the British to leave was to be left to the Jewish underground, its acts of sabotage and even terrorism.

Between October 1945 and July 1946, I could hardly keep my mind on my studies. I was especially captivated by news about the Palmach, the commando units of the Hagana. These units were the only part of the Jewish underground whose members served full-time; they were considered the elite troops. Most other members of the Hagana trained or served mainly on weekends and evenings, and on special occasions. (The Palmach should not be confused with the right-wing Irgun.)

In one daring action the Palmach sprung 208 *olim* from a British detention center in Atlit. Next, the Palmach blew up most of the railroads. Soon it attacked British police stations. A high point of this intensified fight against the British came on June 17, 1946, when the Palmach blew up ten out of the eleven bridges that connected Palestine to neighboring Arab territories.

Twelve days later 17,000 British troops set out to disband the Hagana and especially its commando units, the Palmach. The operation was deliberately started on a Sabbath, which we dubbed Black Saturday, June 29, 1946. Glued to the radio, we learned about the arrest of many leaders and members of the underground. On the highway running by my community, buses well guarded by British army units passed by, packed with glum Palmach fighters. By Sunday, we learned that some 2,700 members of the underground had been locked in detention camps.

Following Black Saturday, the Palmach issued an urgent call for volunteers to fill the much depleted ranks. Several of my friends announced that they planned to drop out of high school and join the underground. I was struggling with the decision. My mother was livid when she learned that I was considering dropping out of high school. She reminded me that I had only recently turned sixteen and she complained bitterly, "How can you refuse to listen to your parents and throw away your future!" My father, who had little taste for confrontation, left me a note on my bed, more hurt than angry. "Why leave now that I am back from the war?"

My parents' concerns were easier to lay aside than my own. True, I was pumped full of patriotism; I wrote to my father, "Everyone may say, 'why me' when the country calls, but then who will rise and serve? If not me, who? And if not now, when? The time has come to get the British out of here and rebuild the Zion from which we were driven 2,000 years ago." And when I asked my diary whether I should dedicate my life to "riches and status" or "service for the common good," I concluded, with all the enthusiasm of a teenager, that service was unquestioningly superior.

My patriotic sentiments found their way into my first published article. I wrote up my sentiments and sent the piece to a publication of a youth organization, which featured it under the title, "A letter to my father." It did not amuse him but it delighted my friends.

What I did not divulge to the readers, friends, or my parents was that I was consumed by doubts, far from confident that when the day came—I would be on that bus taking the volunteers to their secret training place. I feared most that I would be unable to handle the rigors of commando training and service. Images of my poor performance in sports came to mind. During running meets, I was often among the last to struggle across the finish line. When we played soccer, I was typically among the last to be chosen to join one team or the other. In short, there was no way of hiding from the fact that I was much more of a nerd than the stuff from which commandos are made.

My darkest secret: I scared easily. When my friends jumped off high walls into sand piles in one of the many construction sites in our village, a favorite pastime, I often failed their dare. When they walked on the railing of the water tower, I begged off. After seeing the blood-dripping body of the young man shot in Shefayyim, the thought of a bullet tearing up my innards made me wonder if I was cut out to be a fighter.

In the end, the urge to serve won over my fears. In the spring of 1946, together with a group of my fellow students in the tenth grade (ranging in age from sixteen to seventeen), I dropped out of school. With little fanfare and subdued farewells (after all, what we were about to do was illegal) we packed into a bus on the way to some hush-hush location.

There are those who believe that once you make a decision, whether it's quitting your job or undergoing surgery, it becomes easier. But I was more anxious on that bus than when I had been helping to smuggle *olim* through the British lines. And this time I could not let anyone know about the depths of my trepidations. Everyone else seemed so determinedly cheerful.

Life in a Kibbutz

Palmach Training
We had fantasies of undergoing intensive military training and attacking British police stations, bridges, and railroads—to drive the empire out. We saw ourselves drawing arms to protect the arrival of boats packed with *olim*. Instead, we were shipped to a large kibbutz, Tel Joseph. There we were housed in tents and worked for two weeks each month to pay for our keep, doing jobs that kibbutz members were not keen on. My assignments included picking oranges in the heat, cleaning stinking cow stalls, and washing thousands of dishes whenever the giant dishwashing machines broke down, which they did with fair regularity.

During the other two weeks of each month, we did get rigorous training, but not quite the type we had imagined. To our dismay, much of it did not entail guns (the few weapons the Palmach had were well hidden), but was instead dedicated to building up our character and muscles. Long marches were the Palmach's favorite prescription for building up one's physical and psychological stamina. We were made to jump from tall buildings into a river and to glide down a long rope stretched from a hilltop to a tree in a nearby valley. We were dropped after dark behind an Arab village and instructed to find our way home. The rest of the time we were trained in hand-to-hand

Figure 1.3.   1947

combat. Occasionally, especially when the British police were otherwise occupied, we were introduced to old pistols, creaky rifles, and, once, even to
hand grenades.

Somewhere in the middle of all this training, I lost my German last name,
over which I shed no tears. Under the rules of the British occupation everyone was required to carry a British-issued ID card at all times. One evening,
toward the end of 1946, a runner rushed to inform us that the British police
had found a secret card file in which all of our names were recorded. This
meant that the police could find us by simply checking ID cards at roadblocks, a frequent occurrence. We were given two hours to concoct new
names for ourselves, after which the underground would furnish us with new,
false ID cards. I offered "Etzioni," a pen name that I had adopted when I
started writing for a Ben Shemen student newspaper.

I had lifted the name from one of the narratives Ben Shemen used to educate us. This one was a story about a bad boy who broke a branch of a tree.
The boy was called before a court of olive and fig trees (sources of nourishment) and eucalyptus trees (planted to drain swamps and thus fight malaria).
The trees lectured the boy about the great value of trees, which the Jewish

Figure 1.4. 1947

community cultivated to turn bare hills into green woods. The boy promised from then on to cherish trees. He was pardoned by the court, which changed his name to Etzioni, *Etz* meaning tree in Hebrew.

Soon my new name adorned a freshly minted ID card. Somehow, pocketing it cemented my transition from a high school dropout to a bona fide member of the underground. I not only had newly bulging muscles and a stronger grip on my fears, I was also a member in good standing of the revered Palmach, a group about which songs were written and tales of heroism were told around camp-fires. The Palmach had given me a new identity, in more ways than one.

Communalism to Spare

The time spent in the kibbutz during my training provided an opportunity to sort out if I would like to spend the rest of my life in a community that was much more communal than the one in which I grew up. If growing up in Kfar Schmaryahu served as my introduction to communitarianism—life on a kibbutz provided an intensive advanced class.

Kibbutz members had no personal worries. Indeed, one member had a stroke at the young age of thirty and recovered very little; it was taken for granted that the kibbutz would take care of him for the rest of his life. Kibbutz members were very tolerant of one member who was slightly built, short in stature, and rather feeble, but clearly gave his best working in the fields. (He refused an assignment in the small kibbutz office.) In contrast, members kept bitching about another kibbutznik who was much more muscular, but less inclined to apply himself. The motto "From each according to his ability, to each according to his needs" was truly followed here. In short, the kibbutz lived up to its reputation as a community that was highly egalitarian and humanitarian.

At the same time there was precious little tolerance for individuality or privacy. Meals were taken in the communal dining room. In the mornings, kibbutz members would sit next to one another at long tables, at the centers of which were metal bowls full of tomatoes, cucumbers, scallions, and green peppers. The kibbutzniks would, as if all ordered by some invisible command, cut these veggies into small pieces to make a salad, sprinkling the one dressing available (oil and vinegar), eating from the same dull plates, working their way through the meal with the same army-issue "silver." Lunch was often eaten from containers in the field, with one's work crew. Dinner was also collective, although less regimented than breakfast.

Private provisions in one's room (no one had more than a room) or tent were considered a violation of a major taboo. When one kibbutz member received a coffee mug as a gift from a visiting relative, he committed high treason by keeping the mug. His attempt to maintain private property raised a storm of condemnations. When someone did violate any of the long list of other Kibbutz taboos, or neglected to fulfill one of his considerable list of duties, such an offense was known instantly throughout the community. Indeed, members of the kibbutz spent a good part of their time gossiping about who did not do what.

When I asked a kibbutz daughter to "take a walk after dinner" before I ended my relationship with another, three kibbutz members chided me before the day was out. "Nu, nu, I hear you plan to date Tamara *and* Rachel? You are new here but still. . . ." And "Come on, we do not mess around like this here." (In fairness, I should say that an invitation for an after-dinner walk was not necessarily as innocent as it may sound.)

While much of what I saw in the kibbutz seemed excessively communal to me, Tel Joseph was far from a foreboding or gloomy place. Especially heart-

warming were the holidays, Passover in particular. At Seder the whole kibbutz, including the nonmember help (our group and some forlorn young
American Jews who were looking for a utopia), dined together along long tables under the stars. After several speeches by the kibbutz elders about how
they had suffered during the days of true pioneering, we were swept away by
a whole village intoning together various blessings and traditional songs, a
community singing that echoed back from the surrounding mountains.

In toto, the kibbutz seemed too all embracing. It was a place I could last as
long as my Palmach training required, but it was not a place I would choose
to spend my life. Too much community seemed no better than too little.

David Ben Gurion: A Lesson in Historical Sensibility

During my Palmach training, by a sheer coincidence, I attended a most remarkable meeting. It was like being—as a teenager—at a meeting preparing
for the Boston Tea Party, or happening to witness the shot fired at Sarajevo
that was heard around the world. It not only left a lasting impression but also
posed a challenge that I tried to meet for the rest of my days. "Attended" de-
scribes accurately what I did. I did not utter a word. I was quite aware that I
was only invited because I was a member of Mapai (labor party). And, those
who convened the meeting wanted to have "someone young" because "after
all, it is their future we will be discussing."

The meeting, which took place early in March 1947, was composed of
leaders of Mapai, at the time the most powerful party of the Yishuv. Its leader,
David Ben Gurion, headed the informal government of the Yishuv. Those assembled were exploring the position these leaders would strike later that
month at a meeting in Jerusalem. The subject: should the Yishuv settle
merely for a homeland under continued British rule (coupled with more leeway for intracommunity decisions), or should we dare hold out for true independence—for statehood? In other words, should the Yishuv risk losing the
possible, in favor of going for the ideal?

The issue was rapidly coming to a head after years of tense negotiations.
Numerous proposals had been advanced concerning the disposition of Palestine after World War II. Britain had been governing Palestine since World
War I. Faced with growing unrest, Jewish defiance of British rules, some Jewish terrorism, and Arab riots, Britain was growing weary of maintaining its
rule. In 1947, Britain dumped the future of Palestine in the lap of the United
Nations. Ben Gurion and the other Mapai leaders were exploring which of
several proposals before the United Nations they were going to fight for. The
offer that seemed most attainable (although not very much so) was a fair

measure of self-government for the Jewish community; the least plausible was full-fledged statehood.

Several items of business were quickly disposed of. Everybody seemed to be rushing to get to some item of special import, but I had no idea what it was going to be. It turned out that David Ben Gurion was going to have it out with Moshe Shertok (who later changed his name to Sharet and became Israel's first foreign minister) and his supporters about nothing less than the creation of a Jewish state.

Ben Gurion opened this part of the meeting by stating with much gusto, as if speaking to a much larger audience, "It is time to finalize our decision one way or the other." He added bluntly, "The time is right for us to take the ultimate risk and demand and fight for the formation of a full-blown state. Anything less will not allow us to realize the dream of Zion, to defend ourselves, to ensure that there will be a land any Jew in the world who seeks refuge will be able to come to unencumbered; that we shall never again be taken like lambs to the slaughter."

Shertok spoke much more softly. "I realize of course the wonder of having a state all our own. But we could get there gradually, in stages. For now we should limit ourselves to asking for a Jewish homeland, within the framework of the British 'Mandate,' which we should insist be extended and truly implemented. Here, we can base ourselves on the British promise included in the Balfour Declaration, which calls for a Jewish homeland, not for a state. This way we are much more likely to win the support of the United Nations and not unnecessarily provoke the Arab nations that surround us."

Ben Gurion reacted impatiently, almost angrily. He argued, with a rising voice, "The time is now. The British Empire has been weakened as a result of the war. The British people are anxious to focus on rebuilding their land and not squandering their resources by holding on to a piece of desert in the Middle East, especially if we make the occupation of Palestine more costly for them. While we may be the first British colony to push them out, I hear rumblings from India and other British colonies, even French ones; the days of empires are numbered."

Ben Gurion continued: "There are reasons to believe, as difficult as this is to imagine, that even the USSR will support us in the UN, hoping that the Jewish state will be left-leaning and support them." After a brief pause, just as someone else was about to speak up, Ben Gurion added, "The British are now negotiating with the U.S. government for a huge loan, and in the U.S. we have more leverage than in Britain."

Shertok responded, "Goldman [a major leader of the American Jewish community] empowered me to let it be known that the American Jewish community feels that we should not act impulsively; we should proceed very cautiously." Ben Gurion mumbled something dismissively that sounded to me like ". . . these 'shtetl' [ghetto] Jews."

There was considerable give and take. Someone wanted to know if a really tiny Jewish state would be more acceptable to the United Nations; what if it was limited to the area along the Mediterranean coast?

Someone else suggested that we hear from a Hagana representative who was present, known only as "Dov." Dov reported, "The Hagana's unanimous assessment is that while we shall be able to protect many of the Jewish communities along the coastline and maybe in several other parts of Palestine against attacks by the local Arabs, if the Arab armies join the fray, we shall not be able to hold out, given our low level of armament and force."

Many in the room were nodding their heads in approval. They seemed to me to favor Shertok's position but to hold Ben Gurion in great respect, mixed with just a touch of fear.

For a while a heavy silence hung in the room. Then Ben Gurion stood, straightened up, and lifted his head just a bit more than necessary. He looked above the heads of those assembled, toward a place only he could see, and stated resolutely: "I am sure the time has come, and no such opportunity may arise again for centuries, for the dream of the Jewish people to come true. I will demand statehood, and we will have to take it from there." He then added almost mysteriously, slowly, in a deep voice, "Netzach Israel Lo Yeshaker" (a nonliteral translation: "Israel's destiny will not be denied").

Nobody protested, nor was a vote conducted. Shortly after Ben Gurion's conclusive statement, the meeting broke up. People's demeanor was like that of soldiers on the eve of a grand attack: overwhelmed by the weight of the decision taken, determined, now that it had been rendered, to see it through.

Over the years that followed, I often thought about this meeting, as one people after another rose against the colonial powers, during the wars of national liberation. More and more people did what Israel did: drove out the anachronistic European empires to establish their own states. Ben Gurion had correctly diagnosed the new opportunity history had opened and he seized it. The lesson was not that a visionary can tailor history to his design if he is sufficiently courageous and determined. Ben Gurion's genius was greater. It combined historical sensibility, correct reading of the historical situation that made forming the state of Israel possible, and the leadership that was able to marshal the forces that exploited the opportunity that had opened up. Ben Gurion understood that if the people were willing to put their lives on the line, the special constellation of the international forces in

1947 provided an opportunity to realize an age-old dream. He, thus, did much more than fashion a grand new vision; he brought it down to earth and forged a new reality.

As the years passed, I often bemoaned that I was not a much more accomplished writer, able to project a stronger vision, and not better able to convince people to embrace the vision I found compelling. But in my heart of hearts I yearned for nothing more than to acquire a mere smidgen of Ben Gurion's historical sensibility—the gift that reaches beyond grand dreams to knowing what can be realized under the given conditions, when the time is ripe to strike. And to move people to reach for what can be delivered.

As for now, there was fighting to be joined for the yet-to-be-born Israel. The calendar read 1947. It was time to take up arms and put lives—ours and all of those we loved—on the line for the Jewish state that my people were aching for, for centuries. Without such a state, there was no place on earth Jews could call our own, a safe harbor in which to seek shelter if another Hitler set out to annihilate us.

CHAPTER TWO

A Commando Goes Academic

Israel Is Born

My Whole World Is a Stage

What transpired between 1947 and 1949 was heady, historical, and monumental. It would take a much more gifted writer than this one to capture the high drama of the formation of a Jewish homeland after 2,000 years of *galut* (Diaspora). It is a familiar piece of history and my contributions—as a youngster between the ages of eighteen and twenty—were very minor: fighting as a low-ranking commando soldier, mainly around and for the besieged Jerusalem; being one of a force of thousands that repelled the seven Arab armies that invaded Israel; being a member of a commando unit that liberated several Jewish villages that fell to local Arabs and opening a lifeline to the capital—in short, playing a role in shielding the infant nation. Moreover, the notes I did take at the time were sophomoric and personal musings of a teenager about the dramatic events that swirled around me, not some kind of historical overview or analysis.

I was finishing my year of underground commando training in Kibbutz Tel Joseph at the end of November 1947 when I heard a tremendous ruckus emanating from the communal dining room. Peering inside, I saw a scene, never witnessed before or since: kibbutz members were dancing—with their heavy farm boots on!—on the dining room tables! On any other day, even a minor scratching of the communal table would get you a lecture about harming collective property, on acting irresponsibly. How was tonight different from all other nights?

I quickly found out that the United Nations had just approved a partition of Palestine granting us some 5,500 square miles for the formation of the state of Israel. An American may get a sense of this historical moment by imagining that in 1776, after decades of haggling, King George III suddenly granted the United States independence rather than sending the Red Coats.

From here on, everything moved in rapid succession. As the British gradually withdrew from various parts of Palestine, Jews and Arabs were locked in a mortal battle over who would grab the newly freed lands. On May 14, 1948, Ben Gurion declared the creation of the state of Israel, followed almost immediately by the invasion by seven Arab armies. After years of dreaming about a Jewish state and inching toward it, history suddenly jerked forward.

My Palmach unit (known as Ha'Portzim, a subdivision of Har'el) was sent to help defend Jerusalem, which was encircled by local Arabs and under attack by well-equipped and well-trained Jordanian troops. Sneaking through Arab lines to get to the holy city, we took with us some of the new *olim*, guns that had just arrived from Czechoslovakia, and rucksacks full of ammunition. For the next few months, we defended the city and its surroundings from attack and fought to open a corridor from it to Tel Aviv and thus to most of Israel. This was where I saw most of my fighting. This was where two-thirds of the members of my commando unit were either killed or wounded.

My life during Israel's War of Independence unfolded on two vaguely related levels. On one, I was aware of the great historical significance of what was transpiring around me. It was easy to understand what would happen to all those I cared about most and to the whole Jewish community in Israel if we failed to repel the Arab attacks. In my youthful fantasies I was a Samson, able to win the war all on his own, with nobody getting hurt.

On the other level, most of the time I was too exhausted and pained to reflect on the big picture. Much of my effort was dedicated to staying awake (I once fell asleep while under a mortar and artillery bombardment), to ensuring that I had enough ammunition in my belt, to getting my orders straight, to coordinating my platoon's moves with those of other unit commanders, and to finding something half-decent to eat and time to gulp it down. When I had time to think, I joined others to wonder—when will we see the end to all the killing and maiming? And will Ben Gurion's daring challenge succeed? Will the state of Israel survive?

Do You Have the "Beitzim"?

If you drive from Tel Aviv to Jerusalem, you can still see burned-out armored cars dotting the sides of the roads. These belonged to Israeli caravans from Tel Aviv that tried to break through to Jerusalem to deliver food to its beleaguered inhabitants and ammunition to its dwindling defenders. The cars would burst into flame after they were hit by Arab fighters. We were stationed on the hilltops surrounding the steep valley to try to shield the caravans. The days were long and the nights longer when we failed, seeing the caravans blasted a few hundred yards from our positions, drivers stumbling out of the burning trucks, under gunfire, and Jerusalem being denied vital supplies.

One of the most pivotal places in the Arabs' blockade around Jerusalem was a citadel called Latrun. The Arabs had turned it into a major fortification that successfully blocked all travel on the only road leading from Tel Aviv (and the main body of Israel) to the capital. My Palmach unit and several others suffered numerous casualties in repeated attempts to drive the Arabs out of Latrun. All our attempts failed. The road to Jerusalem continued to be blocked and the city siege could not be lifted directly. Instead, an indirect and unpaved road was opened (known as the Burma Road). To make this possible my unit was sent to liberate Hartuv, a Jewish village captured by the Arabs. Its recapture was essential if the Burma Road was to be protected from attacks. "The action," as we called such strikes, turned into a somewhat personal test.

At Hartuv, I had to face a question that had gnawed at me long before I was first fired on: did I have what it took to fight? The Israelis speak of *beitzim* (eggs) instead of balls or nuts, but they refer to the same parts of the male anatomy, when they wonder if one has the courage, the fortitude that combat requires. Could I advance toward the enemy under a hail of bullets? Hold my ground as mortar shells exploded close by as if there were no tomorrow, followed by the thunderous menace of a row of tanks closing in? Could I help pull out those who were wounded, attend their funerals the next day, and come back for more?

Most days and nights, I did what needed doing in the company of other commandos. Having company to share fears with, to console one another somehow made it all more tolerable. When the order "charge" was sounded as I lay in a foxhole next to half a dozen friends with whom I had already shared much, I could not hang back. And when one of them was hit and was screaming in pain, I would dash to help under fire, as I knew he or she would do for me when the bullet with my initials found its mark. But in Hartuv I gained a much clearer measure of the person I had become following months of combat when I did stand out one day—quite literally.

We were instructed to storm an Arab citadel that dominated Hartuv. By that time I had been promoted to platoon leader. The plan called for my platoon to sneak close to the citadel by crawling in a creek that almost reached one of its entrances.

Figure 2.1. Hartuv—Citadel on left

Another platoon was assigned to open fire at that point at the slit windows of the citadel to prevent the Arabs inside from taking aim at us. We would then rush the remaining distance, blow open the gate of the citadel, and storm the fortification.

We proceeded according to plan, but as we closed in on the citadel, heavy fire poured down on us from the back—from where our other platoon was located! They clearly mistook us for the opposition. We had an agreed signal for such occasions when we were being raked by "friendly fire," which is the last thing it is. It entailed putting a sweater on the barrel of a rifle and waving it. We waved as agreed while hiding in the creek, trying to avoid being hit by our own comrades, but to no avail. Streams of bullets kept zinging around us and stirring up the rocks behind which we sought shelter. The fire was sure to not only abort our attack but also, at any moment, cost us lives. Something had to be done, and fast. It did not take long to figure out what this was. Someone had to stand up and expose himself, and it was clear who had to do it: I was the platoon leader; I stood up and waved the gun and sweater; the firing ceased and we carried out our mission.

"You can take me with you on the next attack," said one member of my small troop, grinning bashfully. (Even indirect compliments were not exactly in the Israeli or Palmach style.) "I must say, you have *beitzim*," said another, usually laconic, fellow fighter.

Figure 2.2.   Palmach, 1948 (back row, fourth from right with gun)

For me it was a defining day. I told myself this was because we had liberated Hartuv and secured the road vital for the survival of Jerusalem. I was brought up not only to pretend that compliments rolled off my back like rain off an army poncho, but also not to allow them to reach into myself. But it was on that day that I realized that I had come a long way from the days I considered avoiding the call to serve in the Palmach, because I feared becoming a casualty and being too much of a chicken to fight properly.

A Warrior's Aversion to Violence

Learning to fight, and discovering that I could be quite good at it, posed a new challenge. I had acquired at Ben Shemen the strong notion that Arabs' enmity had to be understood, that they were not a mindless, fanatical, bloodthirsty foe. The tragedy of the Middle East, we were taught, was that both sides had strong historical claims to the same piece of land. Zionism believed that a people without a land could settle in a land without people. But it turned out that the country was not exactly empty, although with good will it could have accommodated both its Arab and Jewish settlers. All these were fine sentiments, which urged me not to demonize those who attacked us.

It was easier in the classroom than in the mountain around Jerusalem. I found it ever more difficult to console a fighter who was blinded by fragments of enemy fire, who had lost a leg, or who had a bullet lodged in her spinal cord—and not to hate anyone for inflicting so much agony. By early 1949, all my friends and numerous other fighters with whom I had merely a pass-ing acquaintance were either somewhere in hastily dug graves or in a hospi-tal. Some seven hundred of them. Fighting was something you did, day after day and at night; however, notifying parents that they had lost their young son or daughter (the Palmach was fully coeducational) was so exhaustingly painful I found that I was trying to avoid doing my share.

Out of all the experiences of the war, two stayed with me more than oth-ers. They are stuck in the forefront of my memory not because they were so extraordinary, but because as horrifying as they were—they became all too common. (My good friend Jessica Einhorn gently chided me: "Can't you dig deeper? This is all?" Somehow my heart—and pen—just won't go there. Much of this chapter remains to be written.)

One occurred during a brief trip home. The car, from which I was getting a ride, stopped for a refill at a gas station near an emergency room entrance. Just then, a truck rushed in. Its bay held a pile of severely wounded people. Some with barely attached limbs; others with deep open cuts across their faces, arms, and legs; a wail of moaning and pierced screams converged into a chorus from hell. It turned out that a group of local volunteers had been sent to dig defense ditches at the perimeter of the town. Each carried a *turia* (a large Israeli hoe). Their truck's front tires were shot out by an Arab sniper. The truck overturned; practically all the elderly volunteers (they must have been in their forties) were mangled. We all rushed to assist in carrying them to the emergency room.

Weeks later, I was leading my platoon across a field not far from Shar HaGuy (on the road to Jerusalem). I was careful to insist the soldiers not bunch together, and, as per Israeli military tradition, I was on point, not somewhere on the side or back as is common in other armies. (The Palmach commanders were instructed not to issue orders such as "forward" or "attack," but only "follow me.") As we were crossing a valley there was a minor ex-plosion followed by a small puff of smoke. I watched with horror as Abraham, my youngest soldier, who claimed to be seventeen but looked younger, was thrown up in the air. Next, his body hit the ground with an ugly thud, jerk-ing violently. A few minutes later, Abraham died in my arms without saying a word. I had marched my troop into a minefield!

We carefully retraced our steps. Abraham's body was quickly put in the back of the jeep, and I held him closely as the car rocked its way back to base. I was angry with myself: "You should have avoided that field." Sorry for my-self, "What can I possibly tell his parents?" I railed at God, "Why take one so young?" I cursed the day I became a platoon leader. And then, "You'd better think about your soldiers; they need to be talked with." It was a very long ride, day, night. And then there were more who died so young.

Yes, I knew that it was the Arabs who had attacked us. I recognized that we were seeking a homeland for Jews who had been persecuted throughout the world for centuries, while the Arabs had many millions of acres across seven countries to live in. The line "The only thing the Arabs understand is brute force" was gaining currency. But I tried to remember that individual Arab fighters were people like us, with families and young lives, people who were duped into fighting us by their rulers. Given half a chance, I believed, we could sit down with them and work things out, if only it was left to us grunts, away from the politicians.

After many months of intense fighting, an armistice was arranged between Israel and the Arabs, which was followed by another round of combat around the clock. Then another armistice, and finally the war was winding down. It left

Figure 2.3.   Posting a call for peace in Arabic, 1948

me with a strong sense that I never wanted to wage war again, however just its cause. But oddly I had also acquired a can-do optimism. We succeeded against all odds to protect the newborn state of Israel. I did have a hand in turning a far-fetched dream into reality. And the fearful youngster who joined the Palmach was converted into someone who was confident that if called to arms again, however reluctantly, he could hack it.

The First Public Voice

During the most intensive stretch of the War of Independence, in the days before the first armistice was to take effect, we attacked Arab strongholds at night and then dashed back to our defensive positions at dawn. (We were instructed to abandon the defensive positions at night because Arabs were reluctant to attack after sunset.) In one of the first of our attacks, we drove an Arab division out of a small town west of Jerusalem.

The following day, a news story about our victory appeared in *BaMachane*, the official newspaper of the Israeli army, which was read by practically everyone during the War of Independence. As the newspaper was very small, many an item in it would become, overnight, the talk of the town, indeed the nation. The paper reported that we had found pages torn out of a Bible strewn in the street of the enemy's town; that blood was splattered on the walls of buildings; and that casualties piled up. All this was said to reflect the ferocity of the fighting. We were appalled at the wildly exaggerated account, written by a war correspondent who—we who had been there knew—had never set foot in the town or talked to any of us. Redhead (the nickname of a woman who commanded my unit), challenged me: "You used to write in high school; why don't you tell it the way it was?"

I had a great deal of respect for this slender, short woman. She seemed never to tire. When we slumped to the ground exhausted after an attack, she would visit each to ensure that we had enough ammunition and water. And she dashed among bullets to command us, to warn us of an expected attack, to direct us to change position, and just to encourage us. I could not refuse her, even if I had wanted to.

The next day I sent along my own account of the recent "action" with a truck that stopped by to replenish our ammunition and rations. It was a pencil-scribbled report written on brown pieces of paper torn out of supply bags. Two days later it appeared on the front page of *BaMachane*, under the title "How It Really Was." Encouraged, I sent in several more first-person, frontline accounts, most of which found their way into print.

By the time the war was ending, I had acquired somewhat of a following. Here and there, on leave, I would run into people who would say something like, "I saw your piece in *BaMachane*—was it really true?" "Keep writing, you're a straight shooter," and even, "What do you think? Will we make it?"

After the war I collected these firsthand reports and ruminations in a book called *A Diary of a Commando Soldier*. The book briefly reached the number two rank on the bestseller list. Its popularity, in turn, led to invitations to write for several newspapers and magazines. Thus, by the age of twenty-one, I acquired a fledgling public voice.

As my life shifted from reloading guns to changing typewriter ribbons, one theme stayed with me. On the face of it, my reportage simply provided first-person, eyewitness accounts of combat. However, the reports contained numerous allusions to the horrors of war. Accounts of a woman soldier who refused to be bandaged by her male fellow soldiers because of the delicate place the bullet was lodged; a soldier blinded by an antipersonnel mine; a girlfriend bidding her last farewell to her boyfriend at the new, rapidly filling military cemetery. When these pieces were collected into a book, I closed it by evoking the vision of the ancient prophets we memorized in school: "They will beat their swords into plowshares, and their spears into pruning hooks. Nation will not take up sword against nation, nor will they train for war anymore."

These were the sophomoric scribbles of a very young man, a seasoned fighter, not a writer. (In later years, I refused all suggestions to have the book translated into English.) But they did contain a sentiment—and that was all it was at first—that I had acquired despite the fierce fighting, or maybe because of it. It was a feeling that one ought to do everything in one's power to work out differences that exist within and among communities and to avoid resorting to violence. Violence is the ultimate degradation. It leaves those subject to it no choices, deprives them of all liberty and rights. Years later, the line "One needs to break eggs (meaning heads) to make an omelet (a new social order)," popular among students on the left, fell on very unsympathetic ears in my case. Coffee shop revolutionaries, who glamorize violence, have never experienced the pain and grief it inflicts, the deep scars it leaves, the vengeance it invites.

Words cannot capture the horror of war, however just and noble its cause. Movies and dramas can be more evocative but they tend to turn wars into entertainment. (Among the exceptions are movies such as *Saving Private Ryan*, which capture well the agony of war.) The best way I can describe what I learned between the ages of eighteen and twenty is for you to close your eyes and imagine—make a genuine effort to truly believe for a moment—that someone most dear to you has just been killed. Now add one more.

Believe me, I know well the arguments for why sometimes a people must bring war to another people. Most recently, during the war against terrorism, following the 2001 attack on America, I joined a group of sixty American intellectuals (including Samuel Huntington and Francis Fukuyama) who characterized the war as a just one. Our main argument, based on Saint Augustine's writings, is that such a war has to aim to protect the innocent (noncombatant) lives, not your own. Even when the Israeli war's nightmare was most vivid in my heart, I did not become a pacifist. However, there is little doubt in my mind that after much bloodshed, pain, and suffering and enormous expenditures of resources during decades of armed conflicts and several wars, the Arab nations, the Palestinian Arabs, and the Israelis may well end up settling into a pattern of coexistence that is much like one they could have had without firing a shot in 1947: a Jewish state and a Palestinian one, intertwined in the small territory between Egypt and Syria. If it were up to me, donor nations would not give one penny or euro or yen to developing nations involved in an arms race with one another, until those nations desisted. And appropriations that we are told are out to aid these nations, which stream right back to our arms manufacturers and dealers, would be banned or, better yet, dedicated to whatever these days amounts to ploughshares. Granted, you hear here the echo of the sentiments of a twenty-year-old, war-weary high school dropout. But after much schooling, I still hold them in my heart of hearts.

I and Thou

As the Israeli War of Independence was winding down in 1949, thousands of soldiers were discharged without much ceremony. I was let loose at the end of the year. After years of being absorbed with fighting for a cause greater than life, for the survival of the first Jewish state in two thousand years, which provided unmistakable direction as to what I had to do all day long and at night—I suddenly had to decide, all on my own, what to make of my life. I had skipped adolescence, the years of wondering what I'd be when I grew up. I could have reenlisted to serve in the Israeli army. Few jobs were as highly regarded as being a member of a force that had just won a war against all odds. Fighting was also the only work for which I was well prepared. Arrayed against reenlisting was my strong aversion to making war. And somewhere buried within me lay a yearning from my days at Ben Shemen, for finding out what great thinkers had written over the ages. However, I did fear civilian life. I wondered how I could make a living, as I was without a high school diploma, the minimum ticket for many jobs.

Above all, I wondered if I could continue my interrupted studies. Three years had passed since I had touched a book, listened to a lecture, or solved an equation. During the war, I became accomplished at throwing a hand grenade a fair distance, bringing down an enemy scout several hundred yards away with a single shot, and keeping my cool when everything around me was shaking violently. Examining a text, writing a term paper, was buried in the far away past. Could I still do any of these nerdy things?

My parents could not afford to support me, and I never asked for, nor accepted, money from them. I had to find a job and figure out in my free time whether my newly awakening intellectual curiosity was more than a passing, postwar mood. So, after turning in my gun, ammunition belt, hand grenades, and machete-sized commando knife, I hit the pavement looking for work.

The memories of the weeks that followed have stayed with me ever since with special pungency. I can still taste the bitter rejection of one workplace after another refusing to even consider a high school dropout, which is what I had suddenly become after years of being a member of a much admired, elite combat unit. I found that my legs refused to carry me to potential places of employment after the first rejections of the day. I usually spent the rest of the day staring into the Mediterranean or hanging out with other former members of the Palmach, at an army canteen on Hayarkon Street in Tel Aviv. Only then could I make myself knock on some more doors the next day, only to be waved away like a nettlesome mosquito.

I lived, in those long weeks, off of selling two articles, one a fairy tale to a children's magazine; the other—a mildly titillating piece about life in the coeducational army (including coeducational tents)—to a satirical weekly. To make ends meet, I consumed a huge amount of watermelon (very cheap and sweet); got off the bus two stops away from the station closest to the room a relative allowed me to use ("but just for now") at the outskirts of Tel Aviv, because the bus fare was a bit lower if you got off at that point. I had one full meal after I collected an armful of used bottles and returned them for the deposit.

Ever since, when conservatives speak harshly about the unemployed, the "underclass," or those on welfare, the sense of those weeks bubbles up; I cannot join such condemnation. I remember vividly wondering where my next meal would come from and if I would still have a place to sleep by the end of the week; gobbling down half of what I had and stopping while still hungry to leave something for the next meal; searching—increasingly despondent—for work but finding none. Worst was the sense that I failed. If I had only listened to my parents and completed my studies . . . nobody gave a damn that I was fighting for them all those years. . . .

I finally landed a job at a prestigious newspaper that was hiring former fighters who had made a name for themselves by writing about their experiences during the war. These included Amos Elon, Dan Ben-Amos, and Uri Avnery who later became members of the Israeli literati. After a few months on the job, an editor took me aside and said succinctly, very much in the Israeli style: "You may be an OK writer but you are an incredible ignoramus. Go study and come back." I did not know what "ignoramus" meant, but I got the point.

The admissions officer at the Hebrew University (the only Israeli university in 1950) sneered. I was advised that I should not waste my ink on applying—"even if you were a war hero, which you are not"—until I earned a high school diploma. He did, though, inform me that this certificate could be obtained through "external" exams, scheduled a few times a year. I did not have to re-enroll in high school.

I was trying to figure out how I could prepare for these special exams and survive—when manna fell from heaven. A newspaper reported that Martin Buber, considered even at the time one of the world's leading social philosophers, was looking for students for the first year of a new institute he was establishing. He offered full room and board and free tuition! In Jerusalem! No questions asked, no high school diploma required!

Best of all, Buber's institute was not going to provide just any kind of learning, but would introduce me to the world of social thinking and analysis. Although I was unfamiliar with Buber's works, I knew from my Ben Shemen days that he was a highly respected, albeit controversial, professor of social philosophy and sociology.

Enrolling was a piece of cake. But then panic struck, again. Whether I could hack it at a college-level institute was a very different question from the one I had faced early in my commando days. Now, the question was: had I lost my study habits for good? Could I really become engrossed in learning the differences between Plato and Aristotle after spending years preoccupied with the differences between Arab and Israeli mortars? Could I find my way around English grammar after years of paying attention to finding the enemy's positions on a worn-out map?

The specifics of the curricula were anything but reassuring. Classes were often conducted in line with Buber's idea of having seminar-like "dialogues" rather than extensive lectures. There would be no place to hide. We were to spend six hours a day in classrooms and practically all the remaining time studying, a hefty diet. Buber's prestige attracted some of the best professors to teach at his new institute, despite their other duties. Biology was to be taught by Joshua Liebowitz, already internationally renowned; Bible by his sister

Nechama Liebowitz, a much-respected scholar; Kabbalah by Gershon Scholem; and social philosophy by Nathan Rotenstreich and by Buber himself. The institute director, the indefatigable Gideon Freudenberg, even expected us to translate operas into Hebrew. I decided I would give this place a try, but I did not unpack my duffel bag right away.

Although everything around me—from hefty books to demanding teachers—was new, I was comforted by our familiar communal lifestyle. We lived together in an old building. We cooked and shared our meals kibbutz-style. Our classes and study halls were in the same building we lived in, which allowed us to hotly debate the lessons of the day late into the night.

These discussions sucked me back into the world of ideas. It was not in my nature to sit back and be left out when people were contesting the meaning of a passage by Immanuel Kant or that of the Talmud. If I had to do some extra reading so I could hold up my end of the debate, so be it. While it did not take long before I was fully absorbed in the give-and-take during and after classes, I continued to be frighteningly underprepared, compared to those students who had graduated from a high school before they enrolled in the institute.

About half of the students were new immigrants and therefore had to study Hebrew while keeping up with the various classes, all conducted in Hebrew. I offered to teach them the secrets of this difficult language, and in return they promised to guide me through the mysteries of subjects they mastered during their studies before they came to Israel. An immigrant from France explained Latin and ancient Greek terms that were flying around. An immigrant from Bulgaria introduced me to the secrets of the basic assumptions of natural science.

Waiting for Buber's first lecture, I expected a Moses as depicted by Michelangelo, a strong, charismatic leader, an overpowering figure, someone to both sit at his feet and salute. Instead, the scholar who quietly took his place in front of the class was a short man, slight in stature, with the weak shoulders of a Jewish teenager. He spoke softly, slowly, and deliberately as if he were weighing each word. He exhibited none of the posturing in which so many Hebrew University faculty members reveled. He hung around some at the end of many of his classes to answer questions. I even followed him to his home and kept nagging him with questions in his dark library, overflowing with used books.

Thus, when Buber turned to speak of God, he said that "God is the super I–Thou, the sea into which all rivers flow," I asked—with the brashness of someone just out of the army and years of combat—"Where is the evidence that there is such a sea?" Buber responded that God was not a person writ large, more a conception than a figure. He was in us, not "up there." A fellow student demanded to know, in typical Israeli style: "Where was that God of yours when the Holocaust consumed His chosen people?" Buber tried again. He never gave up, although at one point, when I must have come close to reaching the limits of his seemingly inexhaustible tolerance, he sighed, tugged at his beard, and fell silent for a very long time.

Sometimes Buber would strike a prophet's pose. He would lecture with his back to the sun, as it was setting behind him on the mountains of Judea. Lifting his arms above his head as if about to bless those gathered, speaking as if in a trance. It was on these occasions that I sensed that I was with a great presence, right in the heart of Jerusalem, a place believed to be closer to God than any other.

Despite late-night reading and more than my share of questioning, I could not follow parts of what Buber had to say. I was slightly comforted by finding out that I was not the only one who found him compelling yet dense. His writing varied a great deal. Some pieces were especially hard to follow; others easier to read but still not easy to comprehend because Buber the mystic mingled with Buber the social philosopher. Nevertheless, I took from his classes several basic concepts and ideas on which I have feasted for the rest of my life.

First among those was the concept of dialogue. Buber did not mean by it simply a conversation, let alone country club chitchat. He meant a give-and-take during which people open up and reach each other profoundly, in which they reaffirm each other's humanity. (He saw the most important dialogue occurring between a person and God.) I tried to follow his ideas in my own work, comparing dialogues to rational deliberations (a term preferred by liberal political theorists) and Habermas's notions on proper conversations. Later, I also worked to dialogue with my students instead of lecturing at them.

Above all I took from Buber (to put it in very quick, simple, and demystified terms) the notion that there was in the world an unending struggle between the forces that pushed us to relate to other human beings as objects, as Its, rather than as fellow humans, as Thous. Moreover, the struggle could never be ended, as It (or instrumental) relations were unavoidable in the world of commerce and work. However, the thicker we could make the realm of Thou, the better the world would be.

Buber also introduced me to my first readings of communitarian philosophy, including his own works. For Buber, community was not necessarily an ideal place. He contrasted it with a place that was pure Thou, in which people treated each other only as objects of love, not labor, a place that could be reached in a moment of excitement and exhilaration but could not be made to last.

I was especially surprised that Buber's concept of community did not contain a concept of individual rights. (We had just learned about rights reading Immanuel Kant.) Here, Buber seemed to be influenced by the Jewish tradition, which, like Islam, stresses our responsibility for others; say, for the poor among us. But neither religion contains a solid concept of individual rights—for example, that those in need have a right to lay a moral (let alone legal) claim to be helped, that they are entitled to assistance from the more fortunate members of the community.

There was much more in the scholarship Buber laid out for us over a year's course. There is just no way I can do justice to it here, even to those parts I did understand, which by no means was all of it.

Another faculty member at Buber's institute opened a door to a different way of thinking, one I was going to tackle in more ways than one. I took my first class in economics from a young American who had just immigrated to Israel, Don Patenkin. He scandalized the stiff academic community in Jerusalem—which was highly influenced by European traditions, especially Germanic notions of "Herr Professor"—by riding around on a bike, with a loose sweater, short pants, and a crew cut. He often smiled, and one could approach him at almost any time with a question. Most consequential for me, in the longer run, was that Patenkin was a graduate of the University of Chicago, the place Milton Friedman called home. Patenkin taught us the foundations of the "dismal science" in the Chicago tradition, that of neoclassical economics. It is worlds apart from other economics, such as humanistic or social economics, or even developmental economics, all little known in the United States but dominant in those days in Europe and Israel.

By the end of the year in Buber's institute, I overcame my doubts about my place in the world of ideas. I hardly remembered how a mere year earlier I could have even considered making the army my career. I was keen to learn more.

The next fall found me at Hebrew University. I was admitted because I passed two exams that qualified me for the equivalency of a high school diploma while at Buber's institute. I did OK on most parts of these exams, except English. I always had a hard time acquiring languages, as I found out when I had to learn Greek and then Hebrew, after German. Having avoided English at Ben Shemen, I barely scraped by, despite fairly strenuous preparation. Moreover, by the end of the intense year at Buber's institute, I also pocketed a teacher's certificate that enabled me to earn a living while enrolled at Hebrew University.

While the year of studying was very placid in contrast with my years of combat, it did turn my life around one more time. My interest in matters intellectual was back where it had been when I graduated from Ben

Shemen. I completed the journey from student to commando fighter and from warrior to one anxious to study.

A Third Way

Early in my studies at the university, I was required to choose a major. It did not take any smarts to note that the society around me was undergoing some very profound changes. Large numbers of immigrants were flooding in from cultures that differed greatly from the Israeli one. Tensions between religious and secular Jews mounted, as did those between Jews from Ashkenazi and Sephardic backgrounds and those in slums and those in affluent suburbs. If I was to participate in the deliberations about the remaking of society, sociology seemed the best tool.

I was barely into my major of sociology at the Hebrew University when I encountered communitarian thinking by leading sociologists. We studied the complex works of Ferdinand Tönnies, known for his distinction between *gemeinschaft* (community) and *gessellschaft* (society). We worked our way through volumes of Émile Durkheim, who stressed the important role of shared values and social bonds in forming and sustaining communities. We sweated over Robert Park's *Human Communities* and prepared to be examined about the concept of the self as a social construction in George Herbert Mead's work. When Buber retired, S. N. Eisenstat became my sociology teacher, and Yonina Talmon, my mentor.

Reading these texts, I found the works of the giants of sociology and social psychology much more complex, intricate, and rich than the summaries in textbooks, my first fare. Indeed, we delved into several volumes by other scholars who argued about divergent interpretations of the tomes of the masters. I was especially captivated by Talcott Parsons's magnificent overview, *The Social Structure of Social Action*. I was astounded by Parsons's ability to weave together works by several sociological greats into a new theory and equally pained to have to read the 817-page book in English.

As I took copious notes during my various classes and readings, two intertwined themes stayed with me. First, the advance of modernity, the march of enlightenment, the rise of new technologies and industries, and secularism were undermining the traditional society based on life in small communities. The new society allowed one to escape the conformity and hierarchy of small towns and villages to live in anonymity in the city as an individual—to be free. Second, at the same time, the resulting loss of social fabric, the increase in human isolation, threatened people's mental health and moral character, resulting in alienation and crime. It made people yearn for a more communal life.

Moreover, people in the modern world were missing not merely community as a place of strong personal bonds, but also a life in which the social order was based on shared values and informal controls rather than on extensive law enforcement. Some of our professors called this yearning "romanticism," which did not seem a flattering label when contrasted with enlightenment, but it seemed wrong to dismiss this profound human yearning.

Long before I felt at home with these ideas, more were loaded on my reading list. It was time to study the young Karl Marx, especially his writings about communes, various Fabian socialists, and Sigmund Freud's work, *Civilization and Its Discontents*, among others. Practically all of these volumes addressed one element or another of communitarian thinking. Having missed any hint of these works in high school, not to mention in my fighting years, I could not read enough. Whatever I read was often applied and sharpened during incessant discussions of these ideas with my fellow students, in the corridors of lecture halls, in guarded whispers in the library, on dates, and in coffee shops. I found it hard to turn off the buzz at night. I would keep thinking about a challenging question someone posed, how I could have better responded, what might be argued tomorrow. A nonstop high.

While I was becoming ever more a student, I did not fully lose my taste for action and for public voice. A minor role in the student government kept me involved in the affairs of the day, but I did not allow the interminable meetings to eat into my new life as a bookworm. And I acquired a new ambition. I tried my hand at new kinds of articles—less descriptive, more analytical—and published them under hefty titles such as "The decline of basic values," "A new Israeli citizen," and even a ponderous piece on "Work productivity and societal rewards." After all, by now I had all the wisdom of a twenty-two-year-old and two years of sociology under my belt!

Sociology continued to be my chosen field, both as my undergraduate major (economics as a minor) and in studies for my master's degree (philosophy as a minor). Absorbing a new way of thinking happens gradually, whether it is sociology, law, or economics. However, after a few years, you see the world (and often yourself and those close to you) through different lenses, noticing that which normal mortals do not, while overlooking features others consider significant.

The fact that I was being sucked deeper and deeper into sociology was driven home to me at a small coffee shop on Ben Yehuda Street where a bunch of us often hung out after classes. We argued hotly and loudly with one another. The owner, rather than throwing us out, often added his voice to the cacophony. One particular line of thought I was pushing troubled most of my friends, a line they attributed to my being brainwashed by sociology on good days and to my sheer mulishness on others. I grew increasingly weary of bodies of thought that based their considerations on one overarching principle.

Aaron Caduri, who studied economics, was after me to recognize liberty as the governing principle, and he mightily labored to reject, downgrade, or dismiss all that stood in its way. He would have made any libertarian proud. While there were all kinds of other views flying around the small table, my fiercest critic from the other side was Dan Dromi, who was working for the youth division of Mapam (a left-leaning party). He believed in socialism and argued with much assurance that equality trumped all other values.

About the only thing Aaron and Dan agreed on was that my sociological training had corrupted me to the point that I would not commit to either principle—or for that matter, to any other one. They complained that I was trying to find social systems that could serve several values simultaneously, which meant that none of them could be truly served.

I responded that philosophers are entitled to see how far they can proceed by following one principle; sociologists recognize that societies must accommodate multiple and partially incompatible needs and values.

"You and your third way" was Dan and Aaron's dismissive line. I responded in the expected style, dismissing their quest for ideological purity. We continued to be the best of friends.

My studies in sociology created another friendship. I spent many an evening comparing notes with another student, Hava, the star of my class. The fact that she had blue eyes, sun-bleached blonde hair, and peachy cream skin—not common colors in Israel—only added to her allure. When a magazine published one of my articles on student life, it featured her picture on the cover. At the end of our first year of studying together, we married.

On completing my master's in 1957, I was fully entrenched in academic sociology. I believed that it provided a master key to most anything there was to be known. It was going to be my vocation and future.

I decided to round off my sociological training with one year of study in the United States. Hava agreed to join me, but with a heavy heart. She was going to greatly miss her mother, who had dedicated her life to bringing up Hava after the early death of her father.

The evening before we left for the University of California at Berkeley, our friends threw a little farewell party. Nobody was toasted with a drink because none of us drank alcohol (including wine or beer) in those days. Coca-Cola was highly regarded if you wished to show that you did not care for the common orange juice.

My friends advised me on how to deal with Americans: "When you get to the United States, and people say to you 'let's get together for lunch,' don't

Figure 2.4.   Hava on a magazine cover

be fooled; they do not mean it," I was warned. Someone added, "Americans are such phonies; you can never trust their compliments." A young woman from sociology had a label for what I was to expect: "pseudo-gemeinschaft," an attempt to make you feel as if you and the other person—say, a car dealer—were members of one community, when actually you were not at all. None of this troubled me any. I was about to study at one of the very best departments of sociology in the world. If my life was going to be that of an academic sociologist, what could be more exciting?

PART TWO

IN OPPOSITION

CHAPTER THREE

A Public Voice For . . .

The Sins of Public Intellectuals

Berkeley: Time and a Half

When I arrived to study in the United States in January 1957, I enrolled at the University of California at Berkeley. (Hava, who joined me later, was working on her first article, soon to be published.) It was a renowned department of sociology, whose stars at the time included several sparkling senior scholars. (S. M. Lipset, Reinhard Bendix, Philip Selznick, Kingsley Davis, Nathan Glazer, and Leo Leventhal. Herbert Blumer was ending his teaching years.) Even several of the young professors had already acquired a name for themselves (including Erving Goffman, William Kornhauser, and Martin Trow). Visiting scholars added to the department's luster (especially a seminar by Talcott Parsons). Even the students were a choice lot.

My first challenge was managing with the $300 I had to my name, the maximum loan a relative could afford. I also had a sealed note from my professor at the Hebrew University, S. N. Eisenstat, introducing me to Berkeley professor S. M. Lipset. I prayed it would deliver me a part-time job. I dutifully handed the letter to Lipset, who read it, grunted something I could not understand, and invited the next student into his office. I was sure my days at Berkeley were numbered. To stretch their number, I joined a co-op, which, in exchange for my attention to massive piles of dirty dishes and other equally attractive kitchen chores, provided room and board.

A few days later, I attended Lipset's first class. At the end of the class he handed me a huge manuscript, some eleven hundred pages. He invited me to examine the work and drop by to discuss it. After struggling through the magnum opus for two long days and much of one night, I knocked on his door. Mindful of what my Israeli friends had said about American manners, I allowed that the book was "indeed a fine one, a masterful work of sociology, a tour de force of political theory."

Lipset grinned: "Come on, what do you really think?"

I let loose a small barrage, as maybe only a young Israeli right off the boat could: "Although the book has immense potential, it is much too long and incredibly repetitious; at the same time, in places it is crying out for more documentation. Above all, the arguments need straightening out." When I left the office, I had a part-time job as Lipset's research assistant. I, together with another assistant, Juan Linz, helped Lipset some as he reworked his manuscript.

The only word that begins to capture what it was like working for Marty Lipset with Juan Linz is *delightful*. Marty, a tall and hefty man, was as exuberant as a teenager given wheels for the first time—as long as he could regale you with stories about some exciting finding he had come across. He had little interest in abstractions, but his tales all had points to them. They helped explain why the United States was different from other nations, why a printers' union was more democratic than others, and so on. Marty rarely needed to take a breath as he shared one story after another. And he scared the daylights out of me when, enthusiastically making some point in the car, he waved his hands and drove with his knees. In later years, he allowed his devoted wife, Sydney, to take over the steering wheel.

Juan often waited with a mixture of respect (he was brought up in Spain) and impatience for Marty to pause, so he could jump in with findings that piqued his curiosity. If Juan had a life other than scholarship, I was unaware of it. He was completely dedicated to academic research (the one exception was his interest in cooking, a subject—I hate to admit—that never made it high on my priority list). It was easy to foretell that he would become a much-renowned scholar.

Decades later, Marty moved to Washington, D.C., and we saw each other often, as colleagues and friends. Following Marty's stroke, I was particularly saddened, when visiting him first at the hospital and then at home, that his ability to express himself remained limited. Marty, I am sure, would have given up an arm and a leg to be able to continue to share his ideas as freely as he did in our Berkeley days.

A psychologist friend, whom I met while visiting Marty, argued that we feel sorry for ourselves when we see him in this condition—"Here but for the grace of God lie I." I have no trouble believing that this may be one element of what I and others feel. But still, I find it troubling when in such situations, and in others such as studies of altruism and charity, social scientists are quick to debunk any sense of true empathy and fellow feeling. I can care about someone even if I fully expect never to find myself in a similar condition; for example, a difficult childbirth.

The book that grew out of the manuscript Linz and I worked on, *The Political Man*, was published to great success. Its acknowledgments note my role such as it was, but they do not mention that without it, I would have been unable to pay my way at Berkeley. Nor does it note that I learned at least as much from the exercise as I contributed to it.

Another major hurdle I faced was my poor command of English. The first book I was assigned was Samuelson's thick introduction to economics. It took me well over half an hour to struggle through the first page, constantly consulting a dictionary. I was sure that soon I would be found out, unable to follow, and be sent packing. It took all my willpower to learn the peculiarities of this foreign tongue. My American friends were surprised at the great difficulties I had in learning English and occasionally became annoyed when I kept asking them why words were spelled in one way and pronounced in another, until they recalled their experiences in acquiring French or German, let alone Hebrew. (Those who fully sympathize with my struggle will understand why I was unabashedly tickled pink—still am—when I found out years later that *The St. Martin's Guide to Writing* was using some of my writings— to teach English.)

Having secured my livelihood and mastered some of the secrets of English, I worked long hours at the Berkeley library on my Ph.D. I paid little mind to the Berkeley around me. I never got to the top of the Campanile, the tower in the middle of the campus, a leading tourist attraction, from which you can admire the striking San Francisco Bay. I missed practically all the rallies that were the harbinger of the Free Speech movement. I earned my doctorate in eighteen months (three semesters and two back-to-back summer sessions, to make for the required two academic years). I was able to complete my degree in record time, in part because I had brought with me piles of data on the organizational structure of kibbutzim and in part because I worked longer, and maybe a bit harder, than many graduate students.

While some of my fellow students were involved in various counterculture experimentations, my main diversions for that year and a half were items that cost nothing. These included occasionally playing chess with other research assistants or watching the *Ed Sullivan Show* on Sunday nights at the home of a fellow student, Fred Goldner. But I could negotiate the library's stacks blindfolded.

Our first son, Ethan, was born shortly before I was awarded my Ph.D. Hava and I lived on the wrong side of the tracks in a small room, in which Ethan's hand-me-down baby carriage doubled as his bed. I could not wait to hold a full-time job. Academic life was dandy, but I had been a student for too long.

As I was completing my dissertation in the first months of 1958, Lipset was placing phone calls to help me land my first academic job. Columbia University was one of the places that showed some interest. None of the other universities that responded came close to Columbia in terms of their sociological standing.

Professor William J. Goode (whom everyone called Si), a highly respected sociologist of the family and stratification (he later developed a sociological theory of his own), was doing the recruiting for Columbia. He asked me to write him a several-page letter laying out my plans for the future, above all "revealing" myself, so that he could "get a feel for what you are like." This request stuck in my craw; he might as well have asked me to disrobe. Aside from feeling awkward and believing that the request was not legitimate, I had brought with me from Israel at least a touch of "in-your-face" attitude. "Hell," I said to myself, "I am not going to talk about my inner self; this is none of his Goddamn business." I continued to fume. "Goode wants a tell-all letter? Here is what he is going to get: a detailed description of my research ideas, the grand and not so grand subjects I plan to study in the coming years. Period." I wrote a letter about my plans to develop organizational sociology, which I discovered while working on my Ph.D. did not really exist. There was industrial sociology, I explained, and studies of governmental bureaucracies, but no attempt to pull together the features of all or even most organizations. I guess I was about to become a true academic: making distinctions where none previously existed, arguing that there are significant tools in bettering our understanding, and so on. With the letter off, I waited.

Nothing happened; weeks ticked by and turned into long months. In those days, appointments were usually not made after mid-May. April was grinding to an end, and still there was no word from Columbia, which continued to be by far the most coveted job of those open to me. Lipset called and Goode explained in his inimitable style: "I asked the guy to write something about himself; he sent me this piece of shit." Well, Lipset took me by my lapel, sat me down, and insisted that I compose a long letter about my inner feelings. I hated every minute of it. It took me longer, and I had to toss out more drafts, than most anything I had written to date. But I did get my first academic job. The move to New York City was an easy one; we had little packing to do.

Two Walks in the Woods

For a while, life in Morningside Heights, during my first teaching year (1958–1959), unfolded smoothly. I was a newly minted assistant professor, but on a tenure track. I prepared my courses diligently and started researching organizations. Moreover, my academic work did not consume my whole day. Ethan was an energetic bundle of joy, who helped me make new faculty friends as I accompanied him to the neighborhood sandboxes and to Riverside Park. I even discovered that I could, as my English slowly improved, regain a public voice. I found I could publish my views in nonacademic terms about matters that concern the public at large. My aversion to violence made me focus on what was and is considered the ultimate threat to our lives, nuclear weapons.

Today, more than half a century since the only time atomic weapons were employed, we've all sort of gotten used to them. (Although, I still see many reasons to expect that sooner or later these bombs will wipe out a Tel Aviv, kill many millions in some Asian country such as India or Pakistan, or wreak unimaginable grief on some other Godforsaken place.) At the time, at the end of the fifties, many agreed with C. P. Snow, who stated that without nuclear disarmament, nuclear war was not a probability but a certainty. If you picture Hiroshima after the bomb and multiply the devastation by 10,000, you see the image that was haunting us. Some even feared that nuclear weapons might melt down the whole world. The whole thing. I tried my hand at writing about the horrors of war and related them to the threatening nuclear holocaust.

"Professor Lazarsfeld will see you this afternoon at 3:00 in his office," I was informed by Esther Davis, the much-dreaded executive secretary of the Columbia University sociology department. Paul F. Lazarsfeld was one of the two "demigods" of the department, widely respected and feared by the junior and not-so-junior staff. (Robert K. Merton was the other.) This was going to be my first audience with his eminence. I approached it with all the assurance of someone caught in the act when nobody was supposed to be around. Only, I did not have the faintest idea of what vile act I was supposed to have committed.

Lazarsfeld greeted me with a mischievous sparkle in his eye, a Viennese accent that many considered charming, and an informality that made me leery. He motioned me to sit down and started with, "I understand that the students love you," like someone anesthetizing the spot before sticking in the knife. With the preliminaries out of the way, Lazarsfeld stated point-blank: "You are a bright guy and may well one day make a fine sociologist, but you'd better cut out this 'social work' stuff. It took us more than a generation to get sociology to be recognized as a science. I know you do not mean to undermine this achievement, but if you continue, you will do so anyhow. Our job is to build knowledge, not to make public pronouncements on things we know nothing about."

My first thought was of fish fat. I could taste its greasy flavor; smell its fishy odor. During my poorest years in Israel, we could buy fish fat very cheaply, and so we had it five times a week. We became adept at turning the fish fat into something that seemed like seafood salad or like a white stew, but for me fish fat came to stand for poverty, insecurity, and powerlessness.

Cornered in Lazarsfeld's office, as he was puffing on his cigar, I sensed that my future at Columbia, an academic life, my dream of a secure job, had gone up in smoke; it was back to fish fat. Still, I did not have a clue what brought on this *gotterdammerung*.

I mumbled, "I am still green; just two years out of grad school; I'm still wet behind the ears. This is something I must think about. Is there anything *particular* I should be watching out for?"

"Well," Lazarsfeld elaborated, "both Merton and I hope that this movie review you wrote is the last one; that it is not the kind of sociology you plan to practice." He then murmured, "The last thing we need is another C. Wright Mills."

Mentioning Mills was as red a flag as Lazarsfeld could have waved, and it got my full attention. Mills was a senior professor in my department. Most senior members of the department considered him a dangerous and rambunctious outcast. ("He is a radical! Never does any research!" "A publicity hound." "And you know what—he rides a motorcycle and wears a scarf around his neck!") About the nicest thing I heard about Mills was from one of his few supporters, who called him "a regular cowboy." Mills was not allowed to teach graduate students, a limitation initially also imposed on me. (Teaching graduate students separated what the department considered the true-blue academics from "mere" teachers, who were relegated to the instruction of undergraduates "in the college," or worse, adults who sought to round out their education, segregated in a special division called "General Studies.")

One must recall that we are speaking about a different age. We were still years away from the civil rights movement and desegregation, before riots on the campus, before Betty Friedan, and before the counterculture. Ivy League universities, Columbia included, were rather stiff places. While only some wore suits, jackets and slacks and of course ties were the rule. Sneakers had yet to be invented. Jeans were something worn by golddiggers in San Francisco and by janitors. Professors were addressed by their last name and treated with considerable respect, most of the time.

All the members of my department, tenured and not, old and young, were white males. The atmosphere can be quickly captured by a brief visit to the admissions committee. We were meeting for hours on end around a longish table, wading through hundreds of folders of students seeking admission. It was considered one of those tedious chores one had to do. Somewhere into the fourth hour, a bit giddy from boredom and fatigue, the file of a female student came up. Her academic promise was borderline. Someone said, only half in jest, "Let's see her picture!" Everybody chuckled. The picture was passed around. "Not bad at all!" "Better than the two we just admitted." "Yeah, let's get her," was the consensus. And we so voted. (If there were any misgivings in the room, they were not because of what would later be called "sexism" but because a nonacademic consideration was allowed to enter our deliberations. Today it is considered highly inappropriate to attach pictures to admission files.)

My injury to that academic culture turned out to be my review of *Hiroshima Mon Amour*, a movie that had deeply moved me. Most reviews of the movie were quite favorable but focused largely on the camera work, the acting, and the soundtrack. Some explored the story line from an individual psychological viewpoint, paying much attention to the trauma of a French girl who had an affair with a Nazi solider while Germany occupied France during World War II. (The girl was ostracized by her village.) The movie also explored her later relationship with a Japanese lover, in which she simultaneously violated three social taboos of the day: both she and her lover were married—but not to each other; their first liaison occurred before she even found out his name; and he was not merely of a different nation—but also of a different race.

I wrote in my review that the movie—which superimposes images of the ominous mushroom clouds of exploding nuclear bombs on the love scenes— aims to make us sense that unless love knows no boundaries, we shall all turn into ashes in the ovens of some horrible nuclear mega-burners. The movie conveys the agony of being subject to violent hatred just because you are different. And it associates these feelings in our guts with the horrifying images of the destruction of a whole city full of people, the bombed-out Hiroshima. It projects the sense of hate on images of miles of roasted bodies, blinded children, dazed survivors lost among the ruins. Whatever the merits of my interpretation of the movie, it was hardly what my senior colleagues considered proper sociology—scientific and free of moral judgments and messages.

I am not sure what I told Lazarsfeld; I believe I thanked him for warning me. I spent the weekend after our meeting trying to figure out where I might go from here. Should I look for a new position *before* I got kicked out? Sociology was my training and love; if I were to be dismissed by Columbia early in my career, other universities would shun me. The best I could hope for was finding a teaching job in some third-rate college in the boondocks. Should I keep myself to the academic grind and my ideas to myself? Refrain from speaking publicly? These questions, in turn, forced me to examine what I was really all about. An anxious young man, keen to secure a paycheck? Someone who believed he had a duty to speak up? And if I had a calling—was I willing to pay my dues? How far was I willing to march down this road—with a two-year-old child in tow and not enough savings to pay next month's rent?

Not long thereafter, Si Goode stopped by my office. Usually, young assistant professors like me would stop by his office to hang around and visit. He served as an older friend, someone you could talk to candidly about the elder members of the department and trust he would not pass it on, someone who would give advice sensitive to your needs. If Si came down from his perch, something was up. Si suggested that we "go for a walk in the woods," which I read to mean "not all the way to the woodshed but. . . ." On leaving Fayerweather Hall, we were drenched by a rain that came down as if God had violated his promise to Noah; we rushed to the closest coffee shop, Chock Full o' Nuts on Broadway.

Si inquired how my housing hunt was progressing: "I hear you want to move out of your dump." I reported that we were looking, but all that we'd found so far was way out of line with our pocketbook. I tried to be brief; I wanted to get through the preliminaries as quickly as possible.

Si explained that he was very fond of me ("Remember? I was the one who hired you.") and was only looking out for my well-being. That entailed laying out the "facts of life" as they were, whether or not he particularly cared for them.

"I know about the meeting you had with Lazarsfeld," he added. Now I knew at least where the conversation was headed. "You must have not been very convinced by that meeting." He let this hang in the air.

Me: "Well, it gave me a lot to think about."

Si: "Look, I don't give a fart, other than I do believe that one owes to one's vocation a full day's work. Let me tell you that word gets around. A friend at Princeton was asked to review an outline of a book you presented to the editors of Collier about peace. We were chatting—I did not call him!—and it came up. He said that your book will be full of value judgments against this and for that."

There was no sense in denying it, and I liked Si too much to play games with him. So I grinned: "Guilty as charged."

Si grew uncomfortable: "What will you say to our colleagues who will point out that you are a sociologist; what do you know about foreign policy? Sure, one could write a sociological book about peace, but you told the department that you were going to work on organizational sociology. You already published four articles in this field. Man, you must specialize. You cannot be a man for all seasons; not in this department, you can't, and not in any other self-respecting one I know."

Me: "I hear you. I do appreciate you laying it all out. I promise you I will think it over carefully. I do."

Si: "You understand, that it is your future I am worried about? I personally do not give a hoot if you write poetry or paint watercolors. . . . I myself have all kinds of other interests, but the department—hell, the whole discipline— is adamant."

Academic or Public Intellectual?

The issue I faced was hardly unknown or mine alone. In effect, every public intellectual—people who have one foot in the academic world and the other in the public marketplace of ideas—has been raked over the coals. The more famous—the hotter the fire. The one I was most familiar with, aside from C. Wright Mills, was Margaret Mead, whose office was but a building away. The lines of criticism were the same: public intellectuals were chastised for rendering pronouncements not fully supported by available data, for allowing themselves a greater measure of certitude than any evidence allows for, for passing normative judgments rather than being value-free, for popularizing, and in the process simplifying, complex thoughts. Several book-length tirades have been written about the failings of public intellectuals (most recently in a book by Richard Posner, *The Public Intellectual*). Academic critics furthermore complained that public intellectuals were overgeneralizing, emotive, given to moral pronouncements, and that they cheapened the academic work.

When David Reisman presented his ideas at Yale which became the basis of his highly influential book *The Lonely Crowd*, economists dismissed him as "lacking in scientific rigor," and sociologists said he was "simply translating into new terminology familiar concepts of 'gemeinschaft' and 'gessellschaft.'" About Harvard's John Kenneth Galbraith, *The New Yorker* wrote, "Even some of those economists who personally like Galbraith dismiss him with the usual tags—'popularizer,' 'gadfly,' or, worst of all, 'journalist.'"

Carl Sagan was not treated much better. After he died, he was described as a "cunning careerist" and, the ultimate put-down, a "compulsive popularizer."

Howard Becker, a perceptive sociologist, observed: "It had once been possible for an American sociologist . . . to be admired by colleagues for serious professional work and simultaneously be a voice in the major political and cultural dialogues of the day. Max Weber did it. . . . Raymond Aron did it. . . . But no American sociologist had pulled this off in a long time . . . and those who had tried it (e.g., David Reisman) were often unfairly criticized as 'popularizers.'"

On closer examination little of this seemed to make sense. There are in any given year approximately 400,000 professors in the United States. Public intellectuals' ranks may number, at most, 100. (Longer lists include havebeens, never-beens, long-dead, and those in other countries.) This leaves only 399,900 to do the specialized, meticulous work the critics of public intellectuals are so keen to defend. Nor is there any evidence that this handful of public intellectuals in some way corrupts the standards of the "remaining" academics. There is not a shred of evidence that in the years public intellectuals were dying out—another common complaint!—that academia was doing better, or that in the years public intellectuals multiplied, it was doing more poorly. Indeed, there is a strong continuous trend toward greater specialization. If anything corrupts academia, it is commercialization not intellectualization.

Nor are pure academics without their own critics—on very much the same issues at hand. The work of many scholars, especially once they have tenure, becomes irrelevant not only to any public or social or moral concern, but irrelevant, period. To give but one example: a whole group of sociologists dedicated their lives to studying when people pause during phone calls, when they say "ah," and such trivia. Granted, one may find some morsels of importance in the deepest junk, but very few (outside the members of this small group) has been able to discern any in these subjects.

At the same time there can be little doubt, as even a young beginning sociologist could discern, that society needs some—maybe 50, or 150—public intellectuals. Someone's vocation must be to think big thoughts, to challenge assumptions society takes for granted, to read back where it is headed, and to suggest new directions it might explore. Moreover, those public intellectuals that are campus-based benefit not only from their familiarity with academic work, which they are able to draw on in their public voices, but also, being tenured, they are freer to speak truth to power at times when others become reluctant (e.g., when a Joe McCarthy looms or when patriotism swells during a war). This point was driven home to me in the Carter White House when most everyone else—with the notable exception of Stu Eizenstat—was fearful of speaking up lest they be sent back to their low-paying, undistinguished jobs in Georgia, from which many hailed. My tenure at Columbia freed me from such worries.

In short, I could see little solid sociological analysis (of the kind the purists called for) in support of the denunciation of public intellectuals. That did not mean, though, that I was willing and able to become the butt of criticism of my senior colleagues. I set aside a weekend to figure out how I was going to respond to Lazarsfeld's message, which spoke for my senior colleagues and, to a significant extent, my academic discipline. On the face of it, my choice was simple. Either suppress my public voice or leave, at least the academic main posts.

Ethicists advise people to use a device to clarify their life goals. They suggest writing your own obituary. Look at your life from the end backward, they recommend, and determine what it is you wish you had accomplished. Then examine yourself candidly to determine if the life you lead is going to get you there.

Instead, I composed an epitaph that weekend that read: "Here lies one who cared, who labored hard to serve purposes greater than self, one who attempted the best he could, within his limited abilities, to make the world better than it would otherwise be." A briefer inscription came to me: "One Who Served."

Reviewing my notes the next day, I scoffed at my empty idealism. To maintain the kind of public voice I hoped to raise, I needed an academic base, to nurse its substance and integrity. Moreover, I wondered, how could I make a contribution to the world if I were out in the street, preoccupied with trying to make a living? I knew several so-called nonstudents who hung around the campus, pursuing their activist agendas, without ever completing their Ph.D. or securing a job. I did not believe that I had the stomach for such a marginal existence. I told Hava over dinner, as Ethan was going about his antics: "I will drop all this activism. No more demonstrations against the bomb. No more peace rallies. And above all, not another line that does not add to the 'glory' of sociology." Hava, who could read me like an open book, was underwhelmed. "That'll be the day," she grinned.

To make a long story short, after some additional agonizing I concluded that I would somehow do both: I would produce so much scholarship that my contributions to academia would be undeniable, and—do peace, too! I was going to be a good sociologist and an active citizen. Images from Hiroshima sufficed to confirm my belief that humanity could not possibly do without my administering to it. The whole world was being threatened with a nuclear meltdown; how could anybody who understood what was coming remain silent? The bomb did not discriminate between combatants and civilians, between men, women, and children, between West and East. How could anyone limit himself to searching for correlations and hunting for footnotes? My Israeli experiences had ingrained in me a strong yearning for action that had some redeeming merit beyond self. I hungered for such action even more than for a secure future. At the same time, I could do little good by merely adding one more demonstrator to the lines in Columbus Circle or Trafalgar Square. I had to find a way to nurture my academic work—and then draw on it to amplify my public voice and to carry it further.

A line came to me, hardly original, but it captures well what was buzzing in me: "Here I stand; I can do no other"; I informed Hava, who was not at all surprised.

Academic Pleasures

Knowing what you wish for is not a bad place to start, but I still didn't know whether I could be both a true academic and publicly active. To serve better my first master, I wormed my way into a cubicle the size of a small cabinet in the main library of the campus. (These were usually reserved for students working on their Ph.D. dissertations.) I spent long days there—including good parts of weekends—examining several hundred previously published studies of corporations, schools, churches, armies, prisons, and voluntary associations.

As I was reviewing these studies, it slowly dawned on me that all these organizations had many elements in common, which in turn combined in predictable patterns. Especially telling were the kind of power an organization employed to motivate or make its members (employees, staff, inmates, pupils, and so on) do whatever needed doing and the members' attitude toward that organization.

The study of organizations attracted me because organizations are the most purposive form of all social endeavors. While cultures, societies, communities, and families basically just happen or evolve naturally (although some of them can be somewhat engineered or organized), organizations—which include corporations, armies, schools, and so forth—are deliberately set up to serve various goals. They differ from other social endeavors the way canals differ from rivers; they reflect our purpose, plans, and managerial capacity. Because organizations often fail in fulfilling their goals, I was intrigued by the question of what forces pull them off target or keep them on course. This turned out to be a huge subject. I tackled only one part of it.

Piecing together a large number of findings, I found that there are basically three kinds of powers that organizations employ to control their members: force (e.g., security guards), incentives and sanctions (paychecks, fines, and bonuses), and "normative" influence (appealing to people's values). The ways members relate to their organizations range from highly hostile (most inmates in prisons) to very involved (young Mormons on mission).

Further examination allowed me to find a hidden pattern in the data I was analyzing: if you measured these two facets of a given organization (the kind of power employed to control people and their basic orientation to the organization), you could "predict" a great deal. For instance, organizations that controlled their members with force, and who faced highly antagonistic members, were less able to rehabilitate or educate them than were organizations that relied less on force (e.g., minimum-security prisons) as long as their inmates were less resentful. Organizations that relied on remuneration (e.g., factories) and whose workers were neither particularly hostile nor dedicated could turn out high-volume work, but it would not be of the same quality or even quantity as that of organizations that also appealed to the values of their members and were viewed by them with considerable approval (e.g., professions). It was all like putting together a giant jigsaw puzzle that had many thousands of pieces. While it took years to see the whole picture, long before the last piece fell into place, there was the joy of seeing partial designs emerge and a sense of the ground covered.

Moreover, it turned out that the puzzle had moving parts! I discovered that if the two cardinal elements (power and orientation) did not line up as the pattern prescribed, the resulting inner tension would be revealed because it would destabilize such organizations. For instance, if teachers of a high school were trying to rely on normative appeals but the pupils were rebellious, either the teachers had to win over the youngsters or use more disciplinary measures. Power and response had to match. These patterns also affected organizational goals, leadership, productivity, and much more. All together, this became an extensive volume of academic sociology.

The work, which at times was tedious and even frustrating (when several stubborn pieces of information would not fit anyplace after several tries), had its own inner rewards. I enjoyed reading and learning about lives of people I never laid eyes on. Scanning reports of life inside prisons, nunneries, and mines was like engaging in prolonged anthropological visits. Also it was gratifying to find pieces of missing data, which had long eluded me; for instance, about the way churchgoers felt about the hierarchy; so was discovering that information collected for one purpose provided evidence in support of a part of the theory that originally seemed utterly unrelated. The best way I can share this sense of satisfaction with someone not so engaged is to evoke the sense of elation one might feel when finally succeeding in assembling a child's tricycle following the manufacturer's obtuse instructions. In short, doing academic work provided for much more than paying my dues to the university in which I was seeking tenure and securing a basis from which I could launch social action. Academic work had its own rewards.

While I was cobbling the book together, I refused to show any part of it to anyone. The book was breaking several academic modes; I feared that my colleagues' displeasure might prevent me from exploring what seemed a promising vein. Before my work, there had been studies of corporations called "industrial sociology," studies of government agencies often treated as "bureaucracies," studies of churches by sociologists of religion, and studies of prisons by criminologists. But as a rule these various social bodies were not treated as members of one species, that of "complex organizations." My study showed that all these rather different beings behaved (and misbehaved) following the same sociological laws.

Although I was fairly confident that I had discovered something that was of sociological significance, there was no way of telling as I toiled away month after month in my cubicle. The rhythms of academic work and public discourse differ greatly. While public feedback is often as close as the applause at the end of a speech or the next morning's newspaper, academic work takes years to complete. Then it's another year until the work is published and still many months pass before reviews in academic journals appear, although one hears from this or that colleague a bit before this cycle is completed. I was particularly apprehensive during this interminable process because this work might well determine my future at Columbia University.

It did not take long to find out. Once the manuscript was completed, I sent it to Jeremiah Kaplan, the owner and moving spirit behind the Free Press, at the time by far the best publisher of academic sociology. He sent it to several scholars for evaluation, as is the custom. A mere three weeks later, a minute in academic time, Jerry himself called me. "We would love to publish it," were his magic words. I barely heard him as he continued to say something about not being able to pay much in the way of royalties. (Jerry's stinginess was legendary. Even when he made it big time, when he took an author out for lunch, you had to watch it or you would be stuck with the bill.)

The resulting book, A Comparative Analysis of Complex Organizations, was published late in 1961. It was rather well received, that is, in academia, while barely anyone off the campus so much as noted its existence. For instance, James L. Price, who reviewed it for the American Journal of Sociology, wrote: "What has been accomplished is impressive. . . . This book is indispensable reading for serious organizational scholars." In the fourteen years that followed, 786 studies were concocted by scholars who tested parts of the compliance theory laid out in the book, augmented it, or challenged various elements of it.

From all these studies, the most intriguing is one by G. William Skinner and Edwin A. Winckler, who showed that the history of the Chinese Empire followed the compliance pattern laid out in *A Comparative Analysis of Complex Organizations*. In 1975, a new edition of my book was issued, which included a summary of and references to the numerous studies that the theory spawned.

In each period, certain books become part of the academic buzz and "must cite" works. Some people keep tabs on who cites whom and how often. Accordingly, between 1969 and 1977 my books (largely due to the work on organizations) were among those most often cited of any sociologist dead or alive— some 2,018 times, right next to those of Émile Durkheim and Talcott Parsons.

My compliance book is a typical piece of academic sociological work. But I did not realize at the time that, aside from whatever intrinsic merits it had, the work was well timed for the development of the discipline. Sociologists in the early sixties were growing tired of the grand theories that had governed sociology. Forming "middle-range" theories, limited to one major phenomenon and less abstract, was the order of the day. My theory fit into that mode. A book review by Peter Fricke for *Political Science Quarterly* called it a "principal text for students of organizations." He also wrote:

> The use of compliance theory as one of "middle range" has been justified in logical and empirical terms in the fifteen years since it was first expounded. The emphasis on organizational properties and the development of a schematic variable analysis which can distinguish between different types of organizations have been the strengths of compliance theory. More important, the book also provides an alternative to the Weberian theory of bureaucracy in the study of social systems, and as such, will continue to be invaluable reading for all students of social systems.

Somehow I wrote a historically sensitive book (in terms of the intellectual history of sociology) without actually being historically aware myself.

The book established my academic credentials. In the following years a new area of specialization developed in my discipline, that of organizational sociology. After the book's publication, quite a few invitations came my way to chair sessions on the organizational sociology that sprang up during annual meetings of the discipline, to review books in this field, and to comment on articles considered for publication on the subject.

Below the surface, *The Comparative Analysis of Complex Organizations* has a normative message, a moral subtext in violation of the disciplinary code, that next to no one noticed initially. The book, in effect, argues that organizations that appeal to the values of their members are superior to those that rely on incentives, and they are better by a long shot than those that employ force.

In addition, the book suggested that organizations were moving toward greater reliance on appeal to values and less reliance on coercion, implying that those who resisted the trend were behind the times. It reflected both my Israeli-born aversion to violence and actual social science data, such as evidence that rehabilitation was more likely to succeed in minimum- as compared to maximum-security prisons, and education was more successful in institutions like Ben Shemen that inspired students than in those that regimented them.

Two of my students in the classes I taught on the subject, Edward W. Lehman and Jerald Hage, both became distinguished sociologists in related areas. They were among the few who noted the normative message. In 1995, Hage explored the notion of moral progress implicit in the book. Ed Lehman wrote:

> A surface reading of *Comparative Analysis* may leave the erroneous impression that Etzioni (at this stage) feels that coercive, utilitarian and normative compliance are moral equivalents and that no one of them is superior to the others; our organization society, after all, depends on all three, and which one organizations should implement depends on what they want to accomplish. Closer reading, however, discloses normative compliance's privileged position.

Outside academia, in the world of real organizations, nobody heard the book's implicit message; indeed, very few, if any, even knew that the book existed. After all, this was an academic book, written in the requisite technical vocabulary and chock-full of sourcing and footnotes.

The book did settle one question: Could I do academic work or did my public work undermine my scholarship? The answer focused around the question of whether or not Columbia (or for that matter, any self-respecting university) would grant me tenure. Gaining tenure is of great interest to practically all professors; it is crucial for academic activists. The ultimate security tenure provides frees one to concentrate on what must be said, with little fear of reprisal. (We were still living in the shadow of the McCarthy era.)

In my case, the decision about my tenure (and academic credentials) dripped out in agonizingly small bits. Reviewers who evaluated the manuscript for the Free Press, and colleagues interested in the subject who had asked to see the galleys, let the word out well before the compliance book was actually published. Lazarsfeld sent for a copy of the manuscript. A few weeks later, one of the junior members of the department, who spent a good part of his time networking and incurring favor with the senior members by doing small chores, confided in me that "the seniors are going to vote on your tenure, after all." I tried to shut this rumor out of my mind; my colleague's gossip was less reliable than weather forecasts. And I dared not believe that the clouds cast by my movie review and rumors about my working on a peace manuscript would lift that readily.

A week later, Esther, the department secretary, requested a copy of all the articles I had published along with names of professors at other leading universities who specialized in organizational sociology. All this meant, I warned myself, was that the department was going to go through the motions before they denied me tenure, motions required by the university's procedures.

A good month passed with not a word, not even gossip. Another six weeks. Then George Fraenkel, the dean of the graduate faculties, left word that I should stop by his office. He was all smiles. He requested, "If you do not mind, maybe you could send me, through your chairman of course, which courses you would prefer to teach in the longer run?" And, "You are currently sharing an office with Professor Terry Hopkins. We are very short of space, but I assure you that we will do our best to find you an office all your own. Or, would you prefer to stay in your current one and that we move Terry?" I thanked him profusely and promised to prepare a course list. I left stunned and confused. Fraenkel was clearly hinting that my tenure was approved, but—I told Hava—"I'll be dammed if I treat these hints as money in the bank."

Shortly thereafter (it was spring 1961), I received a letter. It read, "By direction of the trustees of Columbia University, I have the honor to inform you of your appointment as Associate Professor of Sociology in Columbia University. This appointment, in accordance with the provisions of statutes, will continue during the pleasure of the trustees."

The pleasure of the trustees? It seemed obvious that the letter meant that any time the university did not like what I was writing . . . I might as well pack now. I would rather leave of my own free will than be sent packing after my far-from-academic book on peace sees the light of day.

In my dismay, I went to cry on the shoulders of Si Goode. Si laughed gently and explained that this odd phrase meant the job was mine, that I had achieved tenure for the duration, as long as I wanted it, unless I committed some horrible crime.

The letter thus ended as did a night during my Palmach training, when I was swimming deeper and deeper into a lake, searching for a boat in the dark, increasingly exhausted, doubtful of ever making it—and then I located it.

While a first-year student at the Hebrew University, I'd heard a line that life is like a train ride: all destinations are merely stops on the way. It is a mistake to expect that if you make it to this or that station, you have arrived. Soon, the journey resumes; the train labors toward the next station. Gaining tenure reminded me of this train analogy. While true, tenure *did* provide for a very different ride. It was like being given a life-long pass with a reserved seat instead of traveling without a ticket, in fear of being cast off at the next stop, if not between stations. Moreover, the tone in which many of my senior colleagues addressed me suddenly shifted from gently dismissive to poorly concealed courting: the guy now had a vote! After years of being buffeted about, I had gained a measure of control over my life. Now I could choose to mix my academic work and public activism in any measure I considered appropriate, without fear of economic pressures.

I was going to throw a party well beyond my means (tenure entailed a mere small increase in salary). But, on second thought, it struck me that the other assistant professors, who were still awaiting their fate, might well not be in a mood to party. (I should not have worried. They each—including Immanuel Wallerstein, Johan Galtung, Morris Zelditch Jr., Terence K. Hopkins, and Hans Zetterberg—left Columbia but had fully successful sociological, and in two cases also public, careers.) Instead, I took Ethan on a long visit to an amusement park. I am not sure who shrieked with more joy as we bumped go-carts and hit metal ducks in a shooting booth. This time, I was even game for the Ferris wheel.

Tenure had another especially blessed result: feeling more secure about my future, a year or so later, Hava and I welcomed our second son, Oren. Only parents can fully understand how one can love one child all the way to the stars and back and extend the same love to the second child without that for the first being even slightly diminished.

In the decade that followed, I tried to serve both the academic discipline of sociology and those public causes I found compelling. In other words, I continued to cause mischief—at least in the eyes of several of my senior colleagues. They soon found a way of letting me know their displeasure. But in the meantime, I busied myself doing peace. Sometimes it merely entailed a phone call.

Doing Peace

Activist professors must decide how deeply they want to wade in the sea of action. Some stick to the beaches, formulating ideas that they float in the public realm, hoping that these will wash up on the right shore when needed. Others also jump in and paddle, trying to ferry their ideas to the right harbor just in time. They impatiently call the press when it does not call them and flood editors with op-ed pieces. You hear them on radio call-in shows when they are not on C-SPAN. Still other activist professors are ready to carry their load all the way to dry land, even if it means pushing aside some other stevedores and getting their feet wet and hands dirty. They buttonhole politicians and join public interest groups. They are as much activists as they are intellectuals. They must take note that the farther one delves into this sea, the more one will evoke the ire of those who firmly believe that leaving the confines of the academic ivory towers is bound to undermine one's scholarship.

I discovered early in my Columbia days where my place was. I could not resist going beyond words when I believed there was a call and an opening large or small. For instance—the Cuban missile crisis.

Calling the Pope

In the fall of 1962, President John F. Kennedy imposed a blockade on Cuba because aerial photos showed that the Soviet Union was placing missiles capable of carrying nuclear weapons right under America's nose. Kennedy announced that he would only lift the blockade after the Soviet Union withdrew its missiles from Cuba, and he ordered the U.S. Navy to block further Soviet shipments to the island.

The Soviet Union was deeply agitated. News stories tracked Soviet ships as they continued to sail toward Cuba. The world feared a major direct clash between the two nuclear powers—maybe World War III. The fact that Nikita Khrushchev was reported to be mentally unbalanced further worried observers domestic and foreign.

What was one to do? The fact that this was a ludicrous question on the face of it did not stop me. The notion that a bunch of professors could do anything that might help stop the world from rushing to the brink of nuclear war was at best farfetched. But so was sitting idly and doing nothing. Defusing the situation seemed to call for a third party that could prevail on both sides to step back from the abyss. A call from such a party, one not beholden to or involved with either side, would allow both the Soviets and the United States to save face. But who?

The next day, I broached the idea to a peace-minded acquaintance, Gerard Piel, the publisher of *Scientific American*. He was intrigued; as we explored the question of who could serve, the Pope came to mind.

There was no time to be wasted. But how to reach the Pope, let alone in a hurry? This might well have been the end of our chat had I not recalled that Martin Buber knew Pope John XXIII from his work as a translator of the Bible for the Church. I called Buber and pleaded with him to appeal to the

Pope. The next day the Pope called on both parties "not to remain deaf to the cry of mankind . . . let them do everything in their power to save peace. By so doing they will spare the world the horrors of a war that would have disastrous consequences such as nobody can foresee."

I doubt very much that my call made any difference; many others may well have had the same idea, and the Pope may very well have acted all on his own. And, of course, he was hardly the only reason each side came to its senses. What did matter was that on the next day the Soviet ships changed course, and shortly thereafter Khrushchev sent Kennedy a message offering to withdraw the missiles in exchange for a U.S. pledge not to invade Cuba. The crisis blew over even more abruptly than it had started, to the great relief of the world. I followed the news closely, as if I were one of the president's close advisers. And when it was all over, I felt as if I had achieved a tiny personal victory; I had done what I could. Although placing a phone call for peace was activism lite, very lite, it was more active than, say, writing an op-ed piece.

A New Way toward Peace

Writing a movie review and making some phone calls in an effort to defuse nuclear bombs seemed about as adequate as trying to stop a hurricane by spitting in its face. It was time to try something more active. I joined antibomb demonstrations, wrote memos to congressional committees that as a rule were ignored, addressed rallies. When all this activism had no discernable effect, I tried my hand at forging ideas, at laying the foundations for a different strategy for peace.

I was looking for a new way to frame the basic thinking about nuclear weapons and the relationship between the two superpowers. The approach had to differ from the main existing ones, which reflected two basic ways of thinking, succinctly summarized by the slogans "Better Dead than Red" versus "Better Red than Dead." I was looking, my Israeli friends were sure to complain, for a third, intermediary way.

The first approach maintained that the way to prevent nuclear war was for the United States and the Soviet Union not only to maintain but to keep building up stockpiles of nuclear weapons, rendering it irrational for either of the two parties to attack the other. "Secured mutual destruction" and a "suicide-murder compact" captured the essence of this strategy. Critics (whom I joined) feared that mounting piles of nuclear weapons, bombers, missiles, and submarines posed numerous dangers all their own. These included unauthorized action by some general, usurpation by terrorists, spread of nuclear arms to other less responsible countries, and gross miscalculation by some head of state.

The champions of secure mutual destruction tried to deflect our criticisms by pointing to various safety devices and procedures (e.g., triggering a nuclear missile in the United States required two keys held by two different people, and therefore one madman could not initiate a war). But, above all, they maintained, without such a balance of terror, the free world risked being overrun by the evil empire, the communists. It was better to be in danger of us all frying than for us to lose our liberty, to end up as inmates in Soviet-style gulags.

The only major alternative approach aired in the early 1960s was for the United States to unilaterally disarm itself, as favored by a handful of starry-eyed, well-meaning pacifists. They believed that such a grand gesture would compel the Soviets to follow suit, and even if it did not and they occupied us, we would be "Better Red than Dead." Like most observers, I thought that it was more likely for nuclear weapons to melt away on their own than for the United States to disarm unilaterally. And if we did disarm unilaterally, it seemed even more unlikely that the Soviet Empire would give up its nuclear arsenal in appreciation. (I also had some very grave doubts that I would prefer to live under Soviet occupation; I would rather join those who took to the mountains to fight it.)

In short, while theoretically there were two basic approaches to the nuclear arms race, the first one completely dominated public discourse and public policy (including worldwide U.S. foreign policy: expenditures of hundreds of billions of defense dollars and the very structure of the armed forces). The other approach remained the province of a few far-out advocates and was occasionally backed up by demonstrations.

The challenge, as I saw it, was to find a way to reduce the danger of nuclear war without increasing the danger that the West would be overrun. The thesis I came up with was presented in two books. (One, published in 1962, is called *The Hard Way to Peace*; the second, published in 1964, is *Winning without War*.) The main argument was based on a criticism of the strategy of containment that had guided the free world since 1947. Accordingly, the United States had marked a circle around the Soviet Empire and then had employed all means available—from the CIA's covert actions (e.g., in Iran, Greece, Turkey) to outright war (in Korea and later in Vietnam)—to prevent the Soviets from crossing that line. At the same time, whatever horrible things transpired behind that line were declared off-limits for the West. Thus, the United States steadily warned freedom fighters in communist Poland, Hungary, and Czechoslovakia that the United States would not assist them if they rebelled against the Soviet occupiers. It was true to its word.

My main criticism was that this effort to maintain a global status quo made the Soviet Union, which claimed that it had a superior form of society, tear at the straitjacket surrounding it and cause conflicts around the world as it tried to break out. As I saw it, the United States had nothing to fear if it challenged the Soviet Union to compete with us, using nonviolent means by presenting its ideas, culture, and commerce to any country in the world. We would demand the same right—including in countries locked behind the Iron Curtain. In this way, the Soviet Union would cease to feel hemmed in and see more options than either employing force or giving up on countries behind the containment line. I was confident that if competition replaced containment, we would shine. (After the Cold War, such a strategy was called "engagement" and was employed toward communist China.)

Regarding the arms themselves, I called for a "gradualist way to peace," which contained two parts: one concerned the psychology of the arms race; the other, the dangerous hardware. The psychological part called for a series of small, symbolic gestures whose purpose was to cool overheated tempers. I drew on the work of "peace" psychologists and showed that nations in conflict are caught in an upward spiral. Perceived hostility by one party evokes hostility by the other, which in turn further increases the first party's animosity. The resulting high level of antagonism generates psychological blocks that prevent the sides from working out their differences. Various defense mechanisms are activated, such as rigid adherence to a policy set under earlier conditions.

Further, repressed fears of nuclear war expressed themselves in stereotyping and paranoia. Stereotyping could be seen in the simplistic divisions of the world into good (the free world) and evil (the communist nations). Paranoia was evident in the interpretation of whatever the adversary offered as a means of entrapping us.

The vicious circle of hostile moves and countermoves might be broken, I argued, by a therapeutic technique—improved communication. The way to begin was for one side to show a friendlier state of mind. While such a gesture was surely to initially be mistrusted, if continued, it would be reciprocated, thus reversing the Cold War psychological spiral.

The warmer climate would allow for paving the way to the second part of the gradualist strategy—for the United States to work out with the Soviet Union a *mutually agreed upon* schedule of reduction of the nuclear stockpiles. Specifically, I proposed (1) reducing the arms capabilities of both sides *without* allowing either side to gain a *strategic advantage* at any stage of the process, (2) that arms reductions be *effectively verified*, (3) that the process be *gradual*; no jump toward total disarmament would be expected, but neither would a freeze of high piles of arms. (Charles Osgood outlined a similar psychological strategy but did not see a need for following the psychological unilateral–reciprocated steps with a multilateral agreement. I argued that once we got past the psychological measures to arms, unilateral steps would no longer suffice.)

These ideas incurred some favor—among several colleagues on various campuses and among some peace activists. Anatol Rapoport, a highly regarded mathematical biologist and peace researcher, captured my approach very well in a review of *The Hard Way to Peace*:

> A man trapped on a limb protruding over a precipice still has, in spite of the severe constraint, a choice of several rationalizable courses of action. He can keep sitting there, on the ground that it is too dangerous to move. He can jump off, because it is too dangerous to remain sitting. Or he can try to inch his way back to safety. This last choice would be analogous to "gradualism."

Among those who were reported in the *New York Times* as lending their name in support of my approach were Margaret Mead, Polykarp Kusch (a Nobel laureate for physics), Otto Klineberg (a renowned social psychologist), Willis L. M. Reese (law), Harry W. Jones (law), Walter Gellhorn (law), Wolfgang G. Friedman (law), David B. Truman (government), L. C. Dunn (zoology), and Ernest Nagel (philosophy). Off campus, a few press stories and book reviews were favorable, especially in the *Christian Science Monitor*. In a review of my *Winning without War*, Hubert H. Humphrey, who was running for vice president at the time, called my ideas "idealistic but not visionary" and claimed that the Johnson administration was already following my approach.

But out there, in the real world, nothing budged—at first. In the months that passed after the publication of *The Hard Way to Peace*, the United States and the Soviet Union continued to trade accusations, and arms were piled on top of arms as if there were no tomorrow. I wrote some op-eds advocating my approach, but soon even editors who had been quite hospitable to my articles in the past rejected them out of hand. The Americans for Democratic Action endorsed my position, and I was sent to testify on its behalf before a Senate Foreign Relations Committee. I found that many of the committee members were absent, and those present—with the exception of the chair—were reading their mail. I sent memos about the ideas to President Kennedy and several members of his staff. There was no response.

I tried to feed ideas into the public discourse by debating Herman Kahn before a packed house at Columbia University. Kahn, the most prominent public strategist of nuclear arms, argued that we should not hesitate to "think the unthinkable"—to wage nuclear war—because we could survive and recover after such a war. He was frequently quoted in the press and benefited

from grants by the Pentagon. He testified before key congressional committees and delivered briefings and lectures all over the place. Although some
considered him a right-wing gadfly, he succeeded in moving the whole debate from what was the best way to avoid the horrors of nuclear war to one
that included the option of us starting such a war and "winning" it. The fact
that Kahn—a round-faced, jolly fellow with considerable girth—obviously
got a great kick out of his provocative positions earned him the nickname Dr.
Strangelove.

Kahn's arguments were easy to debunk. For instance, he suggested that
even if we lost a hundred million Americans, we still could regrow rather
quickly. I pointed out that he disregarded that, as the missiles would wipe out
major cities (a major target), they would demolish our medical, scientific,
cultural, political, and economic centers, which would leave the United
States (and the Soviet Union) lacking much more than millions of people.
Moreover, to add even a bit to the likelihood that nuclear war would occur
by openly seeking to reduce our horror of it was morally unacceptable.

Kahn made winning the debate easier by telling jokes about nuclear war
that alienated the largely student-filled auditorium. The campus audience
was sympathetic to my position to begin with, and my arguments were
echoed in the local press the next day. I thoroughly enjoyed the "well done"
comments from a few of my colleagues who were also peace activists, especially Seymour Melman.

The total effect of this and a number of other such efforts initially seemed
limited to forming what is called "constructive criticism" (because our criticism was not merely negative but also offered an alternative approach) and to
mobilizing some public opposition to the arms race. Actually, it turned out to
have legs that carried it much further, but (not to mix the metaphor) hardly
mine. In the months and years that followed, the psychological and arms reduction strategies I favored advanced, but along two very different courses.

JFK and Psychological Disarmament

In 1963, President Kennedy put one part of the gradualist theory to a test,
specifically the idea of psychological disarmament. The first step was a
speech he made at American University on June 10, 1963, in which he outlined "A Strategy of Peace." The president called attention to the dangers of
nuclear war and struck a conciliatory tone toward the Soviet Union. He
stated that "constructive changes" in the Soviet Union "might bring within
reach solutions which now seem beyond us." He added, "Our problems are
man-made . . . and can be solved by man." Given that up to this point we
were involved in a full-blown Cold War of threats and counterthreats ("we

shall bury you"), I was elated. But was the Soviet Union going to respond, as the theory predicted? Without such a response, the United States was not going to make conciliatory gestures for long.

Next, the president announced the first unilateral initiative—the United States was stopping all nuclear tests in the atmosphere and would not resume them unless another country did.

The Soviet response was to publish Kennedy's speech in full in the Soviet government newspapers, *Izvestia* and *Pravda,* with a combined circulation of 10 million readers—a degree of attention rarely accorded a Western leader in those days. Radio jammers in Moscow were turned off to allow Russians to listen to the Voice of America's recording of the speech. This was reported in the United States and had some tension-reduction effects of its own. Premier Khrushchev followed up on June 15 with a speech welcoming the Kennedy initiative.

I followed the news with mounting surprise, avid interest, and then excitement. One of my close friends was a physician; we often played tennis together. He scoffed at my enthusiasm about news concerning public affairs and my interest in public policy. "Treating real people, getting specific results" was what turned him on, he said.

While my tennis partner was not particularly gracious in raining on my parade, he correctly pointed out that neither I nor Charles Osgood had any evidence that our ideas had played a role in Kennedy's sudden and encompassing change of strategy.

The good news continued to flow steadily. On June 11, the Soviet Union removed its objection to a U.S.-favored initiative to send United Nations observers to war-torn Yemen. The United States reciprocated by removing its objection to the restoration of full status to the Hungarian delegation to the United Nations. There were all minor steps whose value was largely symbolic, true, but that was exactly what was called for from the viewpoint of the psychological disarmament theory.

The implementations of a direct America–Russia communications link, proposed by the United States in 1962, was suddenly agreed to by the Soviet Union on June 20, 1963. Next, following the U.S. example, the Soviet Union reciprocated by not testing nuclear weapons in the atmosphere.

On September 19, 1963, Soviet Foreign Minister Andrei Gromyko called for a nonaggression pact between the Soviet-led Eastern European bloc and the North Atlantic Treaty Organization (NATO) and asked for a peace treaty with West Germany. The very next day, President Kennedy dramatically suggested in a speech before the United Nations that the United States and the Soviet Union explore the stars together. Also mentioned repeatedly in the front-page news were the expansion of the test-ban treaty to include prohibiting underground testing, direct flights between Moscow and New York, and the opening of an American consulate in Leningrad and a Soviet one in Chicago.

Gromyko suggested a pact that both sides would refrain from orbiting nuclear weapons. Kennedy indicated that the United States was willing to accept it. An agreement in principle was announced on October 3, and the final resolution was passed in the UN General Assembly on October 19. "Unilateral-reciprocal steps paved the way to negotiated bilateral measures, as expected," I informed my friend over the tennis net with great glee. He said, "I am looking for a better way to manage the diabetes of one patient and how to break the news to a twenty-nine-year-old woman that she has cancer in her hip, and the cancer has metastasized throughout her body."

Not deflated, I continued to follow the news as if international developments were actually the results of some global experiment that was testing a peace-making theory. In confirmation of the psychological disarmament theory, each gesture the United States made was reciprocated by the Soviets. Moreover, the Soviet Union added some initiatives of its own. Last but not least, the unilateral-reciprocated moves gradually led—as expected—to a reduction in Cold War tensions, to a détente, which in turn opened the door to multilateral-simultaneous arrangements to the test-ban treaty and the outer space resolution.

In line with the theory's predictions, the very first steps toward tension reduction were received with much ambivalence and suspicion. The *New York Times* reported:

> There was a new threat of international peace in the air this week, the kind of threat that leaves sophisticates smirking and the rest of us just dumbfounded. The "accommodators," as outraged Republicans call them, were simply delighted. The "Cold Warriors," as the accommodators call them, regarded conciliation as a shrewd new tactic.

When, in early July, Khrushchev offered a ban on tests in the seas, air, and space, but coupled this offer with a suggestion of a nonaggression pact between NATO and the Warsaw Treaty Organization, the *New York Times* referred to the offer as, perhaps, "Another Booby Trap."

As gesture followed gesture, the impact of the new approach reverberated outside the seats of government. In the United States, "from around the country came a generous flow of messages echoing all these responses, but more approving than not. And from around the globe came new bursts of hope kept alive by quick signs of interest in Moscow." A *New York Times* correspondent in Moscow reported: "The ready approval of its contents by ordinary Russians was evident in the reactions of Muscovites who lined up at kiosks to buy newspapers."

While a national poll taken in July, before the negotiations on the treaty had begun, found that only 52 percent of the population strongly supported a treaty, this percentage rose to 81 by September 1963. The tone of the press also changed; there was now an "official amity" between the United States and the Soviet Union.

The assassination of President Kennedy on November 22, 1963, stopped this process dead in its tracks before it could be further extended. It took another twenty-three years before the other element of the gradual way to peace theory was put to the test: were mutually agreed upon, verified *reductions* of strategic weapons possible—without leading to nuclear war?

There is no evidence I am aware of that either Osgood's or my version of psychological disarmament influenced President Kennedy or his staff, directly or indirectly. (There are cases of such influence being evident. For example, Kennedy read a review of Michael Harrington's book *The Other America* and was quite taken by it.) In any event, the satisfaction I got from the turn of events was not that of an activist who delivered, but that of a scientist who designed an experiment that was carried out to perfection by someone else who had never heard of the designer or the design. And the results were as expected! Moreover, the experiment dealt with matter of global import. Often this is as good as it gets.

Reagan Does It, with Spades (Fast-Forward to 1986)

When a few of my colleagues and I argued in favor of reversing the nuclear arms race, between 1962 and 1964, most foreign policy experts dismissed the idea. A frequent response was, "You don't get it. If any one side reduces their pile, the other side will feel that it can gain a winning advantage by hiding some weapons. These will become more important as the total stockpile gets smaller." Some pointed out, "You might be able to put a limit on some kinds of weapons, introduce arms control; but safe reduction is an oxymoron." (David H. Frisch and Louis B. Sohn, two other advocates of arms reduction, encountered similar criticisms.)

Fast-forward: during the next two decades, the arms race barreled ahead. Both sides amassed thousands of missiles, long-range bombers, and nuclear submarines. Hundreds of billions of dollars and rubles were spent, and a great number of the best scientists and engineers were dedicated to building more silent submarines, fitting more warheads into each missile head, and constructing deadlier bombs. I grew utterly frustrated by the fact that the strategy of mutually agreed upon arms reductions gained no hearing, let alone acceptance. So, I moved on to other items on the public agenda as I saw them—first to oppose the war in Vietnam, and then to the domestic front.

Some twenty-three years later, in 1986, long after I ceased to be involved, the idea was finally put to a test. President Reagan had long been uncomfortable with secured mutual destruction and had initiated negotiations with the Soviet Union as early as 1982 to explore a significant reduction of the most destabilizing weapon systems, ballistic missiles, and the number of warheads they carry. The negotiations passed through numerous twists and turns, getting nowhere. One day, President Reagan, considered by many to be naive, made a grand move. Even Secretary of State George Shultz, known for his tendency to keep his shirt on, termed this as "revolutionary." Reagan achieved a major breakthrough when he met with the head of the Soviet Union, Mikhail Gorbachev, in Reykjavik without any staff members; this scandalized the arms control experts and worried sick the president's handlers. Reagan suggested a coordinated, large-scale reduction of nuclear weapons of all kinds, including not merely missiles but also bombers! Reversing the arms race! And Gorbachev agreed!

Once the White House staff got the president back under its wings, they succeeded in scaling back his more ambitious ideas, but the basic new approach survived their efforts to suppress it. After lengthy and complex negotiations, the Strategic Arms Reduction Treaty (START) was signed in 1991. In the years that followed, both the United States and the Soviet Union reduced their strategic armaments by *nearly half*. Large numbers of missiles were destroyed and nuclear warheads disarmed by both sides. Arms reductions were verified through on-site inspection. Military budgets were scaled back. Most important, despite all early fears and hand wringing, strategic arms reductions did not trigger a nuclear holocaust, not even a limited exchange of nuclear blows.

While decades separated the Kennedy experiment from the Reagan initiative, they had one major thing in common: both provided, in effect, experiments in which competing viewpoints and strategies were tested. Moreover, the lessons are far from irrelevant for later generations. In the first years of the twenty-first century, leading generals and civil experts were still arguing that the piles of nuclear weapons maintained by the United States and by Russia were much too high and wildly dangerous. The debate about arms reductions was not fully settled. A typical headline in the *Washington Post* on May 12, 2000, read: "How Low Should Nuclear Arsenal Go?"

There is not a shade of doubt that I had nothing whatsoever to do with Reagan's magnificent initiative. This of course did not stop me from being elated that the world was moving away from a nuclear holocaust. Proud that ideas I helped formulate withstood a major reality test. Sorry that I did not stay with them and do much more to promote them. Painfully aware that the last thing I could do or say to anyone was, "I told you so." Happy that it did not matter. But I had no doubt (a phrase an academic should not use lightly, if at all) that the world was a safer place for what these heads of state had accomplished.

A Soviet Spy, the FBI, and a Civic Refresher

Public intellectuals who mess around in international affairs face dangers usually not encountered in the library. Just as I began to learn to cope with the brickbats of my most academia-minded senior colleagues, I faced an entirely different challenge. While preparing my lectures for the new 1965–66 school year, I was asked to spy for the Soviet Union.

The intrigue started innocently. Someone named Bogdan Walewski called me at Columbia University. Though he was of Polish origin and a Polish citizen, he explained that he worked for the United Nations in New York City. He asked if he could drop by for a quick visit to discuss trends in American culture. Curious, I agreed. Soon, a young man who spoke English well was in my study at Fayerweather Hall. He wanted to know what I thought about several recent Broadway plays and various orchestras that performed in Carnegie Hall in the preceding year. As I did not have the moola to buy tickets to any of these events, I responded on the basis of what I had learned from the *New York Times*. Noting my discomfort, he shifted to talking about movies. After a while, he allowed that he greatly benefited from my sophisticated and learned observations and wondered if my wife and I would be his guests at dinner at an expensive French restaurant in New York. I accepted the invitation without hesitation. I had never set a foot in any of them.

Bringing along my wife was a bit of a problem. Hava and I were divorced in 1964. We had lived for years pretending that sooner or later we would return to Israel and she could be reunited with her mother. We did not put up drapes in our New York apartment and never fully unpacked. But this illusion became more and more difficult to sustain as I gained tenure and Israel made it clear that it needed more sociologists about as much as it needed more dunes or sunshine. After we divorced, Hava immediately left for Israel, taking our sons with her. The boys ended up spending summers with me in the United States, and I, Passovers with them in Israel. Years later, Hava, her new husband, and daughter moved to Australia. To my great delight Oren, when he turned fourteen, moved to live with me, and Ethan went to study at

Columbia. Still, we all suffered a great deal. I still consider the divorce one of my gravest personal failures. We should have found a way.

It was a year after the divorce. I brought with me to the restaurant a Mexican scholar, Minerva Morales, who was visiting Columbia University. We had grown close in the preceding months. I had met Minerva at an unusual seminar at Columbia University, one in which no students but only faculty and UN diplomats participated. The subject was peace. The seminar met during dinners and mixed socializing with intellectual fare. On the evening I was introduced to this tall Mexican scholar who was at Columbia on a postgraduate scholarship, I saw only her smile. People since then have often told me how strikingly beautiful Minerva was, with her sparkling raven eyes, milk-chocolate-colored skin, and fine figure. But it was the vitality and inner warmth that shone through her face that captured my heart. We were married a year later.

A very lavish dinner and pleasant chit-chat were all that transpired this second time I met Mr. Walewski. But all this changed when he called to set a time for a third visit. I marked my calendar for January 13, 1965. This time he was all business. When he arrived in my office, he told me that he was well aware that I was Jewish and a refugee from Nazi Germany. He had read about my adamant opposition to granting West Germany a finger on the nuclear trigger, as laid out in the extensive debate I'd had with Herman Kahn on the subject, moderated by *New York Times* military editor Hanson Baldwin and published in a recent issue of the *New York Times Magazine*.

Walewski explained that the Soviet Union was very concerned about this matter and that I could single-handedly help stop the Germans dead in their tracks if I would get him a report on the subject my colleague Richard Neustadt had prepared for President Johnson. I knew nothing about the report other than that I had read somewhere that it was for the "president's eyes only," which meant it was more highly classified than top secret. It took me a long minute to realize that I was being asked to spy. It is not exactly part of the daily routine of a university professor or, I guess, of anyone else.

I told Walewski to leave my office that instant and that I was going to report this conversation to the FBI even before he closed the door. He warned me, "I will let it be known that Minerva and you are not actually married but merely living together." While this might have troubled someone in some other parts of the United States, it was not a big deal in the campus community. I told him to get going and immediately called the local FBI office. I expected some high-ranking agents to rush over and interview me, maybe even to ask me to set a trap for the guy. Instead, I got someone at some switchboard who, to my utter amazement, was uninterested in my story. The

Figure 3.1.   With Minerva, 1966

person seemed to want to take my name and phone number largely to get me off the line. I had been asked to deliver to the Soviets a crucial document prepared for the president's eyes only! I guess they thought I had made up the whole story. I decided to put it in writing and sent a memo to the agent in charge of the FBI in New York City. In response, I received what obviously was a form letter, appreciating my communication. Heck, I concluded, if nobody cared about Soviet spies hiding in the middle of New York City, on the payroll of the United Nations, I had other fish to fry. After fuming for a few more days, I more or less forgot about the whole affair, although occasionally I still puzzled over it. Was the FBI that inept?

Almost exactly twenty-five years later, in July 1990, I received a letter postmarked from Manassas, Virginia—from Walewski. He asked to see me one more time. He wanted to apologize, he wrote. At the time we had first met, he had been serving as an American agent and was ordered to check on my loyalty to my country. (He later was caught while spying for the United States in Warsaw, and he was released in 1985 in a spy exchange between the United States and the communist bloc. He was planning to write a book about his experiences.)

Walewski's letter was less of a surprise than you might expect. By 1990, I'd had other indications that during the Johnson and Nixon administrations, I—like many other peace activists and those working for civil rights—had been under FBI surveillance. I still resented that my criticism of American foreign policy led to my loyalty to the United States being cast in doubt.

The Walewski letter provided me an occasion to reflect on how different the America of the 1960s (and early 1970s) was from that of the 1990s. In the 1960s, America was deeply engulfed in fervent anticommunism and the Cold War; it was a society that was being dragged ever deeper into a war in Vietnam. Many young people rebelled against its war, culture, and institutions and were roundly condemned by the majority. America in those days was a society in which cities burned following race riots, in which students were shot by state troopers at Kent State University and were beaten up at the Democratic Convention in Chicago. It was the age of the Watergate break-in and Herbert Hoover's out-of-control FBI. As the Church Commission unveiled in 1975, the FBI was spying on civic, religious, and political groups that had no violent intentions but were merely oppositional, and it was providing the Nixon White House with personal derogatory information about civil rights leaders, such as tapes made at a motel where Martin Luther King Jr. stayed. It was a society sharply divided between an established majority and dissenting minorities. I was active among the dissenters. No wonder I was given the "royal treatment," although compared to others I got off easy, very easy indeed.

I never had any doubt about the essential place of individual rights in our life. It did not take a Ph.D. to realize that a free society would not remain free for long if critics could be muzzled, if those who criticized the government were treated like traitors, if those who demonstrated peacefully were beaten or shot. But nothing teaches better than experience. My being treated as a suspect, someone whose loyalty the FBI had to test for the nation's safety—because of some speeches I had made, articles I had written, and demonstrations I had marched in—was so infuriating, it stayed with me for all the years to come.

------ ∞∞∞ ------

CHAPTER FOUR

Further Out: Peace on Earth, Off the Moon (1960s)

Warring the War in Vietnam

In Opposition

The Old Testament speaks of a dark cloud on the horizon, no larger than the hand of a man, threatening to turn into a devastating storm. This image came to mind when I was reading early news about the role the United States was playing in Vietnam, in 1964. Possibly because I had lived at the edge of the Third World, in the Middle East, and had acquired a particularly intense aversion to violence, I had a sense of foreboding about the dangers posed by increasing U.S. involvement in the war in Vietnam. At the end of the day, if and when I come to the gates of heaven and am asked to hand in a resume (or provide my website address), I plan to put near the head of the page the fact that I was one of the first to have publicly opposed the war, in an article published in the *Washington Post* on June 28, 1964, to be precise.

From then on, I participated in various protests against the war. Most were of the "routine" kind activists engaged in, some a bit less so. In all of them, formulating the brief against the war was mixed with actions that sought to call attention to the case that was being made. Public intellectuals run the gamut from those who are sheerly idea smiths to those who also help forge social action. Given my strong feelings against the war, this was the period in which I served much more as an activist than as someone who merely forged critical positions.

Those of us who were among the first to protest the war faced the same difficulties other activists face early in the day: a public whose mind is elsewhere and a national government that gradually digs itself deeper and deeper into a mess without being accountable, as rather few pay attention. The mission was to awaken the public—easier said than done. We were fumbling to find new ways to sound the alarm.

In 1965, the students at Columbia University conducted a novel form of meeting, a "teach-in." It reflected the mood of the time, breaking away from established forms as part of the counterculture and youth rebellion. One such teach-in began at midnight and continued the whole next day, with speakers and audiences flowing in and out. The crowd was often close to the 1,246 capacity of the McMillin Theater. People were free to bring food and drinks. An adjacent coffee shop stayed open all night to accommodate the vibrant assembly.

I was bushed when my turn finally arrived—some ten hours into the talkathon—but the points that demanded a voice were well rehearsed, after repeat presentations before other assemblies: the regime of South Vietnam was corrupt to the core; its people rejected it and showed their disapproval by assisting the north in licking the south. The United States should not use its force to prop up such an authoritarian government. The war was much more one of national liberation and unity than a communist plot. Many thousands of people were being killed on both sides, and we were still shipping more and more men and women over there—and losing. The notion that Vietnam was going to expand the communist empire by joining China unless the United States propped up the government of South Vietnam was farfetched at best, I argued.

Avoiding being merely critical, I outlined a six-point approach to peace in Vietnam that included the withdrawal of all foreign troops, an election supervised by the United Nations, and the insertion of a UN observer force.

A week later, some 250 students from Columbia and five professors participated in a massive demonstration against the war in Washington, D.C. Demonstrations in the early sixties were a public protest tool well employed by the civil rights movement, but not widely used in the more decorous fifties and the patriotic days of World War II. Also, we were just entering the second decade of TV, which vastly amplified the voice of the demonstrators: instead of merely being heard around town, they were seen nationwide. In short, we were attracting much more attention to the cause in this way than was achieved in later decades, when demonstrations became commonplace.

Later in 1965, when I was on leave from Columbia at the Center for Advanced Studies in Behavior Sciences in Palo Alto, California, students at nearby Stanford University invited me to address a rally against the war. The rally was to take place in front of some government building, toward which our protest was directed. In suburban Palo Alto, however, you can find quite a few wine and cheese shops, boutiques, and bookstores, but not much of a federal presence. The students considered taking the demonstration to an Air Force base, but it was too far to reach in between classes and was considered "inconveniently" located. Keen to find some way to express their indignation but also not to be put out too much, the student leaders solved the dilemma ingeniously: they called for a demonstration in front of the local post office!

Following a short march, a sizable crowd assembled at the designated spot, but a new problem arose—how was I going to address them? Standing at street level I could barely see anybody except those closest to me; the rest would hardly be able to hear what was going to be said.

A student leader rose to the occasion: he found a large painter's ladder. Two students held it, and—perching on its highest rungs—I waved my fist as much as I dared and repeated to those assembled my by now well-honed antiwar speech. For decades afterward, my good friend Herbert Stein, who had also spent the year at the center, warmly teased me about my unacademic conduct and precarious position on the top of the ladder. Roasting me at a birthday party, Herb observed wryly that while he was "neither opposed to the war in Vietnam nor was swinging on top of a ladder my cup of tea, Amitai and I got along famously."

Figure 4.1. On the ladder

Speeches, teach-ins, and demonstrations that continued month after month, years on end all over the country slowly, very slowly, helped marshal a growing opposition to the war. Thus, two years later, I was still trying to give it a hand, this time at an eight-hour teach-in at Columbia, organized by Paul Starr, a brilliant, cocky, left-leaning sociology student. (He later played a significant role in devising Hillary Clinton's health care plan and became a coeditor of a liberal publication, *The American Prospect*.)

While the public was frustratingly slow to take note, within my academic discipline tolerance for political action increased some. During the 1967 annual meeting of the American Sociological Association in San Francisco, five of us organized a session on "sociologists and the Vietnam conflict." We were pleasantly surprised when the session drew about 500 colleagues from the 2,500 who attended the meeting that year. Most, though, came to listen, not to act.

Madame Nhu, Immolating Buddhists, and Protest

While the movement against the war in Vietnam was intertwined with the counterculture and the rebellion of young people against institutions that treated them like children—lights out, no visitors of the opposite sex, don't question authority—there still were some strong mores of what was considered proper behavior. I faced those when Madame Ngo Dinh Nhu, the first lady of South Vietnam, was invited to speak at Columbia. Madame Nhu opened her presentation with the comment that there was nothing "more terrible in the world than devils, ghosts, and students," a line that did not particularly endear her to the audience.

She spoke dismissively about suicides of Buddhist monks who, to protest the regime, doused themselves with gasoline and set themselves on fire. Madame Nhu suggested that "suicide and murder are not unusual in Vietnam." She added that in the past immolation had generally been practiced by women; she said she was willing to acknowledge that now that men were also involved, it made these acts of protest significant. But she could not see any connection between these protests and her husband's authoritarian and corrupt regime and the futile war.

Madame Nhu then added facilely, "Victory over the Communist guerillas is imminent and the press and junior foreign service officers are responsible for American misunderstanding of the Buddhist affair. . . . The South Vietnam government would certainly not have suppressed the Buddhists, as the press reports, given that victory is so near." She charged that while her government tried to maintain "peace and order," the foreign press corps tried to create "trouble and disorder" to "make things interesting."

Madame Nhu tried to deal with the reports of South Vietnamese police pummeling American news reporters critical of the regime by stating, "My people would never beat anybody, especially Americans." She gave away more when she added, "Not without some reason."

In those more proper days, no response panel was invited, nor were questions allowed. The Columbia audience was cold but politely silent. I sensed, though, that one should not let the event pass without somehow registering with her that the American people, at least those in this hall, were not fooled by her pronouncements. How could I make the point without disturbing her speech? (Manners aside, disturbing her speech would have been inappropriate; I agree with those who hold that the right to free speech is important, especially for those with whom we strongly disagree.)

At the end of the program, I stood up and requested a moment of silence for the Buddhists who immolated themselves in protest against the regime and the war, a pale gesture, but all I could come up with. The audience was more than willing to comply. For a long minute the hall held a silence that amounted to some speech. Madame Nhu, however, bade us goodbye as if nothing had occurred. At first I thought that ours was one of those gestures despairing activists engage in when they cannot get traction. But then I consoled myself with the thought that protest falls, drip, drip, on hearts and policies made of stone. One more drop was dropped.

Scholarship or Protest?

Not all the protests against the war were solemn. One melodramatic event ended in such an unexpected manner, and so humorously, that I recorded the details as follows:

The scene: more than 5,000 American scientists and scholars milling in the Washington Hilton Hotel during the annual meeting of the American Association for the Advancement of Science (AAAS). While the meeting encompasses scores upon scores of sessions on a large variety of topics, a plenary session, during which all other meetings are suspended, is scheduled for 2 P.M. The main paper to be delivered is by well-known sociologist Professor James S. Coleman; Dr. Harold Orlans and I are to comment on it, in the best academic tradition. Daniel Patrick Moynihan, a sociologist and adviser to President Nixon, is to chair the meeting. We are putting final touches on the plan for the session over a fairly awful meal of hotel food.

Two burly fellows approach our table. The more muscular of the two introduces himself and his companion: "I am an officer of the AAAS. This is the security officer of the Hilton Hotel. The U.S. just resumed the bombing of North Vietnam after peace talks broke down. Your guys down the hall are about to riot."

Moynihan pales a bit. He looks at his watch and exclaims with sudden horror: "Oh my God! I completely forgot! I'm due for a briefing at the State Department—background for my assignment as the ambassador to India." He apologizes, "Sorry, got to dash. Amitai, you chair the meeting." Before I can say, "You miserable chicken," he vanishes.

We make our way to the huge hall; three ballrooms have been combined into one cavernous space. Several thousand people are assembled—screaming at each other. Quite a few stand on their chairs to better project their protests. Many are demanding that the plenary session be dedicated to criticisms of the war (a demand with which I sympathize) while the others insist that we continue with our academic work as promised (a demand whose legitimacy I recognize).

All the way in the back, next to the doors, the security officers are looking on the unruly group with open dismay. They stare at me, alone at the podium, as if to say, "Give us a sign and we shall clean up this mess in a jiffy and with great pleasure." About the last thing I want is to cause a violent melee—all too common these days.

I lift my arms and tap on the microphone, begging to be heard. The din subsides somewhat. I plead with the crowd. "We shall do *both*. Let's first hear Coleman. Orlans and I will cut our comments to a minimum. Then we discuss the war." Many seem to be mollified. A few still shout, "No business as usual!" Others counter with, "This is an AAAS meeting. The S stands for science.!" I repeat my assurance that both conscience and science will be served. Gradually, everybody settles down—but one. One guy still stands on his chair screaming: "*Stop* the war in Vietnam! *No* business as usual!"

I see the Hilton security guard beginning to walk down the aisle behind the last protestor. It is easy to see what will transpire next: the guard will grab the guy and drag him out, causing a major riot. I wish I could tell the guard to take a hike, but I also fear calling attention to him. I stand there paralyzed, frantically trying to figure out what to do. Just when the guard is about two yards behind the last standing protestor, he assumes his seat. A better-timed coming together of a tush and a seat I never witnessed.

I breathe a deep sigh of relief. But just as I am about to introduce Jim Coleman, a new crisis erupts. A young woman, sitting in the first row, stands up and lowers her notebook on the head of a guy seated behind her. As I had prepared myself for the first show of violence, I am about to jump off the stage, put myself between the combatants, and exclaim with as much pathos as I can muster, "Whatever we do—let's not use force!" when I hear the young woman shouting, "If you put your hand on my ass again, I'll kill you!" The audience roars; wave upon wave of laughter sweeps the huge hall. The war critics and academics are giggling together. The tension is broken. We are ready to listen to a learned paper as well as to condemn the ravages of the war. Another day in the life of a public intellectual.

Public Reaction

During the sixties, gradually more and more students, colleagues, and Americans off-campus grew critical of the war in Vietnam. However, the rising opposition was still a minority that had little effect on the war. On the contrary, again and again, the United States was sunk deeper into the Vietnamese quagmire. More young Americans were shipped to Vietnam and more returned home in dark, plastic body bags. Bombing became more savage; unfriendly villages were napalmed. Our B-52s spread their deadly loads from South to North Vietnam, to Cambodia, and to Laos. So did our covert actions, including one in which our agents assassinated civil leaders believed to lean toward communism (Operation Phoenix). In short, between the mid-sixties and the beginning of the seventies, the United States got ever more mired in Vietnam rather than pulling out of the conflict.

While for close to a decade the protest movement had little effect on U.S. involvement in the war, it deeply split American society. The majority of the public considered those of us who opposed the war to be traitors, commies, and draft dodgers. We considered them to be blinded by rabid anticommunism, under the influence of right-wing nuts and rednecks. Recently, as part of conservative revisionism, prodded by Roger Kimball and Norman Podhoretz, the opposition to the war in Vietnam is depicted as a form of "anti-Americanism," which prevented the United States from "winning" the war in Vietnam. Maybe the United States could have prevailed by flattening whatever was left standing in the north and adding other chemical weapons to its defoliants. But I join with those who continue to view this attempt to suppress a faraway people as anti-American. We had no genuine national interest in the place nor a humanitarian cause. Bombing the natives was not justifiable by any American value I recognize.

Most of the time, I was not treated any worse than others. I was subject to the same name calling, taunting, and suspicion. In effect, the hostility was easier to take as the years passed because our ranks did gradually expand. More people attended our rallies. Demonstrations grew larger. But after years, I grew dispirited. Although I continued to be confident that we were on the side of the angels, I was again involved in public action that, at the time, did not deliver. Granted, one can find much justification in merely "bearing witness," in calling attention to acts that are profoundly immoral. True, we did build a case against the war and mobilized the opposition, but for years the war—like some kind of enormous mythical monster—rolled right on, gobbling up thousands upon thousands of young Americans and hundreds of thousands of Vietnamese of all ages.

I asked myself, how many speeches can you make, in how many demonstrations can you march, for how many years can you join teach-ins, while your country is heading further and further at an increasing clip down a road you firmly believe it should not have set foot on in the first place? I did not give up. I helped collect signatures and funds for one more ad in the newspapers protesting the war. I wrote one more op-ed. I demonstrated a few more times. But, truth be told, these steps required ever more effort.

Baying at the Moon (and NASA)

I did not spend all of the 1960s just protesting the nuclear arms race and the war in Vietnam. In effect, in the early 1960s, I opened what jokingly might be called a second front. Peace was about keeping people from the ultimate degradation, of being denied all there is. However, being free of war, to be alive, was only a very basic right. A close second was having an elementarily decent living (what I later came to call a "rich basic minimum"). This led me to consider what the national priorities ought to be. The arms race was eating up many of America's resources, especially absorbing the attention of many of our best engineers, scientists, and labs. At the same time, poverty (which President Kennedy "discovered" and brought to the attention of the nation) and the condition of our inner cities—our domestic, social needs—cried out for more resources. Instead, the nation was turning to put its money into what I considered a technological stunt, a visit to the moon. This plan to invest in a circus instead of in bread invited my ire.

Until 1957, most people in the world did not pay much more attention to space than we currently spend thinking about the inner core of the earth. We vaguely know that it is there, maybe even know what some of its characteristics are, and we may have read a piece of science fiction about a journey to the molten heart of the globe, but that is it. This was basically the way we considered outer space—until the Soviet Union suddenly orbited a satellite, *Sputnik,* around the earth in 1957.

The first official American reaction was to dismiss the matter as a meaningless stunt. President Eisenhower derisively characterized the Soviet satellite as a small grapefruit, adding that it was not going to fall on our heads. Soon, however, the Cold War mentality prevailed. We had to jump higher and further in the skies than the Communists. American space efforts took off.

All this, however, was chicken feed—or stardust—compared to what happened a few years later. In April 1961, the Soviet Union hurled the first man into orbit around earth. In May 1961, President Kennedy told Congress that the stature of the nation depended on the United States matching and raising the Soviet hand by putting a man on the moon. Congress readily obliged. Project Apollo was launched with a budget of $25 billion, a truly astronomical amount in those days. We were off into the blue yonder and beyond.

In 1964, I published a book sharply critical of Project Apollo. (Its title, *The Moondoggle*, reflects its tone.) The book argued that the nation would be much better served if the same resources were invested in the inner cities, in developing America, in shoring up the environment, in an "earth NASA" rather than spending money to put a man on the moon to plant a flag, take a picture, and hurry back. I was particularly concerned that the space effort would gobble up much of our innovative capacity, our research and development resources, all of which were already in short supply due to the high demands of the military.

The book challenged various claims the NASA propaganda machine was spouting on behalf of Project Apollo. NASA depicted capturing the moon as a military necessity (the moon was the high ground). My book argued that if we had to fire at the Soviet Union, shooting from the moon would give them much longer warning time than from any place on earth. And satellites made infinitely better reconnaissance observatories than some U.S. base on the moon.

NASA's spin on the moon was that it contained some fabulous materials. My book countered that there was no evidence that the moon had any hidden treasures, such as gold, diamonds, or any other riches, while our earthly oceans were very much worth delving into.

NASA claimed that putting a man on the moon would lift America's prestige overseas to new heights. The book pointed to public opinion polls that showed that people in many countries would have preferred for us to focus on conquering poverty and disease.

NASA saw in deep space an almighty source of spiritual renewal. The book argued that there was little spirituality in the heavy lifting involved and that banishing cancer or destitution was at least as ennobling.

Finally, the book maintained that if we must invest large amounts of scarce resources in space—the place to go was near space (around the earth) and not outer space. Also, it would be much safer and less costly if we relied on unmanned flights.

The Moondoggle was written in a provocative, polemical style, aimed at my fellow citizens. Many of my senior academic colleagues saw it as one more piece of evidence that I was bound and determined not so much to cross the line between sociology as a science and public advocacy as to ignore it altogether. One reviewer noted, "Although Etzioni is a sociologist who knows a great deal about complex modern organizations and about social change, his scholarship is here set aside in the quest for political action." Another reviewer of the book, in the academic *Journal of Politics*, pointed out that although most political scientists would agree with my conclusions, my problem was that I used words such as "should" and "ought." This, the reviewer noted, was a giveaway sign that I was engaging in moral judgments rather than in unadulterated scholarly work. Given that I was discussing what ought to be done with the resources dedicated to the lunar visit, I was guilty as charged. However, I believed that rendering judgments is fully legitimate. Better yet, that those of us who are tenured and are hence particularly free to act as critics have a moral obligation to so serve.

The press reviews were mixed. *The Chicago Sun-Times* wondered about my refusal to view the trip to the moon as akin to a famous journey by Columbus. It wrote, "One wonders, however, what the benefit to the world would have been if Isabella had been persuaded to use the proceeds of her pawned jewels to finance 15th Century schools instead of Columbus." *The Hartford Courant Magazine* suggested that without interplanetary travel "the human mind, compelled to circle forever in its planetary goldfish bowl, must eventually stagnate. Mankind is going to the stars, Mr. Etzioni—you are welcome to stay home with the other cave dwellers."

More warmly, Edward Edelson, the science editor at the *New York Daily News*, wrote in *Smithsonian* magazine: "This is an excellent introduction for anyone who wants to take part in such a debate. It gives few definitive answers, or there are few answers available, but does raise all the right questions."

I tried to find more legs for my criticism than writing a book. I testified before congressional committees against the size of NASA's budget and the way it was biased in favor of outer space. I participated in some debates on the subject before groups of scientists. But by the late 1960s, it became evident that I was further out of step with the flow of events than I had ever been. Although there were some who favored more investment in near space, and more who recognized the merits of unmanned flights, there were very few who shared my criticism of the main lunar adventure.

The lesson of the day was that a public intellectual who takes on decisions already made—especially those made publicly, particularly if they were announced with great fanfare, and above all if they generate billions for several interest groups—better be good at moving mountains. And if such a righteous soul is unwise enough to take on an agency as politically astute as NASA, he would be better off if he bayed at the moon.

By the time my arguments were aired, Congress had long approved Project Apollo. A considerable lobby, orchestrated by NASA, had been launched, propelled by the space industry and space research programs in universities. The media loved the picturesque take-offs, landings, and, above all, the close-ups of lunar walks. NASA placed space toys in numerous schools and placed its big bucks production projects in the congressional districts of key budget committee chairs. It even retained a Madison Avenue agency to tout its achievements.

Federal agencies are free to inform the public, but they are not supposed to use taxpayers' funds to sway the public. The government is to serve the people's wishes—not to implant them. NASA was and still is in particularly flagrant violation of this rule. It has continued over the years to spin the public more than most, if not all, government agencies. NASA still makes such claims as having found "life" on Mars, which leads many people to expect to hear about an alien civilization, while actually the reference is to traces that might have been left by water or by some amoeba. NASA also claims that spending billions on space stations such as Mir is justified because they will contribute to worldwide cooperation, brotherhood and sisterhood, and peace on earth—hardly a sociologically valid proposition. And NASA's champions continue to argue, most recently, that "there are cultural, political, and economic advantages that accrue to countries that choose greatness"—and this choice is made by building a base on the moon and probing the blue yonder, still deeper in space.

I noticed one day that the pictures from outer space that NASA distributed to the American press were in red, white, and blue. When I inquired whether the creator of the universe was an American, I was informed that the data from outer space actually comes in the form of colorless dots or in black and white, but that NASA had the pictures "color enhanced."

My drive to ground Project Apollo and to urge Congress to unload its resources for work on lowly planet earth had no discernable payoff. Project Apollo continued unperturbed in its orbit, with its busters blasting. And, as every schoolchild knows, it did succeed in putting a man on the moon in 1969; he planted a flag, took a picture, and hurried back.

Over the next twenty-five years it became evident that the moon did not serve as an American military base. It yielded no new or old riches. And—to the extent such a thing can be measured—it failed to lift our prestige abroad or our spirit at home. Moreover, while the space program generated many considerable benefits, *practically all of these were found in near space and through unmanned flights*. These included the development of reconnaissance satellites, a major source of military intelligence; communication satellites, without which nationwide and international communication is hard to imagine; and navigation satellites that allow us to determine our location in air, at sea, and on land with great accuracy. And NASA kept using its well-heeled propaganda machine to promote projects that were likely to burnish its image and appropriations rather than necessarily yield truly significant payoffs.

Most recently, the NASA propaganda machine locked in on its $7 billion (give or take a few hundred million) telescope, the Hubble. Among the claims that are being made for it is that it will explore the "origins of the universe."

NASA claims that Hubble will let us "look back in time and see what the universe looked like thirteen billion years ago." If you believe this, you should be willing to forego all that could be done with $7 billion; but instead of providing evidence that what we are dealing with here is science and not PR, we get one overpowering adjective after another. NASA simply asserts that the project is "the most scientifically significant space project we ever embarked on" and that "it's helping astronomers unlock the secrets of the universe" (but we are not told what these "secrets" are). NASA also claims that "using Hubble, we can see the universe, how it looked when it was less than a billion years old. And we can see what galaxies looked like back then when they were the building blocks of today's galaxies." And again we find that the pictures handed out have been "enhanced" to turn them from a sea of dots and squiggles into beautiful modern art–like pictures of the remote heavens. This is all crowned with the following exchange: in an interview on 60 *Minutes,* Ed Bradley asked Dr. Mario Livio, the head of the science division for Hubble, "So far, the United States has invested, I guess, about $7 billion on this Hubble project. In your opinion has it been worth it?" Dr. Livio responded, "Is it worth it? It has given us the universe. This is cheap."

Some of us thought it may have been the Lord; others, a random act of nature some fourteen billion years ago (some say twenty-eight billion, a meaningless difference for most of us), but to suggest that Hubble has given us the universe is a reach even for NASA.

At the twenty-fifth anniversary of the lunar visit, Walter Cronkite, long considered a starry-eyed space enthusiast of the highest order, interviewed me at The George Washington University for a TV program. He leaned over and to my utter amazement confided: "I always agreed with you." (I was so taken aback by his remark that I later wondered if I heard him correctly. Standing nearby was my secretary Trish Thomas, who doted on Cronkite and could not tear herself away from him during his visit. She was equally surprised.) A young National Public Radio (NPR) reporter, Richard Paul, dug me up from some archives and was amused by the volume and tenure of criticism I'd faced a generation earlier—criticisms leveled by NASA officials, allies on the Hill, and in the media. Especially unkind was Wernher Von Braun, a former head of the Nazi missile program, who together with some others was adopted by the U.S. government at the end of World War II. In contrast, a long essay on the twenty-fifth anniversary of Project Apollo in the *Washington Post* had some nice lines about how prescient I had been.

Such kudos, of course, were welcome, but they did little for my get-down-to-earth drive. The issue, though, did not go away. The question of how to allocate the nation's public resources among various priorities still stands, and not merely because NASA continues to bamboozle the public and Congress. It is, for instance, a key question we face when people complain that the nation is spending too much on older Americans and not enough on younger ones (which I have argued is not the case if transfer of assets is taken into account). It is also a key issue when we debate how much of the gross domestic product health care should be allowed to consume (which led me to ask to which better use would these resources be put if we did not spend them on health—on another NASA project?). Challenging NASA stayed with me for another reason: it raised a nagging question—why are people so unfriendly when one says, however indirectly and subtly, "You see, I told you so."

Contemplating My Navel, the Future, and—
Gore (Flash-Forward to 1976)

I am told that memoirs differ from autobiographies in that not all of one's life is systematically covered, or that one does not necessarily unfold one's life in the precise sequence it happened. Anyway, with the reader's indulgence, I turn to explore two encounters—one (which happened in 1976) with a future vice president of the United States and one (the high point of which took place in 1979) with George Soros—because they played a key role in my assessment of things past. It all began when a night of excessive navel gazing ended with my first encounter with a young member of Congress I had never heard about before, one Albert Gore Jr. But let me tell it the way it happened.

Occasionally, we would have friends over for dinner that often turned into an earnest give-and-take about current events. (An aspiring actress, the wife of a colleague, refused our invitations because, she said, "they always turn into public policy seminars.") One evening the "seminar" revolved around forecasting. Someone was complaining about weather predictions; someone else was making light of economists' projections. I unloaded my pent up disappointment that being right, time and again, did not lead to one's ideas being more widely followed or my counsel sought.

The reaction could not have been more disapproving than if I had gobbled up everybody's yummy dessert right there in front of their eyes. "*Nobody* likes someone telling them that he is right," was the kindest comment. Someone pointed out that if one says that he has completed the marathon in Hawaii and Boston and New York (assuming he did), this may seem somewhat boastful but still impressive. If one adds that one was among the first 100 to finish, this may be a bit uncouth. But to claim to be right is outright obnoxious.

That night I did more tossing and turning than sleeping. This would be a deceptive memoir if I did not divulge that I was pissed about those occasions in which I had been able to see around the corner—on matters of considerable public import—but for which my observations were not appreciated. Why do many people find such claims so annoying? I did the sociological thing and talked to some of my colleagues. The best I could find out was that people sense that when someone declares, "I told you so!" the implication is that everybody else is full of it, is way off base. It is not a characterization people appreciate—whether or not the observation is a valid one.

Why did my sense of being wronged nevertheless persist? A friend offered a psychological explanation. He suggested that public intellectuals must believe that their ideas are valid ones, given how many they must spawn, and how hard they have to push them, before one of them makes it all the way upriver. Without some public recognition, he speculated, it must be very difficult for a public intellectual to persevere. I did not care for this explanation. It somehow sounded vaguely delusional: you had to *believe* you were right to keep going, but truth be told, I thought I was right and wanted people to acknowledge my foresight—for their sake and mine.

The most important mission of public intellectuals is to think outside the box. The "box" is composed of assumptions societies (and individuals) tend to be locked into. They take them for granted. Thus, until 1989 we took it for granted that we would have the Soviet Union as a major power to contend with; next to nobody foresaw the fall of the Berlin Wall and the collapse of communism worldwide. Similarly, until 9/11 we more or less assumed that the United States was protected from major attacks within its continental borders. In these cases major dramatic events made us reassess what we took for granted. But we would be much better off if, instead of waiting until major events hit us over the head, we reexamine our basic assumptions once in a while, spurred by public intellectuals. This is, for instance, what neoconservatives did to the Great Society assumption that government could fix domestic social problems with relative ease given enough money.

One reason public intellectuals are often at least initially ignored is precisely because they break the mold. Most people most of the time resist the hard intellectual labor involved in rethinking their core assumptions about the world and themselves—as was the case, say, in the period when Americans believed that they represented the forces of liberty and light and the Communists were the evil empire. Along came a Harvard professor, one Henry Kissinger, who argued that we should make nice to China. Initially, it was enough to make everyone see red; later, Nixon made it U.S. policy.

The next day, I took to my typewriter and converted my peeve into, you guessed it, another article. This piece did not mention my feelings but pointed out that a nation would greatly benefit if it distinguished among its public intellectuals according to how well they were able to read the future, sort of kept a scorecard. A society that treats all its public intellectuals the same, both false and true prophets, is bound to stumble blindly into the future or follow a false one to the bitter end. Granted, a precise evaluation of diagnoses is impossible for many reasons. Some, like Herman Kahn, safely prophesied about the very remote future (such as the year 2076) or hedged their predictions with so many caveats that they could hardly be proved wrong. Also, all predictions are conditional; they assume that there will be no significant intervention by some external force—for instance, an oil boycott—but such forces act up with annoying frequency.

Still, the article suggested that one can form an assessment of those whose forecasts and prescriptions are, over the long run, less or more reliable than those of others. Someone such as Arthur Lauffer, whose argument that lowering taxes would *increase* the government revenue (an idea "tested" by Reagan's tax cut which resulted in a gigantic deficit), would be laughed out of court rather than lionized. Neither would anybody heed the gold bugs who urged people to amass this metal to secure their investments. In contrast, the projections of the Congressional Budget Office often turned out to be quite close to the mark. (The need for such a scorecard has not decreased since those days. Harvard economist Jeffrey Sachs lost little standing when he argued that Russia could be turned from a communist country into a democratic, capitalist society within two years. An economist joke reflects quite seriously their predictive powers: give them a figure or a date, but never both. It is to the credit of James Glassman and Kevin Hassett that they did not follow this way of protecting their forecast from all possibility of verification. In their book *Dow 36,000*, published in 1999, they guessed the Dow could reach that level within three to five years. Meanwhile, they kept enjoying a following as if this far-out prediction had already come true.) For starters, I suggested, only half tongue in cheek, that whenever someone's predictions are published, that intellectuals last three predictions should also be cited. After all, if you can buy a "poop sheet" on the performance of racehorses, why not have one on those who advise us all?

My suggestion for keeping score for futurologists (hopefully, myself included) fared about as well as my other ideas at the time: it was honored by being allowed to rest in peace. And it turned into another one of those ideas that I floated before moving on to the next one all too quickly. My lesson to myself, which I admit sunk in very slowly—it is so much easier to gain an insight than to follow it—was that I must be more patient. I had to be willing to stick longer with a project, not to take "no" for an answer, and not to let the lack of appreciation deflect that which I believed had to be championed.

Actually, my article about futurology was not a complete dud. It did make me the darling (and frequent keynote speaker) of the World Future Society. It also led to an invitation by young, barely known Congress member Albert Gore Jr. to discuss my proposals before a clearinghouse for the future that he was running in Congress. This was one of my first close encounters with members of Congress (as distinct from the much shorter and more formal occasions when I testified before Congress). I looked forward to the evening.

A group of Congress members slowly assembled for dinner. Gore served as a gracious but not effusive host. He displayed a considerable variety of interests. As I sat next to him during the meal, he explained that 80 percent of cancer was caused by dangerous material in the environment. He next expressed considerable concern about waste in government; he was especially troubled by a growing use of limo drivers and the number of fancy banquets organized by elected officials. I repeated my arguments about the need to edit futurologists. (I was warned to be brief because Congress members' attention spans are far from enormous and that they would rather talk than be lectured.) My presentation was followed by a few comments and questions, most of which were tame and off the mark. One Congress member was keen to know what the future of the Organization of Petroleum Exporting Countries (OPEC) was going to be. Another asked whether I knew a specialist on housing trends. The last question, posed by a congressman who was about to retire, concerned the size of the fees futurologists collect. Gore thanked me, and I rushed back home, complaining about the narrow interests and low caliber of members of the nation's top legislature. Little did I know that that evening was the beginning of a long relationship with a public leader who was going to be very much in the headlines—and at communitarian meetings.

I Mock—George Soros

I do not wish to leave the impression that I claim to be able to read the future the way others read a road map (that is, getting lost but only infrequently). I may as well recount a major development I missed altogether, although it literally walked into my office. I was doing my thing at Columbia University when my secretary said that a guy "with an accent similar to yours" was calling from Wall Street. He had assured her that he was not peddling stocks. He told me, "I would like to stop by and tell you about a new philosophy I developed. It concerns the waves in which history moves forward." I said to myself, "Yeah, that'll be the day, when some stock trader springs a new philosophy on the world," but something about the caller's chatter was intriguing. He came over and we spent an hour talking about philosopher Karl Popper (his hero), the future of the economy, and stock trends. The guy, who at the time was not a public figure, was George Soros.

I saw a lot of him in the following years. Minerva and Annaliese, George's wife, became close friends, and we often had dinner together or were invited—kids and all—to spend the weekend at George's stupendous two-acre estate in Southampton. We played tennis and Frisbee and splashed about in a regulation-size pool. George and I had long conversations, during which he laid out his philosophy and I tried to understand how he made decisions. (Some of what I learned found its way into one of my most often cited articles on humble decision making, called "mixed scanning.")

Maybe we got along so well because I never asked for stock tips. I also refrained from investing in George's mutual funds, which all were "off-shore," making it illegal for a U.S. citizen to invest in them. I hence did not benefit from their stratospheric gains. And when I learned about the grayer sides of the investment business, I did not share the information with third parties. For instance, I found out that some managers of mutual funds can sell a stock short, get a cooperative reporter to do a negative story about the stock, and complain to the banks that finance the related corporation until the bank curtails their loans and credits. Soon the stock collapses; you cover the short, make a killing, and move to the next one.

Over the next few years, George became famous. One newspaper called him "the Michelangelo, Van Gogh, and Beethoven" of investing. He made scores of billions for others and a few extra for himself. We kept seeing each other and neither paid attention to the growing media hoopla about his phenomenal success as an investor. In 1978, George invited me to join the board of a new foundation he was launching. He was going to call it, following philosopher Karl Popper, "The Open Society." George stated its purpose straightforwardly, although with his typical self-deprecating half smile: to lift the Iron Curtain and liberate the communist societies in Eastern Europe.

I tried, very poorly I am sure, to conceal my sense that George had gone off the deep end. Lift the Iron Curtain? Free Eastern Europe? How about finishing off communism? Ending the Cold War? Stopping the earth from spinning as an encore? The last thing I needed was to get involved in another project that would yield little, however virtuous the idea. I demurred, pointing to other duties.

Well, the rest, as they say, is history. George Soros did go a long way toward lifting the Iron Curtain for Hungary and played a role in liberating

Poland and Russia. While Hungary was still deeply locked in the communist grip, Soros put on the payroll of his foundation scores and scores of dissenters. His foundation arranged for hundreds of Hungarian intellectuals and opinion makers to study in the West. And, in a particularly clever move, he donated Xerox machines to many libraries in Hungary, which the Communist regime accepted happily before realizing that the machines greatly facilitated underground communications and newspapers.

I was wrong. This was hardly the only time, but merely the most global miss.

Meanwhile, in Academia

Bert's Blockade

While several of my senior colleagues gradually accepted the inevitable— that I would continue to be an activist academic—one of them hardly agreed. I'll call him Bert Wyman because I do not wish to speak poorly of someone no longer with us. Bert believed that I betrayed sociology with my public voice and activism, and he continued to fear that I would do irreparable damage to the standing of Columbia's department of sociology. (At the time it was ranked as number two or three in the world. Harvard was considered in the lead and Berkeley second or third.) Bert may have harbored other misgivings, but I never found out what those might have been. He took it upon himself to drive me out of Columbia, tenure and all.

The device Bert hit upon is one little known outside academia. When assistant professors are granted tenure, they are usually moved up a rank and appointed associate professors. It is then widely expected that within a few years they will be promoted to the highest rank, that of full professor. When associate professors are not promoted, initially nobody notices. However, as the years pass and no promotion is forthcoming, the word spreads that professor so-and-so is in the doghouse, has evoked the wrath of his or her colleagues. If this condition persists, the perpetual associate professor becomes a sort of outcast locally and is suspect throughout the discipline. Typically, such an associate professor will leave campus for a much less auspicious school that is willing to extend him or her the top rank of full professor.

Because my promotion to a tenure-carrying associate professor position was very fast, I assumed that my promotion to full professor would take care of itself within a few years. However, Bert, who was serving as the new chairman of the department, figured that denying me the promotion would force this activist out of the hallowed halls of Columbia. Just in case I was slow to notice that no promotion was in the wings, Bert—usually a mild-mannered fellow—let me know that I might as well start packing, as I would be promoted to full professor only over his dead body.

Slowly, the word got out. Colleagues, who previously gossiped about the speed at which I gained my Ph.D., appointment to a top university, and tenure (and my publication rate), now traded rumors about the reasons I had lost my standing as a boy wonder. There were a few digs and catty asides during conferences. And for the first time, I was uninvited from a symposium on the grounds of an unexpected budget cut, which I later learned led to only one person being axed—me.

These unpleasantries within academia came on top of disappointments in my public endeavors. Still, while I was here and there in a funk, disagreeable during dinner, even snapping back at a colleague who asked point-blank, "Why haven't they promoted you?" I did slug on. Call it insensitivity, pig-headedness, or perseverance, but if one seeks the life of an activist professor, of a public intellectual, one must be able to take a fair amount of frustration and rejection without allowing it to penetrate to the marrow of one's bones; one must be shielded by what one believes one is trying to accomplish. After a period in which I took particularly hefty amounts of abuse, Bruce Douglass, a professor of government at Georgetown and a friend, once told me, raising an eyebrow: "You are like that Timex ad, you take a licking and keep on ticking." I guess that at least according to one friend I had developed some of the stamina I had resolved to acquire. I was happy he saw the ticking but not the hurt it took to keep clicking.

I am not claiming that the barbs, slights, delayed promotions, and being passed over for this or that prize must bounce off the ego of public intellectuals as if they are made of reinforced concrete; the potshots do leave their marks. But a sense of purpose allows one to stubbornly keep going.

Also, I was less crushed because I expected little. Although I had a strong sense that certain causes command one to serve, I never believed that I was particularly skilled or accomplished at serving them. A line from the Old Testament buzzed in my head when I bemoaned my limited capabilities. The line is the one Moses mutters when God instructs him to speak to Pharaoh on behalf of the enslaved Israelites. Moses says unto the Lord, "O my Lord, I am not eloquent, neither heretofore, nor since thou hast spoken unto thy servant: but I am slow of speech, and of a slow tongue."

Wait a moment. No, no. I do not have even a hint of a Moses complex. I am not crazy enough to think that I can deliver my people from slavery, bring them a new Ten Commandments, march them through any desert, however small. All I'm saying is that the fact that someone is not especially good at public service should not stop that person from doing his or her share. If unpopular causes had to wait until they found highly articulate and accomplished activists, most would never get off the ground.

The Active Society (1964–1965)

In the end, Bert's blockade came to naught, in a surprising way. Out of the blue, the greatest piece of academic manna fell into my lap. Typically, fellowships and awards reach one in dribs and drabs. First, you hear that you might be on the list of potential beneficiaries. Then, you'll learn that a committee decided to grant whatever it is but awaits approval from a higher board; then, the board approves—but funds are not secure. And then, quite anticlimactically, an announcement arrives in the mail, umpteen weeks after you were told it would hit your doorstep any day now.

In contrast, my invitation to academic heaven, to the Center for Advanced Studies in Behavior Sciences, fell into my lap like someone winning a lottery without buying a ticket. The center is a dream think tank, the ultimate answer to a professor's prayers, a place many scholars would give their right arm to spend a year—for very good reason. The center is located just above Stanford, on a small hill overlooking a lake. It does not look like much. It holds a small library, a modest dining room, a bunch of cabana-like buildings that serve as studies, and a few shady trees. But each year it hosts a select group of professors who are flown in with their families and books—all at the center's expense. These professors are paid full salary and provided with research assistants and secretarial backup. They teach no classes, attend no meetings, report to no one. They are firmly instructed to mind no one but their inner light. Sheer heaven.

Granted such an opportunity to carry out a major work, I focused on a set of challenging questions: under what conditions would a people be able to understand history and learn to control their fate—instead of being subject to its capricious whims and vicissitudes? How could we restructure society so that it would respond to our profoundest needs rather than lord over us? How could society end the alienation of modernity and form authentic human relations and communities? If one could address these questions, I thought, both sociological theory and public action were sure to be richly rewarded—and would grow closer to one another.

Given a year without any distractions (other than my occasional participation in demonstrations and teach-ins against the war in Vietnam) and ample research backup, I drafted a 698-page book. After additional work over the next two years, it was published by the Free Press in 1968 under the title *The Active Society*. I discuss it at some length because it is considered my best academic work, by others and myself.

To briefly indicate the book's topic and scope, the volume opens with philosophical questions about the extent to which our fate is subject to our will as
opposed to being predetermined by forces we neither understand nor control.
It examines cybernetic theories that concern steering mechanisms—that is,
those that put people in control—in inanimate systems such as those of machines in factories. It then shows that to develop such a theory for societies,
democratic processes are required; that to effectively control history, people
must be truly involved in developing the signals to which they themselves are
to respond.

The book next highlights the four main components of a social steering
system, the required kinds of knowledge, decision-making strategies, power,
and consensus building.

It closes by investigating whether human needs are inalterably fixed or
subject to manipulation. It asks: if these needs are locked in, how can one ensure that society will be restructured to respond to our needs rather than
vainly trying to tailor them to be what society is willing and able to satisfy?
Such manipulative responses, the book shows, result in inauthentic relations
and false consensus.

Studying all these philosophical and sociological questions, one on top of
the other, makes for a very ambitious agenda. One reviewer stated the book's
scope as follows:

> It is a comprehensive integration of an awesome array of the knowledge and
> concepts of modern sociology and political science. It is a grand program for
> societal action. . . . Above all it is a bold answer to the question: Is it possible
> for societies to become active, that is, responsive to the needs and values of its
> members?

Another reviewer, with a blessed pen and acumen, stressed that although
The Active Society offered a general theory, it was quite specific:

> A rigorous sociological theory is spelled out so that the preconditions for cre-
> ating an active society can be clearly understood. Etzioni's extensive guided
> tour of the sociologist's cosmos is a reasoned and precise analysis of the type of
> sociological theory that is needed to understand the modern world, and also a
> prescription of the priorities and strategies that will improve it.

As the reviewer continued, he provided readers with a fair warning:

> It may seem unusual to praise a book which at the same time cannot really be
> recommended to anyone but a very specialized set of readers. A huge span of

attention is required. . . . Etzioni has given us a coherent and consistent sociological theory of modern society.

I consider this to be one of the most important books in its field in the last twenty years. Apart from its substantive contribution to the strategy of societal activation, it offers a whole focus of immensely valuable perspectives for detailed empirical investigation in the future.

Even the left-leaning *Nation*, which found little to cheer in my work before or after *The Active Society*, praised it. Its reviewer observed that "even on cursory examination [it] will make the lay reader realize how naive and inchoate the ideas subsumed under 'social consciousness' usually are, and how much we stand in need of the sharply focused thinking that professionals like Etzioni bring to bear on social problems."

Other reviews were much more mixed. *The Active Society* did not become the new grand theory of sociology. Aside from whatever intrinsic limitations my theory had—the timing was off. American sociology had exhausted its patience for overarching theories after it had been dominated for decades by several, most recently that of Talcott Parsons. Rejecting them was part of the rebellion and counterculture of the 1960s and a weigh station to a highly fragmented and politicized sociology.

The Active Society did better in Europe, where grand theories often flourish. (In effect, the difference in attitude cut across many areas: American architects tend to be much less Gothic than Europeans. American writers tend to more often be the masters of short stories; Europeans—of grand novels. America gave the world jazz; Europe—symphonies.) The book was translated into German by two of my best students, Wolfgang and Sylvia Streeck. Hans Joas, a towering German sociologist, noted: "*The Active Society* . . . remains, in my eyes, an unsurpassed attempt to develop a theory of macroscopic action."

For a while, I wondered why I was not more disappointed with the American response to the book. I consoled myself with the thought that it constituted the best academic effort I could marshal. While, of course, I would have loved for it to reshape sociology, there was something satisfying about having given the endeavor all I had. And, to put it candidly, I think it is a damn good book.

Although *The Active Society* is a theoretical, academic work, it left some marks in the public realm, as my friend Betty Friedan explained. I quote her at some length for several reasons. Betty is not one who loosely dishes out compliments; hence hers are particularly treasured. Moreover, it is not often that a leader of Betty's stature directly credits an academic theory with playing a role in the formation of her thinking.

Some time before I actually met Amitai Etzioni personally and we became good friends, I happened to pick up a copy of *The Active Society* which some-one had left on a desk I was using at the Frederick Lewis Allen Room of the New York Public Library. I opened the book and it really resonated with me. Its message to me at that time when I was, you might say, starting the modern women's movement, was that you cannot have an agenda for ten or twenty years hence, much less for a century hence. You can only have a sense of how things are and might be on the cutting edge. It was a warning to me of the dan-gers of radical rhetoric in the abstract, rhetoric that does not resonate with cur-rent realities and the concrete possibility of change in the present or near fu-ture. That was a very valuable lesson for me in the early days of the modern women's movement and gave a sort of philosophical grounding for the focus of my own leadership which was, from the very beginning, geared to concrete possibilities of change in the mainstream of American society.

Betty continued to report on how our friendship deepened over the decades:

Since then, Amitai has become a close personal friend. And without giving up any of my concerns for the individual rights of women, I find myself now equally concerned with the values of community. In a certain sense, having spent most of my adult life as a leader and participant-observer on the cutting edge of the Active Society—which the women's movement is and will con-tinue to be if it is in tune with the responsive community—I welcome Amitai's work because it helps give me a theoretical underpinning.

The Active Society resolved one more matter. Even before it was published and reviewed, as the manuscript circulated, the opposition to my promotion to full professorship melted away. I do not know whether Bert changed his mind or the senior members of the department changed it for him, on the grounds that further delaying the promotion might well reflect more on the department than on me. All I know is that suddenly another one of those of-ficial letters appeared in my mailbox, settling the matter. I was promoted to full professor.

CHAPTER FIVE

Dangerous Truths: Seeking a Foothold (1967–1978)

Let My People Be

After Palo Alto, on returning to Columbia, I continued working on the manuscript of *The Active Society* and participating in antiwar activities. In the middle of all this, in February 1967 to be precise, I left for two weeks to try to do some good in a way I never had attempted before or since: a sort of mini personal diplomacy. My journey took me to Moscow.

The trip to the cold heart of the Soviet Empire stemmed from my participation in international meetings dedicated to promoting peace. In these meetings, I formed some personal contacts with Soviet leaders that, it occurred to me, might serve an unrelated cause. One of these leaders, who will stand for all the decent ones I befriended, was Serge Mikoyan. He was the son of Anastas Ivanovich Mikoyan, Khrushchev's close adviser who eventually became a first deputy premier of the Soviet Union. Serge was a soft-spoken peace activist. He reliably represented the views of his country, but did not try to recruit us to spy for the Soviet bloc or ask us to pass on its propaganda. He simply pointed to the dangers of nuclear weapons, searching for ways the two superpowers might come together to defuse this threat to human survival.

The other Russian I came to know, who will stand for all the Soviet representatives I met who were clearly acting as government agents (whether or not they technically were spies), was Professor Yuri Zamoshkin. Zamoshkin would suddenly pop up once or twice a year in the United States. We would spend some time chatting about what was going on in sociology, what good

new books had been published, and who the new stars were. Then, switching his demeanor, Yuri would turn all business: openly, he would inquire how
I thought the American people were reacting to this or that Soviet move, position, or policy. I was obviously on his list of sources he used to assess American public opinion. (Zamoshkin and other Soviets of his ilk did not have
much respect for peace activists who followed their instructions; they called
them "lackeys." But they showed considerable deference to those of us who
favored negotiation leading to arms reduction that was acceptable to both
sides but who strongly opposed *unilateral* disarmament by the West and those
that would not dream of supporting the Soviet's self-serving positions.)

I was willing to let Zamoshkin pump me for information. He learned from
me that Americans were dismayed, flabbergasted, outraged at what the Soviet Union did in Hungary, Poland, and to minorities at home, and other
such "secrets." When Zamoshkin finished checking off whatever list of questions was in his mind, he would visibly relax. We would visit some more,
which allowed me to gain insight into what he and his kind were like. (He
was gaga about buying Western consumer goods and gadgets, especially long-
playing records.)

During a visit with a friend at the Israeli embassy, it occurred to us that I
might be able to draw on my contacts with various Russians to try to convince them to drop their harshly oppressive policies against Jews. The goals
were to seek the release of jailed Jewish leaders, stop the publication of
government-issued and virulently anti-Semitic tracts, cease the appropria-
tion and destruction of Jewish cemeteries, and end the dismissal of employees who applied for rarely given visas to emigrate to Israel. (At the time, the
Soviet Union had launched various de-Stalinization programs, in which
some of the most oppressive measures against average Soviet citizens were
relaxed, but the treatment of Jews remained basically the same as it had
been under Stalin.)

Our idea met with approval by some leaders of the Jewish community in
the United States and by an agency in Israel especially concerned with the
Soviet Jewry. All involved realized that the chances that I could do any
good were small at best. But there was little to be lost by trying and much
to be gained if I could bring about even a small improvement in the treatment of the Jews.

Without much further ado, in the winter of 1967 I found myself in the
Moscow airport, embarking on my first visit to a communist state. The border guard in the airport was suspicious: "What are you doing here in the
depth of winter?" (It was late February.) I told him that I had never been to
the Soviet Union before and that I was between semesters, the only period

in which I could travel. He wanted to know if I had prearranged meetings with any Russians. I thought it would be best to tell him the truth. I mentioned Serge, thinking that my acquaintance, bordering on friendship, with the son of a top Soviet leader would make the border's gates fly wide open. Instead, the guard rushed to bring in a higher-ranking officer, who started the questioning all over but demanded many more details. The fact that in the middle of all this Serge arrived to greet me did not faze the border guards. It took over an hour before they let me enter the country. The airport encounter served as a fair introduction to what was to follow.

Although all the Russians I met were embarrassingly hospitable (especially given their meager means), they were also completely unyielding. Not only Yuri but also Serge maintained that Jews were not treated differently from other ethnic minorities, that Jews had been offered a state of their own called Yevreyskaya (the capital of which was Birobidzhan), but it was they who refused to settle in it. Yuri and Serge further maintained that the Soviet government was trying to liberate all people from all religions that were nothing but superstitions, and that the Jews were not singled out in these "rehabilitation" drives.

At the end of such meetings, I found that I had to go to some pains—especially after evenings in which I was wined and dined, taken to the Bolshoi or to concerts of balalaikas—to leave my hosts with a stern expression of my disappointment and anger. I thanked them for their hospitality, but stressed that neither I nor others in the United States—including the champions of a negotiated end to the arms race—would buy their justifications about the ways they treated Jews. I urged them with as much vigor as I could muster after a long meal during which several glasses of vodka were downed, that the Soviet–American relationship would be best served if they "de-Stalinized" their Jewish policy. I repeated this message about thirty times in various meetings, with growing exertion and fatigue. It was like talking to a wall.

Several of the Jews I met left me with a creepy feeling as they mouthed the Soviet line, either for self-protection or out of careerism. A colleague had advised me to see Vladimir Shamberg, a high-ranking academic who was also Jewish. He certainly had an impressive title: the head of the Information Division of the Institute of World Economy and International Relations, a major Soviet research institute. (Soviet academicians often worked directly for the government.)

Shamberg turned out to be a warm person with a fine command of English. His job included analyzing the American press, and he was well versed in Jewish problems—in the United States. But as far as Soviet policies toward the Jews were concerned, he was a fervent representative of the official line. No, there was no anti-Semitism (except perhaps among some peasants), for anti-Semitism was against Marxism. Discrimination was punished severely wherever it occurred. Most Jews, he assured me, did not want to speak Yiddish or to pray. What did it mean to him to be Jewish? Nothing much, he said with a shrug of his shoulders, looking me straight in the eye, as if saying, "and I want to be sure you know, I mean it."

Aside from recognizing how strongly entrenched the Soviet anti-Jewish policy was, I left with two impressions. The Soviet Union did not look like the superpower the American press depicted it to be. Most of Moscow looked like a cross between a Third World country and a Salvation Army dump. Streets and rooms were poorly lit, if at all. Stores had empty shelves or products that looked like they had been picked up in a junkyard. Vegetables were few and far between and often long wilted. Cars looked as if they were held together with coat hangers. People's faces were withdrawn and glum, with the exception of the children whose cheeks were full and who ran around in good humor in fairly new snowsuits.

The police state was all too palpable. On the face of it, I was an ordinary tourist; it said so in my visa. Tourism in the Soviet Union in those days was overseen by a government agency that arranged sightseeing and kept tabs on foreigners. The agency set me up with a driver and an attractive young blond woman translator. They were quite accommodating when I visited a museum and shopped for gifts for my kids.

But when I evaded them and disappeared for hours at a time (meeting with Jewish leaders or attending a briefing at the American Embassy), they became outright nasty. They insisted that, as they were in charge of my well-being, I *must* inform them where I had been and where I intended to wander next. My phone emitted odd clicking sounds when I picked up the receiver. Even when I was on the U.S. Embassy's most guarded floor, the seventh, in a special room called the "tank," which was specially equipped to prevent Soviet eavesdropping, I was warned to assume that the room was bugged and write down rather than say aloud all important information.

A minor incident stayed with me. Yuri Zamoshkin, Vladimir Shlapentokh, a Jewish sociologist, and I were having lunch. Shlapentokh mentioned that he had conducted a study of Soviet public opinion and cited some figures that seemed hard to believe. I politely inquired if he could explain them a bit more. Shlapentokh offered to show me the study and opened his beat-up briefcase to fish it out. Before he got very far, Zamoshkin turned to him and in a very cold, slow voice, sharply articulating every word, said: "I *bet* Professor Shlapentokh *will not* be able to *find* the study." Shlapentokh took his hand out of the briefcase as if he'd been bitten by a snake and said, with much embarrassment: "I must have left it at home." What a sick place.

When it was finally time to leave, the border guard checked my passport closely and then sent it to a booth for further examination. While it did not take long for it to return, the very possibility that I might be held over made me shiver in the overheated lounge—I could not wait to get out. Together with other foreigners, I was kept in a separate waiting area to prevent us from mixing with Russians. Even after we cleared all formalities, we still had to pass by a Soviet solider, who stood with a loaded gun at the foot of the staircase leading to the airplane. When we landed an hour later in Helsinki, I felt for the first time since I had arrived in Moscow that I could breathe freely and stop looking over my shoulder to see if I was being followed.

What did I accomplish? At best, extremely little. Mine was one of many thousands of drops of protest that were dripped on the rock of Soviet oppression and persecution. Eventually, years later, major historical developments (and continued pressure by the West) softened the Soviet stance. It eventually even opened its gates and let my people go, allowing millions of Jews to escape that cursed land.

Why did I not feel like a complete failure on returning to New York empty-handed? Perhaps it was because none of the Israeli representatives or Jewish leaders who debriefed me seemed particularly disappointed. Maybe because I expected little to begin with. Maybe because I sensed that I had done the best I could for a very good cause.

Parting of Ways: No Cracked Eggs (1969)

Long flights—with the 30,000-foot perspective, the absence of phone calls, and the night's quiet solitude—invite reflection. The flight from Helsinki to New York after my Soviet sojourn was no exception. I decided that it was high time for me to speak up about rising incidents in which American students and other young people were resorting to violence to advance one cause or another.

In the 1960s young people were the engine of social change. They assumed the role Marx assigned to the working class, to be the propellants of history. Young people provided many of the leaders and rank and file of the civil rights movement and the drive against the war in Vietnam. They were the main carriers of the counterculture, the sexual revolution, and the rebellion against practically all established institutions and authorities. (Alan Ehrenhalt described the resulting change particularly well in his book *The Lost City*.)

For a while I was among a small group of older fellows—I had just turned forty—of whom the youth approved. While many professors were still fairly stiff and formal, informality (from sandals to open collars) came naturally to me from my Israeli upbringing. (I still believe that the world would be better for it if no one wore a tie, a completely useless accessory, and dedicated the money saved to some good purpose.) Nor did I mind hanging around at a teach-in until my turn to speak finally arrived, usually at some unpredictable, ungodly hour. And I was one of a small number of professors who joined the students in street demonstrations.

When I reviewed my account on these pages of the popularity I had acquired, and of the long hours I put in as a student and then as a professor, I asked myself, as I have asked about other achievements mentioned in this book—how sure can I be that these claims are justified? In response I have included in this book what many may consider excessive quotations of others' observations as well as numerous references in footnotes. And I have tried to draw on what social scientists consider "objective measurements" (for example, reporting the number of months it took me to earn my Ph.D., write my first academic book, or get tenure rather than relying on my feeling that each happened in record time). And I quote next from letters I got, for instance, from a student who was a member of one of my classes in those days, when I briefly served as a visiting assistant professor at Berkeley. I have not met the student since then or after this letter. She wrote:

> I was an undergraduate in the early 60s and was able to attend your lectures on organizations, and in fact, read "A Comparative Analysis of Complex Organizations." You were the *most interesting* professor. Your class was on Mon, Wed, and Fri's at 3:00. Nobody but nobody ever missed one of your classes even the Friday afternoon classes. We all had to arrive early because if we didn't we would have to stand as so many students audited your class. You tried to explain the concept of charisma, and we all thought that all you had to do was point to yourself and say "charisma."

I enjoyed the popularity I had acquired: being invited to speak when few other elders were; faces eager to listen—rare among a group not characterized by respect for anyone over thirty. What troubled me was that a growing number of the students, the same people who gave me voice and popularity, had turned from peaceful demonstrations to violence. While the number of students who actually turned violent was small, many others condoned, some even romanticized, the use of force. They were full of simplistic interpretations of the role of force in history, confusing the place it had in revolutions against authoritarian regimes with its destructive role in democratic societies. And they embraced some psychobabble about the purging and purifying merits of acting out. They cheered when the underground Weatherman group firebombed the home of a judge and several police headquarters. They applauded the robbing of banks at gunpoint to "finance the revolution," an idea they picked up from Stalin. They admired the Black Panthers who engaged the police in gun battles.

While I shared many of the social purposes for which the students had taken to the streets, I found their means ever less appropriate. I was, though, truth be told, reluctant to confront them. To do so, I knew damn well, would quickly put an end to whatever following and popularity I had acquired. You may think, "big deal," there are people who make endlessly greater sacrifices, and you'd be right, of course. However, walk in my shoes for a moment. My senior colleagues were after me for mixing academic work with activism. My antiwar activism at the time delivered precious little other than rejection. And popularity—ask any actor, author, community leader—is strongly addictive. It was like giving up on a very attractive date because you found her politics to be offensive.

An opportunity to express my dismay simultaneously to several groups of young people about the turn toward violence presented itself during a conference of the New Left. The three-day event was dedicated to debating the applications of power. Some 450 student leaders from all over the country and an audience of about 1,200 assembled at the University of Pennsylvania. Paul Goodman and I were the keynote speakers; the *Philadelphia Inquirer* called us "two elder statesmen of the New Left." The *Washington Post* captured my position:

> Etzioni . . . is concerned, he said, about the "easy talk of violence such as we heard here tonight."
>
> The most alarming aspect of the student power movement, he said, is the "use of violence as a deliberate political strategy."
>
> "Acts of violence against persons are in principle no different than the violence of the Vietnam war, except that a fist may be used instead of a bomb."
>
> There has been a trend among student activists, he said, toward escalation of violence because "everybody is trying to out Vietcong everybody else."

I elaborated my position during a peace rally at Columbia University, as the *Columbia Owl* reported:

> "It is not useful to anyone to blur the lines between civil disobedience and violence," Etzioni said. "It is intellectually dishonest, morally a completely different category and politically unwise."

Etzioni explained that he was against the war in Viet Nam, opposed to the Johnson administration, and favored not allowing the CIA to recruit [on the campus]. However, he said, "The use of force against people who don't agree with you is exactly what the United States is doing in Viet Nam. I see no moral justification for this."

Students did listen, not so much because the arguments were novel but because of whom they were coming from, one who heretofore was on their side. There were only a few hecklers who shouted, "Tell it to the CIA!" and "Stop the bombing in Vietnam!" When I finished, the applause was more than I expected: minimal, brief, and tepid. Later, there were numerous exchanges in the corridors and over Cokes. The students were well versed in all the arguments fashioned by Frantz Fanon, Che Guevara, and other apostles of violence. I tried to refute them, realizing that if I were going to make an impression at all, it would not be so much by what I had to say, but by the very fact that I was more than willing to part ways over this issue. (The same debate ranges these days between the anarchists and members of other groups that participate in anti-globalism demonstrations.)

Students at Columbia were less stung by my disapproval than those at a national conference at the University of Pennsylvania. A year earlier, students had occupied several buildings on campus and held them for several intense days until they were dragged out by the police. I readily acknowledged that they had reason to be peeved. The university's rigid administration largely ignored their requests and representatives. I also granted that occupying a building was a long way from throwing bombs; still, I considered it a form of violence and opposed it. Instead of supporting the students, I joined the faculty who formed a human chain around one of the occupied buildings. We succeeded in preventing the conservative students, led by the jocks, from storming the building and kicking out the occupying students. We thus prevented a major violent brawl. (My own role was a bit more visible than others' because I was chosen to address the crowd, and my picture—waving my finger at those seeking to storm the building—was featured in the *New York Times Magazine* followed by a long article I wrote entitled, "Confessions of a Professor Caught in a Revolution.")

The small drama that followed was captured by a report published the next day in the college newspaper:

Etzioni surprised the student rebels by being critical of them. "This seizure of buildings is a sad mistake. The educational process is not like the manufacturing process. You should not be blocking the way to my office. As much as I sympathize with your aims, I would tell the University not to negotiate any-

Figure 5.1.   Columbia University, 1968

thing so long as you use force and violence to disrupt the educational process."
His colleague Greeman quickly disagreed, "I don't think that the educational
process has been truly disrupted by these seizures. I think it's only beginning!"
A rebel student jumped up to back up Greeman, "This is the biggest and best
class I have attended in my six years as a student at Columbia. Education is
happening *right here!*"

In the years that followed many thousands of students—frustrated by a government that ignored their legitimate protests against the war in Vietnam and
by university administrations that were locked in some remote past—continued
to romanticize violence and, in smaller numbers, to engage in it. I continued to
try to talk students out of following such a course of action and participated only
in demonstrations in which no violent confrontations were planned.

Soon the students stopped inviting me to address their rallies and to line
up with the leaders at the head of protest marches. I wished I had more compelling arguments and personality so that I could have convinced the students
to refrain from the use of force. If I could just have transported the students,
for a few days, to the mountains of Judea, burying friends, consoling their families, witnessing the agony of those at the receiving end of violence—I was

sure—they would have seen the light. But as much as I tried, I swayed only a few.

I had few regrets. Activists, just like politicians, must be willing to draw down their political capital. What I did felt right, although I deeply wished I had accomplished much more.

Science and Society: The Secrets of Policy Research (1970–1971)

As calls to speak at teach-ins and rallies dwindled, I retreated into my cubicle in the library. Here, I knew my way; the stacks offered a quiet peace; my typewriter patter had a reassuring familiarity to it. Still, I was looking for a way not to completely give up on trying to do some good in the "real world." Hence, I turned to explore a question that had long intrigued me: was there a way to bring closer the academic view of the world as-it-is and the quest to recast the world as-it-ought-to-be? Was there a way to bring closer the two masters I was trying to serve faithfully, making one less jealous of the other? Was there a way to bridge the schism between seeking truth and public service?

The answer to these questions, it seemed, required a new kind of social science. It would not replace the scholastic approach but could add to a distinct way of garnering knowledge, one that was action-friendly but also a rock-solid methodology. The more I thought about it, the more I was struck by the intriguing differences between research aimed at increasing our understanding of the world (basic research) and the research required to guide action (policy research).

Once the question was formulated in this way, the next step was to look for books that explored the special methodology that policy research requires, but I found very few. The best book at the time was *The Policy Sciences*, by Harold D. Lasswell and Daniel Lerner. But it did not directly address the methodological issues at hand.

I decided to try my idea on Bert Wyman, my departmental nemesis. As it now was clear that we were destined to spend the rest of our academic lives in the same small department, maybe it was time to bridge our differences. Also, Bert was a basic research purist; if I could convince him about the need for a distinct yet legitimate way of conducting policy research, I might well be able to convince the rest of my colleagues.

Bert listened as I outlined the main differences between the two modes of research as follows: basic research has no a priori favorite factors (or variables); policy research is mainly interested in those that are relatively malleable. For example, policy research is much more interested in the ways people perceive difference in sex roles than in the sex ratios at birth. It sort of follows the Alcoholics Anonymous prayer for focusing on that which can be changed, not taking on that which is given, and building on the ability to tell the difference.

Policy research must encompass all the major elements of whatever slice of the world it is trying to deal with—or it cannot address the needs of action. In contrast, basic research proceeds by fragmenting the world into abstract, analytical pieces and studying one *or* the other. Thus, a basic researcher may study only the prices of flowers (together with other economic factors); a physiologist—the wilting processes; a social psychologist—the symbolic meaning of flowers and other cultural items; and so on. But a person who plans to grow flowers must deal with most, if not all of these elements, and the relations among them. Wilting, for instance, will affect the symbolic meaning of a flower, as any man who ever handed a faded rose to his date is likely to have noticed. And this, in turn, will influence the flower's price.

Bert smiled painfully as I charged ahead, pointing to several other telling differences between purely academic- and action- (or policy-)oriented research. "Academic works are as a rule published; findings of research kept secret typically don't count. The conclusions of policy research are often only for the eyes of a particular policymaker."

And, "The results of basic research are typically written up in extensive articles, even books. The tools of policy research are memos and briefings." Finally, "Basic research has no specific clients; policy research is, as a rule, for those who are supposed to implement it."

Bert reminded me that "sociology models itself after physics, a true science, not some applied or goody-two-shoes approach." I pointed to a different model for a policy-oriented social science—medicine.

"Physicians are not high-powered specialists in any one academic discipline," I said. "They know some chemistry, physiology, anatomy, and psychology. They combine this knowledge with a great deal of practical information that has no basic research base but is very useful. Above all, physicians realize that, given their limits, they actually are experimenting rather than relying on solid answers derived from some science. This is why they typically instruct people to try this or that medication or procedure and then call after a few days. If it does not work, they will experiment with something else. We could do the same."

Bert's response was very much to the point and telling: "No wonder. Given that medicine is much more of an art than a science, they are not even allowed on the main campus! They are segregated in their own enclave uptown. And the university is run by true academics—our provost is not an M.D. but a Ph.D. in physics. The dean is a professor of chemistry." I thanked

Bert for the invigorating discussion and realized—as part of me knew before I visited—that if there was going to be a distinct methodology of policy research, it would have a long row to hoe. Pure academics were going to sneer at what they considered "applied" research with almost as much disapproval as they had for social action.

I proceeded to write about policy research in academic journals and to carry it out. I published what I considered one of my most seminal articles on the subject, unsurprisingly titled "Policy Research." And in 1968 I formed the Center for Policy Research, a not-for-profit corporation, to conduct research along the suggested guidelines.

Centers that specialize in policy research are now commonplace. However, the first of the twenty or more public policy schools that now dot American universities was established just one year before the Center for Policy Research opened its doors; the rest followed. The association of policy researchers (the Association of Public Policy Analysis and Management) was founded in 1976, and its journal, dedicated to policy analysis, was first issued in 1981.

Most policy schools have been (and still are) dominated by economists, who tend to study all kinds of public policies (not merely economic ones), drawing on their mathematical, abstract, and individualistic models. Therefore, even today policy research is often not taught or conducted in line with the multidisciplinary, action-oriented, down-to-earth model. And, while a few books and essays about the special methodologies of policy research have been published over the last twenty-five years, this is not a topic that has been frequently explored to date. If public policy analysis is to improve—and few would disagree that it can stand considerable improvement—more attention must be paid to how it ought to be carried out.

I continued to be involved in a fair number of policy studies in the years that followed, as were a score of others who worked with me at the Center for Policy Research (which I've directed ever since). I soon found an area in which policy research was particularly called for. But first I was awarded an unusual badge of honor.

Making It to the Blacklist

I do not wish to leave the impression that in the second half of the sixties and early seventies I was hidden in my cubicle. I continued, although much more sporadically and with bourgeoning frustration, to lend a hand to the opposition to the war in Vietnam. While a growing number of students, colleagues, and other Americans gradually began to see the merit of our case against the war, we were still considered a deviant and frequently suspect minority. Any doubts about our status were removed when I read a copy of my FBI file, which I obtained under the Freedom of Information Act. (The legalism used by the FBI to justify an investigation in my case was that I spent three days a year as an adviser to a Department of Health, Education, and Welfare committee. This committee reviews requests for funds for mental health research and needs people with FBI clearance about as much as the Audubon Society does.)

The file revealed that in 1972 the Federal Bureau of Investigation conducted a lengthy inquiry into my past. Someone had charged that I "made statements critical of the United States' foreign policy . . . defended the position of Red China and the Soviet Union, and had made unwarranted accusations against the military and intelligence organizations of the United States." The file protects the anonymity of the source of such allegations, but I knew that a far-out right-wing group, the Birch Society, had mailed a letter to the FBI containing such accusations about all the many hundreds whose names appeared as signatories of newspaper ads protesting the war in Vietnam.

The FBI's investigation ranged widely. They interviewed at least ten of my colleagues, several of my neighbors, officials at government agencies where I served as a consultant, and eight employees of the Center for Policy Research. FBI agents combed police records, newspaper archives, and checked files about me at other federal agencies, including the Central Intelligence Agency and the Air Force counterintelligence office. Cables were flashed from FBI headquarters to its field offices in New York, Washington, San Francisco, St. Louis, Baltimore, Philadelphia, Cincinnati, and Columbus, Ohio, with the order to find out whether I—or my "alias Amitai Falk"—was "known in communist circles." All posts reported back that they failed to uncover any incriminating evidence about me or any other.

The investigation told much more about the FBI than it did about me. It showed a remarkable sloppiness, an amateurism in gathering and weighing information that would be unacceptable if conducted by a first-year college student. The FBI file identified me as an "associate professor of Israeli and Jewish studies," which I've never been. It depicted my doctorate as being on Soviet relations when it actually is about Israeli kibbutzim. The file threw together quotes from sources as divergent as *The Washington Post*, local student papers, and *Pravda* (the official Soviet newspaper), as if they were all equally credible.

I was hardly the only one judged on the basis of such a mishmash of facts and factoids. John Seigenthaler, publisher of the (Nashville) *Tennessean*, discovered that his FBI file contained a report listing "allegations of Seigenthaler having illicit relations with young girls" obtained from an unnamed source. Seigenthaler, himself a former high Justice Department official, branded these third-hand allegations as absolutely untrue. He added, "For years the FBI has been engaged in a vacuum cleaner approach to intelligence gathering. . . . Agents will solicit or accept any information, even hearsay, rumor or gossip, and put it into the bureau's raw files."

All said and done, my file concluded, "The Bureau [FBI] has been advised there is no unfavorable information concerning Etzioni, and available information indicates, in fact, that he is anti-communist." And, while I was found not to be a security risk, I was said to be "extremely critical of U.S. foreign policy."

My CIA file also has its share of gems. I include one page for those who have forgotten what those days were like. (Dashes denote names of informants that were blacked out when the material was released to me under the Freedom of Information Act.).

I was unable to assess the negative effects of these files on my activities at the time, because I had no way of establishing who read these files or the summaries that were made of them and widely circulated. I am aware, though, of two consequences; one that I find amusing, and one that was more serious but did me proud.

On the lighter side: a university in Frankfurt invited me to deliver a lecture. This might not have involved the long arm of the government of the United States of America if my colleagues in Frankfurt had not requested that the lecture take place at the Amerika Haus (one of hundreds of cultural outposts the U.S. government maintains overseas). What they did not know was that the scheduling clerk of Amerika Haus was concerned with more than assigning rooms and providing chalk. He also "clears" lecturers with Washington.

So, according to my FBI file, in response to cables from Frankfurt, the United States Information Agency (USIA) headquarters, in the nation's capital, reviewed my record. It learned from the FBI that my attitude toward U.S. foreign policy was "critical" and "negative." Thus, on September 2, 1966, Bonn cabled to Frankfurt that "on basis of available information agency advises against lecture use of Amitai Etzioni."

A year and a half later—the U.S. government grinds as slowly as it grinds finely—another cable was sent from Washington to the U.S. embassy in Bonn: "Security office needs to know if post used Amitai Etzioni which was subject adverse agency recommendation re appearance 1966–67. Advise soonest." Bonn responded a bit defensively that, while by and large they did "adhere to the agency's advice," in my case USIA Bonn recognized that the professor was not an approved speaker, but also had to contend with the fact

18 February 1965

18 February 1965

MEMORANDUM FOR: Chief, Counter-Intelligence Staff

SUBJECT : Communist Suspect

1. On 18 February, [_____] gave me the name of the individual on the name of the attached paper as a member of the faculty of Columbia University, NYC, whom he strongly suspected to be a Communist Party propagandist.

AMITAI
ETZIONI

2. [_____] said that he based his suspicion solely on Subject's tactics in scholarly meetings where he commonly derogated the U.S.S.R. by name, but argued vehemently in favor of its international policies. [_____] characterized Subject as clever, glib, persuasive and very influential with the younger scholars of the New York area. [_____] concluded by saying that something should be done to overtly identify Subject as a Communist agent. I made no reply.

3. I have known [_____] intimately for a dozen years. This is the first time that I ever heard him make such an accusation. In fact, he rarely speaks invidiously of another person. I would judge [_____] sufficiently experienced in contacts with Communists and their sympathizers to give some weight to his suspicion.

4. No file copy of this is being retained.

APPROVED FOR RELEASE
DATE 16 Jan 78

Approved for Release
Date FEB 1982

CIA

CIA File

19 February 1965

MEMORANDUM FOR: Chief, Counter Intelligence Staff.

SUBJECT: Suspected Communist

1. On 18 February, I sent you a note referring to a certain Columbia University professor. I neglected to write that my informant told me that the professor, in a recent public statement, said to his audience, "CIA instructs the Army Special Forces in how to incinerate nuns."

2. I retain no copy of this.

Passed to S.P
26 Feb 65

CIA File

that he was an invited guest of the university. The post felt that cancellation of my appearance "might seriously threaten its relationship with the university. USIA Bonn therefore gave the Amerika Haus Frankfurt a one-time approval with the understanding that *no special effort should be made to attract a large audience.*"

Let it not be said that the government of the United States is feeble. It did prevail: its local representatives in Frankfurt removed all posters and notices announcing my lecture, and I had the smallest audience of all the public lectures I have ever delivered. Less than a handful.

Next, the FBI did me proud, although its benevolence was unintended I am sure. On November 2, 1972, L. Patrick Gray, then acting director of the FBI, sent a summary of my file to an unidentified "Deputy Assistant to the President, the White House" in the Nixon administration. It landed me on a blacklist. The list consisted of people who were to be prevented from speaking under the auspices of the USIA but also to be kept away from government service and contracts.

The list included some of the people I respected most, such as Senator Gary Hart, Madeleine Albright, James Baldwin, Ben Bradlee, David Brinkley, Ralph Nader, Paul Samuelson, and Stansfield Turner. It was somewhat of a badge of honor to be included; I would have considered it a minor indignity if I had been left out. After all, if there was going to be a list of activists, members of the opposition to the establishment, it was a list on which I belonged.

Although the actions of the FBI and other government agencies occasionally seemed so silly they appealed more to one's sense of humor than outrage, other times one could not but feel profoundly troubled. There was nothing about what I said or did (mostly said) that could—by any stretch of the imagination—justify putting me under surveillance, investigating my past and my friends, keeping dossiers on me, or preventing people from listening to what I had to say. I belonged most definitely to the loyal opposition, to those who objected to several unethical and dangerous policies of the U.S. government but who never lifted a finger to try to undermine our form of government. Subjecting people like me to FBI and CIA scrutiny did not protect the United States of America; instead, such investigators subverted the democracy FBI and CIA agents were sworn to uphold.

Bioethics: Man on Top?

My third front (or was it the fourth?) was more closely related to my attempts to ground NASA: it concerned a new technology and its effects on human priorities over those driven by engineers and scientists, of human values over the instruments men and women make. The reason, though, that I was aware of the looming breakthroughs in biotechnologies was highly personal.

After my third son was born in 1967 and he started running around on his own, Minerva and I wondered what we could do, if anything, to have a girl. When our physicians could not provide a satisfactory suggestion, I donned my academic hat and turned to the library. There, I found numerous claims as to what might be done.

Some scientists favored the use of a centrifuge that would separate the X and Y chromosome–carrying sperm, allowing the scientists to select the desired chromosomes for artificial insemination. Others held that it makes a difference at what point in the woman's ovulation cycle she becomes pregnant. Still others favored employing douches to change the acid and alkaline balances of the vagina. None of these researchers had strong evidence to support their claims. (If you are trained in research methods and statistics, you would be amazed at the weakness of data that underlies numerous medical publications.) Bob Zelnick, biographer of Albert Gore Jr., reported that Gore had girls, but he yearned for a boy. He followed the advice of a Columbia University professor—and got a son. He has since advocated the professor's method, which concerns nonmissionary positions and deep penetration. But no one told me about this approach.

While all these articles provided little guidance to us as future parents, the articles did intrigue the sociologist in me. I could not help but wonder what the societal consequences would be if sex selection were to become as easy as washing down a pill. Would people on average "order" more boys or girls? And if it were boys (as the initial data suggested for many societies), what would be the effects on society of upsetting the gender balance inherent in nature? Would the resulting male "surplus" render society more aggressive, war-oriented, macho? Would the gender imbalance leave a large number of men unable to find a spouse? Would this, in turn, increase the value of women and cause parents to "buy" more girls, correcting the imbalance without the need for any governmental intervention?

Soon, I learned that the enigmatic questions raised by deliberate selection of the gender of one's child were merely a part of a much greater array of social and moral conundrums raised by what seemed to me at the time to be the next scientific and technological revolution. In writing *The Active Society*, I started from the observation that, from the onset of modernity, humankind no longer accepted the world as-it-is and set out to reshape the world in humankind's image, in line with its desires and values. Conditions were to be turned into options; nature—into choice. First, science and technology were drafted to subject the environment to our commands—to yield coal and oil, propel turbines to generate electricity—in the service of the industrial revolution. Next, this active orientation was turned on the society itself, seeking to modify the ways classes, tribes, races, and later genders treated one another. Freud extended the active orientation onto the self, showing how it may be recast rather than taken as given. Now, humankind was about to take the body, especially the genetic code, and treat it as if it were malleable rather than an immutable part of nature.

Each of the previous expressions of the active orientation, I noted, yielded a whole cornucopia of blessings, but also opened a Pandora's box of new dangers, including nuclear weapons, social programs that bred dependency and fraud, and psychological manipulation. It was easy to see that new bioengineering might well cure numerous diseases that were fully or partially determined by genes. But it also threatened humankind with genetic-cleansing policies, governments out to breed "superior" races and to eliminate (or at least prevent from reproducing) those with genes the government deemed inferior, Nazi-style.

Among the harbingers of the coming bioengineering revolution, as viewed from the vantage point of 1969, were relatively new findings on the structure of DNA, which—it was hoped—would allow science to manipulate the most fundamental human code. In addition, public officials feared that experiments that manipulated genetic material might generate new bacteria or viruses that could break out of the labs and wreak a plague on humankind. Also, in vitro fertilization was being attempted, which evoked specters of parents and governments breeding people to their specs, engaging in "gene shopping." And there were the first reports of parents using amniocentesis to determine the gender of the fetus—then aborting the pregnancy when the gender did not suit their preference. Each of these developments raised a whole host of social and moral questions.

Soon I was spending much of my time set aside for research studying genetics and learning about public policy and the ethical implications surrounding it. It took me about two years to get up to speed. In 1968, I published my first findings in an article in *Science* on the societal effects of sex selection and the moral issues it raised. The article showed that if there were a widely available, simple, low-cost method for parents to select the gender of their children, this would lead to a 7 percent "surplus" of boys over girls in the United States.

The article further showed that such a surplus would not pose any serious societal harm. This point I could support by examining societies in which much larger gender imbalances occurred. This was the case in the Soviet

Union after World War II, where a much larger number of males had been killed than females. Major gender imbalances also resulted from uneven migration—for instance, to Alaska.

The article in *Science* closed by wondering if we could stop any part of bioengineering even if we found its societal effects undesirable and unethical. Let's say Americans decided to ban human cloning—who would stop scientists in Switzerland or Mexico or some other place from proceeding? One may argue that such research requires a larger amount of money, and hence science could be controlled via its pocketbook. But this is not necessarily the case. LSD was developed and produced in a kitchen sink (and nobody has stopped its production since). And amniocentesis is conducted in India routinely for gender selection, despite the fact that such actions are considered highly dubious by Western ethics boards.

The *Science* article, "Sex Control, Science, and Society," generated more attention than any other article I had written. This may have been in part because many people are keen to select the gender of their offspring, and maybe because *sex* was in its title. There was also, however, growing awareness of the gravity of the issues raised by new developments in biology, which the article examined.

Following the publication of the article, I was invited to serve on the editorial board of *Science* as well as to write several editorials for it and participate in a meeting of an international medical society in Paris in 1972. At the meeting, I was shocked to learn about experiments researchers were conducting on children. To give but one hair-curling example: children who are born without immunological defenses often die within a year. The researchers gained the consent of these children's parents to conduct various tests on the children, searching for a better understanding of the condition, on the way to a cure. The experiments were brutal. They caused one child after another to die, often following severe convulsions, after—as one of the researchers put it—being "dehumanized."

Recent developments highlight how much these issues are still very much with us. Just to cite two: in September 1999, a teenager died undergoing experimental gene therapy. In October 2002, trials in gene therapy, which were attempting to cure toddlers with fatal immune deficiencies—the same diseases we discussed during our meeting—were stopped in the United States and France when the experiments gave the children an illness similar to leukemia.

Although parents consented to subject their infants to these tests, the parents, it seemed to me, were unable to differentiate between assisting science in *one day* finding a cure—and saving the lives of their children. (It was as if they could not tell the difference between working on the design of a better life preserver—and throwing one to a drowning person.) The report by academic researchers about these experiments, and several others like them, made me wonder what true consent entailed. Were the parents—however inadvertently—misled into believing that *their* children might be cured, although the researchers knew that this was extremely unlikely? Would the parents have consented if they were fully aware of the suffering to which their children were going to be subjected by the researchers? And were the parents or the children better off living a year without immunological defenses or dying in short order, following severe convulsions as a result of the scientific experiments? Not easy questions.

Other researchers reported to the meeting about attempts to find "criminal genes" (XYY), believed to render people aggressive and predispose them to criminal behavior. A sociologist could not help but ask whether these genes *made* people into criminals, or whether there was merely some kind of a correlation between the presence of these genes and criminal conduct? And, if there was a correlation, how strong was it? Could it not be explained in some other manner, as correlations often can?

Most important, should parents be informed that their future children are carriers of XYY and should they be encouraged to abort such fetuses? Would children born with XYY be labeled "dangerous" and hence become dangerous? And was the mere study of such genetic abnormalities an area science should avoid in the first place, a piece of the apple of knowledge we'd best not bite into?

Only a few of the researchers attending the meeting seemed to be concerned about the moral dilemmas raised by their work. Most were so deeply engrossed in their academic work, and believed in science so religiously, that they seemed to tune out the moral and social implications of what they were brewing.

The concerns brought on by the forthcoming bioengineering revolution seemed to me too important to be left merely to the researchers, just as questions concerning warfare were too important to be left only to generals. But how could one involve the public? To be frank, I drew one blank after another. Nothing came to mind that in any way came close to the profound challenges to human primacy that biotechnology was foisting upon us. The modest suggestion I put before the meeting was the formation of a Health-Ethics Commission, which would include medical researchers, ethicists, and community leaders. The commission would hold hearings on the moral and social effects of biological engineering. Such hearings would allow the public to become informed, mobilized, and have its say on these vital matters before the commission formed recommendations for action.

During the closing session, Professor Jean Hamburger leaned over a row of chairs to ask me if I would formulate a formal resolution for the meeting to endorse, calling for the establishment of an international commission to explore further the troubling issues at hand.

I scribbled:

> The conference recommends that the Council for International Organizations of Medical Sciences and the World Health Organization should explore the possibility of establishing an international body to explore and study the moral and social issues raised by new and forthcoming developments in biology and medicine.
>
> Such a body would include biological, medical, and social scientists; humanists; religious leaders; and science policymakers; and will be backed up by a research staff.

After some revisions and amendments, the resolution was unanimously adopted. It was at best a small step, but one in the right direction.

Leaving Paris, I concluded that more had to be done to get the word out about the experiments that were being conducted and the ethical issues they raised. I had copies of the papers the researchers presented as well as a tape of the give-and-take that occurred during the meetings. I requested permission from all those who participated in the conference to quote at length from their papers and the tape. To my amazement, they all wrote back granting permission.

As a result, I was able to publish a diary of sorts about the cutting-edge developments in biomedical research, the moral and social challenges they posed, and how we might cope with them in a book entitled *Genetic Fix*, published in 1973. (The German title was much more telling: *Die Zweite Erschaffung des Menschen*. Roughly translated, it means "the second creation of man.")

The book was welcomed by a good friend. Betty Friedan wrote:

> Beyond the fantastic implications of *Genetic Fix* itself, Amitai Etzioni's existential act of courage in writing this book seems to me to point the new political road we must all map for ourselves now—beyond scholarly dispassion, passive compliance, or radical rhetoric mechanically fixed to the past—to take active personal responsibility for the human future.

Even more supportive was a note by a scholar who I greatly respected but whose path I never crossed. John H. Knowles, M.D., president of the Rockefeller Foundation, called *Genetic Fix* "a most important book . . . scholarly, provocative and extremely timely." One reviewer called the book a *"Silent Spring* of biomedical research." Another reviewer wrote: "This is a book that all those interested in the future of humanity should read, taking into account that the author is a recognized activist, but one who has an important message."

The book was nominated for a 1974 National Book Award in the science section, which is like being a runner up for anything else: nice to be on the list, nicer if the book had won the award. I consoled myself with the knowledge that I was not a natural scientist and, hence, being on the list at all was recognition of sort. I was further flattered by the invitation to continue to serve on the board of *Science*. (If you fault me for bragging, think about your area of specialization or interest; go invade some field which is very different from yours; read up for two years and gain a foot in the door, and you may be more forgiving.)

The idea of forming a bioethics commission and all it entailed was noticed as far away as Australia: Monash University philosopher Peter Singer wrote to me that he hoped the United States would continue to take steps toward creating a body similar to the one that he consulted for in his own country. (He has since become a world-renowned, albeit somewhat controversial, figure. In 1999, he was appointed to a professorship at Princeton University, where he struck some unusual positions, such as favoring animal rights over those of infants or mentally disabled persons.)

To bring my case to my colleagues, I followed *Genetic Fix* with several articles in scholarly publications about the moral and social implications of amniocentesis. However, in the years that followed, not much transpired. The main bioengineering breakthroughs were still far down the road. Neither the public nor my colleagues were ready to lock in on bioethical issues. Stem cell research and human cloning were still the stuff of science fiction. Thirteen years later, in 1985, Congress established the Biomedical Ethics Board and then, in 1988, the Biomedical Ethics Advisory Committee, which were somewhat similar to what I had suggested. I continue to believe that the issues I raised are valid ones, and in the years since, I have continued to follow developments in biotechnology and bioethics with extra interest. However my timing was such that I practically ensured that my voice on these matters was barely heard.

Nor did my study of genetics pay off as far as its original purpose was concerned. In 1969, my fourth son, David, was born, and the fifth, Benjamin, in 1974. Like most other parents, once the children were born we could not have cared less about their gender and were delighted that they were healthy and vigorous. In effect, we did not have the slightest doubt that they were incredibly cute, smart way beyond their tender ages, and otherwise vastly superior to any other children we knew, a fact we had a hard time keeping to ourselves.

Figure 5.2. From left to right: Shira, Eli, and Danielle—the "older" grandchildren

My grandchildren are correcting the gender imbalance in the Etzioni family. I am now the proud grandpa of three granddaughters and two step-granddaughters, and only two grandsons. They are remarkably different from one another, reminding me not to put too much credence in the increasingly popular notion that genes shape much of our behavior. Each of the seven is a bundle of joy, easy to love and loving, a magical remedy for the aches and pains of an aging man.

Figure 5.3. Noa (Tel Aviv) and Noah (Seattle)—the younger grandchildren

Historical Sensibility: Taking Stock (1978)

The years zoomed by. Suddenly, I had been out of graduate school for twenty years and was about to face turning fifty. There was gray hair all over, and I had to let my belt out for the third time. I had a hard time keeping up with my youngest son, Benjamin, who was racing about on his four-year-old legs. Obviously, I was well past the midpoint of my journey; it was time to take stock. How did my plan to try to be both a solid social scientist and effective social activist work out? And what lessons did I learn on the way? Above all, how could I serve better? I wrote some of this down, in case it would be of interest to other activist professors, public intellectuals, and those interested in how it is done—or mucked up.

My academic record at the time did not trouble me. I had written six scholarly books, more than a hundred academic articles, most published in refereed journals. (These journals publish articles only after peer reviewers determine that they pass academic muster.) The journals included several in disciplines other than sociology, such as *Psychiatry*, *The American Political Science Review*, *World Politics*, *Administrative Science Quarterly*, *Public Administration Review*, and *Science*. (Because professors live and die by footnotes, a measure of the acceptance of their work, here is a note about footnotes: to judge by statistics kept by Professor Richard Coughlin, my academic books and articles were cited frequently enough to satisfy even a Bert.)

I even served as the chairman of the department of sociology at Columbia University (1969–1971), although God clearly did not intend for me to be an academic administrator or administrator of anything else. Icing on the cake (or should it be on the mortar board?) were some prizes I got, topped by a Guggenheim. Looking over my academic work, there clearly was room for improvement, but it seemed to me fairly close to the best I could do and—by prevailing criteria—the work was by and large relatively well received. (Sociology is known as one of the most contentious fields. Extremely few works are universally lauded while many are roundly criticized.) All in all, let me say with some false modesty, not a shabby record.

Also my academic colleagues groused less about my activism. I hoped this was largely because my academic achievements were not easy to dismiss. Also, more and more academics were becoming engaged in public action.

The irony that stuck out in my fifty-year stock taking was that, while not failing academically, it was my social action record that was far from reassuring.

One of the first signs that my public voice carried at all is on the funny side. In 1968, *The National Observer* published a list of people its editors considered young, up-and-coming stars in various fields, displaying a picture of each, including those of Julian Bond and Robert Coles. In the middle of the page there was an empty box, as if a picture had fallen out. The text in the box read:

> In social circles that regard themselves as sophisticated, there is a whole sub–*Who's Who* of people and things, casually mentioned names that sound familiar, but names you really couldn't identify fully if your next Martini depended on it. And in the spirit of sophistication, it is a rare listener who will interrupt to ask, "Pardon me, but who is Amitai Etzioni?"

I have since written several books addressing my fellow citizens instead of professors. I wrote op-eds and essays in publications such as the *New York Times, Washington Post, Wall Street Journal, The Public Interest, The Saturday Review,* and one even in the *Village Voice.* And I tried to get the word out by testifying before Congress and making presentations to most any public group that put up with me. Also, over the years, I ended up in the Rolodex of a fair number of reporters and TV and radio producers. Hence, I was often able to broadcast my views on a considerable number of occasions.

Still, I felt inadequate; not a failure, but like someone who has labored long and hard but squandered some of his efforts and mistargeted some others. Over twenty years I had shifted the focus of my attention several times, moving from arguing in favor of rolling back the nuclear arms race to opposing the war in Vietnam to shifting major public investments from lunar visitations to domestic social programs and near space to making research more socially relevant to bioethics.

I was not the only one who noted my shifts from one front to another. *Time* pointed to my "bustling omnipresence" in a profile on my forty-sixth birthday. Under the banner "The Everything Expert," *Time* wrote:

> Sometimes Amitai Etzioni seems to be a one-man profession. . . . Etzioni, 46, has written two books on foreign affairs, debated Werner von Braun on the space race, helped Betty Friedan start a "think tank" for women, testified as an expert on an abortion bill, and received a National Book Award nomination for a book on genetics. Two weeks ago, he was hailed by a New York *Daily News* headline writer as a "sexpert" for a talk on sexual ethics, and the same day he was named staff director of a politically sensitive investigation of New York State's spreading nursing-home scandal. . . . The American Sociological Association's newsletter has received complaints that he is quoted entirely too much in its pages.

As if this was not enough, *Time* continued:

But his influence is not doubted. Etzioni is one of the new social science mandarins now beginning to dominate the profession: a politically astute opinion maker . . . showering newspapers and magazines with articles on every conceivable subject, and producing hard-nosed, workable programs that politicians like.

The *National Journal* followed suit. It reported that, in a short period, ten different newspapers carried my comments on various aspects of contemporary American society, which the journal recognized as my specialty. But my colleagues, it reported, were aghast, although neither my colleagues nor the journal claimed that any of my observations were invalid; there were just too Goddamn many of them.

At first I felt both complimented and maligned. A full page in *Time* magazine dedicated to listing many of my achievements, peppered with a few deflating lines—this was something one could live with. At the same time, I railed against the writers who did not understand that I applied the same basic insights and sociological tools to all the projects I took on. Thus, my analysis of bioethics very much reflected ideas presented in *The Active Society*, on the question of whether and how we can get on top of new scientific developments and guide them in line with our values. The same theme was played out in *Moondoggle* and in my earlier treatments of nuclear weapons. They all concerned protecting our values from being overwhelmed by the means we forged to serve them. They all dealt with what might be called the "human priority" (think Frankenstein, the Golem, or Sorcerer's Apprentice).

Looking back on basic positions I had formed and advocated, I concluded that if I could start all over again, there was no reason to change any of them. This, I recognized, was no small claim, given that a fair number of my colleagues moved over the years from supporting communism to becoming liberals to metamorphosing into arch conservatives or from hawks to doves to hawks again. But checking over what I had done one more time, I concluded that I may have been pigheaded but I did not waver, nor did I see, in retrospect, a reason that I should have. This conclusion did give me some comfort.

I double-checked: stopping the war in Vietnam? Reducing nuclear weapons? According higher priority to domestic needs over outer space? Developing special methodology for policy research? Reviewing the social and ethical issues surrounding biological breakthroughs? Which should I retract? There were several other domestic policy issues on which I had weighed in briefly, none of which I regretted taking. These included my efforts on behalf of nursing home reform, for a less tightfisted Federal Reserve, and my scheme for an antipoverty insurance. (As a result, I was ranked first among thirty "major contributors to public policy analysis between 1969–1980." I did not do the ranking.)

Was I switching from championing one policy to another because I continued to be a restless person, despite all resolutions to stay the course? This was surely part of my problem, but there seemed to be more to it. After all, if you are simply impatient, you would hardly write books, each of which takes years to complete and another small eternity to be published, and more eons before you are rewarded with reviews—if they are rewarding. Anyone who seeks rapid gratification in the academic world should dedicate his or her life to teaching. When you do it right, the students' faces light up; they are eager to hear more; and they are free with their appreciation.

It dawned on me that what I was after—and what was eluding me—was the special high that I tasted in Israel, of participating in a project that was larger than life, greater than self. For accomplishments that changed something in the real world, beyond just bearing witness, composing protesting briefs, and working to mobilize people on their behalf, although these all had their place and purpose.

The public voice, I noted, has two different ranges. The narrower of the two allows those who command it to join the public dialogue, to add to the thoughts and beliefs of people. This was a range I believe I did reach on some occasions. The second public voice ranges further. It influences that which people and officials actually do: behavior, policies, institutions. Many public intellectuals are content to enrich or redirect the public dialogue; activists, like myself, hope to reach further. It was fine to point to the dangers of nuclear bombs and to lay out ways to scale them down. However, I regretted not having been among those who finally did succeed in significantly rolling back the superpower arms race. Sure, it felt right that the United States finally extricated itself from Vietnam. And it was rewarding to note that this small country did not join the Chinese or Soviet bloc, or even remain much of a communist society, two developments that were used to justify U.S. intervention in Vietnam. However, whether or not I deserved brownie points for being among those who helped build opposition to the war, there was no denying that when, finally, the main shift in U.S. policy did occur in the early seventies, I was drumming up opposition on some other front. And I played no role when the bioethics commission was finally formed, and I contributed nothing to the formulation of bioethical policies that followed.

Toward the end of this exercise in self-assessment, my childhood friend Emmanuel dropped by. Whenever he visited, I found that important luncheons could be readily rescheduled, and meetings I thought I had to attend could be easily skipped. We could pick up the conversation as if we had talked last week, although actually several years had passed.

We reminisced about the days we had kicked each other under the table as children and about our first double date. He reported that he continued to enjoy his job as an accountant in Tel Aviv. He also had news about our third playmate, Yitzhak. He had become a manufacturer of aluminum windows and lived in New Jersey.

When Emmanuel asked, "So, which book are you working on this time?" I unloaded a litany of self-doubts. After listening attentively, my friend asked with considerable astonishment: "But aren't you a critic?" I responded plaintively: "And look what writing a movie review got me into!" Emmanuel clarified: "I don't mean *critic* this way. You dump on the government and its policies, right? How can you expect to be in opposition and think you can have on impact on here-and-now policies?"

On reexamination of the projects in which I was involved, a pattern emerged—I lacked historical sensibility. I may have earned an A for effort, and possibly a C– or less for public impact, but I deserved a big fat F for failing to account for that which changing historical conditions tolerated. The nuclear arms race was *heating up* when I joined those who tried to cool it down. The United States was *getting deeper* into Vietnam when I worked with those who tried to bail it out. The commitment to outer space was *firmly made* when I first challenged it. Bioengineering was still in the purview of a few researchers. Being far ahead of one's time may be admirable, but it guarantees one's effect will be minimal.

True, history does not follow a predetermined course set by the stars, but neither is it putty we can shape to our desire. If you plan to apply whatever leverage you can marshal and—by pulling with others—alter the flow of events, discerning where history is headed is an imperative. Now that I understood how much I lacked even a smidgeon of Ben Gurion's grand historical sensitivity, could I acquire some?

PART THREE

IN THE CORRIDORS OF POWER

CHAPTER SIX

The White House (1979–1980)

A Changed Nation

Looking for a way to carry ideas closer to their consequences, I did not hesitate long when the opportunity arose to spend a year (1978–1979) as a guest scholar at a highly respected think tank, the Brookings Institution. The fact that it was located in Washington, D.C., only added to its attractiveness. True, New York City had its own policy issues. Still, the center of national as well as international policy was obviously in the capital.

My move to Washington was eased by the ways the country had changed over the preceding years. The war in Vietnam was finally behind us. The deep divide that it inflicted on American society was being bridged. Political protests were replaced by shared, nationwide concern over the fate of the economy. On campus, students were catching up with their books; professors with their research projects. I was ready to dismount my horse as an outsider critic and move closer to the seats of power, bringing ideas to those in charge rather than mobilizing public opposition.

Memories of the shooting of students at Kent State and the beating of demonstrators during the Democratic Convention in Chicago were receding. The main visible signs of the 1960s riots and burning of the inner cities were several boarded-up houses in Washington. The counterculture was subsiding not only because hippies had cut their long hair and gotten jobs but also because American society had begun to tolerate long hair and all that it stood for. The civil rights movement had scored its greatest victories. The Great Society was in place. The women's movement was making its mark.

137

Watergate reforms were introduced. The old American political structure was shaken. American society had passed through one of its relatively rare extensively progressive phases.

For me, all this meant that I did not so much feel that I was softening up (or "selling out," as the left would have it), but that the establishment was yielding. It eased my transition from a critic to a participant.

Returning to Washington brought back a memory of one instance in which I could nurture my quest for the action high I acquired in Israel: I played an extremely minor role in one of the most important events of the era. In 1963, I was elected to serve on the National Board of Americans for Democratic Action (ADA). The ADA was a progressive group that differed from many to its left because of its strong anticommunist posture. ("Cold War liberals" was the name its detractors gave it.) In 1964, the ADA was part of a large coalition of groups that worked feverishly to help pass the Civil Rights Act, arguably the most important law ever to begin to redress the injustice done to African Americans.

Southern opponents of the new law knew damn well that if it was enacted, it would have a great multiplier effect. If African Americans had an effective right to vote, this in turn would bring a major change in the power balance in the South (as well as in Washington), forcing open many public positions such as mayors, sheriffs, and school board officers, and it would provide much needed political muscle to numerous other reforms.

On the eve of the critical vote in Congress, the ADA and other coalition participants feared that the vote would be lost for a trivial reason. While Congress members from the South with safe seats often stayed in town for the weekend, liberal members—including the considerable New York City delegation—usually rushed home long before the weekend to tend to politics in their districts. The coalition feared that Southerners would schedule the pivotal vote for late Thursday, when they knew many liberals would already have gone missing. A whole slew of us were sent to visit with liberal delegates, to plead that they stay around this time—and to ensure that they lived up to their word.

There was nothing glorious or edifying in sitting in the small and crowded reception areas of various Congress members, waiting for a moment of their time, being squeezed into their schedule. Although our words were gentle, the message was firm: "If this bill fails—and you were not counted—you will never hear the end of it!" Then some more visits—"Is the Congress member still around?" we queried receptionists until they would not speak to us any more. But then—headlines. On February 10, 1964, the House of Representatives passed the measure by a 290-130 vote. On July 2, 1964, President Johnson signed the Civil Rights Act into law.

Having a beer at the euphoric party that followed, whites and blacks together, my main sense was not of accomplishment. My role was much too
marginal for that. However, it was one of partaking in a major piece of social
action that delivered an unquestionable good. And for once I was there when
pushing and shoving ended up with the establishment yielding. The gates of
Washington were pried open for a major, society-transforming reform.

On my return to Washington some fourteen years after that, in 1978, I was
looking for more of such good action and for the high that goes with it. But
this time it took place inside the White House.

A "Ticket" to the White House

I spent one stimulating year (mid-1978 to mid-1979) at the Brookings Institution. I had no teaching duties. Although I missed the challenge the
students at Columbia threw my way, there were numerous colleagues at
Brookings who provided all the stimulation one can hope for. The mixture
of scholarship and policy research was very much to my taste. Most delightful were the Friday lunches. At Friday noon, twenty-five people,
many from Brookings, some from other parts of town, would lunch together and comment, in rapid fire, on the events of the week. Joe Pech-
man chaired these lunches, and he was especially good at getting people
to speak their minds unafraid to go out on a limb. It was the best intellectual football I ever experienced.

As a guest scholar at Brookings, I was free to choose what to study. I
chose a mighty subject: the condition of the American economy and society. By the late seventies, the condition of the economy could only be
characterized as lousy. Growth was sluggish; inflation and unemployment
were troublingly high; productivity and saving were woefully low. In contrast, while our sun was said to be setting, it was said to be rising in the
West: the Japanese economy was performing miraculously. Over there,
growth was remarkable—employment was guaranteed for life, inflation
was minimal, and productivity and saving were nearly unparalleled.
Japanese students regularly outperformed American students in numerous
tests. Crime and drug abuse and gun violence were as rare in Japan as they
were common in the United States.

Americans streamed to Japan to study its production, management, and
teaching methods, looking to find ways for us to copy or imitate the Japanese. Several leading public intellectuals were writing off the American
way. They held that America's time had passed; the next generation, if not
century, would be the domain of some other superpower. (Over lunch, we
talked about which Japanese stocks we bought and whether we were
"long" on the yen.)

I did not share the prevailing sense of pessimism about the future place of the United States in the world. In the past, when challenged, the United States had often shown that it could rally and come from behind and do more than catch up. (I also sensed that some of those who predicted the decline and fall of America wished it to collapse so that what they considered a just world could be erected on its ruins. The left has forever been predicting the collapse not merely of the United States, but of capitalism.) Also, the sociologist in me could not see how whatever was working for the Japanese could be transferred successfully to a country as different as ours is from theirs. Japanese ideas such as lifelong employment and worker "quality circles" were all the craze in the United States. They reminded me of the numerous Latin American republics that copied our Constitution without gaining our form of democratic life. Out of such deliberations came a decision to dedicate my Brookings year to studying why the American economy and society had deteriorated and what was required to renew them.

As the resulting paper made the rounds, a colleague introduced me to Richard Harden, who was in charge of one of the less illustrious units of the White House, one that deals with budget and organization. But Richard had one great virtue: he hailed from Georgia and had known President Carter for a long time. Richard acquired all kinds of things he decided the White House required, including new computers and—a Columbia University sociologist. I accepted his invitation to be the only behavioral scientist in the White House, as of July 1, 1979. My contract accorded me the august title of "senior adviser to the White House," although the definition of my duties was at first very vague.

It is said that where your office is in the White House is all important. Well, Richard and I found ourselves as of July 1, 1979, in the White House's West Wing, but we were soon relocated to the adjacent Old Executive Office Building. We were, though, able to avoid the ultimate exile to the New Executive Office Building. In short, we were somewhere between the very center of power and out in the cold. In any case, our lease was temporary. A year later, after Carter lost his reelection campaign, our stay was unceremoniously terminated.

The tense but rich year taught the activist in me several disparate lessons all sharing one theme: the difference between being a public intellectual out on the hustings as compared to being a member of the king's entourage. These lessons all concerned ways of bringing ideas to the seats of power, seeking action. Although I was involved in several White House endeavors, two stand out; one concerns the role of government in dealing with our social problems; the other, ways the economy might be rejuvenated.

Economic and Social Renewal: An Immodest Proposal

The Brookings Paper

By far my most extensive and time-consuming White House endeavor concerned what might be done to reverse the deterioration of the American economy and society. The ideas behind this project were not developed in the White House and probably could not have been formulated within its confines. Most White House days lasted from early in the morning until late in the evening. Working during weekends and holidays was common. Fatigue shading into exhaustion was the typical state of mind. Stress was immense, given the high stakes of the issues at hand and the continuous tug and pull among various staffers, advisers, interest groups, political hacks, agency heads, Congress members, and the press. On a typical evening, I jogged a bit after dark, watched the news on television, numb, called Minerva and my sons (who spent the year in New York City), and fell into an uneasy sequence of dreams, only to be jerked awake by the alarm clock. Like many other White House staffers, I drew largely on the intellectual capital I had brought with me.

I came up with the basic concept of my American renewal White House project in the year I spent at the Brookings Institution, just before I joined the White House. My study sought to determine what made America's economy so strong in earlier periods, overtaking that of countries that industrialized before us, especially Britain and Germany. I read a fair amount of American economic history, a treat for someone like me who is trained in sociology, which often offers much less enticing reading. It was fascinating to read about a period during which it took thirty-three days or more to get a message from New York City to San Francisco and how, with the introduction of the telegraph, the time was suddenly cut to minutes. Also, there was the joy I had experienced most strongly while working on *The Comparative Analysis of Complex Organizations*, when numerous details find a home around a thesis I was hammering out.

The study found that for an economy to run well, seven specific "needs" must be well attended to and that these needs were well satisfied between 1820 and 1920. As a result, America's wealth (gross domestic product, GDP) more than doubled each generation or so. The U.S. economy slowed during the Great Depression and then revived during World War II. However, in the postwar period, between 1949 and 1979, the services to six of what I found to be the seven basic needs of a strong economy had deteriorated.

Here's one quick example of what the study revealed: a well-functioning economy must be able to move people and goods expediently and at low cost. If workers or steel or rubber products concentrated in one place are needed elsewhere, the shorter the wait and the lower the cost of moving them, the more efficient the economy.

In the golden period of the U.S. economy, between 1820 and 1920, the country's transportation system vastly improved. A nationwide grid of railroads replaced slow and unreliable modes, such as horsedrawn carriages, mules, and barges (in canals that froze in the winter). However, during the era of deterioration, between 1950 and 1980, most railways deteriorated to the point that some trains had to travel at ten miles an hour in several areas. In the same years, many highways were poorly maintained. Ergo, for the economy to revive, it needed either to fix the old transportation system or come up with an efficient new one. Similar findings showed what happened to our energy sources, training of workers, and so on: rapid rise followed by considerable deterioration on a wide front. All this now required fixing on a grand scale. I called the needed drive "reindustrialization."

My paper further concluded that economic renewal had to be accompanied by a social and moral renewal, that one could not treat the economy as if it was a world apart from the rest of society, as the field of economics so often does. I found that a major source of social deterioration was the rise of selfishness. The paper next pointed to what it would take to shore up families, schools, and communities. For instance, I showed that it was not enough for schools to teach better academics; they also had to do more for character development.

Although I fully realized that some of my academic colleagues were likely to claim that my paper covered too much ground (it was very sweeping) and that I did not sufficiently document this or that point, I believed the basic scheme was sociologically sound. I also thought that the paper was timely, speaking to an economic and social malaise that was greatly troubling my countrymen and women, not some faraway cloud I discerned on the horizon. It was historically sensitive, or was it?

My sense that this paper hit the mark was strengthened when, as a result of a series of flukes, it quickly acquired some public attention. I presented its findings at a Franklin Foundation Lecture Series lecture at Georgia State University. A local press report about my Georgia talk triggered a query from the *Wall Street Journal*'s representative in Washington, and the newspaper published— just six days before I joined the White House staff—a front-page report on my reindustrialization thesis. "The hard truth is that the once mighty U.S. economy, following years of neglect and overuse, is aging and tired . . . what's required, in the view of an increasing number of experts, is a long-term commitment to rebuilding America's industrial base. . . . Some of the most provocative thinking comes from a sociologist rather than an economist—Amitai Etzioni."

The paper helped transform me from a public intellectual who was casting his visions on the water, hoping they would wash up on some shore just when needed, to a staff member of the president. It became the main focus of my White House endeavors, after my brief stint on the refugees task force. I entered the White House with high hopes that, finally, I had found a way to not merely form ideas that spoke to the historical condition, but also to carry then further down the action chain, where they would directly do some good, instead of merely prepare the ground.

Reindustrialization in the White House

Shortly after I joined the White House staff, we were informed the president was to deliver a major speech. We gathered in the West Wing office of the chief of staff, Hamilton Jordan, to listen. Something was wrong with the TV set—the president's voice came across as weak, his image on the tube was pale and washed out. Someone tried to adjust the various knobs and dials, but the picture remained fuzzy. It made me ask (myself, to be sure), if they can't get a TV set to work properly in the White House when the president delivers a pivotal speech—how can they get anything accomplished? (It was the third year of the Carter administration, and it had already acquired a reputation for being a gang that could not shoot straight.)

In the speech, Carter proclaimed that America suffered from a decay of the spirit and that coming to terms with the energy crisis was to be a measure of our spiritual revival. It is often stated that this so-called malaise speech was badly received because Americans do not care for the kind of "blood, sweat, and tears" speeches of the kind that Churchill delivered when Britain was under siege. Actually, public and editorial reaction was initially favorable.

The real malaise, and the sense that the Carter administration was floundering, came a few days later. Carter wanted to oust two cabinet members who did not follow his policies. Not having the gumption to fire them, he made the whole cabinet resign and then reappointed all but the two. The resignation of the whole cabinet, which was merely a tactical maneuver, was seen around the world as a governmental crisis. From then on, the Carter administration never regained a sense of competence, which it had not exactly exuded before. Increasingly, laboring in the White House was like participating in a race—it was an election year—in which the other participants were miles ahead and nearing the finish line. While some did not realize that our team was falling ever farther behind, most pretended that we needed merely a lap or two to catch up. About the only people I could find to have a candid conversation with about our poor condition was Carter's national security adviser, my Columbia University colleague, Zbigniew Brzezinski, and a bright woman working with him by the name of Madeleine Albright. Although being able to talk freely did serve to vent mounting frustrations, none of us had any viable ideas as to how to move the administration forward and to win the forthcoming election.

Looking for some way to turn things around, I reworked my Brookings paper into a memo. The first hurdle I had to surmount was that economic policy was not my turf, and sensitivity to turf was considerable, to put it mildly. My excuse for dealing with reindustrialization varied according to whom I was trying to pitch the idea, but, as a rule, it was that the paper dealt with sociological data and concepts. I also pointed out that the paper provided a sort of home for many specific policies that the administration was already pursuing. Some, especially Charles L. Schultze (the chairman of the White House Council of Economic Advisers), quietly objected to my mixing in where I did not belong. Others, especially Stuart Eizenstat, Alfred Kahn (adviser to the president on inflation), and Curtis Hessler (assistant secretary for economic policy, Treasury), were somewhat intrigued. An interagency group also examined my paper on reindustrialization. But basically my memos were filed and my briefings ignored.

Meanwhile, to my mixed chagrin and delight, other presidential candidates formulated similar themes. (My marker was the term *reindustrialization*, which was new at the time.) First, Governor Jerry Brown, during a meeting with *The Washington Post* editors and writers, called for the "reindustrialization of America." He stressed the need for greater collaboration between government and business, for more planning, for use of credit and tax incentives for reindustrialization. Next, Senator Edward Kennedy called for an American Reindustrialization Corporation to launch a massive public and private Marshall Plan providing grants, loans, and subsidies to businesses and individuals involved in revitalizing the economy. John Anderson, who ran as an independent candidate, and several Republican candidates unfolded similar agendas.

The *Wall Street Journal* cracked, "If you close your eyes and throw a dart at a map of the U.S.A., it would land at a place where someone is holding a seminar on reindustrialization." *Life* used this line as one that "characterized" 1980. *Business Week* issued a special issue on reindustrialization. Lee Walczak, Washington bureau chief of *Business Week*, wrote: "Within the Carter camp, the reindustrialization issue, still in the study stage, is being examined by an informal interagency group. Separate papers on reindustrialization policy are being prepared by Amitai Etzioni, who has been quietly at work for months on the problem in a White House office." He continued with a concise summary of the thesis.

Inside the Carter administration a split of sorts developed over reindustrialization. The president was viscerally and intellectually committed to the fiscally conservative perspective. He made no bones about the fact that he felt very strongly that a balanced budget was the way to fight inflation. Anyone who explored economic policies that entailed increased spending was swimming upstream from the get go. And he was not a man easy to reason with. Carter has been such an exemplary ex-president in recent years that people tend to forget what his record as president was like. Very often, he was caught between lofty principles ("deficits are evil") and managing minutiae (believe it or not, Carter determined who got to use the White House tennis court). He consulted mainly with a very small number of key staffers he knew from Georgia. As a rule, others approached him with memos that had to pass through channels. Such memos he would mark not in the expected "yes" or "no" pattern other presidents followed, but with "maybe," "I'll think about it," or "more information needed." When you did see him in person, he studied you with cold, steely eyes, a smile affixed on his face as if to show how well he whitened his teeth, and he listened attentively. Giving kudos was not his favorite management device; implied dismissal of what was put before him came more readily.

As I saw it, Carter's balance-the-budget-come-what-may approach would not address the underlying weakness of the economy and was political suicide in an election year. (Presidents are supposed to inflict the pain of deflation their first year in office and then reap the benefits of reinflating the economy when they seek reelection.) But Carter's approach had the support of the main economic policymakers, including the secretary of the Treasury (William Miller), the head of Office of Management and Budget (James McIntyre), and, to a somewhat lesser degree, Charles Schultze and Alfred Kahn. Given that reindustrialization would initially entail considerable public outlays, it found little favor on this level.

On a lower level, there was a greater interest in reindustrialization. Van-Doorn Ooms, OMB assistant director for economic policy, was much less strongly committed to balancing the budget than was McIntyre. And Curtis Hessler, Miller's assistant secretary for economic policy, and his deputy, Richard Syron, were much more open-minded about reindustrialization than Miller himself. Assistant Secretary of Labor Arnie Packer wrote several memos in favor of industrial policy and promoted it in the press. I worked long and hard to convince these lower-ranking staff members about the merits of reindustrialization. But, whatever they thought in their heart of hearts, they did not sway their superiors. The weeks zoomed by. Soon Carter's term would run out without my grand design being put to the test.

I attempted an end run by trying to get reindustrialization incorporated into a presidential speech, preferably the State of the Union address. This would have legitimated the theme and provided a policy cue for various federal agencies. Although such a maneuver had been successfully carried out previously by others, by this time a new vetting system had been introduced by Al McDonald. Accordingly, the staff checked suggested items for speeches against established policy. When no such basis was found for my choice paragraphs, they were unceremoniously dropped from a draft of the president's speech.

Moreover, as the election campaign heated up, I lost control of the concept of "reindustrialization." Editorial writers and candidates for public office used it, each for their favorite recommendations for curing the economy. I tried, in editorials in the *New York Times* and the *Christian Science Monitor*, to protect the concept, but to no avail. While the concept grew in popularity, it grew fuzzier and fuzzier. Still, by May 1980, many of the candidates for election signed off on one version or another of reindustrialization—except the man I was working for, Jimmy Carter.

Carter was doing poorly. Inflation and unemployment continued to rise, his approval rate had dropped to a low 20 percent despite his promises to balance the budget. To add insult to injury, Senator Kennedy was challenging Carter in the primaries, seeking to become the candidate of the Democratic Party. The Carter administration now became more actively concerned about labor's support. If the labor unions supported Kennedy, Carter might lose the renomination of his party—particularly disgraceful for a sitting president. The White House and the AFL-CIO had previously negotiated a "national accord" which called for close consultation with these unions on matters of short- and long-run economic policy. This now led to two specific suggestions: one was the creation of a national reindustrialization board, which would formulate reindustrialization policies; the other, the formation of two industry-specific committees to help the auto and steel industries, which had been especially hurt, to turn around. While these were relatively small reindustrialization measures, I could not but hope that they might be parlayed into something more encompassing. Was there going to be a last-minute break for the idea, after all?

After the Kennedy threat was overcome, reindustrialization survived as part of a larger package of new economic policies advocated by the Carter campaign, which was now facing Reagan. Carter unveiled much of this package late in the election campaign, at a point when the whole campaign had been widely written off as likely to fail. I wondered what would have happened if the president had embraced the promise of reindustrialization earlier and on a much grander scale.

My grand scheme was not tailored to the president to whom it was pitched. The design as advanced required a forceful leader, maybe even one willing to look beyond his own political fortunes, ready to incur large-scale public costs for the country to reap longer-term benefits once the economy was back on track. I could hardly approach Carter directly and tell him to find his—well, let's say backbone. Instead, I wrote an article called "The Lack of Leadership: We Found It—In Us." After it was published, I sent it to the president. Carter responded with a handwritten note. It speaks volumes for itself. "To Amitai Etzioni, Thanks—A good article—when a president has *authority* to act uni-laterally [as in a crisis] his leadership can be exerted. Otherwise, compromise, delay, and confusion are more likely. It's our system. I like it. J. Carter."

In the decade that followed (1980–1990) much was done along the lines suggested by the reindustrialization scheme. Railroads and highways were fixed, new sources of energy were used, schools were improved, civilian R&D

Figure 6.1.   1980

budgets increased, and so on. The extent to which these improvements in the economic infrastructure account for the great success of the American economy in the next decade (1990–2000) requires a study that has not been carried out, as far as I know. If I had to guess, I would expect that reindustrialization played a significant role, but so did other factors, such as the end of the Cold War, the weakening of OPEC, and the elimination of the deficit.

A New Way to Settle Refugees

Shortly after I joined the White House staff, the Carter administration found itself facing a crisis as mounting tensions in Southeast Asia rapidly increased the number of people seeking asylum in the United States. In addition, Soviet Jews began immigrating in larger numbers after the Soviet Union finally relaxed its emigration restrictions in 1978. The Carter administration responded in the tradition of other Democratic administrations: it expanded the role of the federal government. The office of U.S. Coordinator for Refugee Affairs was created in February 1979 to "coordinate" various governmental efforts on behalf of the rising wave of refugees.

Until 1979, voluntary associations handled a good part of the settlement of refugees. Among the better-known were Church World Service, the International Rescue Committee, the United States Catholic Conference, and the Hebrew Immigrant Aid Society. The largely private method of refugee resettlement was strained by the fall of 1979, not only because of the rapid increase in the number of refugees but also because many of the new immigrants were more difficult to assimilate. This strain did not go unnoticed by the White House staff. An in-house memo warned of "a serious crisis—the inability of current resources, public and voluntary, to meet the needs of the Indochinese refugees, a crisis which, both in human terms and politically needs stronger attention and attack."

Stuart Eizenstat (assistant to the president for domestic affairs and policy) formed a task force headed by Ellen Goldstein and Frank White, two junior staffers, to review the matter. On joining the task force, I read a draft report prepared for it that struck me as having a leitmotif that, although never explicitly stated, ran through all of its long and belabored parts. All leaned toward the federal government taking over the handling of the refugees. Government agencies would provide housing, jobs, welfare, health services, Americanization—direct this and coordinate that.

The approach troubled both the sociologist and the activist in me. True, I disagreed with libertarians who believed that the government should be minimized, that immigrants—like most anybody else—should be left to fend for themselves. I believed that the government had a considerable legitimate role. But it seemed to me that when there were missions that communities and voluntary associations (the Third Sector) could carry out well, it was unwise to preempt them, further weakening the social fabric and increasing public costs. Moreover, the Third Sector was particularly good at absorbing immigrants. American ethnic groups have taken care of their own for generations.

The activist in me could not help but note that inflating the government's roles and burden was the number one topic Republicans were using to attack in the Carter administration. It was a powerful theme that swayed many people. Allowing the Third Sector to play a major role would show that Democrats were no longer the tax-and-spend party and were open to new ways of treating social problems without throwing people in need to the not-so-tender mercy of the marketplace. Moreover, communities could be the state's partner rather than being replaced by it. (These conceptions were much less widely held in 1979 than they became later, although even in recent years both the underlying assumptions and their policy implications are still often contested.)

To deal with the flood of refugees, I suggested that the government help launch a National Emergency Coalition for Refugees, composed of voluntary agencies, religious groups, and private charities, and turn the matter over to the coalition.

Goldstein and White initially raised some objections to this approach. Goldstein wanted to be sure that turning to the major charitable organizations would not squeeze out the smaller ones that had traditionally settled immigrants. White sought to ensure that minorities would not be treated less well than new immigrants. I modified my memo accordingly after which they both signed off on it and sent it on to Stu Eizenstat. I was elated. This is the way things get done, I thought. From ideas to framing new policies to action! I finally hit my stride, I believed.

Almost immediately, I hit a king-sized bump in the road. Victor Palmieri, the newly appointed U.S. coordinator for refugee affairs, objected to the Third Sector approach. He was confident that the voluntary agencies would refuse to take on the burdens of the mission. First, I grew hot under the collar: I had a workable concept; I was in the White House proper, getting someplace; here comes this guy and shoots down my idea. After I calmed down, I offered to prove that the concept was a realistic one by informally exploring the agencies' responses to the idea. I was delighted when their responses varied from cautious endorsement to considerable enthusiasm.

Bill Aramony of the United Way conditioned his support on the understanding that the United Way executives would play a key role in the suggested coalition. Better yet, he invited me to a meeting of the heads of seventeen major voluntary groups. I thought that I had made my case when all the assembled leaders indicated that they would be quite willing to participate in the coalition. The head of the Red Cross, George Elsey, was outright enthusiastic about taking on a new mission. Even more enthralled was Landrum Bolling, chairman of the Council on Foundations. He offered to personally take the suggestion directly to Mrs. Carter.

I was pleased with the results of my quick survey and suggested that, as a next step, Palmieri should meet with the heads of the voluntary associations to launch the nongovernmental Third Sector project. To my dismay, all that Palmieri said was that he would think about the matter. He then wrote: "While I think your suggestion is a good one, attempting to organize this right now would complicate some of my first priorities." Palmieri's "first priority" was to have his federal agency take on the mission.

White and Goldstein prodded Palmieri to proceed, but Palmieri was not to be moved; he responded:

> Carol Hecklinger informed me that at a recent meeting you expressed a strong interest in acting on Dr. Etzioni's "voluntary option."
>
> I think Dr. Etzioni's idea is useful because one of our major problems in the resettlement area is the incapacity of the traditional organizations to maintain contact with the refugees and to follow up with support after the initial reception activity. Right now, however, given the other priorities in the picture, I do not intend to try to follow up in a major way.

The lesson was as important as it was elementary: ideas have no wings; if they are to fly, one must find some other way of carrying them forward. That means power, in plain English. This is the stuff out of which Political Science 101 is made. But initially, I believed (and to some extent still do) that when you work in the White House, you are part of a small group of people who work directly for the president of the United States. If you have a significant policy recommendation that is substantively and politically sound, no other considerations should prevent it from reaching the president.

Facing Palmieri, I quickly learned how naive my view of White House workings was, but not how one could push an idea through in the face of opposition. I had next to no experience with this kind of micro power play. People say that academic politics are contentious and thus a good preparation for Washington. However, I had avoided academic politics with a vengeance with the exception of the years I had served as chairman of the department of sociology at Columbia. And during those years, my performance as a power broker was at best tolerable. Now I was far from sure how to build sup-port. Above all, I simply lacked the personality traits that make people into good politicians.

Palmieri, the staff explained, was heading a very small agency. Without more missions, budget, and power, he could not play a significant role. Also, as a successful manager who came to government from the private sector, dealing with a bunch of voluntary associations seemed to him, I was told, like herding cats. He would only change his position if he were overruled by someone high up in the White House, either Chief of Staff Hamilton (Ham) Jordan or Stewart (Stu) Eizenstat, in charge of domestic policy. Ham had much more pressing matters to attend to. Hence, if Palmieri was to be over-ruled, it was up to Stu. Stu was known among the staff as the "honest bro-ker," who would deal fairly with the staff, listen carefully to their ideas, and try to sort out what was the right course to follow rather than be driven by considerations of ego or office politics. Consensus building was his style. But confronting someone was not something Stu was inclined to do. I saw no way to marshal the needed support, and so Palmieri's decision was the final word on the matter. Well, almost.

I found some comfort in what happened next. Suddenly, the challenges we faced with the waves of Indochinese refugees were topped by still higher waves of Cuban refugees. In mid-1980, over a very short period, some 125,000 Cubans escaped to the United States. This huge influx of refugees initially seemed to vindicate Palmieri's position. If the government was needed before, surely it was now indispensable. Indeed, Congress granted Palmieri more funds and staff, and he was on his way to expanding his fiefdom.

As the months passed, however, despite the huge increase in the number of refugees, various voluntary associations and communities absorbed most of the refugees on their own! The U.S. Catholic Conference alone resettled about two-thirds of the incoming Cubans. Cuban American associations raised funds and provided social services. All said and done, approximately 100,000 Cuban refugees were resettled over the summer, mostly with families or friends. Many refugees simply "disappeared." Cuban Americans found the new immigrants places to live and work and tutored them in the ways of America. By November 1980, only 6,900 Cubans remained to be resettled, mainly felons, mental patients, and handicapped persons.

Both the core idea that the government could solve our social problems (the old-fashioned Democratic idea, embodied in the Great Society) and the notion that the private sector was the savior (the key theme of the incoming Republican Reagan administration) were missing a major fact. There was a very important role for communities, voluntary associations, places of worship—for the body society—to play in dealing with the problems that plagued our society. Later, these ideas became popular following numerous writings about the civil society by various communitarians (including me) and still later by the works of Robert Putnam and Francis Fukuyama. They also featured in the debate between Old and New Democrats. However, at the time, the Third Sector was barely visible.

The fact that Carter was tone deaf to the Third Sector communitarian message, to the extent that it was raised in those days and was within his hearing range, was more reason among a hundred and one others that he lost the election so decisively. I was on my way to the Democratic headquarters for the traditional election night party, early in the evening to await the results and to celebrate or share the grief, when I heard on my car radio that Carter was not just defeated, but trounced. The polls in California had not even closed yet.

For me, participation in the refugee task force and the pursuit of reindustrialization drove two points into the inner core of my bones: first, promoting policies that have long-term payoffs but short-term costs—in places where people have a short-term lease—is an uphill struggle, at best. Second, when a public intellectual roaming in the corridors of power faces opposition—a common occurrence—marshaling arguments on behalf of one's ideas is woefully insufficient. Strong debating points may carry the day on campus, but even when one works directly for the president, on his small staff, one must be skilled in the politics of power if one's ideas are to have a prayer.

Don't Meet the Press

The lesson from my White House encounters with the press was rudimentary: the press, which can work wonders in conveying a professor's ideas to the public, can undermine a person inside the government more quickly than you can say "fired!" As a staff member, everything you say may be held against you. One can work with the media here, too, but it requires much greater caution than I brought with me after two decades of talking freely with members of the press.

One early morning, entering my White House office, I noticed that my secretary's eyebrows were raised about as far as they could go in a mixture of warning and bemusement. She said, in a voice full of what-have-you-done-now: "The organizers of the White House Conference on the Family want to see you *pronto*. In effect, they would prefer to have your head and skip the rest." I felt vaguely guilty as I quickly ran through the events of the last few days, but nothing specific came to mind to which I could attach my concern. I asked my secretary if she knew why I was being summoned; she did not have a clue.

It turned out that I was quoted that morning in the *Wall Street Journal* in a way that some in the administration considered highly damaging. This was about the ninth month of my year at the White House. In the preceding months I had firmly refused to grant any press interviews. Initially, there was a measure of curiosity when a Columbia University senior professor was appointed to the White House. But after I did not return any of the calls and instructed that they all be referred to the press office, the calls became infrequent. Before I joined the White House, I did not mind seeing my name and picture in the press one bit, although after seeing it a few times I found it much less intoxicating. Also, the press compresses one's ideas. Often, I would wince when reading about what I had supposedly stated. At the same time, I realized that if I wanted to get the word out, I had no choice but to work with the media. Now that I was an insider, I worried that an inaccurate report in the press would get me in trouble.

But toward the end of my term in the White House, I yielded once. When a reporter from the *Wall Street Journal* called and suggested that we have lunch at Maison Blanche, an "in" restaurant across the street from the White House, I was tempted. With my family in New York, I had nothing in my Washington fridge but plain yogurt and carrot sticks, and I had "lunched" at the Old Executive Office Building snack counter more times than I could remember. The invitation for a full meal at a fine restaurant was enticing. I checked with the White House press office and was assured that the reporter was "OK; you can trust him."

I still played it safe. The Carter administration was a rudderless sinking ship, although many on the top bridge believed—or pretended—that it was sailing true. I was not going to air my misgivings to a reporter, even if the conversation was going to be "off the record." So, I told him that Zbigniew Brzezinski was a brilliant national security adviser, Stu Eizenstat was the most accomplished domestic adviser the country could pray for, and that Carter could walk on water, or something to this effect. Our policies were clear and focused and so on. He grinned but seemed to appreciate my loyalty. As we were about to leave, the reporter asked what I thought about the White House Conference on the Family. Searching for something bland and safe to say, I uttered, "Well, it is not our first priority." Hell, I thought, we are not talking about the family but a conference on it. Anyhow, the mucked-up economy and the hostages in Iran were obviously what commanded our primary attention. True to his commitment, my lunch host asked at the door, "May I quote you about this?" I shrugged, tempted by God only knows what—being nice? Appreciation for the lunch? The desire to see my name in print one more time after all these months? Fatigue? I replied, "Sure, why not?" The next day, the *Wall Street Journal* stated, "Governor Reagan says the White House merely pays lip service to the family. Professor Etzioni, a senior adviser to the White House, agrees." It took two days of mea culpa, promising to keep my brilliant ideas for the White House away from the media, and allowing fingers to be waved in my face before I was sort of forgiven. I am not saying that when one works somewhere in the shadow of those in power one must keep mum. The press has often been used for power plays, especially by various well-timed and well-placed "leaks." However, anyone who is accustomed to the freewheeling ways in which a campus-based public intellectual can converse with the media will need considerable retooling if he or she is to draw on the media from the inside to try to move policies in the right direction.

White House Lessons on Ethics

Power Tempts

The year in the White House also sensitized me to the moral dimension of even the smallest decision we make. I do not mean to sound melodramatic. Compared to what one reads about the various kinds of hanky panky that go on in the White House, and not merely in the Lincoln bedroom, the temptations to abuse my White House power (such as it was) that I faced were minor, at most. I readily resisted using information about yet-to-be-announced changes in economic policy to trade in the stock market. Such trading would have been a serious, major offense. But twice I crossed the line—once without even noticing it.

Most weekends I rushed to New York to spend time with Minerva and the boys, light-years away from Washington. We missed each other a great deal, which made the weekends especially precious. There is little more joyous than a bunch of kids rushing to the door to throw their arms around you, shouting, "Daddy! Daddy!" One late Friday afternoon I found that the line of people in the Washington airport waiting to fly on the shuttle to New York snaked throughout the terminal and spilled onto the sidewalk. Something was wrong in LaGuardia and we were told that we had at least a two-hour wait for those of us at the end of the line to make it. I suggested to two guys in front of me sharing the driving to New York. Soon, we were in my car on the highway. About a third of the way to New York, the car was running out of gas—but none was to be had. Carter had ordered that half the cars in the country could be refueled only on odd weekdays and the others on even days to conserve energy. Mine was an odd-day car. Indeed, as we rolled into a gas station, we saw that already several cars were parked on the side of the road, waiting for midnight to be able to fill their tanks. With much reluctance, I was about to join them even though it would cost me a much-treasured evening with my family.

My companions argued otherwise. They had long since learned about my White House post, and they pointed to a White House decal on the windshield of the car (used as a parking permit). They suggested that I tell the gas station attendant that I was on White House business and had to be helped. I demurred. I explained that the White House lawyer had repeatedly warned us against any personal use of government stationery, phones, cars, and so forth. I was not on White House business, and I was not going to pretend otherwise. After considerable give-and-take, I yielded, sort of. I allowed one of the guys to drive my car toward the pumps; the other approached the attendant and said something I could not hear but that was easy to surmise as he kept pointing to the decal. I was home for a late dinner, feeling that I cheated. The fudged arrangement did not help. Acquiescing was no different from having acted myself, only less honest. Yes, there are greater sins, and it was all for a good cause, but this is exactly the type of excuse people use when the violations are much more serious. Good place to stop, right here, I said to myself. Little did I realize that the next seduction was going to be much more subtle.

A Presidential Tracking System: How I Crossed the Line

In July 1979, a *New York Times* reporter called the White House press office with what at first seemed a routine query. A year earlier, he said, the president had promised to study the role of coal in solving our energy crisis and to report to the nation within thirty days. The reporter wanted to know the results of the study. The press officer did not know. He called around to other White House agencies to no avail. He checked with the Department of Energy, but no one could recall the president charging the department with such a task. Eventually, it was established that the Interior Department was working—still working—on the study.

This incident was one of many that fostered the sense that the president lacked follow-through. It underscored that the president had no procedure for keeping track of what he assigned people to do, no systematic follow-up to establish whether his instructions were carried out.

To remedy this situation, Richard Harden suggested using a computer to provide a tracking system. I participated in trying to develop the needed program. The first difficulty we ran into was trying to answer the seemingly simple question of what constitutes a presidential directive and hence something that should be tracked, and what was merely a presidential political gesture, a promise to be forgotten, a threat not meant to be carried out. For instance, during a speech, the president reassured a group of American exporters that he had every intention of helping them increase exports the next year and that he would seek to open twenty new trade offices overseas for that purpose. Did this constitute a directive? Was the president merely seeking to placate the delegation, and if so, would he be served if this and other such political gestures were systematically recorded? And was our role to help cover his tracks or foster systems that would keep him honest? Many other questions arose, including who would be in charge of acting on what the tracking system showed, for example, chiding those behind schedule, and who would be allowed to access the tracking system and thus be free to see exactly what the president charged whom to do, whether they were on schedule, and so on.

Soon, Harden and I discovered that the White House did not have an appropriate computer and it feared acquiring one more. In those days computers were very bulky and costly and could do much less than PCs can readily accomplish today. Moreover, many computers were programmed to specifically carry out one mission. Most disconcerting (to the White House) was the fact that the public feared computers the way some people these days are troubled by FBI databases; these machines were considered the tools of Big Brother.

Although the White House had several computers, these were small and specialized. The Secret Service had one strictly for its purposes. Hugh A. Carter, special assistant to the president for administration, had one, but it served mainly housekeeping purposes. The Office of Management and Budget and the National Security Council each had its own. None of these were suitable or available for presidential-tracking purposes. Moreover, the very idea of creating a central computerized system to shadow the work of all government agencies smacked too much of Big Brother. "What will the press say?" was a rhetorical question often raised.

A solution was eventually proposed—hide the computer in the military! There, one more computer would hardly be noticed, and the White House could plug into it without having to own up to having one more. I was sent to work out this arrangement with John Carabello, director for data automation in the Pentagon. He flatly refused; his computers were for the use of the military, not the White House. He did not exactly show me the door, but he made it clear where it was located.

I was infuriated; I was representing lord and country, the president. Here was this civil servant, insisting on some kind of bureaucratic or childish division of computers: this is mine, not yours. I returned to 1600 Pennsylvania Avenue and had Ham Jordan pen a handwritten note to Harold Brown, the Secretary of Defense. It said:

Memorandum for: Secretary Brown
From: Hamilton Jordan
Subject: DOD support
    Your department has been extremely helpful to the White House in dealing with information and communications problems. The president has asked me to develop some systems to help us monitor the implementation of the administration's initiatives, and I would appreciate the assistance of some of your senior people in determining how best to approach the task and to implement and appropriate the system.
    Richard Harden has had some informal discussions with John Carabello. If you would have him, or whomever you consider appropriate, contact Harden, he can discuss our needs in more detail.

And in handwriting at the bottom, "We would appreciate your help on this! Thanks, Hamilton."

Soon after I delivered the note, we had access to all the military computers we could use, and then some. Only years later, when I read about Colonel Oliver North's commingling of funds, I understood that I crossed not merely the Potomac in my shuttling between the White House and the Pentagon. North employed funds he garnered from weapons sales to Iran to finance the operation of the Contras in Nicaragua. Congress had banned the allocation of additional funds to this group. Well, similarly, Congress jealously guards its right to set the budget for each government agency, including the White House. (For instance, the number of staffers we were entitled to hire was severely limited. We got around this limitation by having staffers from various agencies "detailed" to the White House, but the amount of time they could be so assigned was also strictly limited.) In my case, I in effect drew on funds Congress meant to be used by the Department of Defense for White House needs.

Granted, there are larger offenses; I did not stay up nights, agonizing at great length over my violation of the budgetary regulations. But I was shocked that when I was dashing about, trying to help set up the presidential-tracking system, I crossed the line without even noticing that there was one. I did not deliberate whether I could justify, at least to myself, my actions, because I was unaware that was something that called for such a consideration.

My main lessons were several: there are few, if any, innocent decisions, decisions that do not harbor immoral and illegal trapdoors, considerations that can be overlooked with impunity. There are not two categories of decisions, one for moral (or legal) decisions, the other for economic, social, and technical ones. Most, if not all, decisions have a moral dimension. Second, under pressure of hard work, commitments of loyalty, and political considerations, it is very easy to overlook subtle lines that often separate what is right from that which is wrong. We all need devices to help us be more sensitive to these traps. For instance, requirements to clear new initiatives with lawyers can serve as such a device. Above all, we all can benefit from greater attention to the moral and legal implications of our decisions, a sort of inner red light that flashes when we so much as get close to the line.

An Ironic Moment

Shortly after Carter lost the election to Reagan and the new president was sworn in, I was surprised to receive an invitation to a White House briefing, which was to take place in the Old Executive Office Building. To this day, I believe it was simply an error based on some staff list the White House maintained. The briefing was conducted by Murray Weidenbaum, a professor of economics from Washington University, the incoming chairman of the White House Council of Economic Advisers.

Weidenbaum had much to say and often did so with a keen sense of humor, but one comment stuck with me. He told the assembled group that the new administration would generate such a deficit that if the Democrats ever made it back into office, they would be unable to spend much on their favorite social programs. (Not trusting my memory, I checked with Murray, who confirmed my recollection.) The Reagan administration lived up to this promise, with a vengeance.

President Clinton had to (at least he believed he had to) abandon many of his plans in order to wipe out the Reagan deficit. He ditched his plan to Put People First, to invest great amounts of public funds in education and training, a cardinal part of his 1992 campaign. Instead, overruling liberals such as Robert Reich and Donna Shalala, siding with Robert Rubin and Alan Greenspan, Clinton gave priority to eliminating the deficit. He—and the nation—were richly rewarded. Ending the deficit was a major factor in reducing interest rates, which in turn helped generate a fabulous economy in the 1990s and which left, at the end of his administration, a giant surplus. But, far from it being used to fulfill Clinton's initial commitment to invest in people, it was largely consumed by the Republican administration that followed him to provide tax cuts, mainly for those better off. It is quite possible that when the Democrats find their way back to 1600 Pennsylvania Avenue,

Murray Weidenbaum will be on the money for a second time. Lesson for the day (or decade): politics is a strange business that follows different rules than economic theories, doctrines of fairness, or giving just desert where it is due. Take note, those who enter these gates.

Speaking Personally

I am often asked what it was like to serve in the White House. For me, it was a very painful year—a year I never want to live through again—yet one I would have given my right arm to have had. My inability to transform my ideas into policies, to do what I was sure the country needed, was distressing and depressing. I was both so close—right next to where decisions on the highest level were made—and so far from influencing them. The fact that the policies the Carter administration did follow fared very poorly provided little comfort. The administration's dismal failure just made me regret even more that I could not contribute to reshaping its policies. It is far from self-evident whether I could have helped if I had played more of a role, but one thing is abundantly clear: although Carter has become arguably our best ex-president yet, while in the White House he made every mistake in the political science textbooks and even invented some new ones.

At the same time, I learned a great deal about the ways activist academics must work if they are going to have a fighting chance in the inner sanctum, what might be done and how, and what cannot be done. Being right is nice; being able to marshal enough support for an idea is a hell of a lot nicer. Only, being nice has nothing to do with it.

Real Power

After leaving the White House staff and becoming firmly ensconced in my new academic home at The George Washington University, I tried to live up to my commitment to myself to stick to my study of and action on behalf of the American economic and social renewal project, but I got distracted one more time. This time it was a power play that made all those I had experienced in the White House seem like child's play. Like many stories in Washington, it started at a party. I ran into a highly regarded albeit controversial professor of sociology of law, Ilene Nagel. She told me that she was serving as a member of the U.S. Sentencing Commission, about which I knew diddly-squat. She explained that the commission was initially formed in 1984 to study what should be done about great discrepancies in the penalties dished out to individual offenders in different states. For instance, in those days, smoking a joint could get someone a twenty-year prison sentence in Texas, but only a suspended sentence in New York.

By 1987, the commission formulated a suggested national scale for judgments that Congress enacted without any significant changes and with unusual dispatch. Penalties imposed by judges all over the nation had to, as a rule from then on, stay within ranges provided by the sentencing guidelines.

Flushed with its success, the commission got its mandate extended to encompass the study of another category of crimes—corporate ones. It started by conducting a study of the then-prevailing penalties. It found to its utter amazement that between 1984 and 1987 the average penalty for multibillion-dollar corporations (when not dealing with environmental crimes, à la *Exxon Valdez*) was $48,000 and 67 percent were fined less than $10,000.

At this point the commission conducted hearings about what should be done and what would be just. I testified before the commission and thereafter closely followed its work. The commission initially concluded that much higher penalties must be imposed if corporations are to be chastened. In 1989, it drafted a thirty-two-level scale of fines, ranging from two to three times the amount of damage caused or illicit gains achieved, and which could range still higher depending on the severity of the offense. Fines could range up to a third of a billion dollars—enough to get the attention of even the largest corporation with the deepest pockets. At this phase of the commission's work some economists opposed the direction it was taking, but the business community seemed to be completely unaware of what was about to hit it.

The commission published its recommendations in November 1989, in preparation for a public hearing to take place on February 14, 1990. Suddenly, all hell broke loose. Corporate leaders called on the Bush White House, and it alerted the Justice Department. The commission rushed to redo its recommendations, scaling back the penalties—*some 97 percent!* The new maximum penalty was dropped to $12.6 million. Talk about leverage.

Moreover, the commission added ways for corporations to greatly reduce these low fines by a set of mitigating factors. For instance, if a corporation had an effective compliance program, it could subtract three points off a possible culpability score of five and thus reduce its fine by 60 percent.

In the years that passed since then, corporate penalties have increased. Still, given that the likelihood of being caught is small, most penalties imposed on sizable corporations are not particularly daunting. For instance, in June 2001 the Sara Lee Corporation pled guilty to "producing and distributing adulterated meat and poultry" and was fined $200,000. In the fiscal year ending that same month, the company's net sales were over $17 billion. In another instance, in 1996, Archer Daniels Midland pled guilty for its role in "conspiracies to fix prices to eliminate competition and allocate sales in the lysine and citric markets worldwide" and was fined $100 million. Its net sales and other operating income amounted to nearly $18 billion in the same year. Russell Mokhiber, editor of the *Corporate Crime Reporter*, studied what he called "the top 100 corporate criminals of the 1990s." The imposed penalties on ten corporations were $50 million or higher; 71 were fined $10 million or less, and 16 were fined less than $1 million. The low deterrence effect was all too evident when the Enron scandal made the headlines in 2002.

Back in the 1980s, the commission flip-flop drew my attention to other such power plays by other lobbies, including banks, real estate agencies, and labor unions. One more time, I donned my social critic hat. The more I looked into the matter, the more evident it became that although corporations and other lobbies had power for several reasons—including that they generated jobs and tax revenues in various congressional districts as well as promised jobs (often as lobbyists) to members of Congress if they were to lose an election—a major reason these lobbies commanded so much power was their campaign contributions. It seemed clear to me that if Congress (and state legislatures) were to be reformed so that they would be able to pay mind to the public interest—and not be swayed on most matters by the highest bidder—these contributions must first be curbed.

I say "most" because, once in a while, when the issue is of especially great national interest, at least during the time the press is very attentive, Congress does what is right. Often, though, once the public limelight moves elsewhere, even these policies are corrupted by deep pockets. One example should stand for all the others that could be cited. Congress passed a bill in 1996 requiring the Immigration and Naturalization Service (INS) to put in place a system of documenting every foreigner entering or exiting the United States. Pressure from groups such as the U.S. Chamber of Commerce, which argued that such regulations clog the borders and hurt the bottom line for many nearby businesses and towns, lead to Congress scrapping these measures all together.

Cynics argue that it is impossible to stop money from flooding politicians. If one approach is dammed, the money just finds another. They should look at Britain. Election costs there are much lower, because campaigns are basically limited to four weeks. Each candidate is allowed to spend a small, fixed amount. (The amount is determined by a complex formula, but is on the order of 9,000 British pounds, about $15,000 dollars—a puny amount compared to the millions spent by most American candidates.) If a candidate spends more, the election results are invalidated and the campaign manager may be punished by a jail sentence. Candidates are entitled to mail one leaflet to each constituent free of charge, and the parties get free television time.

Many Americans abhor the idea of the government covering election costs. The fact is that if clean elections could stop even a few of the laws that favor lobbies over public needs, then paying for campaigns from the public till would be a tremendous bargain. Thus, if we could kill some of the weapons systems that neither the Pentagon nor military experts favor, say, buying an extra Sea Wolf submarine (estimated cost: $3 billion) or the LHD-8 ship, a helicopter carrier (estimated cost: $1.5 billion), we would already be able to pay the costs of the next presidential and congressional elections (which are estimated to cost about $3 billion).

Apologists for the current system argue that all that money buys is access. But in a democracy, access should be based on how many voters you have lined up, the potency of your case, and the service done for your country—not the size of your bank account. And access leads to influence. Corporations, unions, banks, and real estate agencies would have to be stupid beyond belief, as well as in violation of fiduciary duties to their shareholders or members, if they rained millions on Congress members without any payoff.

By pointing to those who have lost elections to others who have spent less, some suggest that money does not buy victory. But these are rare exceptions that prove the rule. Still others maintain that money goes to legislators with whose general philosophy (conservative or liberal) one agrees. Hardly. It goes to members of both parties as long as they serve on the right committees that control whatever the deep pockets are after, especially if they chair these committees.

Others point out that lobbying is a constitutionally protected activity, meaning that citizens have a right to petition their elected officials about whatever specific causes or interests concern them—whether or not they are in the general "public" interest. But gaining influence by paying cash on the barrel is a form of lobbying the Constitution hardly favors. I laid out all this in my book *Capital Corruption*.

It is also an area in which those of us who are public intellectuals have a legitimate beef with several of our academic colleagues. Several political scientists, who have studied campaign contributions without leaving their desks or computers, report that they found no correlation between funds donated and legislation later enacted. What they did not take into account is that funds flow in all kinds of ways, including those channeled to law firms, who then provide them to members of Congress, and to donations made after the promised legislation is enacted. This last point is especially nefarious because it allows a lobby to pay up only after delivery.

You may say that this amounts to outright bribery and, of course, you are right. Campaign contributions are little more than legalized bribery. However, until laws are changed—they are legal, no matter how unethical and undemocratic. I became aware of the relevant small print by a fluke. I wrote an article for *The Washington Post* in support of Abscam. The FBI had a bunch of agents pose like Arab sheiks offering members of Congress oodles of money in exchange for favors. All but one congressperson pocketed the money (on tape) without hesitation or qualms, with both hands out. My article, which argued that no entrapment was involved, led me to be invited for lunch with the head of the FBI, William Webster. Not much was said by him or me. But I was richly rewarded by a meeting with one of his assistant directors, Buck Revell. He explained the finer points of legalized bribery to me. These included the fact that Congress set a shorter statute of limitations for itself (if congresspersons are ever caught red-handed) than for the rest of us. Moreover, the law allows a lobbyist to come to a member of Congress and state something like, "Here is a donation; more will be forthcoming after you vote on bill such-and-such next week." The only thing that cannot legally be said explicitly, is, "If you do not vote, no money." Quid pro quo are daily and openly traded, you just cannot say it in so many words. Even the dumbest members of Congress can find their way around this hurdle. Worse yet, members of Congress are now regularly calling on lobbies for money, unabashedly soliciting contributions, and broadly hinting at payoffs. It matters little whether they are good or bad people; a member who does not raise tons of money in a hurry is very unlikely to be there. It is the system that is corrupt and corrupting. Take it from the mouth of those involved. They tell you privately, long before the third drink, that Congress has become a whorehouse. I cannot say it better.

I suggest to anyone, student or activist, who finds such harsh criticism of Congress (and state legislatures, many of which are worse) hard to believe, that they should go and study the course of any piece of legislation that is not in the limelight. (Easy to do, most are not.)

Over the years that followed, many joined the drive to reform campaign financing. Among others, Elizabeth Drew and Bruce Jackson wrote fine books. *Common Cause* and *Public Citizen* struggled to make a dent. Finally in 2002, Congress enacted a bill, promoted by John McCain and Russell Finegold, that curbed one part of the problem, soft money. Long before the ink dried on the bill, it was already being challenged in the courts, and lawyers and lobbyists found ways to begin to circumvent it. This does not mean that the crablike movement of Washington—one step back for every two forward—is all wasted. But it does suggest that the work of public intellectuals interested in reform is never done. Passing a law, as difficult as it might be, and even if it is 100 percent on the side of the angels, is often just one more step in a never-ending process. Those who enter politics better have the patience of Job and the stamina of a triathlete.

CHAPTER SEVEN

The Moral Dimension

"Things Will Never Be the Same Again"

On Saturday July 17, 1999, I landed in the small airport at Martha's Vineyard, on my way to a short vacation. There were many grim faces. Word was spreading that a small airplane, due in the night before, had not made it. Some believed that John F. Kennedy Jr. was on it; others whispered that his glamorous wife was also missing. By the time I checked into a B&B in Edgartown, the television networks reported that the plane had nosedived into the ocean. A few days later the bodies of Kennedy, his wife, and his sister-in-law were pulled out of the wreckage.

Many people grieved as if they had lost a distant but loved member of their own family. Numerous reasons were offered to explain why people were so perturbed by the death of someone they had never met. One reason I could best relate to was the deep sense that you can form plans, launch projects, develop strategies—and be thrown off course by a force fiercer than the perfect storm. Out of the blue, you can be sent tumbling down into a bottomless void. As the saying goes: man proposes; God disposes.

I came by this mourners' lesson, the universal Kaddish, the hard way. As 1985 was winding down, I had stuck to my course trying to serve both my academic and public masters. The five years that had passed since my White House service were largely dedicated to fleshing out the case for America's economic and social renewal both in academic publications and in the popular press. My book on the subject, *An Immodest Agenda*, published in 1982, had been reasonably well received. There was the usual stream of invitations

165

for lectures, testimonies before congressional committees, and even a few honorary degrees. For a while, I was distracted by studying the way election campaigns were financed and their corrupting effect on our political system, but most times, gritting my teeth, I did stay the course.

Staying the course was no mean feat during the first Reagan administration, between 1981 and 1985, a period during which laissez-faire, neoconservative ideology had its heyday. Tax cuts, deregulation, and unfettered market forces were said to suffice to solve our economic and social problems—which were believed to have been caused by the government to begin with. While Reagan often spoke glowingly and movingly about family values and against keeping God out of the classroom and chastised permissiveness, neither his personal life nor the policies he actively pushed for spelled moral renewal. As a previously divorced man who was estranged from his own children and not one to frequent church, this was not an area in which he was much of a role model. And while the religious right was heartened by what Reagan said, it was crestfallen by what he did not do, in terms of the policies they favored.

The economy was not performing particularly well either. The deficit sky-rocketed; unemployment was high, while economic growth was sluggish;

Figure 7.1. My largest audience: speaking at commencement following acceptance of my honorary degree from the University of Utah

crime and teen pregnancy swelled; drug abuse continued to break records. I was confident that sooner or later closer attention would be paid to what truly must be done to shore up the economy and society as a whole. I was planning to stand in the wings until an opening occurred. But suddenly, the stage collapsed; the whole set fell apart. I was thrown into a dark and bottomless pit.

At the end of my service in the White House I decided to resign my tenured position at Columbia University, where I had served for twenty years, some as chairman of the Department of Sociology. Instead, I accepted a "University Professor" position at The George Washington University. (This title means little to most people off campus. Many universities have a few professors, five, in the case of GWU, who are given this title. They can teach a wide array of subjects and draw students from all over the campus rather than being boxed in by their department. Universities believe that such professors add to their reputations.)

My move raised some eyebrows, as professors usually do not move from more prestigious universities to those significantly lower in the reputation pecking order. (Since then, GWU president Stephen J. Trachtenberg has greatly lifted the quality and standing of the university.) My reasons, though, were simple: public life and family. I found myself more and more involved in public policy, testifying before congressional committees, participating in task forces, consulting for government agencies, zipping down on the shuttle from New York and back several times a week. Living in Washington was going to make all of this easier.

Also, the condition of the community around Columbia University worsened. My young children suffered from living on Riverside Drive next to the university. Dogs relieved themselves in the sandboxes. Mike's sled was taken from him in the park, and he was left tied to a tree. Another day—someone viciously kicked his bike as he rode by and he sailed into a park bench, damaging his front teeth. Much more seriously, a fellow professor was killed a few blocks from us because he was slow to surrender a wristwatch. Another professor was knifed when he walked on the "wrong" block early one evening. There was a steady flow of reports about other assaults. And at all times there were nagging fears, when I had to walk home in the dark, or when a child or spouse was late. It was a relief to leave all this behind. Prestige is ephemeral; safety is real, especially when children are involoved.

When we moved to Washington, we ended up in a large house in a Washington suburb that we could barely afford, where there was no need to wash the soot out of one's shirt everyday, step over dog shit to cross the street, or be assaulted by the heavy urine smell wafting from subway passages. The children could safely ride their bikes or walk to school. We did have to keep our lawn closely groomed, and we had trouble finding reliable gardeners and a pool service—a quite lighter set of worries. My wife, Minerva, loved her new garden, where azaleas bloomed in a dazzling array of colors at different times during the season. She soon formed several friendships with neighbors. During workdays, the streets were mainly empty, but in the late afternoons and on weekends people worked in their front gardens and visited. It was no kibbutz, but somewhat of a community.

In the years that followed our marriage, Minerva moved in the opposite trajectory of many women of her generation—from successful professor to accomplished homemaker. She was born and educated in Mexico City, studied international relations at Stanford, and served as a Rockefeller fellow at Columbia University. Before we met, she wrote a book, in Spanish, on Latin American diplomacy. Soon after we married, she wrote a book in English, *The Majority of One*, on the role of the United States in the Organization of American States, which garnered rave reviews.

Minerva's heart, though, was not in what she called "the academic rat race." She disliked departmental politics, the pressure to publish, being away from home. As soon as our first son, Michael, was born, she declined all teaching offers and never wrote another word for an academic publication. Instead, she decorated Mike's room, redid the kitchen and the living room, and within a year and a half, proudly delivered David. Her afternoons in New York were spent in the sandboxes of Riverside Drive, at ice-skating rinks, birthday parties, and swim meets, and visiting with other faculty mothers, and driving kids to school. She became a very creative cook and sewed her own evening gowns. She also chose religious instruction; brought up a Catholic, she converted to Judaism.

When our older sons began to grow increasingly independent, we chose to have another child, Benjamin. Thus, in a few short years, Minerva, the young professor, transformed herself into a full-time mother and homemaker. Anybody who knew her had no doubt that she enjoyed every moment of her "traditional" life. She had a radiance about her that brought dancing smiles even to our sourpuss of a butcher and my dean.

She made friends effortlessly. We had left all our friends in New York, but shortly after we settled in Bethesda, we acquired a whole new slew. She often had the neighbors' children over, unless she was visiting them with our children. When there was a community event, Minerva would prepare one of her special dishes for the occasion, help serve, and clean up. When there were several burglaries in our area, Minerva and a neighbor organized a crime

Figure 7.2. Left to right: Minerva, Oren (David in front), Mike, Ethan (Ben in front), December 1978 family vacation

patrol composed of volunteers. As a side effect, people spent more time together and got to know each other better, making our neighborhood more of a community and less of a commuter suburb.

On December 20, 1985, the radio reported that less than one inch of snow was expected but warned listeners, at 2 P.M., about an early rush hour. "Typical Washington fuss about nothing," I thought. Minerva was to call me from the airport where she was going to pick up our youngest son, eleven-year-old Benji. I was to say hello to him before she rushed him to a dentist appointment.

When I had not heard anything by three o'clock, I called the airline: "No, the flight was not delayed," I was told. I assumed Minerva had heard about the evolving traffic snarl and headed immediately for the dentist, skipping the call to me.

Soon, I set off for our home in Bethesda; the traffic inched along on Massachusetts Avenue. An hour later, I was no more than halfway home. I tried a side road, but it was icy and the car was slaloming. I abandoned it at the side of the road, hitched a ride in a car with four-wheel drive, and found myself, another half hour later, close to home.

While I walked the last stretch, a cab stopped, and a neighbor invited me in. His voice was shaky. He was saying something about an accident. "My God," I thought, "it must be his wife Barbara."

"Minerva is critical," I finally heard him say. "Benji is fine," he said. "It happened on the way to the airport."

By now the cab was at my door. In the kitchen two of our neighbors were holding back tears. "Tell me," I said, turning to Sid, "is she alive?" He gave me the phone number of the physician at the emergency room of the hospital closest to the scene of the accident, which occurred on the George Washington Parkway.

The voice on the phone was grim. "Could you get here?" I told him I had been in combat and seen many of my best friends killed. "Give it to me straight."

"She died instantly and did not suffer. Her car shot off the icy road into a tree."

I felt too many things at once. This could not be; why hadn't I picked Benji up? I cannot handle this! What will I tell the children? How could we live without her? Did I say a good good-bye when we parted after breakfast? The children, the children, the children.

A neighbor drove me to the hospital. The police brought Benji there from the airport. He hadn't been told about Minerva's death and was watching TV next to the emergency room.

There was a brief conference with a nurse and a physician, who mixed condolences with assurance that they had done all that could be done. They asked me if I wanted to see Minerva. I could not.

I told Benji, "It's time to go home." Benji lifted his small face to me, "What about Mommy?" I kneeled next to him, took him in my arms, and whispered: "Mommy will never come home again. . . . She died. . . . I will take real good care of you. . . . I love you very much."

He cried, and so did I. I kept repeating that I would take care of him. He quieted down a bit, and then said something that would echo hauntingly in the weeks, months, and years to come: "Things will never be the same again."

I was utterly lost. I did not know how to sleep alone or how to talk out the day's problems with only myself. I could not find the pilot light of the heating system, the keys to the cedar closet, the office of the orthodontist.

After the funeral, friends and neighbors came to what used to be our home, for a prayer service. Many had offered to bring food and libations, but I could not stomach the atmosphere that often surrounds wakes. When I explained my feelings ("not even coffee will be served"), many seemed to understand.

Instead of milling around as if at a reception, we sat in a large circle and talked about Minerva. A friend spoke of jewelry Minerva made; she showed us a piece of it she was wearing. Someone else remembered how Minerva saw a picture of a dress in the *New York Times Magazine* and successfully copied it.

These stories were not exaggerations. Minerva had two golden hands that could make or fix virtually anything. Yet, as I sat in the middle of all this chatter, I grew nauseated. Ever since I had been hit by the news I wanted to throw up but could not. I could cry, and did at the slightest provocation, but this did not alleviate my sense of having been hit in the stomach with a giant fist.

Over the years we had been married, our bond grew stronger. I refused all invitations to international conferences and to lecture away from home, whatever the fee, when Minerva was close to giving birth, holding hands and breathing with her during three deliveries. We brought the babies home together and shared the struggle of the first months and the joys and tribulations of bringing up youngsters in a challenging age. When I was hospitalized with what was incorrectly believed to be heart trouble, Minerva sat at my bedside hour after hour. I, in turn, held her in my arms when she miscarried and she believed she would never be able to conceive again.

Together, we cared for her mother, dying from a malignant tumor, in our home for thirteen months and shared with her the last moment of her life. And we cried our eyes out in each other's arms until it became clear that our son David did not have a similar tumor, as a careless physician had implied.

Our relationship was not all bliss. There were years when we were each wrapped up in our own projects. Minerva devoted a lot of time to Judaism. She invented new dishes, cooked, and deep-froze one-and-a-half freezers full of refined sauces, Mexican canapés, and soups (some of her recipes ended up in the *Washington Post* and in a cookbook). She spent what seemed like years in her sewing room, making ever more dresses, skirts, gowns, Halloween costumes for the children, even colorful swimsuits and muumuus. For my part, there were years when I did more writing, research, and traveling than I ought to have done. I was not merely trying to balance family and career but also my sense of mission. Now that it was too late, I had grave doubts about whether I had found the right balance.

How I wished we had spent more of those years truly together! But there was never a question about the depth of our commitment to one another. We would grow old together, dance at our sons' weddings, and Minerva would hold my hand in my last days (I was ten years her senior). We had just announced that on our next wedding anniversary we would supplement our original civil marriage with a Jewish one, to add one more band to our bond.

Each of the children reacted differently to our loss. One spoke of it openly, which everybody told me was a good thing.

With one of my sons, then a college freshman, I made a mistake. In the first weeks, he expressed his sorrow by being very attentive to me, helping me with the endless chores, answering the doorbell, ushering mourners in and out, hugging and consoling me. I came to lean on him. As the weeks passed, he became quite depressed and a bit irritable. He slept late and woke up tired. He locked himself in his room for hours. When I asked him whether I should accept an invitation to a dinner scheduled a month later, he exploded: "It's up to you."

Two days before he returned to college, we talked it out. I apologized for leaning too much on him, and we parted as the good friends we had become over the preceding years. Against my rule never to act behind my kids' backs, I called his dorm counselor as well as a friend there who had studied with me in grad school and asked them to keep an eye on him.

Another son kept his grief to himself, as he used to do with most of his other feelings. But his dark eyes grew darker and his face was drawn and shadowed. He worried me a great deal when he refused any coat or jacket when we set out to bury his mother on an icy afternoon on a windswept little hill at King David Memorial, just outside Washington. Over the years that followed, he found his way to talk about our loss. And he did not let me go alone to King David when I visited the gravesite and reserved my place close to Minerva.

Oren and Ethan, my sons from my previous marriage, often visited for weekends, doing chores, trying to get me out of the house, and putting their arms around me. People sometimes tease me for having as many as five children. I wish they could see us together.

A psychologist explained to me that people in our position must follow the "grief syndrome," with its appointed stages of denial, anger, and accommodation. Denial? Well, though I occasionally found myself turning to address Minerva about this or that, most of the time I had little doubt about what fate had dished out to me and my sons. As for anger, I felt little—whom could I blame? I often felt punished, beleaguered, and down, but I had little sense of "accommodation."

A tragedy tells you volumes about the community in which you live; it sorts out one's friends and neighbors. Some drove me deeper toward the edge, some pulled me back. I do not refer to suicide, as I did not seriously consider that. The thought of my sons, their need for me and love for me was sufficient to keep at bay my more extreme moods. But some friends made me feel rejected. I never expected anybody to cross to the other side of the street or stare right past me to avoid having to express condolences and deal with death and grief. Others, who were out of town and found out late about Minerva, were sort of angry with me—not so much for neglecting to inform them, but for having passed the first period of grief without them. How could they grieve properly if I was no longer tearing out my hair?

One evening, a kind invitation backfired. My sons and I were invited to join friends for a Friday night meal. As the lady of the house lit and blessed the Sabbath candles, just as Minerva used to do, I never felt more heartbroken. Somehow, at that moment, the realization sunk in that my sons and I would never be part of a whole family again.

I did not function well for about two years. Often I would just stare out the window or sit in a darkened room, doing nothing. I tried to help my boys cope, but did far from enough. Slowly, the black hole I would regularly sink into became less deep and dominant, although I never worked my way out of it. By mid-1987 I had to move on. I sold our house and donated most of the furniture and clothing to the Society for the Blind. One son was off to college and the other returned to his boarding school. (The older ones were already on their own.) I was invited to serve as a visiting professor at the Harvard Business School, to fill a chair (the Thomas Henry Carroll Ford Foundation Professorship) previously held by Alfred Chandler, Samuel A. Stouffer, and George C. Homans, among others. I was quick to accept the invitation, although I had a hard time remembering the chair's name.

Living in Cambridge took me hundreds of miles away from our Washington suburb. I rented a place to live in which the only constant visible reminders of my truncated life were some photos. They mattered little. The day on which I do not miss Minerva has not yet dawned. I was ready to resume my project though. The "B" school, as most everyone at Harvard referred to the business school, seemed like a promising place. Many of the members of its faculty worked on various economic issues, and it was planning to introduce a new program in ethics, both close to the core of my interest in America's renewal.

The Moral Dimension: Toward a New Economics

Ships Passing at Night

Slowly, I settled into the routine of a new life, in a new town. I found out where to buy ready-made dinners; people I had previously known, who would add a single person to the dinner's guest list; places to listen to jazz in Inman Square; lots and lots of economists (and very few ethicists) to talk with on campus.

When I was working on my original paper on economic renewal at the Brookings Institution, I drew largely on economic history and sociology. I found the works on economic development written by economists surprisingly thin. Moreover, returning to economics proper (which I had not read since my days at the Hebrew University), I was distressed by the unrealistic

assumptions about human nature and the workings of society that economists continued to rely upon and by the immoral implications of their governing theory. It seemed obvious that the kind of economics (often referred
to as neoclassical) that dominated American universities and spilled
from them into public thinking, especially via libertarian ideology, could
not accommodate the kind of redevelopment conceptions America's renewal required.

My quest for other social scientists interested in a different kind of economics brought me to a conference conducted by a small group of "behavioral
economists" in San Diego. The conference was dominated by a ferocious debate between economists and the other social scientists present. The main arguments can be readily captured; the heavy tone of mutual derision and contempt is hard to replay. The main points of the exchange were as follows:

Sociologist to economist: "Your theory is full of completely unrealistic assumptions. People are not self-centered, cold-blooded, rational creatures.
Yours is a flat-earth theory."

Economist to sociologist: "As Milton Friedman pointed out, it does not
matter whether the assumptions of a theory are unrealistic, as long as it leads
to the right predictions."

Sociologist: "But your predictions, again and again and one more time, are
way off. In effect, as your own Nobel laureate Wassily Leontief has shown,
many of the leading works published in your official journal, the *American
Economic Review,* have no data at all! They are full of mathematical mastur-
bation that may satisfy you, but bears no fruit."

Economist: "Look who's talking! Sociologists live in a never-never
land, in which nothing has a price, people have no choices to make, their
lives are predetermined by culture and history. And there are no two sociologists who can agree on anything, maybe other than that Tuesday follows Monday."

Sociologist: "Your theory undermines morality, whatever is left of it. Take
your notion of 'free riders.' You argue that if people work as a group, and one
cannot measure how much effort everyone puts in—people will slough off,
benefiting from the hard work of the others. If you are half right, every time
a truck is stuck in the mud at night, and people jump down to help, since
they are in the dark they will just pretend to push, hoping that when the others are done, they can simply climb back on. What shitty behavior to extol."

Economist: "And what makes you . . ."

Sociologist: "Let me finish. Almost done. When Gary Marwell conducted
an experiment, using twelve groups of students—to establish if people free
ride as your theory claims—he found that only the members of one group out
of twelve behaved in that cynical a manner. This group, it turned out, was

composed of graduate students in economics! This is proof positive that your theories make people more selfish than they would be otherwise."

Economist: "We are not against morality; we are amoral. You are nothing but a bunch of bleeding-heart liberals who hide behind a cockamamie theory."

I was just as happy that Daniel Kahneman, with whom I studied at the Hebrew University and became even friendlier when we both spent time at Berkeley, was not in attendance. I respected him too much to see him mired in this kind of discussion. When Danny got a Nobel Prize in economics in 2002, this gave a great boost to unorthodox economics, whether you call it behavioral economics, socio-economics, or communitarian economics. But he was hardly the first. Among others of such vintage are Herbert Simon and Arthur Lewis, for instance.

The meeting, though, was not a complete waste. It completely convinced me that there was little merit in expanding and repeating the criticism of economics. One cannot beat a theory with nothing. It was all too clear what was wrong with the economists' mousetrap, but was it possible to build a better one? The specs were obvious: the new theory would have to draw on realistic assumptions about human nature and society, yield better predictions, and be morally defensible. "All" that was missing was to find or form one.

This point was driven home when I served as an after-dinner speaker for a meeting of the Washington, D.C., Banker's Association at the fancy Greenbriar Hotel. I often learn much from conversations before and after my presentations, especially when I deal with people I normally do not see. Once, in 1968, following the police's roughing up of scores of young people who rioted during the Democratic Convention in Chicago, I found myself at a cocktail party in Arlington, Virginia, where guests included some of the Pentagon brass. I chatted with one General Kelly, who I had never met before. He was rubbing his hands with glee. "Today, we finally gave these bastards their due." It obviously did not even occur to him that he would be attending a cocktail party where there might be someone who would be taken aback by his views. And although I vaguely knew that such people existed, I had never laid eyes on any.

During the Greenbriar dinner, I asked a banker sitting next to me, "Why do you pay economists good money to predict interest rates when their predictions either tell you that tomorrow will be similar to yesterday or they miss the mark by a country mile?" The banker chuckled and explained, "What do you want me to do? Go to my board and say that I do not have the foggiest idea what the rates are going to be? I tell them my economists predict 4.6 percent and three months later I 'correct' and say now 5.3 percent is expected, and so on." Obviously, until one could provide bankers—and all kinds of other policymakers—with a sounder foundation for their decision making, they would continue to rely on economics as a crutch, however feeble.

My visits with the behavioral economists and D.C. bankers added to the dismay with which I had long observed the nefarious effect of economists on the American government and public. Their theories caused the government to impose unnecessarily high interest rates, which caused substandard economic growth and high unemployment. Put this way, it sounds as if the economists caused some dials to be set on the wrong digit, which may not seem like anything to be agitated about. However, an unemployment rate even 1 percent higher than can be justified means that many hundreds of thousands of people will be thrown out of work and will be unable to find new jobs, which in turn forces many to go on welfare and to lose their homes, families, sanity, and even lives. (Divorce, institutionalization in mental hospitals, and suicide are all correlated with unemployment.) And I remembered all too vividly the indignities unemployment entails. Similarly, 1 percent less of economic growth may sound like small potatoes, but it means that numerous social needs—from housing to health care, from environmental projects to schools—will come up short.

The San Diego conference brought back my pent up resentments over what the economists were perpetuating and the sense that cussing them out was senseless. The challenge was to find out whether I could help formulate an economics that was more realistic and humane than the prevailing one by building on the work carried out by others. The conference returned me to the manuscript of a book on a new approach to economics that I had been working on, but which had been collecting dust since the end of 1985. The Harvard Business School was just the place to finish it: there were numerous colleagues interested in economics, I was assigned a fine research assistant, and the facilities—from the duplicating machines to the library services—were better appointed than I ever had.

A New Approach to Economics

The manuscript led to a book, *The Moral Dimension: Toward a New Economics*. It speaks in my academic voice; however, I often summarize its main points in public lectures. Basically, the book reflects a fundamentally different way of thinking about human nature, society, and economic behavior than that followed by the dominant school of economics.

The book focuses on three questions: first, what are the purposes for which people are engaged in their endeavors, what are their goals (their "utilities")? Are people truly egotistical creatures out to "maximize" themselves and nothing else? For instance, do they give to charity only to get a tax deduction?

Once people have chosen their purpose, the book explores the second question of how they determine which way to proceed, which means to employ. Do people really act like two-legged computers, cool and rational? Or are they also deeply affected by their moral concerns and emotions? For example, will Orthodox Jews start to eat pork if its prices are sufficiently slashed?

Finally, the book asks: who are the "actors" who render all these decisions—free-standing agents, individuals, or people who are members of various families, peer groups, and communities, which deeply affect their choices? Thus, do teenagers buy Nike sneakers at $180 a pair because *they* conclude that they need these sneakers, or because their peer culture and friends persuade them that they do?

During my first year at HBS, I was invited to conduct a seminar for the faculty on my approach to economics, which I called "socio-economics." The lively discussions served as a vivid reminder of economists' objections to my approach and allowed me to develop my arguments and manuscript.

What Are People After?

Moderate neoclassical economists in the seminar advanced the cynical view that all that people seek is to "maximize" their self-interest (their happiness, their profit) in all matters concerning economic behavior. Immoderate ones made another giant leap: they presumed that self-seeking ends are what all human behavior is about. In support of their beliefs they claimed, for instance, that people attend church to gain prestige, to make business contacts, and to buy salvation points.

I had a hard time responding with as little emotion as possible as I argued that people are conflicted between their desires and their moral commitments. The simple statement "I would *like* to watch a football game on TV, but I *ought* to take out the garbage and paint the fence" captures the essence of this human condition. All human beings, except psychopaths, find that some moral values command their respect. These values typically require steps that are *not* pleasurable, such as fasting, refraining from having sex, or giving a tithe to the church. Human behavior reflects a continuous tug of war between our desires and our values.

In response, two diehard economists engaged in what academics call "reductionism"; they argued that every decent thing we do actually reflects some hidden self-interest. Charity is given to show off. Blood donations? They make you feel better about yourself.

I pointed to studies of the level of savings, of great importance for any economy. Economists have been unable to explain why some people (Americans, for instance) save very little, while others (e.g., the Japanese) save much more. Some economists maintained that the Japanese save more because of self-interest, because they have a weaker social security net than we do and hence need to rely more on their own savings for their old age (i.e., they save out of self-interest and nothing else). But this explanation is blown away by the fact that western Europeans, who have much more social security than we do, save more than Americans do.

Instead, I pointed out that the more conservative people are, the more they believe it is morally wrong to depend on the government or on their children. Thus, people in small-town America save more than in the more liberal cities, and earlier Americans saved proportionally more than contemporary ones. Ergo, what people believe is the right thing to do affects their economic behavior.

Asked for another example, I mentioned the reasons people pay taxes. True, their fear of being punished if they are caught cheating is one factor. But numerous studies, summarized very well in a book by Alan Lewis called *The Psychology of Taxation*, show that people are much more likely to pay taxes if they believe in two things. First, that the goals for which the taxes are used are legitimate—that is, in line with taxpayers' values. (American tax compliance fell during the war in Vietnam, which many considered illegitimate.) People also comply better if they believe the burden of taxes is fairly shared by their fellow citizens. What is considered fair is, of course, a matter of moral judgment. I was rewarded with some nodding of heads that suggested that I was making some inroads.

How People Choose Instruments

Many economists at the seminar held to a flattering view of people's intellectual capabilities. People facing a decision, they held, review various alternative means, building on factual information and drawing logical conclusions from the evidence. In short, economists believe that people choose their course rationally.

This line of argument did not offend me, but I claimed that it was incompatible with the evidence. Several noneconomists at the seminar rallied to help me, citing mountains of robust data showing that human beings' capacity for rational decision making is surprisingly limited. For instance, studies found that people's judgments are more influenced by horror stories in the press than by statistics. (Hence, they believe that in the United States more people are murdered than commit suicide, which the press reports about less often, while the data show that the opposite is true.) Especially striking are the findings that people cannot make the kind of calculations that typical rational economic decisions require, whether they concern mortgage rates, interest rates on student loans, or price differences among items that have different weights or sizes.

Aside from suffering from poor intellectual capabilities, our choice of means (and not just ends) is deeply influenced by our values and emotions. For instance, some people will go out of their way to use recycled paper because of their environmental beliefs, whether or not such use is the most cost-effective.

I half joked that instead of studying why people err, it would be better to assume that most decisions we make are faulty—and study the exceptions, the times when we make solid choices. For instance, education helps some, as does working with others (two minds are better than one on most issues).

Not everyone in the seminar was convinced, to put it mildly. In trying to buttress my case, I rolled out my Alzheimer's story. The power of internalized values is evident in that—despite the high legitimacy that divorce attained in U.S. society in the 1960s and 1970s—few spouses leave their husband or wife when they are afflicted with Alzheimer's (as well as other prolonged, incurable diseases such as cancer and severe paralysis following stroke). None of the "rational" explanations work: the caregivers cannot expect that those who are ill will pay them back. They cannot benefit from "psychic income" of appreciation from the patients, because the patients soon do not even recognize their caregivers and tend to become abusive. Nor does it make sense to claim that caregivers stick around for years on end to provide very challenging care because of what some neighbors might say if they moved away. People seem to persevere out of a strong sense that they ought to, that it is the "right thing to do," although not, by and large, an enjoyable one. I closed my argument by stating: "I am not saying that facts and logic play no role, but much less than economists assume, and values and emotions deeply affect not merely the goals we pursue but also the means we choose."

The Alzheimer's example seemed to carry some weight. The word got around that the seminar was of some interest, and the number of faculty participating in the seminar grew to about twenty. When I ran into the dean of the B school, John McArthur, he slapped me on my back and said, "I hear you are making quite a splash; come and see me sometime." Back at my office, I reached for my phone to call Minerva to share the flattering news. It took a second for me to remember that this was not going to be.

Free Agents?
Whatever popularity I gained in the seminar quickly evaporated when I touched the economists' holy grail: the assumption that people are free to make choices. This assumption is not merely at the heart of economic theory,

but also libertarian ideology—the dominant political belief of the 1980s, the core ideal of Reaganism and Thatcherism.

I pointed to a great deal of evidence that shows that people are deeply influenced by the social groups of which they are members; teenagers, for instance, by their peer groups. I stressed that I was not suggesting that the individual has no freedom, but that it is best to think of people as individuals and *also* as members of groups and not simply as free agents.

Several economist members of the seminar reacted angrily. "People *choose* the groups they join!" Well, hardly those that they are born into and raised in. "People may listen to what others have to say, but ultimately, they make up their own minds! Don't you?" Well, *no*. People often are unaware of the ways groups (of which they are members) influence their thinking and, even more important, their beliefs and feelings. And, "This is some kind of liberalism, blaming society for one's irresponsible conduct." One can take into account the social conditions that affect people's choices and still hold them responsible for what they do, given that they have some measure of independence.

The clearest sign that I was exhausting the patience of some of my colleagues was that the attendance of the seminar declined, although as a semester grows older, such dropping off is not unheard of. I consoled myself by saying that whether or not I was reaching many of the economists who participated in the seminar, I greatly benefited from the give-and-take as I put the final touches on my book on the same subject. Some authors are able to retreat into some isolated place and write their tomes. I find arguments that need to be countered and challenges to better explain what I am trying to say very helpful—the kind of give-and-take this and other such seminars provide. No seminar I ever led or attended was better at goosing me than the Harvard B school faculty.

It took me nearly 300 pages to lay out all the findings showing the merits of building socio-economics based on three assumptions: first, that people are not merely pleasure maximizers but are conflicted between their self-interests and their values; second, that they often act nonrationally; and third, that to a considerable extent they behave as members of groups rather than as free agents. Such a theory, I argue, provides a much more realistic and morally sound foundation for the study of economic behavior than the prevailing theories of economics that dominated the field in the United States at the time. Neoclassical economics had been highly compatible with the individualistic and neoconservative 1980s. But the eighties were ending and there was a palpable need for what George Bush called a kinder, gentler society. Was my socio-economic approach more compatible with the coming decade? Was it historically relevant? An answer came more quickly than I expected.

I Find Plenty of Company

By the end of my stay at the Harvard Business School, my book containing my ideas about economics, *The Moral Dimension: Toward a New Economics*, was published. The B school provided the venue for a meeting of a few scholars to discuss the book close to its publication date in March 1989. When the word about the conference spread, several other scholars asked to join in, offering to pay their own expenses. Soon, several others, who taught or conducted research in the greater Boston area, sought to participate. As the date approached, the number grew. In the end, some 108 professors attended.

Among the speakers were scholars who paved the way to socio-economics: Amartya Sen, who wrote a powerful critique of neoclassical economics called "Rational Fools," and who was later was awarded a Nobel Prize in economics; Neil Smelser, who wrote a major book bridging economics and sociology; and Albert O. Hierschman, a renowned development economist. Harvey Leibenstein, a Harvard economist who had suffered a stroke, nevertheless attended the meeting. (I later made these few honorary members of the new association dedicated to socio-economics that we formed at the end of the meeting. My move prompted Michael McPherson, a philosopher who edited a fine publication called *Economics and Philosophy*, to quip, "Etzioni created an instant pedigree and history for socio-economics.") Participants in the conference included many other scholars whose works I had previously studied and learned to respect.

The principle that guided the meeting, on my request, was to avoid arguing with neoclassical economists. Few such economists were invited; those who were, were maverick economists who had already rebelled against what economists call the "orthodoxy." I felt that we had to see whether we could formulate an alternative theory by talking with those who shared such an agenda rather than keep trying to justify the need for such an enterprise.

The result was nothing but astonishing. People at the meeting were buzzing with excitement. They were like lost souls, each on his or her own journey, who suddenly discovered that they had spiritual and intellectual brothers and sisters. Many of the participants led either a marginal existence in an economics department where their way of thinking was considered deviant or served in other social science departments or professional schools.

Given that my book obviously had occasioned the meeting and the good feelings generated by it, finding many new soul mates was heartening. For the first time, a cause I was championing not only found rich support off campus but also significant pockets of endorsement on campus. Better yet, it turned out that the interest in socio-economics was not limited to a one-meeting wonder. It extended well into the future.

Toward the end of the conference, it seemed natural not to allow all this good energy and excitement to dissipate. My suggestion to form an association of scholars committed to developing the new discipline was well received. We did what academicians do: elected a board (which included Paul Lawrence from the Harvard Business School and Michael Useem, at that time from Boston University). We formed an organization that we called the International Society for the Advancement of Socio-Economics (SASE); I served as the first president.

Regrettably, at the time, we were not clairvoyant enough to realize that closely related, important work was going to be carried out by Robert Frank, Richard Thaler, and Robert Shiller.

A statement of SASE's main thesis was formulated and approved. It reads: "Socio-economics assumes that economics is embedded in society, polity and culture, and is not a self-contained system. It assumes that individual choices are shaped by values, emotions, social bonds, and judgements—rather than by a precise calculation of self-interest."

Building on this platform, SASE's goals were stated as follows:

- To advance an encompassing understanding of economic behavior across a broad range of academic disciplines
- To support intellectual explorations and policy implications of economic behavior within the encompassing context of psychological, societal, institutional, historical, philosophical, and ethical factors
- To balance inductive and deductive approaches to the study of economic behavior at both micro and macro levels of analysis

The group readily agreed to meet annually. We needed a journal. Richard Hattwick, the editor of the *Journal of Behavioral Economics*, changed its title to the *Journal of Socio-Economics* and included our members on his editorial board; overnight we had a journal. A publisher was delighted with our approach and published over the years several collections of papers on socioeconomic topics in a series of books.

In the following years, the group's main events have been annual meetings in select European cities such as Paris and Stockholm and in some American ones, ranging from Irvine, California, to Washington, D.C. Unlike the contentious meetings of the small groups of behavioral economists, ours are congenial. Aside from adhering to our policy of largely avoiding debates with neoclassical economics and of focusing on "doing" socio-economics, the agreeable atmosphere results from the fact that people who attend come because they are interested and committed, rather than for some ulterior motive, such as networking or trolling for jobs in their discipline. Ten years later, SASE had 675 members in thirty-five countries. In short, over the span of a decade, socio-economics turned from a gleam in my eye to an academic discipline with all the trappings.

Originally, SASE was run out of my office, and I had considerable influence over the subjects of the topics addressed during the annual meetings, the keynote speakers, and other such matters of content and organization. After four years, it seemed to me that SASE was strong enough to survive on its own rather than being carried (and controlled) by me. During the New York meeting in 1993, I suggested that the office be moved elsewhere and that control be taken over by others. Bill Frederick, the dean of business at the University of Pittsburgh and president of SASE at the time, was openly skeptical that I would turn over the reins. Soon, however, the first independent executive director of SASE, Richard Coughlin, took over and did a fine job running SASE from New Mexico. From then on, SASE kept flying without me at the controls or anywhere near them. Some later SASE presidents—especially Barbara Bergman—took it in different directions than I would have taken it, but no one wondered anymore whether I would try to prevent my "child" from being adopted by others. While each year I did receive a round of applause when I was introduced as the founder and the first president of SASE, and here and there I delivered an address, I no longer had any say about the ways the meeting program was composed and very little influence over other decisions made by the association. How independent SASE grew was driven home to me when I shared a cab with a young man who was also rushing to a SASE meeting from our hotel. After we introduced ourselves and chatted for a while, he turned to me and said, "You know, this is really a good organization; you should consider joining it."

Looking back on SASE at its tenth birthday, in 1999, I derived a measure of satisfaction from having initiated and helped launch a new academic society dedicated to a new discipline. Much had been achieved in the first ten years. SASE developed many of the instruments of an academic discipline, such as annual meetings, a journal, and books. It grew in the number and stature of its members and the countries from which they hailed. While the journal has been quite poor, publishing many papers irrelevant to socio-economics and weak ones to boot, at least it limped along while the journals of other budding groups collapsed. Individual members and new SASE-based research networks (the brainchild of Rogers Hollingsworth) have produced several strong pieces of scholarship.

At the same time, SASE had yet to generate the kind of economics I was dreaming about: one that is empirically valid, theoretically sound, and based on communitarian ethics rather than individualistic assumptions. Recently, a dialogue between Rogers Hollingsworth, Wolfgang Streeck, Dennis Wrong, and myself on the subject appeared in the first issue of a new publication, *Socio-Economic Review*, edited by David Marsden and Alexander Hicks. Much has yet to be done to consolidate the numerous socio-economics studies into one disciplinary core. And, to serve more fully, it has to break out of academia and reach the public. Currently, policymakers, opinion leaders, and large segments of the public continue to rely on "flat-earth" neo-economics, especially in the United States and increasingly elsewhere.

One reason socio-economics took off in the 1990s, although it has yet to soar, was that the societal atmosphere was more favorable than in previous decades. In the 1980s, neoclassical economics was riding high because it was ideologically compatible with Reaganism and Thatcherism. The reaction to excessive individualism in the 1990s, Clinton's New Democrats in the United States, Blair's New Labour in Britain, and Third Way parties elsewhere favored a new kind of economics. Socio-economics rose in response to the age, but has not quite met its challenge.

CHAPTER EIGHT

Harvard: Peculiar Ethics

Harvard Business School: Peculiar Ethics

To Lie or Not to Lie Is a Question?
Harvard Business School is different from most university departments. It is like a tiny village in which most faculty members know one another personally. Moreover, this community has a strong culture. Unlike Harvard proper (and many other universities), the Harvard Business School culture is hot on teaching rather than on research. A typical discussion in the faculty club during lunch is not about some research project, but about new teaching devices, better usages of the sidebars of the blackboard, or a new instructional film. Before I was let loose on the MBAs, after teaching for twenty years at Columbia University, and after I was invited to conduct a seminar for the HBS faculty—I was given a semester off with full pay (what a luxury!) to prepare for teaching my classes!

It was shortly after I joined the faculty as a visiting professor in 1987 when, during a lunch at the faculty club, I first heard about "the crisis." A professor, colleagues related in muted voices, was teaching the Braniff case. The Braniff case is about an airline that was headed toward bankruptcy. A customer called the head of Braniff, after hearing that it was in financial trouble, and said that he wanted to purchase a bundle of tickets but wondered if the company would still be up and flying a few months hence. The head of Braniff, the story goes, responded that he was not sure. The students argued that the CEO should have lied, that he endangered the shareholders' equity by being candid, that he was representing the shareholders, not the customers.

The faculty was troubled. People dropped in and out of offices to discuss "the situation." Although, theoretically, a classroom is free to draw its own conclusions, it is widely expected that a skillful instructor will guide the discussion to the "proper" conclusions. But in this case the professor himself was puzzled—what was the right answer? Should the CEO have lied?

The professor called on Tom Piper, an associate dean in charge of the school's evolving ethics program, for guidance. Tom was unsure himself and made some phone calls, questioning me among others. When Tom discovered how divided opinions were, he arranged for a faculty-only seminar, in collaboration with political philosopher Dennis Thompson. (Dennis was later appointed by Harvard to foster ethics programs in all of its professional schools.)

The seminar included about twenty faculty members, among them Amy Gutmann (a leading political philosopher from Princeton, visiting for the year), Thomas Schelling (a highly regarded but unconventional economist), Howard Raiffa (a pioneer in decision and negotiation analysis), and Sissela Bok (a philosopher and author of the oft-cited book *Lying*). The seminar coordinator was Arthur Applbaum, a rising young star.

Numerous arguments were made by seminar members to justify lying. One was that in many social situations lying is common and expected, such as bluffing when people play poker. Others pointed to a "market" approach to truth telling: people who are found out to be lying will lose their customers, while those who are trustworthy will gain them. To the extent that this does not occur, it shows that the customers do not appreciate truth telling enough to meet its costs to them.

Many based their assessment on a philosophy called utilitarianism (or, better yet, on a utilitarian consequentialism). In simple English, this philosophy maintains that there are no absolute values; what is moral depends on the consequences of one's actions and on what their utility is. This, in turn, can be established on the basis of a calculus of harm. "By telling the truth, the CEO could have caused the already troubled airline to crash economically, causing harm to the shareholders, employees, and creditors; therefore, the CEO should have lied, even if this harmed some customers" was one way this idea was expressed.

Only two members of the seminar insisted that the CEO should have told the truth. Sissela Bok argued that in all but the most unusual circumstances, lying is not called for; she said: "Deceit and violence—these are the two forms of deliberate assault on human beings. Both can coerce people into acting against their will. Most harm that can befall victims through violence can come to them also through deceit."

Bok evoked a rich image in support of her point: "Even Othello, whom few would have dared to try to subdue by force, could be brought to destroy himself and Desdemona through falsehood."

I argued that truth telling is superior to lying, one of those self-evident truths that speaks to us directly in an unmistakable voice. True, we recognize some exceptions—for instance, when a cancer patient asks if all hope is lost, we have reason to wonder if he really wants to hear the answer. These are cases in which we clearly lie for the benefit of the other, so-called white lies. But these exceptions, whose scope is clearly defined, do not a rule make. (The philosophical camp that supports this position is less well known in the United States than utilitarianism; it is called deontology, from the Greek word *deon*, meaning binding duty. Such a moral sense is subject to critical examination, but the basis is our sense that it is "self-evident" that truth telling is more moral than lying. To nonacademics, the differences between deontology and utilitarianism may seem like an arcane academic debate. It is. But in its own way, it goes to the essence of the difference between true morality and situational ethics or, worse, glorification of self-interest.)

Applbaum, who wrote a detailed account of the seminar, credited me with supplying "important direction [to the seminar] and a stream of challenging ideas." However, these ideas did not carry the day by a long shot. Although the seminar did not seek or reach any official conclusions, it was strongly leaning in the utilitarian direction and, in effect, toward situational ethics.

I felt inadequate and inarticulate and resolved to redouble my readings of ethics to be better prepared if another such opportunity should arise. I was also troubled by some members of the seminar, most from the business school, who seemed to try to find a justification for their peculiar business teachings and practices. At the time, the Harvard Business School included classes that taught students that one could make tons of money by breaking implicit contracts. For example, one buys the shares of a company like Delta Airlines, which in those days had an informal understanding with its employees that it would stand by them through thick and thin, and not fire them even in a recession. In turn, Delta and other such companies assumed that the employees would work harder than they would otherwise and would demand fewer raises and benefits. As a new owner of Delta, the students were instructed to announce that they are not bound by such implicitly agreed to understandings, and then to thin out the labor force. The stock, much data show, jumps up on such news. Then you sell the company and move your nicely fattened investment to another corporation with similar implicit contracts. This, future CEOs of America learned, was one way among others of making money that is a much safer bet and a quicker way of gaining a fortune than developing a new product, producing it, and finding a market for it.

When I first learned about these teachings, I was furious; I had a brief day-dream of grabbing the professors involved by their lapels and telling them, right then and there, how debased their way of thinking was. But on second thought I realized this was a cheap sentiment. It was like going to the movie *Erin Brockovich*, fuming about the ways a corporation maltreated people, and then forgetting the whole thing—until reading about some outrage in some other place and venting again over a meticulously prepared cappuccino and gourmet shrimp salad. I had to find a way to convert my anger into some-thing that had more staying power and social import than simply expressing my dismay. And I was sure some other faculty must share my misgivings. Per-haps they could guide me as to what might be done.

Asking about soul mates, the first thing I was told, in a lowered voice in the posh faculty club, was that the Harvard Business School fired, eased out, or removed those it hired to teach ethics, year after year. Among those let go were Barbara Ley Toffler, Laura Nash, and Joanne Ciulla.

I found out, though, that not all the B school faculty shared the dominant culture. George Lodge was teaching communitarian economics and was very mindful of human and ethical considerations. Paul Lawrence was deeply con-cerned about the fate of the more vulnerable members of society. Howard Stevenson, Al Chandler, and Michael Porter were among the others. How-ever, they did not change the culture of the place.

Could the B school be reformed and turned into a place that would prop-erly educate the future CEOs of America? The answer to this question jumped at me in a critical faculty meeting and in the very class on ethics where I was supposed to teach these incubating business tycoons.

A Pivotal Vote on Teaching Ethics

In 1987, the Harvard Business School received a $20 million grant from John S. R. Shad, chairman of the Securities and Exchange Commission, to support ethics teaching. To overcome faculty resistance, a popular associate dean, Tom Piper, was chosen to promote the program. He spent nearly a year meet-ing with small groups of faculty, trying to allay their concerns and gain their support for teaching ethics. "Some faculties," he explained, "said that if the school insisted that ethics be integrated into all teaching (instead of being taught as a separate course), they would have to close shop." Tom said that this was what several teachers of finance had informed him, without detailing their reasoning. The marketing faculty was also concerned, because it was to a considerable extent in the dissembling business, such as teaching managers to put small products into large boxes and distract consumers from the small print by using brilliant colors on the packaging. Brilliant colors are also believed to encourage compulsive buying; that is, purchasing items people would not get if they considered them rationally. Several other professors wanted the ethics course to be a short one and an elective rather than required.

After months of consensus building, the faculty met on April 21, 1989. Dean John MacArthur introduced as an item of business: "*Tom's* ethics program." He moved his chair to the other end of the platform, as far from Thomas as possible. A masterful politician, the dean had a good sense where his faculty's minds and hearts were. Tom made a fine "spiel" about the need for more ethical CEOs and the leading role Harvard Business School could and should play in their moral education. He had barely finished when Michael Jensen, a diehard economist, stood up and questioned the whole program on the grounds that the faculty was there to teach a science, economics. Others joined in. The few who had some kind words to say about Tom's effort expressed themselves haltingly.

Despite all the ground laying, Tom's ethics program had little support. After the meeting, in effect, it was returned to the drawing board. The overwhelming majority of the HBS faculty did not see a need for teaching ethics and, in effect, felt threatened by it. A sad observation to make about any college, let alone our most renowned one. At the end of the 1980s, one could hardly be in the B school and not be deeply troubled by the absence of an ethics teaching program for the next generation of American business leaders—leaders who also have considerable influence on the whole society.

Since then, HBS has changed some. It now has an ethics program and it finally did grant tenure to a solid scholar to teach ethics, Lynn Sharp Paine. Especially after the Enron et al. scandals, many B schools have added courses that do promote values other than the maximization of investors' and managers' income, and Harvard has been praised as at the forefront of this trend with its "Initiative on Social Enterprise." Such courses generally favor social values, and usually liberal ones, such as concern for the environment or the well-being of minorities and workers in the Third World, rather than traditional values, such as personal integrity, veracity, and loyalty.

Most business school professors choose to steer clear of teaching morality, pointing out, with some justification, that while it is relatively clear what economics dictates and even what the law dictates, what is "ethical" is far from obvious. What appears ethical to one person is not to another, they say, and what is ethical under some conditions is not under others.

A recent Aspen Institute study of about 2,000 graduates of the top thirteen B schools found that B school education not only fails to improve the moral character of the students, it actually weakens it. The study examined student attitudes three times while they were working toward their MBAs: on entering, at the end of the first year, and on graduating. Those who believed that maximizing shareholder values was the prime responsibility of a corporation increased from 68 percent upon entrance to 82 percent by the end of the first year.

In another study, students were asked whether, given a 1 percent chance of being caught and sent to prison for one year, they would attempt an illegal act that would net them (or their company) a profit of more than $100,000. More than one-third (35 percent) responded "yes." In light of the corporate scandals, some B schools will surely attempt to strengthen ethics education. They should recruit more faculty members to teach ethics. And ethics courses should be approached not as a way to circumvent challenges by outsiders, but as moral obligations any decent person heeds. The ethics requirements set by the Association to Advance Collegiate Schools of Business, which is responsible for the accreditation of B schools, should be more straightforward: no MBA student should graduate without having taken at least one full-term course in a class aimed at heightening students' ethical standards. Best, ethics would be integrated into all classes.

Students Teach the Professor a Lasting Lesson

Back in 1987, I was wondering if members of the faculty were not lined up enthusiastically to teach ethics or to cheer its being taught, what about the students? Could they be reached? When I came to Harvard Business School, I saw myself as overprepared to teach ethics to a bunch of MBAs. I said to myself, "So what if these are the best and brightest of future corporate America?" To me, Harvard Business School students were just as bright-eyed, eager, and open to new ideas as any I had had in thirty years of teaching at Columbia, Berkeley, and GWU. Working on a book about economics and ethics, I was loaded with teaching material.

An early indication that these business-leaders-to-be were not to be easily swayed happened during a discussion of persuasive advertising. Most students in my first class firmly believed in "consumer sovereignty," in letting the market provide whatever legal products for which consumers were willing to open their wallets. I challenged this view by asking: "But what about John Kenneth Galbraith's view?" Prolonged silence.

"Galbraith," I elaborated, "argues that corporations actually produce the demand for their product together with whatever they wish to sell—say, male

deodorants. Rather than serving true consumer needs, corporations manufacture needs by advertising aimed at our emotions or subconscious minds."

"Is that ethical?" I asked. One student responded, "I'm not sure there is
such a thing as the subconscious." Another insisted, "If I don't want it, no ad
will convince me to buy it." Well, I continued, years ago male executives
wore only gray-flannel suits and white shirts to work. No one knew they
"needed" shirts in umpteen colors until the industry decided to do to men's
clothing what it already had done to women's. The class did not buy this
point. "We have a built-in desire for variety, for color," a student explained
to me. "Why not satisfy it by enjoying nature?" I asked. "What is it that dictates that we have to buy products to satisfy our need for color, if there is such
a need in the first place?"

My final undoing came a few weeks later, when the subject was moral duties. I told the class that we find duties such as our obligations to our children
compelling; we sense we ought to live up to them. They significantly affect
the way we act, how much we save, how we spend money, and so on.

Most students didn't accept the notion that we are doing things for other
purposes than self-interest. "You expect your friend to visit you when you are
in the hospital—so you will visit him when he is sick," confided one student,
suggesting we do good only to get good in return. "You're trying to impress
your friends with how 'good' you are," offered another. "It makes you feel
good; that's the motivation," declared a third. These future MBAs had
picked up the notions of reductionism, of boiling down whatever is noble in
human behavior to base motives (self-interest, the quest for reputation, or
simply whatever is fun; no wonder they rushed to buy sneakers with the slogan "just do it"). They could not get to first base in their moral considerations as they were denying the very existence of the realm.

So, I tried a different approach. "A delegation from a Middle Eastern nation just arrived to visit," I told the class. "The VIP delegates let their host
know that they expected to be entertained in the style to which they are
accustomed: they expect young boys to join their quarters for the night." I
asked my MBA class if there were any takers, hoping to evoke outrage—an
indication of a moral commitment.

"You did not tell us what the fee is," noted one student, only half in jest.
"Yeah," another picked up, "at first I thought 'no,' but then I wondered how
much was involved." Just as I felt that I reached the end of my rope, had exhausted all the educational moves I knew, one student exclaimed: "Not my
husband; he ain't going." And another muttered, just loud enough to be
heard, "What a disgusting deal!" Others found their voice. This was something several disapproved of—whatever the price.

The class concluded with a divided sense: many held on firmly to the notion that moral statements were merely fig leaves trying to conceal naked self-interest. However, a fair number of others said they could see that there were some moral dos and don'ts that even people in business had to abide by, even when they were not ("necessarily," one added cautiously) good for business.

There were few other encouraging signs that my efforts were not a complete bust. In subsequent classes several students warmed up to the idea that there is considerable leeway in corporate management, that a corporation may do some measure of "good" without becoming uncompetitive. And, while most students were highly unfriendly to labor unions, many came to agree that it was wrong to fire old employees on some fabricated pretext, even if one could get around the law. One student dropped by my study to discuss how he might cut costs in his family business without firing longtime employees, which is what his father was planning to do. However, by and large, I failed to help a class full of future business leaders see that there is more to life than money, power, fame, and self-interest. If I ever had any doubt that the time had come to work not merely for the economic but also for the moral renewal of America—the B school removed it.

"No Family Values, Please; We Are Liberals"

Harvard is like a giant intellectual candy store: there are so many treats everyday, one finds it difficult to choose which to feast on. I picked another faculty seminar, this one convened by two philosophers, Sissela Bok and Daniel Callahan. The seminar's subject was the moral condition and future of the American society. The first meeting explored which topics we should cover. Various people suggested poverty in America, racism, maltreatment of women, and the lessons of the war in Vietnam. I added "the future of the family." No nodding of heads, no additional discussion, no—"interesting suggestion." Next seminar: the chair summarized the topics mentioned last time and nominated one to get us started, but "family" was nowhere on the list.

I raised my hand. The chair, however, didn't seem to see me. Once the discussion was on its way, it was difficult to return to the question of the agenda of the seminar, but I tried. When I was granted the floor, I said "Would an examination of the major moral issues facing American society be complete without discussing the moral infrastructure, especially the family?" No response. The discussion merely continued as if no challenge had been posed.

After the seminar, I walked out with a colleague. "Question," I said to him softly. "I often encounter disagreement, sometimes enthusiastic support, but very rarely no response at all. What gives?"

He explained, "Liberals are afraid to discuss the family. They fear that if there were a widely held agreement that the family must be saved, this would lead to bans on divorce and other coercive measures. Hence, they prefer to let sleeping dogs lie."

I protested: "I am not speaking about coercion, but a *discussion* of what is right and wrong, of changes in our convictions that may lead people to change their conduct *voluntarily*."

"I see your point," he observed in parting, "but the liberals fear that one thing will lead to another."

That evening in my diary, I noted: "Liberals leave the moral agenda and infrastructure to the Religious Right; the country needs a 'democratic' moral center." While I often lacked historical sensibility, this time the liberals seemed to me the dense ones. They continued to focus on unemployment, inequality, racism, and other such important issues. But it made no sociological, ethical, or political sense to cede issues raised by the deteriorating moral foundations of the society to the religious right. These crucial matters also had to be addressed, but in a new way.

I was jerked out of these weighty considerations by a call from my oldest son, Ethan. Ethan is a strong man, who served in the Israeli Air Force, one who does not wear his emotions on his sleeve. But his shaking voice revealed what he was trying to keep under control. "Hedva's [his wife] water broke. We are in the hospital." Such news is sure to delight most expecting parents and grandparents, but a quick count, and then alarm: Hedva's pregnancy had two and half more months to go! Suddenly, the fate of my first grandchild was nothing but a heart-wrenching doubt. Two hours later, I was at the hospital in Manhattan.

Three very long hours passed, and a surgeon emerged, exhausted, milking the moment for all it's worth: "I worked hard," he asked to be appreciated, "but I did it," he finally let out. A tiny Danielle was born. She was in an incubator and would have to stay there for weeks. "We can now do wonders for these preemies, but it was really tough," the surgeon repeated for the third time.

For the next two weeks, Ethan and Hedva spent long days by the incubator, feeding, holding, caressing, and speaking to Danielle, who was barely larger than Ethan's hand. At first, she lost some of the minuscule weight she was born with, which the family followed ounce by ounce. Finally, she pulled through. She gained weight and stature, moved home, and grew up without any ill effects. Somehow, as if she mysteriously sensed my presence in those trying first hours, a special bond formed between us. But this I did not realize until well after I returned to the seminars, books, and students at the B school.

Figure 8.1. Danielle's bat mitzvah with her mother Hedva. Tel Aviv, 2001

Rights and Responsibilities, the Communitarian "Apple"

Newton is said to have discovered the forces of gravity when an apple hit his head. I stumbled over my communitarian "apple" preparing for a class at Harvard Business School. I already mentioned the finding that young Americans, while anxious to maintain their right to be tried before a jury of their peers, were far from keen to serve on one. Much more generally, millions of Americans at the time were more aware of their rights and entitlements than willing to assume their responsibilities for themselves, for those close to them, and for the community as a whole. Welfare reform was still in the future. A common pleading in courts was the "devil made me do it" (fill in for "the devil" your favorite defense—abusive parents, drug addiction, mental illness. These are all extenuating circumstances, but none should be used to argue that one has no free will, has a license to violate the laws and mores of society). All these tendencies called for a correction, not to curtail rights, but to encourage members of society to assume corollary responsibilities.

When I discussed these ideas with my colleagues at Harvard Business School, several mentioned that the roots of excessive me-ism had been exposed in *The Habits of the Heart*, a highly influential book by a group of scholars headed by Robert Bellah. The book finds one major root of me-ism in expressive individualism, the result of the let-it-all-hang-out counterculture of the sixties. The other—in the instrumental individualism of the eighties in which profit and self-interest were raised to the level of a high principle by the ideologies of laissez-faire conservatives (including Thatcherites), libertarians, and certain kinds of liberals.

I added Bellah's book to my reading list, which included other books by sociologists and political theorists who studied the balance between the individual and the community, some of which I covered as a student at the Hebrew University (Durkheim, Tönnies, Park, Mead) and others I read while in Cambridge (including the works of Charles Taylor, Michael Sandel, and Michael Walzer).

After two years in Cambridge, I was more than ready to leave the piles of snow and long months of dreary gray skies behind and return to Washington. I was looking for a place to live, at one point fairly deeply in Virginia. I chatted with the real estate agent about what was happening in the country. I briefly mentioned the lessons that I had brought back from Cambridge: individual rights are to be cherished. However, over the last few decades, social responsibilities have been neglected. We must restore the delicate balance between rights and responsibilities. The moral infrastructure of the country is decaying—we must shore it up, although in the process it may well need to be reconstituted. We must have a dialogue about moral values to bring to the surface shared moral understandings rather than shying away from moral issues out of fear that we would feed a right-wing frenzy.

The real estate agent was glowing. "This is what I've been looking for. All these liberals tell me to be 'tolerant.' The moment I say anything, they treat me as if I were some kind of religious fanatic. They see only two kinds of people: either good folks, willing to fight poverty and racism—or bigoted troops of the right. You make it 'kosher' to speak about moral issues." He made me feel that I was on to something, that this time my ideas were in step with the times.

PART FOUR

LAUNCHING THE COMMUNITARIAN PROJECT

CHAPTER NINE

Fashioning the Message:
Creating a "School"

Three Stages

Usually, I try to keep the "public" side of my life as a public intellectual out of the classroom, but one day, late in 1989, shortly after my return to The George Washington University from Harvard, I was so caught up in my deliberations about how to get the American renewal project off the ground that I did not keep my "public" thoughts to myself. I opened my Contemporary American Society class with a question: "What does it take to change society in a truly significant way?" Without waiting for an answer, I continued, "First, second, and third: a social movement. If you look throughout history, American and otherwise, you will find numerous religious and secular social movements that melted old beliefs and social arrangements and cast the foundations for new ones. The resulting transformations were not always for the better, but only social movements command this kind of blazing force. These include national liberation movements (which blew away colonial powers that dominated large parts of the world and founded national states in Latin America, Asia, and Africa), socialism, fascism, the civil rights movement, the women's movement, and Zionism, to mention only a few."

Now even Heather, who usually passed the class daydreaming, was taking notes, and Jim stopped exchanging whispers with his girlfriend, who practically sat in his lap. I plunged ahead: "Social movements are not organizations or associations, although they may have a core of such. They draw on highly evocative, shared symbols (such as a new flag) and work to formulate new shared values (for instance nationalism). They mobilize the masses by creating social drama through devices such as demonstrations, sit-ins, and boycotts."

The students looked intrigued. Lenora, the best of the lot, wanted to know: "What does it take to form one?" I answered, "Good question; I have been asking myself this for the last few weeks." I avoided disclosing why. My new and tentative grand plan for the renewal project would bridge the divide that separates the academic classroom from the world of public action. "I've found that all movements pass through three stages. At first, they formulate a new message. The environmental movement started with Rachel Carson's book, *Silent Spring*. The contemporary women's movement was launched with Betty Friedan's *The Feminine Mystique*. Martin Luther nailed his new theses to the doors of the cathedral."

I added: "Stage two entails disseminating the new message, bringing it to the people, mobilizing them. Stage three entails embodying the message in the habits of the heart, social arrangements, and public policies."

As I was speaking, it hit me that the term *stages* might be misleading. "*Stages* seems to imply that these three elements come one after the other. They do, but they do not replace one another; they are additions. Thus, in stage two the message is still formed and reformed, but dissemination is added, and so on.

"Stage three is by far the most difficult and important one. Ideas come relatively easy, dissemination takes a great deal of time and effort, but changing people's conduct is particularly challenging. In a successful social movement, as people explore new ideas, *they become convinced of their merits and change their conduct voluntarily!*"

Jim did not seem convinced, so I elaborated, "Let me give an example. Once the environmental movement took off, those who came to believe in its values recycled voluntarily, bought environmentally friendly appliances and cars, and voted for politicians who minded the environment."

Several of the students might not have bought my theory, but I sure did; the only way I could envision large-scale societal renewal was if a social movement could be formed. I did not fantasize that a movement could be formed around this issue of the scope and power of the civil rights movement; I was dubious if one could even match the Moral Majority. I had, though, one clear model before my eyes: the neoconservatives.

In the 1970s, the neoconservatives, a small group of public intellectuals, some campus-based and some freestanding, began to leave their mark on American public life. Although they are often referred to as a group or "school," this movement's members typically wrote as individuals. The group did not meet regularly or issue joint proclamations. Several of its members rejected the "neoconservative" label. They did, though, share several main themes, including a rejection of the counterculture and the welfare state, a sharp criticism of the Great Society programs, and a call to rely on applied social science and pragmatism to sort out what limited social roles the government could play. The group included Irving Kristol (often referred to as the godfather of neoconservatism and the group's most visible member), Daniel Patrick Moynihan, Daniel Bell, Nathan Glazer, James Q. Wilson, and S. M. Lipset. The fact that I knew all these people personally helped. They all came in fairly human sizes; none walked on water. If they could form a school, another similar group might repeat the feat.

The neoconservative school had considerable influence on American thinking (and beyond), gaining broad-based public support and contributing to major changes in public policy and in the ways the nation conducts itself. As a group, it had many times more influence than its members would have had if they were merely acting as individuals. The fact that they constituted a group or school added credibility and leverage to each of them. When one or the other was speaking, people did not say "John Doe thinks . . ." which makes one wonder, "So what? Jane Doe thinks otherwise," but they gained considerable hearing because each person was considered to be speaking for a whole way of thinking. And the group was a known commodity; its members were assumed to be people who had something valuable to say about the times.

Now the times were changing. A reaction was setting in to the excessive individualism that neoconservatives and their followers helped to foment. The country was yearning for a less one-sided way of thinking, a third way between the worshipers of the market and state-hipped liberals and an approach that would not ignore core social-moral values. To effectively respond, the American renewal project needed a school rather than merely individual thinkers, each working on his or her own.

A "Historical" Lunch

I often have lunch at the faculty club, but it never occurred to me when I started on my public intellectual journey that one of these lunches would be the subject of reports in newspapers and become part of the annals of the communitarian movement.

The notable luncheon took place at The George Washington University Faculty Club, to which I had invited William A. Galston, a professor of public affairs at the University of Maryland, to join me for a bite and some dialogue. The invitation followed my reading of Bill's book, *Liberal Purposes*, which suggested that our ways of thinking on social and moral issues over-lapped considerably.

I had met Bill before, when he served as the issues director of Walter Mondale's presidential campaign between 1982 and 1984. (Bill was on leave at the time from the University of Texas, Austin, thus himself one who straddled academia and public life.) On several occasions during that period, I dropped by and tried to palm off some ideas. Bill always listened attentively, welcomed my memos, and implied that he would pass them on to Mondale. However, I could never find a trace of these ideas in the positions Mondale embraced or in his speeches.

I was unsure what Bill thought about my ideas. Given that I believed he would make a sterling member of the yet-to-be-formed new school of thought, it was time to find out.

During our lunch, as the fall semester of 1989 was under way, Bill and I had one of those conversations where one need not complete a sentence because the other already nods vigorously in agreement or adds the remaining fragment. I laid out my views on the American condition and the call for renewal; Bill outlined his views on the civil society and liberal virtues. We spoke at length about the need for a different way of thinking than that of the left and the right, a social philosophy that relied less on the government *or* the market—but more on a sense of responsibility people have for taking care of themselves and other members of their community. We toasted (with D.C. water) the importance of two-parent families; we sang (metaphorically) the praises of the civil society. There must have been something about which we differed, but it was lost in the celebration of finding a kindred spirit.

Two themes came together. I talked at length about the need to replace the culture of self-centeredness with one that would balance self-interest with concern for others and for the common good. And I argued that the rise of the religious right showed that moral issues could no longer be ignored, that our charge was to find democratic responses to the issues religious fundamentalists were raising, instead of ignoring them.

Bill saw the same historical juncture when he talked about the need to move the Democratic Party from its left-liberal agenda toward the American center, drop its preoccupation with Big Government, and insist that the welfare system be reformed, so that those people who are able to take care of themselves will feel obligated to do so. He mentioned that a group called the New Democrats, with whom he worked, was pulling in that direction. The chair of the group was a governor I had never heard of before, one Bill Clinton.

The George Washington University Faculty Club is not a formal place, although some of my colleagues tease me when I march in wearing shorts and sandals during the summer. This time eyes were turned as I left, making short rhythmic steps as if dancing to a tune no one else could hear. When ideas fly fast and furious, they carry me back to my student days in the coffee shop in Jerusalem. It is a high unlike any other. It is intoxicating without numbing the mind; it is filling without tipping the scale. I felt that I might have found a partner. The troops of the communitarian project doubled: from one to two!

Listening to Bill, during lunch and in numerous meetings and phone calls that followed, provided another bonus: I often benefited from his extensive knowledge of the subtleties of political theory and social philosophy, subjects in which I became increasingly interested but in which I was not schooled.

In the process of working together, which continued long after that pivotal lunch, I've gotten to know Bill quite a bit better. Aside from being erudite and politically savvy, he is a *mensch*. Early in our acquaintance, we attended a meeting of about twenty people. As the discussion turned productive, someone suggested, "We ought to take minutes." Another, scanning the room, said, "Nancy, how about acting as secretary?" Bill, sensitive to the sexism and touch of authoritarianism involved, said very softly, "Nancy has not finished her lunch; I will do it." He spoke so gently that nobody felt rebuked.

On many other occasions, I watched with admiration as Bill accepted one thankless chore after the other: chairing a session at a conference in some faraway place; participating as the last discussant on a panel, condemned to be squeezed for time; or attending one more meeting of the Democratic Leadership Council. The only times Bill was reluctant to add another chore to his overburdened schedule was when it conflicted with his family's needs.

During the weeks that followed our lunch, Bill and I formed a list of colleagues from different parts of the country who seemed to us to have shown an affinity with our way of thinking. Next, we issued a joint letter of invitation to some fifteen people.

We had no idea what kind of response we were going to receive. Invitations to meetings are very common, and most contain one form of inducement or another. Some are to coveted places (Aspen, Colorado, a cool place in the heat of summer, or Key West, a warm place in the depth of winter); others entail a handsome fee (sometimes for a paper to be written, sometimes just for showing up). Some invitations even include tickets for "Significant Others." Many are to meetings of academic associations where one meets colleagues who work in the same field and can network, and maybe open the way to a better job. Bill and I could not offer any of these inducements. We invited colleagues to come to Washington to discuss an ill-defined new beginning, to a meeting of people of different disciplines, not only without a fee, but also—at their own expense. We did, though, send them an extensive letter that laid out the purpose of the meeting: to determine whether there was a group of academics who shared the distinct line of thinking we outlined very briefly and to establish where such a shared perspective might lead us.

When twelve of the fifteen we invited agreed to come, I had the first indication of the promise of our idea. How much, or even what it was, was still to be seen. Indeed, I had good reason to approach the meeting with trepidation; academics, especially if they hail from different disciplines, have a hard time agreeing that Tuesday follows Monday, let alone finding common ground on matters concerning social philosophy and its public policy implications.

Groundwork

The first meeting took place in March 1990 at The George Washington University. Those attending formed an impressive group, by any measure. They included a highly respected senior sociologist (Philip Selznick), two firebrand political scientists (Benjamin Barber and James Fishkin), one equally established but much more even-keeled political theorist (Thomas Spragens), a progressive political science star (Jane Mansbridge), a professor of city planning (Seymour Mandelbaum), a senior professor of philosophy (Terry Pinkard), and a younger philosopher (William Sullivan), as well as two activist lawyers (James W. Moorman and Roger Conner).

The discussions that took place are difficult to reconstruct. Only brief minutes were taken and the deliberations were fairly general. Several things, though, were quite clear: the same sense of excitement that emanated from my lunch with Bill was palpable here, and intensified as the meeting progressed. Many of those who attended the meeting shared the sense that we were thinking along lines that diverged from those already established, thinking that could not be characterized as either liberal or conservative. We sensed more that we were onto a new perspective than we were able to define it. Most everyone agreed that we had to break out of the debate about the merit of free market versus big government and recognize the full importance of community; we had to be concerned with the moral foundations of the country but not by simply trying to restore the old ones. While most of the discussion was general, two specific issues were faced.

Rights *and* Responsibilities

The first subject we delved into was the explosive growth of individual rights, accompanied by the loss of a sense of social responsibility. The thesis I put before the group was that even when it comes to rights, there can be too much of a good thing. Certainly, one must ensure that society fully respects the rights of individuals and vigilantly protects them. However, there is little sense to claiming that drivers have a right to refuse to be stopped at roadblocks to determine whether they are drunk or that drug dealers have a right to loiter on street corners. Also, people have to accept that they have social responsibilities and not just rights, especially the responsibility of taking care of their near and dear and themselves. Finally, people have to be willing to make some sacrifices for the common good.

William Sullivan, a soft-spoken, modest, solid philosopher and one of the coauthors of *Habits of the Heart,* captured the essence of my long-winded opening with a few choice words: "What is rational becomes irrational when pushed to an extreme."

Bill Galston warned that we should not imply that the more rights one gains, the less responsible one becomes, and vice versa. Jim Fishkin, Jane Mansbridge, and Benjamin Barber all shared Bill's concern.

I was slow to join the evolving consensus. I held that some rights had to be trimmed—for instance, such manufactured claims as Americans have a "right" to credit cards (as the companies that peddled them maintained). And I believed that one can add new responsibilities without trimming any rights, such as our duty to help the poor and our responsibility to the environment.

After much more discussion, by midafternoon a consensus did emerge. Before a twice-delayed break, we all agreed: "We are not against rights. We fight for strong individual rights paralleled by an assumption of social responsibilities. We object to rights talk that assumes that the whole moral turf belongs to rights without any attention to other considerations. This may entail some reinterpretation of rights or greater attention to the common good."

What's in a Name? Different Kinds of Communitarians

After the break, Benjamin Barber took the floor to "object strenuously" to the term *communitarian,* which had come up several times during the preceding discussion, and one I suggested our group might adopt as a name for our way of thinking. Words spring out of Barber as if every other one is armed with an exclamation point. He projects so well, one can hear him loud and clear from the other end of a sizable hall, without any amplification. He can be very insistent. Moreover, what he opposed worried me, because he had a valid point.

The term *communitarian* has a checkered history. The term was first introduced in 1841 to refer to communists, of all things. The term was rarely used in the next few decades, but, when applied, it was in a similar manner. Even today this would not be a welcome association; it was much less so in 1990 as the Soviet communist empire was just crumbling.

In the 1980s three scholars, Charles Taylor, Michael Sandel, and Michael Walzer, became known within academic circles as "communitarian," although, oddly, they themselves almost never use the term in their own works and did not describe themselves as communitarians. One reason for this aversion might have been that the term *communitarian* was adopted by authoritarian East Asian leaders who made short shrift of rights for the sake of social order (and their dictatorial posts), such as Prime Ministers Lee Kuan Yew in Singapore and Mahathir bin Mohamad in Malaysia.

Barber demanded: "Why would we wish to become associated with such an authoritarian camp?" I countered, "No other term would allow us to stress that community is our central concern, not the state nor the market." I also pointed out that often one term is applied differently by different groups. Socialism, for instance, refers to democratic labor parties in Scandinavia, communists in the Soviet Union, and even Nazis, which stands for "national socialists."

The discussion dragged on. There were moments when it seemed that despite our agreement on basic principles, we were going to break up over a name. Finally, we concluded that we would add a qualifier to set our communitarianism apart from that of others. Our brand was going to be "responsive communitarian." The term, I explained, stands for deeply democratic institutions that respond to people, not those that lord over them. It would surely set us apart from both communists and East Asian, authoritarian communitarians.

As the day-long meeting neared its end, it was evident that if we were to form a school of thought, we had to go beyond articulating a few shared but general principles. At the same time there was an unspoken concern that if we tried to tease out what these principles meant for specific issues and public policies, we might well end up splintering the group. Still, without some such specifications we were going to be left merely with the delight of sharing some abstractions. I took the plunge and called for a second meeting. There was much hesitation in the room. It took a good half hour before the group agreed to reconvene.

The group zeroed in on three very divergent and hot topics for the next meeting: the future of the two-parent family, HIV testing and disclosure of the results to previous and prospective contacts, and mandatory community service in high schools. We decided to ask three colleagues to open the discussion on each of these topics. A time was set, six months down the road.

While I was elated about the meeting, indeed, it greatly exceeded what I had hoped for, I feared that once enthusiasm waned, few would show up for the second meeting. That would not make much of a school. One way to improve our prospects was to expand the circle of those invited.

A New Partner: Mary Ann Glendon

In the months that passed between the first and second meeting, I asked Mary Ann Glendon from Harvard Law School if we could get together. My purpose, I told her up front, was to brief her about the first meeting and explore whether she would care to join the next one. I was very taken with Glendon's new book, *Rights Talk*. In it, she shows that out of the sixties a language emerged that greatly damaged American discourse. It biased people to examine every issue in the legal terms of claiming rights, which—unlike expressions of needs or interests—are much more absolutist in formulation and less open to compromise. When A says I need a raise and B says she cannot afford to give it to me, nobody claims a priori that the other is in the wrong. There is room for negotiation and for splitting the difference. However, when A says more money is my right, I am entitled to it, by law and by all that is right, any counterclaim is framed as a violation of a legal and moral principle. There is much less room for give-and-take—one does not trade in rights. And there is more of a tendency to state, "If you won't honor my right, see you in court." All this leads to a litigious and conflicted society on matters that might well have been settled through mediation and compromise.

When one first meets Mary Ann, one notes her warm smile, easy conversation, and highly supportive style. (After we became acquainted, Mary Ann often sent me short, congratulatory messages on one article or another.) Slowly, I got to know the other Mary Ann, the one who does not mince words in giving voice to her very strongly held Catholic values, especially her opposition to abortion. (A few years later, she headed the delegation of the Vatican—not often represented by women—at the United Nations World Conference on Women in Beijing in 1995.) I was smitten by this gentle true believer and awarded myself a brownie point when she agreed to join our nascent group. I knew there was no shortage of firm pro-choice members of the group; with Mary Ann among us, we were sure to speak not only to the liberal part of the world. And, given her stature as a law professor at Harvard and as the author of what was, in effect, a highly communitarian book, she would add much to our luster.

The fact that Mary Ann strongly favored social justice only added to my respect for her. She was equally ecumenical in her personal life. She mentioned the black civil rights leader she had been married to, and their child whom she adored. And she introduced me to her Jewish husband, Ed Lev.

Breakthrough

Mid-October 1990 was the time set to test our new approach: could it truly cast a new light on significant matters of public concern?

I realized, of course, that this was going to be an unusual meeting. At other meetings, you get a second, even a third chance. If your department does not approve your idea for a new course, there is always next semester. If a congressional committee refuses to allow you to testify about whatever troubles you (and about what you believe must be done to save the world)—there is always another committee. But this time there was no fallback. If the group at this meeting did not buy into the communitarian project, if the members departed without sensing that we shared more than a vague conception, the whole school would come to naught. There was no way we could continue after such a failure or reassemble the group for a third time. Indeed, if many of my new colleagues in arms did not show up for this second meeting, it would hardly be surprising. If I'd had a strand of worry beads, I would have worn them out.

I tried to scold myself for making such a fuss about what was, after all, just a meeting, nothing like the agony of waiting for the medical report about the black moles that had appeared on the skin of one of my sons (melanoma, the cancer from which his grandmother had died?), or the scary thirty hours of hard labor before another one agreed to join the world of the living and we found out he scored well on the APGAR scale (which measures the physiological well-being of newborns). There was no denying, however, that it mattered a great deal, if the communitarian project was to be born and grow.

HIV Testing, Contact Tracing, and Fair Warning

The first sign that the second meeting would not be a bust was when practically all of those who attended the first one showed up, as well as a few new ones. The meeting opened with a discussion of HIV, led by James Childress, a professor of religious ethics from the University of Virginia, whose writings on bioethics were distinguished. The issue Childress addressed was sharply drawn: AIDS was a horrible epidemic, yet public authorities were not treating it like other infectious diseases such as TB or hepatitis. Public health authorities heeded gay and civil libertarian groups, who maintained that it was fine to provide information about AIDS to one and all, but beyond that it was each individual's purview to decide how to conduct him- or herself. Their right to autonomy and privacy trumped all other concerns (some of these groups even opposed closing gay "bathhouses" in which visitors had numerous partners, most of whom they hardly knew, often without taking precautions).

AIDS activists and civil libertarians had many arguments on their side. They pointed out that public knowledge of HIV-positive status put one's job, housing, and health insurance in jeopardy and added further stigma to people who were often already stigmatized. Moreover, they maintained, everyone should engage in safer sex anyhow, at all times; hence, warning a new sex partner that one was HIV-positive was not called for.

On the other side were several overzealous social conservatives who viewed homosexuality as a grave sin and sought to ban homosexual activities (for instance, by trying to enforce antisodomy laws) and to segregate those infected with HIV from society. Whatever respect for individual rights these social conservatives held, they evidently did not extend it to homosexuals.

The question we had to address was toward what course communitarian thinking should point. Childress argued, "HIV-infected individuals have responsibilities to others and to the community as a whole, as well as rights against others and the community. Ideally, everyone at risk of HIV infection would seek testing and if infected would avoid putting others at risk. In addition, he or she would disclose this fact—or authorize others to disclose this fact—to people who may be at risk as a result of sexual contact or needle sharing."

Childress's language was dry and carefully measured, but his point was pivotal: we had to find a way to both serve the society's need to stem the spread of the dreadful disease—and to respect individual rights. This led Childress to an important distinction that seemed to me at the core of the communitarian position: the difference between persuasion and coercion. As he put it, we must "distinguish *expressing community* from *imposing community* and to argue that we can protect the public health more effectively if we first develop policies that express community rather than rushing to impose community (through coercive laws). Even though it is sometimes necessary to impose community (against recalcitrant individuals), it is likely that the expression of community will engender widespread voluntary cooperation, for example, in contact tracing and partner notification, and reduce the need to impose community."

I cheered Childress on by adding: "The emphasis on the moral culture is a cardinal insight of the communitarian perspective. Liberals object even to moral censure of HIV carriers who do not inform others; conservatives rush to call in the state. Communities lead with their moral voice, appreciating those who act responsibly, and chastising those who do not. When the law is called in to enforce a social position on a broad basis rather than dealing with a few recalcitrant individuals, it is a sign that the community is failing."

Benjamin Barber asked urgently: "Do we have a right to override the rights of HIV-infected people?" He answered his own question: "No one has a right to have sex without informing one's partner of one's HIV status. This is one's responsibility to the community."

Sullivan, speaking for a moment like a liberal, believed that the core of "our position must enhance personal dignity and autonomy."

I added, "If we're to call on people to 'be responsible,' we also ought to say, 'we're going to do all we can to ensure that you will not suffer from discrimination.' We will act to protect people's jobs, housing, and health insurance, which are often endangered for those known as HIV or AIDS carriers."

Barber introduced an important consideration: "We don't want to encourage policies that *disempower* people. You shouldn't take away people's sense that they must act responsibly by forcing them to act properly. Once the state becomes the agent of moral enforcement people feel that they no longer need to sustain their own obligations."

At this point, Jim Fishkin, Roger Connor, and Terry Pinkard all jumped in, addressing finer points of ethical and legal considerations at issue.

I feared that the shared understanding that was evolving was about to evaporate. Before I figured out how to get the discussion back on track, Sullivan offered to summarize the emerging consensus: "You are morally derelict if you don't inform your prior and prospective partner(s). We shall strongly advocate this moral claim. The community should protect you from discrimination and loss of your job."

Everyone seemed satisfied with this last formulation. We had reached a shared position on a major social, moral, and policy issue! And it was a distinct one! Moreover, our evolving position was also politically savvy. It provided a much more democratic and humanitarian response to an issue that liberals were very reluctant to address but the country had to face and that social conservatives used to beat up on people.

While I tried not to show it, who could fault me for being elated? A whole slew of academics combined to formulate a major, new, shared public position. Trust me, this takes place only when the stars are properly aligned. This time they were shining on the communitarian project, and they were not done.

Pro-Family and Community Service

What happened was truly surprising; at least, I had never attended a meeting that evolved the way this one did next. Two more topics were explored: the value of the two-parent family (a discussion initiated by Bill Galston) and mandatory community service for high school students (a give-and-take directed by Benjamin Barber). Both explorations unfolded in a way similar to our discussion of HIV, despite the fact that on the surface, they concerned very different matters, thus boosting our sense of the value of our communitarian approach.

In examining the future of the family we set ourselves apart from the liberal view, which held that all kinds of family—single parents, two parents, gay marriages—were all "alternative lifestyle" options of equal value. We also disagreed with social conservatives who campaigned for a return to traditional marriages, women in the nursery and kitchen, "graciously submitting to their husbands." We wanted no part of a way of thinking that was all too ready to force people to do what the community considered moral, for instance, by banning divorce, as was done in the 1950s in many states and still is in other conservative parts of the world. We argued that on average a two-parent family was better equipped to bring up children than are single parents, but fathers and mothers had the same rights and responsibilities. Various measures were suggested to promote such a family, including teaching high school students strategies in conflict resolution intended to help sustain their future marriages and removing the marriage penalty imposed by the tax code.

Galston tied our view of how the family should be promoted to the same core theme that emerged when we discussed HIV: "There can be little doubt that whenever a meaningful choice exists, it is preferable to create moral incentives for socially desirable behavior rather than to employ directly coercive measures. But in family policy, as elsewhere, this choice is not always available. The law— the moral voice of the state—must sometimes command as well as cajole."

Fishkin added, "We have created economic incentives for the single-parent family in our welfare policies. If the community is to provide support for the family—then the government must change these incentives."

Terry Pinkard stressed, "This is not about poor people's problems. The middle-class family is also being undermined. We must address all families." This, I thought, was a point communitarians could not stress enough. Too many public policy discussions sounded as if the social-moral crisis the country faced was limited to the underclass.

After much more give-and-take, Pinkard moved us to closure: "What have we agreed to? First, we raise a moral voice in favor of a positive child-rearing environment. Second, build a community infrastructure to support this child-rearing environment. Third, we're encouraging a two-parent and interactive/effective family. Fourth, making sure to prioritize women, so that our position will not be misunderstood as an attack on feminism." (We later learned to call the concept we favor—a two-parent family but one in which fathers and mothers have the same rights and responsibilities—a "peer marriage." We owed the term to sociologist Pepper Schwartz.)

A Heated Discourse

In the last presentation Benjamin Barber strongly urged us to support requiring high school students to do community service as a condition for their graduation. They should be made to volunteer a fixed number of hours, in a soup kitchen, hospital, or local library. Barber emphasized that community service was not just a matter of altruism, doing good deeds, but that it benefits youngsters. "Community service teaches citizenship, the ways to participate in the civic society." It also exposes students to people of different social and economic conditions than their own.

Someone suggested that mandatory volunteerism is an oxymoron. Barber rushed to respond, "95 percent of what is taught in high school is required." He added that community service is basically the practicum of civics classes.

Laissez-faire conservatives and libertarians—I knew—were vehemently opposed to community service, let alone mandating it. Among the nicest things they had to say was that all "public schooling was tantamount to government indoctrination of the nation's young—citizenship training is just an extension of a bad idea." And, "What mandated service is teaching is that it's selfish or evil to pursue your own goals. It is teaching that it is your duty to service the government."

The discussion took me back to a meeting on voluntary service at the Hoover Institute at Stanford. Doug Bandow from the CATO Institute, who was attending the meeting, opposed even voluntary service on the grounds that its advocates really were after compulsory service. Bruce Chapman, founder of the Discovery Institute, compared national service to an illness that flares up once in a while and that acts like a tax on people's time. All this was small potatoes compared to Milton Friedman, who, during the same meeting, compared voluntary community service to the Hitler Youth. (Nothing personal here; his comments on my paper were moderate and conciliatory.)

Returning to the discussion at hand, I asked if "mandatory" was the way to go. "My experience in Israel taught me that voluntary community service can be very appealing," I said. "At least we should start advocating it before mandating it."

Barber responded somewhat assertively, "A fundamental need of democracy is to educate for citizenship. Community service provides such education. Hence, it should be mandatory."

Galston objected gently, "If the point is that people aren't good citizens unless they're doing community service, then I can't endorse it. I think you can learn citizenship in other ways."

There were many more exchanges along the same lines. Most members of the group except Barber were learning toward voluntary community service, but nobody wanted to close the long and productive meeting on a note of disagreement. So, without anybody openly stating it, we moved to close, leaving in the air the understanding that most of us favored community service as part of a newly invigorated moral culture, but not as a state requirement.

At this point in most meetings, some people leave, saying that they are sorry but they have to catch a flight or they have another obligation. Others fidget, check their watches, and assemble papers. Some engage in private conversations with those seated next to them. None of this was happening this time, it was as if people regretted that the meeting was ambling to an end.

I checked, "How does everyone feel?" Galston: "I'm encouraged. There is clearly a center which holds us all here. Let's write it down. There is more than overlap here. We can affirm and agree on principles." Right on!

Fishkin: "We must remember to separate ourselves from communitarian extremists who believe community concerns should trump individual ones. We're searching for an in-between."

Glendon urged us to "not be afraid of the complexity of the matters at hand." I was unsure of the implications of this valid observation but did not ask. Pinkard was the least "sold" of the group: "Let's not rush into claiming we have a great deal in common." Most others talked with considerable excitement about the joy of coming together, of finding a "third" approach. However, no specific next steps were discussed. A school was born, but could it find a voice?

Hammering Out a Platform

First Principles

Were we ready for the next step—raising our voice in public? And if so, how was that voice to be raised? Issuing a joint statement that articulated the principles of our school, I realized, would be to venture further than the neoconservatives had. They were acting as individuals, whom the media lumped together into one school. I believed that a joint written statement of our principles and core positions would serve both to formulate our message, the starting stage of social movements, and move us into phase two, disseminating the message.

It did not take particular smarts to realize that it was one thing for a group of professors to be excited by the coming together of minds in a meeting or two, and quite another for them to be able to craft and endorse a shared written statement. At the same time I feared that if I drafted it alone, my colleagues might object, even if I drew directly on our joint deliberations. They might feel that I was trying to foist my views on the group.

After consultations with Mary Ann, Bill, and some others, I concluded that we'd better take the risk, lest our whole thrust will peter out. I drafted the platform and sent it to Bill and Mary Ann, who each made numerous suggestions for revisions, additions, and omissions. The result was a document that read better than most statements born to a committee.

The revised draft, which we called "The Responsive Communitarian Platform," was sent to those who attended the two founding meetings and to several others, leading to extensive give-and-take. Faxes were flying one after the other. My long-distance bill for those months was, well, long. Most suggestions for revision were readily accommodated, but one major issue did arise. Robert Bellah objected to the phrase "universal values" or any other such wording that might imply an endorsement of absolute values. Philip Selznick objected along similar lines, although in his own very gentle way. Any notion of moral absolutes scares progressive people, who recall the influence of totalitarian regimes and the Church.

In contrast, I believed that without recognizing universal principles, of which human rights is but one, and social responsibilities (expected of all, although the communities to which they are responsible may vary), communitarianism was but a form of relativism. If we did not recognize any values above and beyond those upheld by various communities or cultures, we would deny ourselves a basis on which to rest moral claims. Nor could we challenge other nations' practices of stoning adulterous women, chopping off limbs of thieves, jailing dissenters, and trading sex slaves, not to mention child labor, forced marriages, and female circumcision. And these nations would lack a moral foundation to justify their call on us to better respect our elders, abolish nuclear weapons, limit our military interventions in other nations, and so on. Based on my deontological inclination, I argued that there must be a few select moral causes that all people would find compelling—once they were able to examine them in a free dialogue. (I granted that historically these universal values have been hidden from people in oppressed countries.) To my regret, I failed to convince my colleagues, and the platform merely states that "our communitarianism is not particularism. We believe that the responsive community is the best form of human organization."

The final draft that resulted was circulated to provide one last chance for comments. No one else volunteered or could be volunteered, so I stepped forward and "managed" the processes of getting comments, securing revisions, ensuring that those whose suggestions we could not accommodate stayed with us.

My experience serving on the National Board of the ADA (Americans for Democratic Action) served me here. The board followed a very unproductive procedure; once a year it would present to the annual meeting a huge number of resolutions on everything from the disposal of the Panama Canal to treatment of Castro to better ways to fight poverty, pollution, racism, and crime, among other matters of great and not-so-great social import.

During the annual meeting, these draft resolutions would be hotly debated with numerous suggestions concerning minor rewording. At the end of the meeting these resolutions would be "published," which meant that a copy would be mailed to the yawning press and busy policymakers—as a rule without any discernable notice, let alone effect.

To avoid futile quibbles and to keep attention on the essence of our message, I added, at the end of the draft platform, the phrase: "Signatures signify that we are of one mind on the broad thrust of this platform and the necessity of this intervention into the current dialogue, without necessarily agreeing to every single, specific statement." It worked. People who had minor objections found that they could nevertheless endorse the platform. (People were also accorded the opportunity to endorse the platform but indicate that they did not support one of its planks. Only four availed themselves of this option.)

The final text of the platform, the guiding document of the communitarian project, has been republished and translated often. It opens by stressing the importance of community and a readiness to assume social responsibilities:

> Neither human existence nor individual liberty can be sustained for long outside the interdependent and overlapping communities to which all of us belong. Nor can any community long survive unless its members dedicate some of their attention, energy, and resources to shared projects. The exclusive pursuit of private interest erodes the network of social environments on which we all depend, and is destructive to our shared experiment in democratic self-government. For these reasons, we hold that the rights of individuals cannot long be preserved without a communitarian perspective.

To avoid even the appearance that we opposed individual rights, we stated:

> A communitarian perspective recognizes that the preservation of individual liberty depends on the active maintenance of the institutions of civil society where citizens learn respect for others as well as self-respect; where we acquire a lively sense of our personal and civic responsibilities, along with an appreciation of our own rights and the rights of others; where we develop the skills of self-government as well as the habit of governing ourselves, and learn to serve others—not just self.

We stressed the role of the moral voice versus the state or market and called for the formation of a communitarian movement:

> Moral voices achieve their effect mainly through education and persuasion, rather than through coercion. Originating in communities, and sometimes embodied in law, they exhort, admonish, and appeal to what Lincoln called the better angels of our nature. They speak to our capacity for reasoned judgment and virtuous action. It is precisely because this important moral realm, which is neither one of random individual choice nor of government control, has been much neglected that we see an urgent need for a communitarian social movement to accord these voices their essential place.

The rest of the platform speaks to more specific issues such as our responsibilities as members of families and communities, educators, and citizens in the polity.

When the process of rewriting and revising the platform was completed, I let only my two closest friends know how tickled pink I was. Only those who were with me during all the years and decades of working on projects that tackled important issues but did not take off could fully appreciate why this time I was showering in imaginary confetti and bathing in metaphorical champagne. I beseeched my friends to keep mum because I feared that if the word got out that the whole initiation of the communitarian project was the work of one or two colleagues, this might distract from its appeal. But in my heart of hearts I was proudly celebrating. Finally, after all these years, something of promise was beginning to happen. I knew how much of the work was done by whom, and that had to do.

Working with Bill, I brought together some of the best minds of my adopted country to issue a compelling and rich statement, one that reflected a worldview and values close to my heart. The first step toward a social movement, forming a message, had been taken. Most important, the message could not have been more timely, responding to the moral crisis but in ways that would take the wind out of the sails of the religious right. (At the time, the religious right was much more powerful than at the beginning of this century. It played a key role in several state governments, numerous school boards, in formulating the Republican platform, and selection of judges and government elected and appointed officials. The right was also much more active at the time in public condemnation of gays, liberals, sex education, school reforms, and much else. Pat Robertson and Jerry Falwell were major public figures with substantial political influence. Moreover, the religious right's power, at the time, seemed set to continue its rise, stoking the fear that a point might be reached at which the right could impose its values on the rest of the nation.)

At the same time, my personal life was also mending. Jewish tradition has it that whoever arranges for a match has a secure place in heaven. Susan Tolchin, a colleague and friend of many years, took me under her wing after I returned to Washington from Cambridge. Her first attempt was a bust. The woman she introduced me to had just earned millions from her second, gossipy bestseller. She was so preoccupied by the lawsuits she faced, tons of dough she had to invest, and the movie rights she was angling for that she had little room for anything else. Susan scored much better on her second try. Pat Kellogg and I hit it off from the start. After a while, we felt ready to meet each other's children; we married toward the end of 1991. On a typical evening Pat would unload some of the troubling cases she faced during her day as one of the most sought-after physicians in Washington, and I found a patient and sympathetic ear for my anxieties.

One evening, after gloating a bit (or was it more?) about our achievements, I noted, more to myself than to Pat, that it very much remained to be

Figure 9.1. With Pat, 1991

seen how much following our communitarian "school" would engender. All we had so far was a declaration by a small group of academics. While we had grown from two to fourteen, this did not quite make a crowd, let alone a social movement. My celebratory balloons came down to earth quite quickly. At best, we were at the very beginning. We did formulate a message, but could we end up like someone who invited one and all to a party, but no one came? Could we get the word out, and if we did, to what effect?

CHAPTER TEN

———— ⊗⊗⊗ ————

Fashioning the Message:
From One to Many

Endorsements: A Big Tent

The Diversity Conundrum

After the drafting and redrafting of the platform was completed, I invited those involved from the outset and an assortment of other colleagues and public leaders to endorse it. There was no way of telling how many people, if any, who did not participate in our deliberations would see their way clear to endorsing a twelve-page-long document. This was especially true because many of those invited to endorse the platform had heretofore identified themselves (most publicly) with a liberal or a conservative camp. We had dreamed up a school and invited people to join, but there was no way of knowing whether anyone would come be a part of it. Declarations are rather common; endorsements are a diamond a dozen.

There was no specific rationale for the selection of those invited. I included people of different political viewpoints, excluding only the extreme left and immoderate right, to highlight our nonpartisan position. I also sought out people whose stature would add prestige and visibility to the platform—and thus to the communitarian project—and people of diverse social backgrounds.

The first two criteria were straightforward; the third was anything but. Anyone who is involved in the selection of people for any position—from the president of the United States to an assistant professor, from Pulitzer Prize winners to blue-ribbon recipients for the heaviest hog in the county— is painfully aware of the contested issues involved. Debates typically arise between those who favor making choices strictly on what they consider merit and those who believe that such selections should also help correct for past and present discriminatory practices. (Later, during the year I served as president of the American Sociological Association, these issues demanded more attention than all the others combined.)

I found the debate about diversity and representation particularly tantalizing because I could see some merit in both sides of the argument. I tried to find a third way, which left me with an eclectic, hardly novel, and unsatisfactory position. (In my search I was particularly influenced by the works of Harvard law professor Randall Kennedy, Yale law professor Stephen Carter, and University of Chicago sociologist William Julius Wilson.) Maybe because of my childhood in Nazi Germany, I found merit in the argument that one should take into account all of a person's past social history (including social class), instead of focusing exclusively on race. I asked, rhetorically, should not a poor, handicapped, white person from Appalachia at the top of his high school class garner more admission points to a college than, say, the son of a multimillionaire member of a minority group? Still, I could not ignore that often, despite a great deal of change, minorities and women continue to be poorly represented pretty much everywhere.

Certainly, it could be debated whether one ought to secure equal representation of women and minorities in all vocations and positions and if it must always be proportional. But as far as we were concerned, we could hardly speak of the national society as a community and not include all parts of it. Moreover, there are few matters that can turn out to be more contentious and divisive—and thus subversive of community—than fights over the criteria for admission. My brief membership in the Cosmos Club was an object lesson that stayed with me as I was struggling with the list of people invited to endorse the Communitarian Platform.

Women to the Back Door

After I moved to Washington in 1978, I joined the Cosmos Club, a private club dedicated to "the advancement of its members in science, literature, and art." A few months later, I discovered that its bylaws stated: "This club shall be composed of men." As late as 1980 women were not allowed on the upper floors and could visit the lower floor only as guests of male members. And, I realize this is hard to believe, but fully true—until 1973 they were expected to enter via a back door, labeled the "Ladies' Entrance." Repeated efforts to open club membership to women were defeated by a small clique of old fogies. They protected the discriminatory policy by calling for board meetings in midmorning, when younger members were at work. They even got sixteen former presidents of the club, even older fuddy-duddies, to claim that to admit women would begin "the transformation of one of the world's distinguished men's clubs into a mere luncheon group." Now you've heard it all.

Although some of the younger members grumbled and signed petitions, only a very few resigned in protest. I was among those who did. (Please shed no tears; the food—in the roast beef, mashed potatoes, and buttered peas tradition—and the membership, left much to be desired.) In deciding to resign, I argued that even if one concurred that some private clubs had a right to exclude some people—these reasons did not apply to the Cosmos Club. The club's membership was based on "accomplishment and achievements," not on being an alumnus of an Ivy League institution or being the descendent of a deckhand on the *Mayflower*. It was preposterous to the nth degree to maintain that there were no women who could match the accomplishments and achievements of the club's male members.

Shortly after some of us resigned, the club warned its members to stop *discussing* the matter or they would be kicked out. Moreover, new members were required to sign a statement that they were joining a "men's club," and that they would not campaign or even think about admitting women into the club. When I was asked about these dictates by a reporter, I responded, "My knowledge of history is limited, but I think the last time an organization told its members to stop thinking about a certain issue was in the seventeenth century." The lesson was that ensuring diversity was not merely a matter of elementary justice but also crucial for avoiding bitter, even silly, confrontations.

By Definition, Community Excludes

Shortly after the invitations to sign the platform were mailed out, I found myself lingering next to my inbox when the mail was due. I also made sure that the fax machine had plenty of paper. As the responses trickled in very slowly, at least for my taste, I called several of the invitees to ask, "Are there any questions I can answer as you consider endorsing the platform?" The frequent responses were, "Why, no, I already mailed the thing back," and "Did you also invite so-and-so?" These reactions were the first indication that our endeavor might be taking off. This impression was soon backed up by a steady stream of endorsements. As more and more endorsements piled up, I organized them in groups to determine to what extent we were achieving the diversity we required.

Endorsements from African Americans included those of the ebullient Sylvia L. Peters (a founding partner of the Edison Project, which was created in 1991 and is the country's leading private manager of public schools), eloquent Kenneth Tollett (a higher education policy scholar from Howard University), Anthony Cook (Georgetown University law professor), and Joyce

A. Ladner (a highly respected sociologist and high-ranking public official). Orlando Patterson's (Harvard University sociology professor) endorsement was important, not only because he is a particularly well regarded scholar, but also because he is known to kowtow to no one.

From all these endorsements, none generated more delight than that of Enola Aird. Enola, who refers to herself as "an activist mother," is a strong advocate of the two-parent family and consistently practices what she preaches. She is also active on behalf of the African American community and the community at large by serving on commissions, producing radio programs, and writing op-eds. We met by sheer chance while watching a taping of a Fred Friendly TV show in which her husband Stephen Carter, the renowned Yale scholar, participated. Her endorsement of the platform was a good omen.

From then on, Enola frequently spoke for the communitarian movement, participated in our meetings, and participated as a key member of our task force on the family. In the process we became friends; not the kind who call each other regularly with "you know what happened today?" and share intimate details of their personal lives, but of the kind who work together well and enjoy each other's company.

I was hence taken aback when one day over lunch Enola mentioned that she was ever so pleased that the summer was approaching; soon, she and her family would retreat from the Yale community to Oak Bluffs. "Oak Bluffs?" I inquired. (I knew it to be the home of a middle-class African American community in Martha's Vineyard.) "Yes," Enola explained, "to be with my own kind." As my face must have registered some astonishment, Enola elaborated, "You know, to be able to let our hair down, to tell our kinds of jokes."

These brief comments evoked many deliberations. It does not take a Ph.D. in sociology to realize that it is essential that community members be "comfortable" with one another and that this is much more readily achieved among people who are "of the same kind." But, at the same time, this means that communities exclude people who are different, which goes against the grain. There may be no way to expunge this tension inherent in the nature of community. There is just no way around the fact that communities draw a line between members and nonmembers—they aren't a railroad station. That is, by definition they exclude some people, typically many more than they include.

It saddened me, nevertheless, that the base for de facto exclusion so often is race. What would it take before a very successful, much-respected, African American family would feel fully at home in the white part of Bethesda, where I used to live (and for me to feel comfortable in Enola's parts of Oak Bluffs)? Maybe communities of the future could build their affinity on some other social base, such as working for the same college or a shared interest in the arts. One cannot help but long for a day when communities will be made on the basis of what kind of life people choose rather than with what they inherited at birth.

While I was drafting this memoir, I checked with Enola about our conversation on Oak Bluffs, which took place several years earlier. This led to a number of candid exchanges by e-mail about the relations between blacks and whites, culminating in a lunch to which Enola brought her fifteen-year-old daughter Leah. Enola explained that she and her family are members of many "affinity" groups that are either largely white or racially mixed and feel "comfortable" in them, but it was also true that they had special bonds with African Americans, in black-only groups. It was especially important, Enola elaborated, for her to be a member of the Jack and Jill society. Here, it was not even clear whether racially mixed couples should be admitted. A key purpose of this society is to encourage young African Americans to marry within their race. Enola pointed to the many successful African American men who marry white women, which sends a message to African Americans that they are not as worthy as whites are, feeding their inferiority complex. Hence, the need to allow, even encourage, some measure of separate social relations by race. Here is a verbatim transcript of the dialogue that ensued.

Amitai: We are talking about social life. We obviously are integrated in the classroom and at work. We can go from here in two directions. We can either segregate the social fabric and say there's nothing wrong with it—both sides do it—or we can see we need a mixture. We need some occasions where we can meet in our groups but we need also some situations where we meet socially across those lines. Because, otherwise, we're going to be a very divided society.

Enola: First of all, I don't think we have a problem. Maybe because I'm so alarmed about the rate of interracial relationships and marriage and the implications for black women, but I don't think we have a problem when it comes to people meeting socially across racial lines. . . .

Amitai: If you had a magic lever, would you increase the separate tables (in campus and school cafeterias in which students tend to self-segregate by race) and decrease the social interaction?

Enola: I think, to be perfectly honest with you, I think that I'm a dying breed. I would. . . .

Amitai: You said you are alarmed about the interaction?

Enola: I am because of my children. Because I have become more and more convinced through my research and my work that there's a lot of unfinished emotional business in the black community that needs to be taken care of. Particularly around issues of self-worth and relationships that we've just not attended to. As Orlando Patterson has argued in "Rituals of Blood," slavery was devastating in its effects on relationships between black men and black women and those effects are still with us today. And I think that has an effect on this whole issue.

Amitai: May I ask Leah about the same thing?

Enola: Sure.

Leah: I think that it's partially just a function of the way that I've grown up that I'm basically pretty much in favor of really integrating. The school I'm at is mostly white and a lot of my friends are white. And, they're just my friends. And I wouldn't give them up. I wouldn't give them up just because they're not my same race. And about the issue of intermarriage. I don't know it sounds like, I guess, hard to know that it might be hard for me to find someone to marry me because I'm black. But I think if people are really in love with other people they shouldn't really have much regard for their race.

Amitai: I don't think it's going to be hard for you to find people to marry you. Mark my words. Leah, one more question please. My older African American friends, present company not included, often tell me they feel discriminated against every day. When they try to get a cab, it won't stop for them; when they go to a shop, the shopkeeper keeps an eye on them thinking they're going to steal and such. Do you feel that way?

Leah: I have to admit that I don't really do a lot, mostly I just go to school. And I don't really feel that way. There was one incident when there was a lady in a store, I was there with my brother and a friend of ours and she was following us around. I mean it might have been because we were teenagers and it might have been because we were black, I don't know. But I don't feel that generally happens to me a lot, but I do believe that it does happen to some people.

There was much more of a three-way conversation along the same lines, but the high points for me were Leah comments. She was clearly able to put behind her whatever feelings of inadequacy and need to self-segregate her parents had. In that sense, her parents had succeeded. They aspired to nurture young African Americans that could leave behind the psychologically damaging effects of the past. In Leah, they fully achieved their purpose. This was good news for all of us. I believe there is a growing sense, on both sides of the divide, not only to do right, but also to bring the matter to closure. There is a desire to bring an end to the charges and countercharges, the guilt and shame, the sense of racial "apartness," and to move toward a world in which people are judged by their personal journeys rather than by the past of the group of which they are members—by birth and pigmentation. Leah told me that this was not an idle dream.

Noah's Ark

Next to African Americans, I was particularly keen to enroll Hispanics, not merely to add diversity, but also to break out of what I deemed an unfortunate tendency to view race issues in black and white. My three half-Hispanic sons only added to my commitment to this quest.

The endorsement of several Hispanic leaders thrilled me. They included Rodolfo Alvarez (a scholar and friend from UCLA), Alejandro Portes (a Cuban American scholar and the first Hispanic to become the president of the American Sociological Association), and powerful activist Raul Yzaguirre (the head of La Raza, the largest Latin American organization in the United States). Yzaguirre's endorsement was the first sure sign that the communitarian platform appealed to major public leaders, not merely to academics or intellectuals. The endorsement of Henry Cisneros (the former mayor of San Antonio, and later a secretary of HUD in the Clinton administration), followed, as did that of Dennis DeLeon (commissioner of human rights for the City of New York, a Mexican American, a particularly accomplished orator, and an openly gay leader).

The platform's endorsers were beginning to form a diverse group—with one exception. I failed to find Asian American endorsers. I called various contacts in an attempt to find some and was repeatedly told that the few public leaders of that community were primarily local. During a visit to San Francisco, a rich donor I was courting confided in me, "We have a hard time finding even one to serve on the board of the opera." (Francis Fukuyama, one of our most illustrious endorsers, sees himself as an all-American intellectual, not as one of any particular ethnic or racial group. In the following years, he wrote two strongly communitarian books, one on trust and the other on what he called remoralization of the society, entitling it *The Great Disruption*.) Much of this has changed since 1991; Asian Americans have become more publicly active. But in 1991, I failed to find them.

In addition, endorsements from the academic community included those of several highly respected scholars well known within their respective disciplines and beyond. Rarely has opening the mail been more exhilarating or receiving faxes more welcome.

Additional endorsements trickled in from moderates on the left and the right, from community leaders and nationally recognized public figures, and—to my surprise—from reigning and not merely has-been politicians. I could hardly restrain myself from calling Bill every other day, exclaiming "Guess who endorsed this time!" I did not even try to refrain on the day we gained, from the liberal side, the endorsement of David Cohen and Michael Pertschuk (the two codirectors of the Advocacy Institute) and—of Betty Friedan.

Betty and I have had a long-lasting relationship. I figured she might have endorsed the platform more out of friendship than complete agreement, the lack of which she never hesitated to express in public. Our love–hate relationship spanned more than thirty years, since Si Goode first introduced us. Betty could go from zero to sixty-five more rapidly than any sports car. In a booming angry voice, she repeatedly announced that although she shared

Figure 10.1.   With Betty Friedan at her home in Sag Harbor, 1999

our basic concerns for community and our objections to excessive individualism, "This call for a return to the traditional family will not be; the family
is kaput, gone, history. Women will never agree to be sent back to the
kitchen. Get used to it." I learned that responding that we never called for a
return to a traditional family would only raise the debate's temperature and
that if I ignored Betty's outbursts she would cool down in a jiffy.

While I hardly cherish Betty's outbursts, I admired her keen historical sensibility. Feminist books had been written often over the decades that preceded the publication of *The Feminine Mystique*, but Betty's book was issued
just when the women's movement was ready to take off. Betty also timed well
her book *The Fountain of Age*, as it became evident that we were facing a
growing aging generation. In the book she urges seniors to view the last stage
of life not as a decline and fall, but as a golden age. And just when the majority of Americans, including many women, were growing tired of strident
feminist claims, Betty called for a cease-fire in the identity wars, building
bridges to the male species, and creating a grand coalition for social change.
The fact that she joined us was one more sure sign that our time had come.

On the conservative side, Chester E. Finn Jr. (a well-known authority on
educational matters), David Blankenhorn (the president of the Institute for
American Values, an indefatigable advocate of social conservative causes),
David K. Hart (from Brigham Young University), and Richard Shuber (CEO
of the Points of Light Foundation) endorsed the platform, as did Sanford N.
McDonnell (Chairman Emeritus, McDonnell Douglas).

While McDonnell's endorsement spelled potential difficulties, the trouble
Father Richard Neuhaus's endorsement produced was far from potential.
When his endorsement came in, I rushed to call Mary Ann Glendon with
the news. At the time, we all considered his signature a strong sign of how
far to the right of center our appeal reached. Neuhaus was a Lutheran who
had converted to Catholicism and became fairly immoderate, as converts
sometimes become. I first met him during a meeting organized by Mary Ann
Glendon at the Harvard Law School on the "Seedbeds of Virtue," the social
conditions that foster values. Father Neuhaus spoke with such confidence
and authority—one got the impression he had reflected long and hard about
his positions, until he was left with few, if any, doubts or reservations. Indeed,
I sometimes thought that Neuhaus could not speak with such certitude on
grave and complex moral matters unless he believed that the Lord was whispering into his ear, telling him what to pronounce.

Several years after Neuhaus endorsed our platform, he wrote that he wished
to withdraw his assent. Initially, I was taken aback by this request. You can resign from a board or quit a post. You can even endorse a declaration and later

indicate that you've changed your mind. I wondered, however, could you make it seem that you never subscribed to the communitarian position in the first place?

In his publication *First Things*, Neuhaus explained himself:

> The communitarian movement has come in for a good deal of attention in the last few years. It is the baby of sociologist Amitai Etzioni, and its platform is at least a movement toward the side of the angels in our political and cultural wars. That is why this writer signed on to its original manifesto, although not without misgivings.

Whatever these misgiving were, Neuhaus kept them to himself at the time. But what new sin brought them into the open?

> Recently, Etzioni expanded the manifesto in the form of a book, *The Spirit of Community: Rights, Responsibilities and the Communitarian Agenda* (Crown). Joshua Abramowitz reviews the book in *The Public Interest* and, in our judgement, puts his finger on a serious, and potentially fatal, weakness in the communitarian vision: "Etzioni is mindful of two institutions that stand between the individual and the state—The family and the community. But that's it. He goes two for three. In other words, Etzioni's plans for a 'moral revival' pay almost no attention to religion. . . ." For communitarianism to ignore religion is to ignore the largest associational (i.e., communitarian) pattern in American life.

In 1996, I responded indirectly (in my book *The New Golden Rule*), arguing that although being religious did not guarantee that one was ethical, and one could be ethical without being religious, it was true that religion could be a major source of communitarian commitments. I did not turn this into a personal issue and did not add that back in 1991, when endorsing the platform, Neuhaus did not raise any of these concerns. I respected his wishes, and he is no longer listed as an endorser.

At a snail's pace, the mail continued to deliver endorsements from some sterling figures of American public life, many from the great political center. None ranked higher in my book than John W. Gardner. He served as Lyndon Johnson's secretary of health, education, and welfare, founded Common Cause and the Independent Sector, and served as the chairman of the National Urban Coalition—among another half dozen public posts. Gardner often made time in his very full life to advise us. Soft-spoken and a consummate moderate, Gardner listened attentively before he provided counsel. On the infrequent occasions we did not follow it, he took no offense.

Two Watergate heroes were our next endorsers: high-ranking moderate Republicans who stood up to Nixon and refused his order to fire Special Prosecutor Archibald Cox, who had been examining the Watergate-related charges against the president. As a result, both were themselves fired. One was William Ruckelshaus, often referred to as Mr. Clean, who also served as acting director of the FBI, and twice as the head of the Environmental Protection Agency (EPA). The other Republican star who stood up to Nixon, at the time serving as attorney general, was Elliot Richardson. We also gained the endorsement of Nicholas de B. Katzenbach, former attorney general of the United States under Johnson.

There were many more good people, mainly from the center of the political spectrum, including former Kennedy whiz-kid Newton N. Minow, who made his reputation by taking on the television industry when he served as head of the FCC, calling it a great wasteland; Stuart E. Eizenstat, whom I respected greatly from our days in the Carter White House; William F. Schulz (president, Unitarian Universalist Association), whose group found our ideas attractive and often invited us to speak at its local churches and once even to address some 4,000 people at one of its general assemblies. Albert Shanker, the gutsy and innovative president of the American Federation of Teachers and a personal friend, also signed the platform.

The last thing I expected was that politicians still in office would endorse a twelve-page-long text, any line of which could be held against them during an election campaign. Nor could a politician seeking election or reelection expect that we would make campaign contributions or line up our volunteers to mobilize voters. Indeed, very few politicians did sign on. The fact that John B. Anderson (presidential candidate, 1980) gave us his John Hancock did not invalidate my expectation; he was a professional maverick. John Brandl was another exception who did not disprove the rule. He was both a Minnesota state senator and a professor at the University of Minnesota, more of a public intellectual than a typical politician.

But no such qualifications applied to other politicians who endorsed the platform. When I met Kurt Schmoke, the mayor of Baltimore, I approached him with some prejudice because he was a politician. I did not expect him to be reflective and thoughtful. But after a long conversation with Kurt at a Belmont conference, I concluded that few, if any, of the endorsements we got were based on more careful deliberation than his. It also provided additional evidence that we were reaching way beyond the academy.

The endorsement by Daniel Kemmis (the mayor of Missoula, Montana, who wrote a strongly communitarian book well before he laid eyes on our platform) alarmed me. I called him posthaste and told him how much we appreciated his unqualified endorsement, but would he please reread our very strong plank against guns, which called for the removal of firearms from all private hands. I feared that his chances of being reelected were nil, indeed, that he might be recalled, if the good citizens of Missoula found out about that part of our platform. Kemmis, bless his soul, did not revoke his endorsement but modified it to read, "signing with exception to Second Amendment section."

Every additional endorsement added more luster to our platform and project. "These people," I exulted to Bill, "by endorsing the platform are not merely increasing its legitimacy. They are declaring to one and all that they are 'communitarians.' And from now on, they'll be asked, 'Why are you a communitarian?' or 'What does it mean to be a communitarian?' and they naturally will become ambassadors of the communitarian cause."

Because the endorsements dribbled in, one or two at a time for weeks, it took a while before the full importance of what was happening dawned on me. It was only toward the end of 1991 that the full scope of our achievement became evident. By that time we had 104 endorsements. (The full list, attached to our platform, is available on our website at www.communitariannetwork.org.) At this point we decided to close the list in order to publish the platform and the list of its initial endorsers. (We reopened endorsements in 2001. I am not sure it is good manners to make a pitch in a book like this, but what the hell, in for a penny in for a pound. I have been calling on people for most of my life. So, if you can find it in your schedule and heart to read our platform, posted on our website—www.communitariannetwork.org—and feel right about it, we would love to have you as an endorser. Nobody will solicit you and we do not sell our list to telemarketers or anybody else.)

Though tickled pink, no champagne was uncorked. True, the communitarian project had clearly taken one giant step forward. There was now a platform, a social-moral message, which we considered not merely significant and timely, but also one that commanded a measure of public support. However, much remained to be done.

One evening after dinner at home, Pat observed: "You look like you made it up Mount Everest. What's up?"

"Well," I explained, "this project is very different from the others I've gotten myself into. This time, out of every ten people I talk to, eight say that they could not agree more, that indeed they have been a communitarian for a long time but didn't know what to call themselves."

Add a Journal

In the social movement "business," one day's crowning achievements are quickly discounted as money already in the bank and are best viewed as a source of investment for the next stage. Shortly after the platform con signatories was issued, various colleagues and public leaders inquired how the platform could be augmented as new ideas arose and new situations developed. If we are going to be an effective social movement with an active public voice, we could not limit ourselves to a twelve-page text, and one that was largely a statement of principles and thus left uncovered our position on numerous policy issues. At the same time, gaining the consent of all those who originally endorsed the platform for a steady stream of additions and revisions would be extremely difficult, if not outright impossible. We needed a venue in which to continue developing our message and tease out its implications for numerous ethical and policy issues.

We could have limited ourselves to publishing our ideas in various existing publications, as, indeed, we soon started doing. However, it quickly became apparent that although there were many academic journals in which to publish high points of theory, there were very few magazines in which public intellectuals could publish their thoughts. Moreover, those that did exist tended to reflect a particular perspective—but hardly a communitarian one. *The Public Interest* was the flagship of the neoconservatives, *Dissent*—of the old left, *National Review*—of social conservatives, and *Reason*—of the libertarians. After we got several rejection notices, I suggested the formation of a new journal devoted to communitarian ideas.

Jim Fishkin, Bill Galston, and I met in my home for a long dialogue. We quickly agreed on the merit of a journal, but disagreed about details. Jim wondered whether there would be enough material for a journal dedicated only to communitarianism and suggested that we start with an annual volume. I feared that there would be no reader identification if we published that infrequently. Bill raised the possibility of following communitarian articles with liberal ones on the same topic.

Hours of conversation later, we concurred that the new publication should be largely limited to explorations of communitarian viewpoints. It would welcome expressions of differences within communitarianism and publish challenging commentaries by people of different persuasions. And it should mix academic or policy-oriented articles with those descriptive of community life. In short, it should be a public intellectual—and not strictly academic—publication.

We named the new publication: *The Responsive Community: Rights and Responsibilities*, stressing our theme that we were not opposed to rights; however, we held that they needed to be matched by an assumption of social responsibilities. (Hence our motto, which long adorned our mailings to potential subscribers, "Strong rights presume strong responsibilities.")

The responsibility of becoming the editor fell on me; Bill and Jim agreed to serve as coeditors. I was delighted when Mary Ann Glendon consented to become the third one. I invited William Raspberry to serve on the editorial board; I greatly respected his judicious writing in the *Washington Post*. Unfortunately, Raspberry turned down the invitation, explaining that he could not join any group he might wish to write about one day. (I soon learned that the same was true for other members of the media.)

We readily found colleagues from academia and a few public intellectuals to serve on the first editorial board. However, not everyone we invited accepted our invitation. An explosive rejection by Roger Wilkens (professor of law and history, George Mason University) was particularly distressing. When I contacted him, to follow up on our letter of invitation, he chided me right off the bat. He said angrily, "So, you wanted to start a journal—dedicated to community!—without an African American on the board?" I exclaimed, "No, no, wait a minute. We invited William Raspberry on the first day." Roger was not mollified, and I felt unfairly treated. I was sorry for failing to convince him to join us. It turned into one of those unhappy conversations whose ill aftertaste lingers. For years after that phone call, we approached one another warily when we ran into each other at one meeting or another. One more black–white dialogue that was not. (I should have taken pains to revisit it.) Soon, I had to face other disappointments.

Some of those who did join the board resigned over the years, pleading increased workloads, burn out, or that we'd strayed too far from the liberal line or academic purity. Among those I was especially sorry to lose were Martha Nussbaum and Jane Mansbridge. But most board members stayed on, and once *The Responsive Community* was launched, we had no difficulty in finding others to keep the roster complete.

The Responsive Community, first issued in 1991, includes in practically every issue one article that deals with some question of communitarian philosophy or theory (for instance, an essay by Charles Taylor on "The Dangers of Soft Despotism"), one or two essays dealing with communitarian public policy issues (such as community policing, gated communities, and curfews), and a descriptive essay (for instance, Alan Ehrenhalt's fine-grained description of life in a small town after Wal-Mart rolled in). And finally, each issue includes an assortment of book reviews, op-eds, and brief comments on current events in which we make digs at social conservatives and liberals and hand out commendations to the communitarian side.

The Responsive Community (like its editor) tries to serve both the academic master and the public. Hence, it is not surprising that it has occasionally been criticized by some of our more academic colleagues for not being academic enough and chided by some community activists for running too many "abstract" articles. At the same time, over the years *The Responsive Community* has gained its share of kudos, especially in the form of its articles being quoted or cited or republished by other publications, such as *Current*.

If you think that being the editor of a quarterly is a fun, prestigious thing to do, please think again. Likewise, if you have an urge to publish a journal, I urge you to lie down until you feel better. Well, at least read on so you will be well prepared. It did not take long to discover the special pains reserved for those who edit such publications. Rejecting an article all too often results in sullen faxes, angry phone calls, and flaming e-mails. The fact that the articles we publish are reviewed by all the coeditors and the managing editor gives me some protection. However, there are still a fair number of colleagues who have not forgiven me because their masterpieces did not see the light of day on our pages. The feelings of some of those whose articles we *did* publish were ruffled by our editorial suggestions, and some were even displeased when they found themselves in the back of the book rather in the front.

The least enjoyable part of editing *The Responsive Community* has been learning more about the business of publishing small quarterlies than I ever wanted to know. We had to find a printer and subscribers (who forever need to be courted and replenished), struggle with the post office rules for mass mailings by not-for-profit entities, and read and reread page proofs. And we forever lose money. Hence, I am forced to court foundations and people of means to keep the publication afloat. This is the part of being an activist I could do without.

Editing *The Responsive Community*, though, is not without its rewards. One of the main ones is working with an exceptionally talented group of young people who have served as managing editors and assistant editors, working together with my research assistants or splitting their time between the two jobs. Their names are listed on the masthead of the publication. (And on the dedication page of one of my books.) Most of them come from the country's top universities and work with us for a year or two before they leave to continue their studies or to work elsewhere in the not-for-profit sector. They do not exhibit the failings often attributed to our young generation; they are well educated, informed, and public-minded. Practically all of them brought or developed a style that allowed them to criticize freely whatever copy they worked on, without being disrespectful. Most years, they formed a community of sorts, playing cards during lunch breaks and hanging around together after work. The division of tasks among them was very informal and fluid; so, if one needed assistance, others would chip in to fix a computer or find an elusive site on the World Wide Web. Cookies appeared next to mailboxes when someone had a birthday or returned from a trip overseas. We attended with glee the elaborate wedding of a staff member whose parents initially did not want to have much of one because she was already living with her boyfriend. (They relented largely because she was crying as if she'd lost her favorite dog, but also because I promised to pay for a "real" wedding if they continued to refuse.)

As far as I could tell, there was no office politics. Very rarely did a staff member hint that some other one was poaching on what the first one considered his or her turf. Once an older member was too bossy; the younger staff bristled, and we agreed that she would help introduce new staff to office routines but try to cease ordering them around. A minority student reported that he was being discriminated against by other staff members, who denied treating him differently. He kept complaining to me. The staff wanted me to encourage him to resign. I argued that past evils and political practicality advised against it. We met several times and worked things out. Most days I felt good about our little community; it made me miss the office on days I could not be there.

Over ten years, some twenty-five young people have worked on *The Responsive Community* and communitarian projects. I am sure that most, if not all, will be heard from. But the account of one of them in particular should not be deferred for a later day. Ben Wittes, a young aspiring writer, took over as assistant managing editor of *The Responsive Community* in 1993. He was especially interested in legal matters. Interspersed among many discussions we had about which articles to run and how to edit them, we had stimulating give-and-takes on the justice of conducting mandatory drug tests, requiring youngsters to wear school uniforms, banning hate speech, and other such issues.

Like many young aspiring writers, Ben was keen to break into print, but at the time his only published piece was an article for the *Washington City Paper*, a throwaway. While he often pitched articles to a variety of publications, he was particularly keen to write for the *New Republic*, which he regarded as a leading intellectual magazine. But, as the months passed, the *New Republic* repeatedly rejected his various bids.

Ben's big break came when Andrew Sullivan, then the editor of the *New Republic*, invited him to write an article for the publication. But there was a catch. Sullivan invited Ben to do a profile on me, but added that I had grown too big for my britches and needed to be knocked down a peg or two. Given that Ben worked for me, Sullivan was confident that Ben could easily uncover some dirt about me. Ben offered to compose a balanced piece and to write about me honestly, the way he saw me. Sullivan stated that the *New Republic* was not interested in such pieces; take it or leave it. Ben, crestfallen, declined.

Aside from being relieved that I was spared a hostile profile in a national magazine, I was deeply impressed and moved by Ben's integrity. I was also concerned that his writing career would be set back. After all, he blew off a major opportunity to break into print. I racked my brain to come up with what I could do to help him, but nothing came to mind. It turned out that I need not have worried. Soon thereafter, Ben was hired away from us by *Legal Times*, and next—he was invited to serve as a member of the editorial board of the *Washington Post*! I did not lift a finger— even to write a recommendation letter—on his behalf. His rapid rise was based solely on his own merits.

The Spirit of Community

The next step was to make the new communitarian case in a full-length book. Speaking in a public voice to my fellow citizens, I wrote *The Spirit of Community* in 1990–1991, and it was finally published in 1993. One reason it took that long for the manuscript to see the light of day was because the gestation period of most books is still nine months, about what it was forty years ago. The publication was further delayed because an editor at the publishing house did not care for my position on HIV testing. My position, developed during our founding meetings, was that people at high risk for HIV should be expected (by the moral culture of their communities) to volunteer to be tested, and if the results were positive, they should be expected to inform previous and prospective sexual partners.

The openly gay editor, David Groff at Crown, stepped out of his editorial role and into that of an advocate. While for most of my manuscript he raised no substantive objections and made numerous helpful but limited stylistic suggestions—when it came to the passage about HIV testing, he attached a note that opened with, "I absolutely object to this." Just in case "absolutely" was not strong enough, he underlined it. Then he spelled out his reasons:

> First of all, there is no compelling public health reason to gather the names of HIV-positive people. There is no point to making such lists unless they do *not* remain confidential, for contact tracing—which makes *no practical sense* for the two groups thus far most affected by HIV, gay men and IV drug users: gay

men *know* they are at risk, and most IV drug users are too disorganized to render contact tracing very effective. And the risk of loss of confidentiality makes no sense either because the risk of discrimination—losing your job, home, *health* insurance—are so great that *no one* would take the test—including *me*— if anonymity (not confidentiality) were not guaranteed.

The note put me in a difficult position. On one hand, although Groff did not threaten to block the publication of the manuscript unless I modified my position, his strong objection led me to believe that the manuscript's publication would at least be delayed if I did not yield. I could have demanded that Crown release me from my contract, but this would have meant an even longer delay. I could have complained to higher-ranking editors, but this might have resulted in a messy fight, which I did not care for. At the same time, I did not find Groff's arguments compelling and I was not going to alter my position.

So, I settled for a series of discussions over the phone, over lunch, and in his office. I argued, "There is no contradiction between the claim that lists of names of those infected will be used to trace previous contacts and—confidentiality. HIV-positive individuals must be told so that they do not further spread the fatal disease. Informing people involved that they have been exposed (without even telling them by whom) does not mean that their employers, landlords, or insurers need to find out."

Groff responded that all gay people, indeed everyone, should conduct themselves at all times as if everyone they encounter has HIV. I countered that, because human nature is what it is, when people get a specific warning that a particular prospective partner has HIV, they will be much more likely to act safely. I asked: "Would you maintain that because everybody is advised repeatedly to wear seatbelts in an airplane, that a pilot does not have to warn people to be sure to put them on when she knows that the plane is about to crash?"

We went around and around several more times. Throughout, it was a civil confrontation. Groff did not claim that I was homophobic, and I did not ask what right he had to try to impose his view on an author. We just firmly laid out our respective views, repeatedly. In the end, I wore Groff down, although he did manage to wring some minor rewordings out of me. But the book's delay—which the world handled quite well—left me frustrated and anxious to get the word out.

My purpose in the book was to lay out the case for our central thesis, that there is an urgent need to rebuild the moral foundations of society, but it must be done in a democratic, nonauthoritarian way. The book opens with a declaration under the subtitle "We hold these truths. . . ." I repeat some of it here because it captures the essence of new or responsive communitarianism as I see it:

"We hold that a moral revival in these United States is possible without Puritanism, . . . without thought police controlling our intellectual life.

"We hold that our call for increased social responsibilities, does not call for curbing rights. On the contrary, strong rights presume strong responsibilities.

"We hold that the pursuit of self-interest can be balanced by a commitment to the community, without requiring us to lead a life of austerity, altruism, or self-sacrifice. . . .

"We hold these truths as Communitarians, as people committed to creating a new moral, social, and public order based on restored communities. . . ."

This opening declaration reflects an attempt to break out of the age-old debate between the left and the right, between liberals and conservatives. It suggests that the nation faces a whole host of social issues whose textures are fundamentally different from the important socio-economic ones.

The Spirit of Community lays out a moral agenda based on convincing people rather than coercing them, on a sense of responsibility people truly assume rather than on duties imposed upon them. (I used to tease my colleagues on the right who wanted to ban divorce, abolish abortion by law, make homosexual activities illegal, and mandate prayers—that they have no faith in faith.)

Central to the book is the thesis that instead of relying on the law to promote a good society—we should primarily use the moral voice. Antisocial urges such as aggression and inappropriate sexual drives cannot be expunged, but if young people are brought up properly, they can acquire an inner moral voice that countervails these drives. For instance, my first reaction is anger: honk the horn, pass the driver, cut in front of him. But before I proceed, I often hear another voice. It calls on me to keep my shirt on; it reminds me that I don't want to contribute to a world of angry retaliations, in which one act of aggression leads to another. I do not always heed this voice, nobody does all the time; but people who hear no such voice are dangerous psychopaths, and people with weak moral voices are human beings whom we failed to properly educate.

Moreover, because even the moral voice of educated people from well-formed families and good schools tends to wane over time, it must be nurtured constantly. This is the central purpose of community. It is not merely a place that is warm and supportive, but also a group that draws on the affection members have for one another—to make them nobler than they would otherwise be. People are especially mindful about the admonitions and gentle chiding of those close to them. Thus, the moral voice of the community is added to and reinforces one's conscience. John Grisham, in his book *Skipping Christmas*, provides a very effective feel for the guilt (one form of inner moral voice) and social pressure (a communal one) that engulf a family that decides not to send gifts or decorate a tree.

I later found out, when I delivered public lectures and responded to callers on radio talk shows, that many people question the concept of a moral voice. Some feel that if behavior is to be regulated, say, if drunk driving is to be prevented, smoking in public to be discouraged, and recycling to be encouraged—"this is what laws are for." I respond by pointing out, "When we call in the cops, we have already failed; encouraging people 'to behave' through their friends and neighbors is much more humane, less alienating, more tailored to special circumstances, and less costly." Other people stress, "No one likes to be told what to do." I concur, "When I was jaywalking in Seattle and a man on the sidewalk hissed at me 'stupid!' my first response was, 'What the hell?' but then I realized that he was upholding one of the mores that make Seattle a more civilized and communitarian city than most."

Often I add, "We should let people be—unless at issue are matters the community needs to regulate. Then the moral voice is vastly superior to the law." When asked, "Are you saying that the law has no role?" I respond that although the law helps to express the values of the community and undergirds the moral culture by going after those who ignore the moral voice, if it becomes the mainstay of social order, society has lost its communitarian quality.

Because the concept of the moral voice is so pivotal, I decided to go academic with it and developed a simple tool a researcher can use to assess which moral tenets people are willing to speak up for and to what extent they are willing to speak up at all. In effect, anybody can use it to assess one's own moral voice or that of others. Here are a few sample statements. About each matter the respondents are asked: "Should you say anything? If you choose to speak, what would you say?"

- You are walking down a trail among some very old trees. A young couple is carving their initials into the bark of one of the trees.
- Walking home from the bus station you see a child whose parents you vaguely know from the neighborhood. The child is throwing stones at a cat that is stretching itself next to the sidewalk.

- You see two nine-year-olds, a boy and a girl, using a spray can to mark a swastika on a mailbox.

If people are unwilling to speak up on these and other such issues, their moral voice has been lost. We are each other's keeper. (When I made these points in *The Spirit of Community*, I did not have the data nor the analysis of the American moral voice that were provided years later in Alan Wolfe's books *One Nation After All* and *Moral Freedom*.)

As our society lost its moral confidence and the moral voice waned, speaking up became increasingly considered uncool. More and more, not only those who wave their fists in people's faces, or are self-righteous, have been considered "judgmental," but all those who took a moral position to others. This was reflected also in the way the phrase "my brother's keeper" has been reinterpreted. For many, denying such an obligation no longer means concealing a crime and avoiding a moral duty, but not butting into other people's business. That is, the meaning from being morally troublesome to commendable. I hold that we need to return to the original intent: not to be judgmental, but to recognize that we have responsibilities to one another, including encouraging one and all to be better than they would be otherwise. Actually, this is the main reason I chose "My Brother's Keeper" as the title of this book. It is not only that I did butt in, but that I consider it something we ought to do.

Much of the rest of *The Spirit of Community* addresses the question of what else it would take, beyond the moral voice, to provide the building blocks of the social-moral reconstruction. It explores what kind of family, education, and community bonds bind communities into a society and make the best building blocks for a good, communitarian society. In the process, it examines various issues, such as freedom of speech, drug searches, and the relationship between the white majority and various minorities that are frequently discussed from a liberal or conservative viewpoint from a communitarian perspective.

The book is written in a breezy style, with no jargon and no footnotes. It seeks to speak to my fellow citizens, not my academic colleagues. To stress that it was not meant for professors, I put a cartoon on page one. About 25,000 copies of the book were sold in English and several thousands in other languages; far from an earthshaking number. Yet, as the major newspapers reviewed it, many more people found out about the communitarian message. And, to my astonishment, several college professors have used it over the years as a popular communitarian text.

Several of my academic colleagues made it clear that they were not enthralled. One complained that I did not footnote Durkheim, who made related points a century or so ago. Others pointed out that I did not define community. I was thoroughly pissed. I held that this book should be evaluated on whether its normative message was a sound one, whether it was based on valid social science, and whether it was written in a way that would reach the "masses"—not by typical academic standards. However, I also recognized that my colleagues had a point, even if they made it in reference to the wrong book. We had not provided the kind of justification for responsive communitarian thinking that would meet philosophical or sociological academic criteria. This remained a job yet to be done.

A Distraction

The communitarian drive was humming right along when I hit a bump in the road. A young, lanky woman applied for a position as a research assistant. I interviewed Jean in the same format I always follow: door wide open; my secretary within eye line and earshot. The reason I follow the open-door policy is that I have seen professors' careers ruined after they have been charged with sexual harassment, even if, in the end, the courts or hearings fully cleared them. (I, of course, do not speak of those actually guilty of such actions.) Hence, I bend over backward to avoid such accusations. I even avoid riding in crowded elevators, just so nobody can claim that I touched them.

Jean brought with her an impressive resume and answered questions brightly. A few days later, when I called to tell her that we were ready to hire her, she informed me, "You ought to know that I am applying for a job at the CIA. However, my security clearance is going to take many months because I used to live in Poland." This seemed to make sense, and Jean started working for us, doing a credible job, although she did not quite click with the other staff members.

After a short period on the job, Jean suggested that her work would improve if she could take a course that she believed was germane to her research assignment. She asked that we pay several hundred dollars for the course. I reluctantly agreed but wondered, "What if you do get clearance in a few days?" Jean countered, "In that case, I will pay you back the tuition fee." She had barely started when her clearance came through, and within a day she packed to leave. When I asked for the refund, she refused.

At this point, I made a clear and regrettable mistake. I instructed the university to hold her last paycheck until the matter was resolved. When she found out about it, she stopped by. She spoke briefly and calmly: "If I do not have my money by five o'clock, I will accuse you of sexual harassment and tell your wife that we had an affair." I should note that we had no personal relationship of any kind, not even a cup of coffee nor a walk in the campus yard. I realized, though, that I was defenseless and soon called the university to release the funds. I never heard from or saw her again.

For quite a while, I felt violated. True, I *was* wrong to block her pay. People who work are entitled to their compensation even if they did not abide by some agreement they made. Despite this belated insight, I felt pushed around and unable to defend myself against ludicrous charges. Worse, I had to face the fact that the same thing could be done to me, again, any time, by anybody.

My sense of being abused and powerless festered for a while until I decided that these feelings might help me be more empathetic to true victims of harassment. When a research assistant working at an institute nearby came crying to my motherly secretary, and I mean crying, because his professor was giving him a hard time, I visited with him. I very well may not have done so before Jean taught me a lesson. When one of my colleagues jokingly complained about coeds rejecting his advances, suggesting that they should enjoy older, experienced men, I did speak up with a little more vigor than I might have done before my short course on what it is like to be at the receiving end of such treatment.

The incident had another lasting effect on my relationship with the young people who work with me. When one of them was mugged and brutally assaulted in Georgetown, I helped her regain her composure over the weeks that followed, but did not feel free to show her how deeply concerned I was. I wanted to give her a shoulder to cry on, but I kept her at arm's length. The same was true when the father of one of the younger staff members suddenly died, and she was grief stricken. Another young staff member dropped by my office often and unnecessarily, looking deeply into my eyes, and asking to accompany me to meetings to which I was invited, often at the end of the day. I tried to transfer her to another part of the university, but she refused to be reassigned. Luckily, she was accepted into a top medical school and broke away.

The "communitarian" lesson of all this is far from easily drawn. All too often in the academic world in which I live, there are young women—and sometimes young men—who are pressured to engage in sexual acts by people who have power over them, coeds by their professors, junior faculty by those who will rule on their tenure. There is not and never was any doubt in my mind that those who so do abuse others—and academic standards—should be exposed and properly punished. But there should also be a way for someone to fully clear his or her name. Currently, even those who are found not guilty in various hearings are still assumed to be guilty by many in their campus communities.

There must also be some clarification of the code of conduct. A colleague was charged with sexual harassment because a coed claimed that he was staring at her through his goggles in a swimming pool. The charge was brought under the rule that harassment can take the form of creating a "hostile environment" and that what constitutes such an environment is determined by those who declare themselves to be its victims. These kinds of rules are too fungible and undermine any notion of due process and fairness that should be extended even to old, white males.

Maybe it is impossible to have a warm personal relationship with one's staff or students—without fearing that it might be misunderstood, mischaracterized, or exploited. It is a crying shame.

Task Forces and Position Papers

There was only so much time to mope. We were still missing a tool. We had no way to develop, as a group, positions on specific policy issues from a communitarian viewpoint. Task forces turned out to be an effective way to close this gap. Our task forces were composed of a group of leading scholars, experts, public intellectuals, and in some cases, activists. Members served as volunteers; indeed, they typically covered the expenses entailed in participation from their own resources.

I take some pride in the way I set up these task forces. Like many others, I have attended numerous meetings of researchers and scholars in which prepared papers are presented, one following close on the heels of the other, allowing precious little time for dialogue. These kinds of meetings have their purpose, but their sociological design is particularly detrimental to developing new and shared positions. "My" task forces proceeded in the opposite way: no papers were presented; the task force meetings were all dialogue.

The task forces worked best when the members were available for an evening and a day. Shorter time periods did not allow for the development of a new perspective, and the members often could not be kept for longer periods. Ideally, we met first for a dinner, during which members of the group became acquainted and presented an initial overview of what would constitute a communitarian treatment of whatever subject they had agreed to take on. The next morning was dedicated to a brainstorming free-for-all. By the end of the morning, the differences of opinion often seemed considerable. After lunch, a long break was typically scheduled during which small groups of members went for walks or chatted over coffee. In the last hours, often, albeit not always, a shared outlook did evolve. Once a basic approach was found, the group dispersed. One member—best not a committee—drafted a position paper, reflecting the evolving consensus. This was then sent for review and comments by all other members. Rewrites and endorsement usually followed. (It was also necessary to carefully moderate the meetings to ensure that once a subtopic was brought up, the discussion stayed with it, rather than ambling all over the place.) Numerous position papers, prepared by our task forces, have been issued over the years. These include papers on pro-family policies, character education, criminal justice, gun control, and health care reform.

A bit more about these task forces, by the way of visiting one—this one concerned sex education in public schools. We started by noting that sex-ed was required in most schools, though at the same time many people objected to teaching values in public schools. Those on the political left feared that such teaching would lead to religious indoctrination, and those on the right, that it would lead to the introduction of permissive liberal values. The result was that sex-ed was often taught as if it were a biological issue that had no moral context or content. (Individual teachers often did better but not the curricula or texts.)

The task force met several times before a consensus was formed. Initially, the members were sharply divided between those who believed that sex should be deferred until marriage and therefore schools should teach abstinence, and those who held that sex is a natural urge and that denying it leads to unhealthy frustrations. Furthermore, some argued that young people should be taught to engage in safer sex because they would engage in it anyhow. After much give-and-take, the task force came up with a position that leapfrogged this debate.

Our position was that sex education should be folded into a much more encompassing treatment of interpersonal relations, family life, and intimacy. The intimacy program assumes that sex is neither inherently good nor evil, neither pure nor sinful; the context makes all the difference. Sex is somewhat akin to nuclear energy: properly contained, it is a boon to the world; let loose, it can be a highly destructive force. The fact that must be shared with the younger generation, gleaned from both historical and contemporary experience, is that both attempts to repress sex as well as to let it roam freely cause much human misery. Properly contextualized, sex is not only a precondition of our future but can well serve to cement relations that have been properly constructed. In short, sex should be viewed and taught within the context of values and relations.

We urged educators to explain to young people that while sex is a source of much joy, it is much more than "recreational"; it is an act that can carry serious consequences. Responsible persons weigh the moral issues involved. They take into account that yielding to impulse leads to dire consequences for the child to be born, restricts the life options of the parents, and corrodes the values of the communities of which we are all members.

The task force urged teaching teens to defer *both* sex *and* marriage on the grounds that they are not likely to be ready to make a responsible decision in either department. Maturity is measured by behavior and not merely by chronological age, but it is more common among those who are older.

The position paper went on to spell out the specific ways this orientation should be taught and its communitarian origins and links. It was well received. Its ideas were reflected in articles published in *Educational Leadership* and in the magazine *Tikkun*, among others. When we put our ideas in an Internet magazine, *Intellectual Capital*, it generated a lively dialogue.

William Raspberry wrote in the *Washington Post:*

> Two things strike me about the "Communitarian Position Paper on the Family" just released. The first is that most of its proposals are, apart from legislative detail, essentially unarguable. They may be hard to state in a way that is entirely free of sexism or left/right political partisanship, but their essence is common sense. The second is a question: Why, if these things are so self-evident, haven't they been embraced and translated into public policy? . . . It all makes sense—including an interesting section on the need to restore childhood. Not only must we stop encouraging the premature preoccupation of young children with physical attractiveness, the authors say, but we need to look again at the way we do sex education. "The heart of our message must not be safe sex or mere technique, but rather responsible behavior as one feature of our mature identity."

We could not have written a more supportive column ourselves, and we sent copies to numerous educators and parent groups, as one more way to get the word out.

An active participant in the task force meetings on intimacy was one of the original endorsers of the Communitarian Platform, Isabel Sawhill. I had a great deal of respect for her. Although an economist by training, her interest in social and ethical issues was as keen as her willingness to consider other bodies of knowledge. However, I also learned to steel myself in dealing with her because she did not suffer (what she considers) fools, patiently or otherwise.

While Sawhill was working for the Clinton White House, I assembled at her invitation a group of noneconomists to lay out alternative approaches to welfare reform. I feared that the group would come up with umpteen different notions, many conflicting with the others, and we would lose our chance to influence the drafting of the reforms the White House was planning, which I considered were veering in an excessively harsh direction. (I felt this was especially true about the plan to cut recipients off of all benefits after a given number of years.) Before the meeting, I discussed with the members what joint or at least complementary positions we might take, who would start the ball rolling, and so on. (Note to activists: never walk into a White House meeting as if it were a seminar or brainstorming session. Often, this is going to be your only shot, and a bewilderment of half-cooked ideas will not carry the day.) However, soon after Belle (as most everybody calls Isabel) and Bruce Reed settled down and I introduced the participants, Belle interrupted me by stating that she wanted to ask the participants about some points that were on her mind, never mind the prepared presentations. And so it went—for the next five hours.

It was hence with a considerable amount of delighted trepidation that I watched Belle's participation in our task force on intimacy. I need not have worried; she helped bring the divided group to a shared, very sound conclusion. When Belle left the White House, she put together a large-scale and highly successful national drive to curb teen pregnancy. In it, she drew on communitarian ideas, especially on raising the moral voice of the community and on striving to change the normative culture instead of focusing on economic incentives, which her training could have easy led her to consider. Here, our message, combined with those of others, entered stage three, that of actually leading to changes in people's conduct. In the wake of Belle's drive and other developments—teen pregnancy declined significantly.

Although forming the task forces and keeping them going often entailed numerous phone calls, generated tedious scheduling problems, and required the ironing out of intellectual and personal differences, I found them an exhilarating part of the communitarian drive. In the process, I had a chance to meet and work with stimulating people who shared our basic perspective, but who brought insights and ideas all of their own to the discussions. There is a special joy in listening to people tackle a very taxing problem, one that they approach from different perspectives (ethical, legal, sociological) and on which they first talk past each other, but then find a common definition of the problem, work through it, and—as a rule—find a new handle on it.

CHAPTER ELEVEN

Getting the Word Out: Take Off

Enter Stage Two

For society to change, the communitarian message had to be widely accepted and implemented. We needed more than ideas that were sound and right for the time; we had to find ways to share them with our fellow citizens.

In taking the communitarian idea public, we faced an obvious obstacle. At any point in time, scores of people are scurrying about, each confident that they have found an idea that deserves full attention. How could we get above the noise, raise our voice above the clamor? Ours was a new "philosophy." This is not the stuff that makes headlines and that politicians stop their wheeling and dealing to study. True, we had outlined several specific policy positions, but these were largely calling for a new moral culture, not for concrete policy measures that might intrigue the media or that a legislature might enact.

What happened next, the story of how communitarianism gained entry into the public dialogue, is somewhat complex. It entailed working simultaneously on several fronts. Once we got a foot in the door leading to the public square, we delivered more than 800 (I counted) public lectures, press interviews, radio call-in shows, TV appearances, and briefings of public leaders, over a nine-year period. In the process, advances on one front helped on others: reports in the media about us whetted the interest of politicians and led major public groups to invite us to address their meetings. The fact that we captured the interest of major groups intrigued politicians. Their statements about us further fed the media's interest. For instance, media representatives attended public meetings in which presentations of communitarian ideas elicited long rounds of applause and standing ovations, such as at a major conference of the Points of Light Foundation in Orlando, Florida, and at the end of a General Assembly of the Unitarians in Rochester, New York, attended by Unitarians from all over the country.

By the end of 1991, there was so much demand for communitarian presentations that we set up a small speaker's bureau. In the process, I learned that many communitarians preferred writing and teaching to public speaking. Among those who did take to the road, Bill Galston provided quite a few very well received public lectures, until he joined the White House staff. Mary Ann Glendon was particularly effective, but she ceased to speak for us after she was called to represent the Pope at the United Nations Fourth World Conference on Women in Beijing in 1995. Philip Selznick's scholarly audiences particularly valued his addresses in the United States and abroad. After Phil published his communitarian magnum opus, *The Moral Commonwealth*, he was sought after even more. Enola Aird was so much in demand that she restricted her appearances so as not to neglect her family. Susan Anderson, a psychologist from New York University, was available to talk about her ideas concerning community service. William Sullivan often gave us a hand, especially when people wanted to learn more about the communitarian ideas expressed in *Habits of the Heart*, of which he was a coauthor. And David Anderson, a lecturer at The George Washington University, although junior to us in years, turned out to be one of our most dedicated emissaries.

Others could be counted on to occasionally speak about communitarian thinking. Still, most presentations fell on me, either because no one else was available to fly to places like Battle Creek, Michigan, or San Diego, California, between classes, or because, once I was recognized as the titular head of what was increasingly referred to as the communitarian movement, those who sought speakers insisted that they wanted to hear it from the horse's mouth.

The process of reaching out hardly followed a carefully laid out plan, based on some profound—or even not so profound—sociological insights. The three-stage model required getting the word out; it did not provide so much as a hint on how to proceed. What actually happened was much more a matter of being ready to respond to opportunity than of having a master plan. It involved a bit of luck and, above all, the fact that our idea was one whose time had come.

To wear my academic hat for a moment, I will first account for the "inputs" (what we did) and the "processes" (how we did it). I turn later to the "outcomes" (results). It should be noted, as they say in academic journals, that stage two (dissemination) started well before stage one (fashioning the message) was completed.

"Communitarians Are the New Zeitgeist"

Take Off

Pondering how to get the word out, I was distracted by sunny southern California. During the summer of 1990, I was offered a position at the University of California, Irvine. Although the offer was very attractive, I was unsure whether I could adjust to life in southern California. So, when negotiations with the university became serious, I moved with the kids to live for a week in Laguna Beach, so we could all share in the decision.

In the middle of trying to find out what people do in southern California once they get off the highways, tennis courts, golf courses, and sailboats, I received a message to call a *Business Week* reporter. She said her beat was "social issues" and that she had heard about my communitarian ideas; we had a good chat. Still, I made little out of her call. I had learned long ago that you can never tell by the interview if a published story will follow, let alone how extensive it will be.

A few days later, *Business Week* carried a full-page story. The magazine told about the struggle of Ramona Younger, a black community activist who supported a local antiloitering law aimed at curbing street-corner drug dealers. The American Civil Liberties Union (ACLU) and the National Association for the Advancement of Colored People (NAACP) were challenging the ordinance "an infringement of individual rights," and as a "racist." But Younger claimed that the ordinance helped "to get the drug business off our streets."

The article read:

> Younger has company in her concerns. An emerging group, sometimes called "communitarians," believes that the cause of the individual has gotten out of hand, jeopardizing community needs and public safety. For some in this movement, the problem is an overemphasis on individual rights. Others are more troubled by what they see as rampant, irresponsible individualism throughout American society.

The article closed with the lines:

> Etzioni goes further. He backs drug tests for train engineers, fingerprinting of children to foil kidnappers, weapons screening at airports, drunk-driving checkpoints, and the Alexandria anti-loitering law. These "acceptable intrusions" on rights

meet key criteria, he says: They are minimal, respond to clear and present dangers, and no alternative measure would produce the desired effect.

The *Business Week* article then added what, from our viewpoint, was the most important point: "The tension between individual rights and the common good is built into the U.S. Constitution, with a preamble that gives the government power to promote the general welfare and a bill of rights affirming basic freedoms."

This story was followed by several articles in the "idea" sections of major magazines, extensive commentaries from columnists, and—even more surprising—news stories. I quote these at length, perhaps excessively. However, I have found no other way to document that the claims made about the responses we received—at this stage in the media, later by elected officials and the public at large—are justified. Also the quotes allow readers to judge for themselves the tenor of the responses.

While the initial press stories focused on one of our primary themes— rights and responsibilities—John Leo, in a column in *U.S. News & World Report*, captured our community-building, restoring-the-moral-foundations theme. He was also the first to call attention to the misunderstanding that communitarians believe that the majority is always moral and just. Leo wrote: "Community ethics have been used for so long to mask prejudice or to exclude minorities that communitarian thinking is likely to be suspect. But it is not simply majoritarianism. It does not exalt the group over the individual. It asks for social responsibility and laws based on connectedness."

Soon after Leo's article was published, we were the subject of an article in *New York Magazine*. Coverage followed in an analysis in *Time* by Michael Kramer, a *Newsweek* article by Howard Fineman, an article in the high-powered *National Journal*, and in stories in respected local papers, such as the *Star Tribune* of Minneapolis.

To my utter amazement, in a matter of months, the communitarian school was on the map. Our stunning takeoff was largely due to changes in the American condition that invited a movement like ours. In the eighties, individualism got out of hand. By 1990, American society sought to repair the moral foundations of the nation. The age of Thatcherism and Reaganism, which had attempted to correct the liberal excesses of previous decades, itself called for a major correction. At the same time, most Americans found the religious right's prescription for whatever ailed America too dogmatic and condemning. Communitarianism, in contrast, provided a moral message that was much more inclusive and loving.

We faced no competition in the moderate moral "business," as there was no third group to offer a moral agenda for the nineties and beyond. Both liberals and laissez-faire conservatives were absorbed in the old, yet important, socioeconomic issues (jobs, inflation, the role of the state) and were very reluctant to touch the new sociomoral ones. While "communitarian," a term heretofore almost never used by the popular press, did not become a household word, it became an oft-used one.

Most important, with surprising speed, the media started to refer to communitarianism as a third way of thinking. For instance, in a major essay in *Time* on the politics of virtue, Robert Wright listed communitarianism next to liberalism and conservatism as a third body of thought. He defined it as providing a moral language that both moderate liberals and conservatives could embrace.

The Personal Is Public

Following several press stories that depicted me as the "guru" of the new communitarian movement (the *National Journal* referred to me as "the godfather of the new communitarian movement"), some newspapers published profiles on me, to personalize the news in a tradition long established by *Time*. On these occasions I tried to push our points instead of talking about my personal life, both to serve the cause better and because I see my private life as, well, private. Thus, when Michael D'Antonio prepared a five-page story about me for the *Los Angeles Times*, I divulged so little information about my personal life that he ended describing how I ate.

Our conversation grew heavier when D'Antonio wanted to know "if the death of your wife is what made you into a communitarian." I resented such questions not only because they were tugging at a very painful memory, but also because I do not believe that arguments should be judged by what caused them. I responded, "Either the communitarian ideas can be justified in their own right and should be embraced or they cannot and then should be rejected, but it should not matter if I got them shaving, listening to rock and roll, or at a funeral." D'Antonio explained, "But this is an article about *you* and your ideas." He had a job to do, as did I. I considered mine to keep profilers focused on our message.

Another reason to avoid profilers is that they fear coming across as fawning. Hence, regardless of what they might actually feel, the published report is sure to include some unflattering details. They will always try to quote someone who is critical of you. When I complained to Pat about these barbs, she reminded me: "You chose to be a *public* intellectual."

Anyway, whether the focus was on the message or on me, to my amazement the media continued to be intrigued by communitarian thinking and by what I had to say about it well into 1993—and in many cases, even later. Clearly, the media also sensed that the time for a moral renewal had come and saw communitarianism as a major way it might be achieved.

Courtesy of the ACLU

Social movements are often defined not merely by the social-historical conditions they seek to correct, but also by the opposition with which they contend. As we provided a democratic response to "the moral deficit" (in an era when most politicians spoke of the budgetary deficit), I assumed we would clash with the religious fundamentalists and their extremist right-wing allies. Instead, to my regret, from our very first day in the public eye, we were attacked by the ACLU.

The very first story about us in the press reported: "Ira Glasser, executive director of the ACLU, says complaints that the balance has tipped are nothing new. 'Communitarian really means majoritarian,' he says. 'The tendency is to make constitutional rights responsible for the failure to solve social problems.'" In the years that followed, we had numerous clashes with the ACLU in the forms of face-to-face debates and quote-counter-quote reports in the media. As a result, all too often we were portrayed as being in opposition to immoderate civil libertarians rather than to the religious right. At the same time, the ACLU's barrage of criticisms and accusations were not all a loss; these attacks—and our criticisms of the religious right—firmly established us as a centrist group, the place I thought we should occupy. There is no way of knowing what would have happened if the ACLU had simply ignored us, as the right wing initially did.

Because of the media interest in our message, I was able to place several articles in mass-circulation newspapers about our ideas. The first appeared in the *Wall Street Journal*, the second, in the *Washington Post*. In response to my *Wall Street Journal* article, the ACLU's Ira Glasser jumped in with this:

> It is ironic indeed that at a time when the early American idea of individual rights as the highest purpose of government is reasserting itself all over the world—in the Soviet Union and elsewhere—Prof. Etzioni would choose to revive in this country the profoundly dangerous and statist notion that individual rights and the common good occupy distinct and oppositional spheres. If this be communitarianism, who needs it?[18]

I responded that there was a world of difference between Eastern Europe's former Communist party regimes and our philosophy. Laws in the United States are arrived at democratically, not imposed by a tyrannical government. They are limited in scope and are neither omnipresent nor totalitarian. Moreover, their enforcement is subject to public scrutiny, democratic approval, and constitutional checks; gulags, secret police, and torture chambers are indeed alien. Second, laws democratically enacted do represent a proper method of expressing social and moral values and of signaling conduct that the community considers proper or abhorrent.

These exchanges were but the opening salvo. Over the years that followed, Nadine Strossen, president of the ACLU, and I debated on eight public occasions. And often, when our group promoted a public policy, for instance, favoring protecting young children from violent and vile material on the Internet by allowing libraries and parents to use filters, the ACLU would protest.

A word about my two main ACLU adversaries. Ira Glasser is a hard-hitting advocate who is not held back by complicated moral conniptions. In debating Roger Conner, the executive director of the American Alliance for Rights and Responsibilities, and me on network television, Glasser repeatedly, grossly misstated the ACLU position when he found it difficult to defend it. One example will stand for the others.

Drawing on our general position that individual rights need to be balanced with concern for the common good, we have argued that those who have the lives of others directly in their hands, such as drivers of school buses, train engineers, pilots, and air-traffic controllers, should be subject to mandatory drug testing. The ACLU protested that such searches violated a major constitutional principle that people should not be subjected to "suspicionless searches." Searches were legit only when there was specific evidence—before the search—that a crime might have been committed. For instance, the ACLU would not oppose testing the breath of pilots who had been seen by witnesses downing several drinks in a bar and stumbling out on their way to their cockpit—but objected vehemently to the testing of all pilots.

In line with this position, in 1972, the ACLU adopted a policy resolution opposing the introduction of screening gates in airports that routinely searched the luggage and bodies of millions of passengers—without any specific, prior suspicion. The ACLU maintained that such gates would "condition Americans to a police state." The courts disagreed and allowed the screening gates to stand. The gates eliminated practically overnight the hijacking of airplanes. And there are no signs I can detect that these screens have conditioned Americans to a police state. Drawing on the same logic, I argued that the prevailing legal doctrines should be modified to allow for suspicionless searches, but only when there was a compelling public need. For instance, sobriety checkpoints might be introduced to remove drunk drivers from the roads.

In trying to respond, the ACLU found itself in an awkward position. By the early nineties, it still had not repealed its resolution defining screening gates as unconstitutional, but it realized that attacking these safety devices was unwise as they had proven to be effective in stopping hijackers. At the same time, the ACLU correctly perceived that these gates were setting a precedent for "suspicionless searches" and hence did not openly drop its opposition to them. To avoid seeming inconsistent, the ACLU stopped referring to its opposition to screening gates, but kept attacking "suspicionless searches." When I pointed to this contradiction—Glasser maintained that the ACLU had never opposed screening gates.

I fumed: how dare he deny such a well-established fact? It soon became clear why and how: we had between us three and half minutes on nationwide network television. There was no time to find a document and hold it up to the camera to show the world what his representation of the ACLU was made of.

In contrast, Nadine Strossen is a charming model of a reasonable yet powerful ACLU advocate and critic of communitarians. In the "green room" (where the media parks guests until airtime), Nadine never failed to inquire about my family's and my well-being. We often chatted about her husband, Eli Noam, a colleague of mine from my Columbia University days. During one such event, Nadine broadly hinted that she had tried to reverse the ACLU position on the screening gates and that she was also uncomfortable with another ACLU position that I found particularly troubling.

The "other" policy is based on the notion that "money is speech," which are code words for saying that no limitations should be placed on how much money rich people, corporations, and labor unions should be able to give to politicians, a practice that corrupts our political system to the core. To understand how corrupt such a position is, think about a town meeting in which the rich are allowed to use amplifiers, which the rest cannot afford. Those who are able to buy more public opinion polls, consultations, and TV ads have a significant edge over all others in election campaigns. As a result, one-dollar, one-vote is replacing one-person, one-vote in our election system under the money-is-speech rule.

While Nadine was a fair opponent and wisely avoided issues that cast the ACLU in a poor light, she firmly opposed the essence of our message. On the air she did not mince words. When I faced her on the *Today Show*, she called our position "unprincipled" because, she said, it violates basic constitutional rights. On another occasion, Nadine stated, referring to what she called "The Communitarian Manifesto," that: "A lot of people and politicians would rather do away with the Bill of Rights than look at the underlying structural problems."

I responded:

> This is the worst kind of McCarthyism. Not a single person or politician was quoted or named. Above all, what such nuts have to do with us communitarians was not even hinted. Our quarterly is called *The Responsive Community: Rights and Responsibilities*. . . . To suggest that we have anything to do with doing "away with the Bill of Rights" is about as valid and fair an argument as for someone to suggest that the ACLU is a bunch of New York Communists.

ACLU charges against us fed into the media's interest in conflict. Soon, it seemed as if there were two camps—the civil libertarians and the communitarians! These depictions never ceased to surprise me. There were hundreds of thousands of civil libertarians—long established, major organizations, with armies of lawyers and multi-million-dollar budgets, while there was only a handful of us, a meager network run out of one professor's office, with an overdrawn account. Still, in less than a year our message had achieved some of the visibility that the neoconservatives had acquired when the media propelled that line of thinking into a "school." We not only had a message for society, but also a voice.

First Politicians and Bipartisans, Too

A Teach-in
To keep getting the word out, to move us further into stage two, I briefly considered crafting a pseudoevent. I had read somewhere that to gain the media's attention, something had to happen, not just talk. If all you had was a bunch of ideas, you had to "create" an event that would dramatize your cause. That is why the suffragettes chained themselves to the fence of the British parliament in their quest to call attention to their demand for a right to vote for women, African Americans held "sit-ins" at segregated lunch counters, and environmentalists buried a brand-new car. But the academic in me stopped me from manufacturing an incident or contriving to make drama. Instead, I decided to revive a sixties idea, to form a "teach-in."

The first obstacle to a communitarian teach-in was that we did not have the funds to rent a hall. It turned out that you can get a free room on Capitol Hill, in the building where Congress does its business, if you can find a member to sponsor you. Two scores of phone calls later, we found one.

Next, I wrote to members of Congress and others, informing them that on November 18, 1991, at the Russell Senate Office Building we would "unveil" our communitarian agenda. I invited them to drop by and speak whenever it fit into their schedule, but asked that they commit themselves to come at some point so that we could inform the public and the media.

Two senators, Al Gore and Pat Moynihan, were the first to accept the invitation, which made my day—and caused a problem. It was important that the communitarian movement not be boxed into a partisan pigeonhole. I saw the communitarian movement as the second environmental one; the environmentalists are concerned with protecting nature, we are concerned with the body society. Like the environmentalists, I argued that we should appeal to all comers and not just one political party.

Given our nonpartisan posture, the first communitarian teach-in could hardly proceed until we found at least one Republican to participate along with the two Democrats. Several scores more phone calls later, we gained the participation of Senator Dave Durenberger, a moderate Republican from Minnesota, and Alan Simpson, a less moderate Republican from Wyoming. Both have remained strong supporters ever since. Durenberger wrote simply, "I found your platform intriguing and consistent with many of my views."

Senator Alan Simpson was often chided by the press because he was very outspoken. I found him to be bright, witty, and highly supportive of our ideals. He wrote, "I have come to know your work and I have great respect, admiration, and regard for you. I am very intrigued by the communitarian agenda and I admire you so much for presenting it to our countrymen."

Simpson regaled our audience with stories about his misspent youth, about leaving pot marks on stop signs and considering beer the only suitable college nourishment. While his anecdotes at first sounded merely amusing, in accumulation they had an uplifting message: we may all start our journeys flawed, but this does not mean we cannot grow up to be upstanding human beings.

Gore said more by his presence, by staying an hour and responding to numerous questions, than by any specific statement he made. He was too cautious to endorse any of our positions, let alone a whole philosophy advanced by a new group. The highest accolade Gore made was that the communitarians "really are on to something." Coming from a man who was very wary, who had nothing to gain and much to lose by embracing politically untested thoughts, this was about as high a praise as one could expect from him.

While Senator Bill Bradley and Jack Kemp (at the time secretary of HUD in the Bush administration) could not attend, they responded to my invitation by sending strong letters of support which we proudly read to those assembled. From then on, the press often reported that Jack Kemp was one of us. Indeed, he had some ideas that could be considered communitarian, especially his interest in empowering people and in developing the inner cities' economies.

Now that we had a bipartisan lineup of speakers, we issued announcements about the teach-in. Given that on any day in Washington there are scores of public events to choose from and that we convened our teach-in on a work-day, I was very concerned that the audience at our first public event might be meager. I was pleasantly surprised when several hundred people showed up, as did the press, which allowed us to get the message to many more.

What happened at the teach-in and how the press reacted was well captured by Paul Taylor of the *Washington Post*. Taylor started by conveying the essence of our position on the moral infrastructure, families, and schools:

> How's this for a political platform for the 1990s? Fathers and mothers, consumed by "making it" and consumerism, come home too late and too tired to attend to the needs of their children and cannot discharge their most elementary duty to their children and their fellow citizens. Though divorces are necessary in some situations, many are avoidable and are not in the interest of the children, the community and probably not most of the adults either. Divorce laws should be modified, not to prevent divorce but to signal society's concern.
>
> Education institutions should provide moral education. We ought to teach that the dignity of all people ought to be respected, that tolerance is a virtue and discrimination abhorrent, that peaceful resolution of conflicts is superior to violence, that generally truth-telling is morally superior to lying, and that democratic government is morally superior to totalitarianism.

Taylor, moving from the specific to the general, then added a very succinct summary of our basic approach:

> The exclusive pursuit of private interest erodes the network of social environments on which we all depend, and is destructive to our shared experiment in self-government.
>
> This is not the kind of stern catalogue of shoulds and shouldn'ts that either the Democrats or the Republicans are likely to serve up. That's because the platform comes from a different realm altogether—the Communitarians.
>
> They aren't a political party. They are a loose alliance of academicians and social thinkers who believe there should be a political discourse grounded less on the language of rights and entitlements, and more on the language of responsibilities and obligations.

A picture of Senator Pat Moynihan and me reviewing the proceedings accompanied the article. My mother pointed out that I looked exhausted. Putting together a public meeting, sweating about attendance, and shepherding a whole day of talking, with senators dropping in and out and a public keen to break into the conversation, left their marks. But, as bushed as I was at the end of the day, I celebrated another major step forward. Senators came to address us, adding to the visibility of our ideas, and in the process they learned about our message. Now that we had acquired momentum, the question was: what next?

The Bush White House

An invitation by James Pinkerton, President Bush's deputy policy planner, to address a breakfast of the staff of Bush's White House on October 11, 1991, was particularly welcome. It allowed me to further demonstrate that we would talk to all sides. Pinkerton was one of those moderate Republicans who readily took to our message, largely because he and others like him had been thinking along similar lines themselves. (Pinkerton later put his communitarian ideas to print in a book called *What Comes Next: The End of Big Government and the New Paradigm.*) When Pinkerton called, he expressed the hope that "you will convince my colleagues that there is more to the world than deregulations, tax cuts, and smaller government."

I had no idea how many staff members would be interested in listening to a professor, even a public intellectual who had served in a Democratic administration, during an election year. Sixteen people showed up, including Jay Lefkowitz, Connie Horner, and Todd Buchholz. I briefly outlined our position.

The reaction of Bush's staff was fully underwhelming. Most of the questions that followed concerned our economic policy, of which at the time we had none. I explained, "We are just at the beginning of formulating our ideas and we choose to focus on social-moral issues." One staffer wanted to know why we did not attack outright "the sexual permissiveness, relativism, and multiculturalism of the Democratic Party." I responded, "We are trying to advance a positive agenda of what needs to be done to shore up the moral infrastructure and not beat up on anyone." Pinkerton tried to change the tone of the meeting with a question about the civil society. Before I knew it, breakfast was over and it seemed that I had not won over a single person.

Clinton's First Election and the New Zeitgeist

Bush's loss of the 1992 election was in part due to the same forces that generated much interest in communitarian ideas in the early nineties. Granted, numerous forces were at work. For instance, commentators made much of Bush's lackluster campaign. Questions were raised about whether he truly wanted to win; his aloof Yalie style was compared to Clinton's engaging communication skills, especially during town meetings on the all-important television.

As I see it, however, the 1992 election was deeply affected by the fact that Bush did not respond to the profound needs of the time, and those were not merely economic, by a long shot. Polls showed that nearly two-thirds of all Americans yearned for a moral message. Bush's pale response—his call for a kinder, gentler nation—never amounted to more than an election slogan.

Beyond being blinded by a laissez-faire conservative ideology, Bush was prevented from championing a communitarian moral message by a profound division within the GOP that continued to plague the party throughout the nineties. It was a division between laissez-faire conservatives, who were basically libertarian, and social conservatives, who were dominated by the religious right. The fight about the place of abortion in the Republican platform was but the most visible sign of the rift. The first camp continued to focus on cutting government, taxes, deficits, and regulation. The second camp was concerned with the fraying of the American moral fiber. Bush did not develop a message that could speak to the concerns of this group without offending the laissez-faire Republicans.

In contrast, the Democratic Party revamped itself by advancing a new social message, a rather communitarian one, under the influence of the New Democrats. The left-liberal wing of the party resisted and was dragged along complaining, but learned to accept the need for great personal responsibility and mutuality, less reliance on government, and more concern for community. The result was a coming together, however uneasy, around a centrist party, a position that eluded the GOP at the time.

The New Democratic movement was spearheaded by the Democratic Leadership Council (DLC), a group that moved the Democratic Party toward the political center and thus played an important role in winning the 1992 election. The group was founded in 1985, and Governor Clinton became its chair in 1989. In this period the DLC developed the Third Way, which contained many communitarian themes.

The New Democrats had their own think tank, the Progressive Policy Institute (PPI), which was launched at about the same time as the Communitarian project and promoted similar themes. The main New Democratic figures, Al From and Will Marshall (Elaine Kamarck also played a key role, as did Robert Shapiro on economic matters), participated in several of our meetings, and we in theirs. Moreover, Bill Galston was much more active in the PPI than he was in the communitarian project. We read each other's drafts of position papers and exchanged ideas informally at book parties and during Q&A sessions following public lectures.

To provide one example of the linkage: a somewhat different version of the paper on pro-family policies that Bill Galston presented at our first meeting, and which was the lead article of the first issue of *The Responsive Community*, was also issued as a major position paper by the New Democrats.

The three core concepts of the DLC were opportunity (for all, privileges to none), responsibility (for self and one another), and community. The last two concepts are communitarian par excellence. The main difference between the two groups was that the New Democrats were much more concerned with making the government leaner and with matters of public policy such as welfare and social security reform, while we were more interested in community building, the moral voice, and in the philosophical and ethical principles that undergirded our specific positions. And we were bipartisan.

Representative Dave McCurdy (D-OK), a chair of the DLC, captured the reception of communitarian ideas at the time when he wrote:

> In recent months, events have sparked me to rethink the nature of the New Democratic message and to probe its connections with the political philosophy of communitarianism. I am committed to the success of Bill Clinton's presidency, and believe he could benefit from an explicit embrace of communitarian themes—themes which match very closely those he articulated during the campaign.

On November 3, 1992, election night, I stayed up late. (Usually, I am early to bed, early to rise.) After midnight, I was rewarded when the new president-elect sounded a strong communitarian theme by stating, "We need more than new laws, new promises, or new programs. We need a new spirit of community." This was about as communitarian as it gets.

Over the years that followed, the media claimed a much greater communitarian influence on Clinton than I could see. The *Village Voice* put it simply: "Bill Clinton is voicing the credo of the Communitarians." However, even if one disregards Bill Galston's two and a half years of service in the White House; and our meetings with the president, the vice president, the first lady, and their staffs; and that these leaders let it be known that they had read *The Spirit of Community* and various other communitarian publications—one thing is clear: many of the ideas that the president and his associates drew on were communitarian, wherever they got them from. Other publications carried similar reports. Later, Clinton's personal conduct raised severe moral concerns. These were much less visible during his first term, during which most of our involvement with him took place.

Working with the Clinton White House

There were several reasons I was delighted when I found ways to work with the Clinton White House in the early years. It greatly enhanced the visibility of our message and, in some circles at least, added legitimacy to our approach. Also, the White House has a very strong convening power; (I knew from my Carter days that when you invite people to come to a White House meeting, most will ask "when" and "for how long" rather than saying that they need to check their calendars.) Two examples of how and about what follow.

The Communitarian Crime Task Force
The first event I organized in collaboration with Bill Galston in the White House was a "White House Conference on Public Spaces." Our basic thesis was that communities are formed in parks, plazas, sidewalks, and other such public places; if these spaces are unsafe, people will not venture outside their homes and cars. Ergo, communities would be set back.

Whom to invite? The natural tendency is to invite those you know and respect; maybe some of your friends who are keen to join a meeting in the White House's Roosevelt Room. Instead, I worked hard to find a broad range of people, including academics and community leaders, people of diverse social backgrounds, from different kinds of communities, as long as they were knowledgeable about public safety and showed some communitarian inclinations.

As people were ushered into the West Wing in mid-March 1994, the labor of the previous months paid off. From the community (in my mind I called them "real" people), we had two African American police chiefs from Virginia (Rubin Greenberg and Melvin High), a well-known district attorney from Texas (Ronnie Earle), and a deputy police commissioner from New York City who was a key architect of the policy that sought to suppress minor crimes as a way to build up community action against more serious ones (Jeremy Travis). The group also included several experts such as George Kelling (author of *Fixing Broken Windows*), Mark Kleiman (a brilliant policy wonk from Harvard), and innovative city planner Oscar Newman. We even had an African American Republican, Vincent Lane, the head of the Chicago Housing Authority, as well as a handful of others.

It is easy to depict the Roosevelt Room and difficult to capture why it evokes such an awesome sense of presence. The room is warmly colored, with creamy yellow hues, a light brown carpet, and darker brown leather armchairs placed around a long table. The walls are covered with paintings of the two Roosevelt presidents and a landscape. A fireplace rounds off the feeling that you are in the oversized living room of some cozy family. Maybe it is the pictures that say, "Wow, you are in the White House!" More likely, it is the fact that if you walk out the wrong door while searching for a bathroom, you find yourself at the door to the Oval Office. The fact that you are prevented by an armed Secret Service agent from trying to relieve yourself in the wrong room is a strong reminder that the most powerful man in the world works right here and lives upstairs.

The day was deliberately structured along the task force model. No papers were presented. After a brief round of getting-to-know-you and an unstructured discussion, we identified several topics that kept popping up and explored those in some depth, one at a time. The next day I composed a memo that summarized our main conclusions, which Bill passed on to the president and to key staff members. It contained thirteen pages of single-spaced recommendations.

The task force strongly favored the then new policies of going after what were previously considered minor, "quality of life" offenses (e.g., defecating in parks, playing boom boxes too loudly). We agreed with those who argued that such moves (including driving drug dealers out of public spaces by the "pram brigades," parents with their infants) help boost the moral voice of the community. Once it is fortified, it can speak to much more serious offenses. (Critics scoffed at "wasting" police resources on such small stuff.)

We argued for truly involving the community in community policing, beyond what was commonly done, just getting cops out of their cars to walk the beat. We pointed to the importance of involving community leaders in setting priorities for the police and discussing modification of those tactics that minorities found especially offensive.

We strongly criticized the trend to increase the severity of punishment and pointed out that the data showed that the "certitude" (increased likelihood) of apprehension and punishment served as a better deterrent to crime than tougher jail sentences.

We were persuaded by remarkable accounts from Oscar Newman about the merit of erecting barriers to cars at entrances to neighborhoods. He showed that these barriers (which did not keep people but merely cars out) both reduce crime and enhance community identity. And we favored certain kinds of curfews for youngsters and drives to reduce truancy.

"Not bad," I thought, "for a day's work." Of course, the ideas were not formulated in a day; what we did do was to draw on a lineup of experts and practitioners, to cull out some policy ideas that together amounted to a communitarian public safety package.

Our Character Education Gets Quite a Hearing

Vacations were never high on my priority list, but summers in Washington, D.C., leave much to be desired. Pat, who must have been a mermaid in a previous incarnation, needs to be near water. So, we are off to Camden, Maine, to kayak. But, almost immediately after I bought a sweater and a poncho to cope with the cold weather, the executive director of the Council of Chief State School Officers called to say that the commissioners in charge of education in all fifty states were about to meet in Salt Lake City. There had been a last moment cancellation and the caller wanted to know if I could come, in two days, to talk about communitarian ideas on character education. This was good news; fifty commissioners were not merely one more audience, but an audience that could take our ideas to stage three, to actually implementing them. But I was also reluctant to leave cool Camden, so I set an unreasonable condition: I needed *two* hours. I explained that it would take one hour to lay out our approach, and that unless there was another hour for discussion, I could not properly justify our viewpoint. Next thing I knew, I was on my way to the airport, to one of our best meetings ever.

The commissioners' interest in character education was but one more indication that there was a great need to attend to the moral agenda. "Character education" is a term often employed by people who realize the political risk of speaking openly about value education. The right wing fears that liberals in public schools will use value education to push their ideals, and the left fears the same education will serve the promotion of religion. Hence, politically savvy educators long shied away from the subject and focused on teaching academics. However, by the early nineties the need for value education became so pronounced that many educators were looking for new ways to proceed. Communitarian ideas provided a way.

I started my presentation by suggesting that the need for character education in schools arises because families—even when fully intact and dedicated to the moral education of their children—cannot complete the process of making children into good members of society. Hence, I stressed that schools must be concerned not merely with teaching values but also with education in the deepest sense of the term. I added, "Schools are best viewed as a series of experiences generated by the ways teachers do or do not discipline their students; whether they evaluate homework and exams fairly; whether or not there is social promotion; whether the corridors, halls, and parking lots are orderly or out of control." (Shades of Ben Shemen?)

I concluded, "The total environment of the school must be used to help young people develop two personality characteristics. The first is self-discipline, the capacity to keep one's urges under control. We all have aggressive and sexually inappropriate urges; these cannot be expunged. The best education can do is equip us with a second voice, an inner moral voice, one that is activated as a countermeasure when these urges swell in our chest."

When I saw many commissioners nodding their heads in approval, I moved to the second essential characteristic: "The trouble is that if one has only strong self-discipline, one may become an efficient killer. Empathy, the capacity to feel another person's pain and joy, is essential for good character education. It ensures that self-discipline will be pro- rather than antisocial. Once people have these two essential character qualities, values can be crafted on them, but without these qualities, even if people *know* what is good—they will not have the capacity to *do* good." Right or wrong, it was nothing like what anyone else in the character or value education "business" was presenting.

When you lecture, it is somewhat like a first date. When there is "chemistry," the audience responds by listening attentively, furiously taking notes; when it is missing, the audience is restless, whispering, even unfolding newspapers. Well, this felt like my best "date" in a long time.

In the discussion that followed, the first question was: "But which values can we teach?" This question is frequently raised and many educators consider it a "killer" because it implies that because communities cannot agree which values to teach, value education cannot take place in public schools. I responded by stressing that no reasonable person could object to teaching children self-restraint and empathy. I asked rhetorically, "What would a Moral Majority representative claim? That permissiveness is better? . . . Anyhow," I reiterated, "we are talking character education, behavior development, not abstract values." This seemed to go over well because this approach met two criteria at once: it was substantively sound as well as politically helpful. Commissioners must keep their eyes on both balls.

Another commissioner said, "I like your emphasis on the school as a total environment; give us another example." I responded that sports—we have known since the ancient Greeks—are the best character-building activity. It is unfortunate that some schools are carving gyms into classrooms and most treat sports as an *extra*curricular activity; it should be part of the core curriculum." This comment raised several eyebrows. More were raised by my next caveat.

"Note that the sports program I am talking about is not one that focuses on winning at all costs, but, on the contrary, on teaching young people to play by the rules, accept legitimate authority, control their emotions, deal with defeat, and be fair to the other side." After some more give-and-take, I was on my way. I read into many of the invitations that followed to consult with various educational departments and into requests for more information about our ideas a sign that the message was well received. Unfortunately, I was never able to determine whether and to what extent it found its way into school reforms in the following years, as increasing attention was being paid to character education in numerous schools.

Character Education in the Clinton White House

Another sign that our character education message was falling on open ears came when we organized, working with Clinton's Secretary of Education Richard Riley, our first White House Conference on Character Building in 1994. The White House provided the all-important venue; that is, legitimation and its enormous convening power. I did the rest, working with a small staff at the Communitarian Network, a not-for-profit corporation I had founded by that time. More than 250 leaders accepted our invitation to attend.

As our first White House conference got underway, we were crowded into room 450 of the Old Executive Office Building, a place one often sees on TV because it is the room where the presidential press conferences are held. We were waiting for the president. I dashed back and forth between the green room and the podium. I would check in the green room, adjacent to the stage, to see if the president had arrived and then would rush back to the podium to reassure the restless group that the word was the president was going to join us any moment.

After a while, a presidential aide showed up and pinned the presidential seal on the podium, a sign that he was nearing. However, when there was still no president in sight, several members of the audience, led by gold medalist Jeffrey Blatnick, jumped on stage, stood behind the podium with the seal, waving their arms as if campaigning, and had their picture taken.

As the host, I was frantically trying to figure out what I could possibly do if the president did not show. At just about this time I was beckoned back into the green room: *he* had arrived. We exchanged a few pleasantries and notes about the Third Way and communitarianism while the president gulped down a Diet Coke. (The green room had a considerable bowl of fresh fruit and several Cokes. When I reached for one of them, the president's steward blocked me, politely but firmly: "For the president *only*.")

Finally, we were on stage. I introduced the president and sat down to listen to the message he was going to share with the assembled educators. Clinton opened with words that few would take with indifference when they come from the president of the United States addressing a packed room: "Thank you very much, Dr. Etzioni. Thank you for that introduction and for the inspiration that your work has given to me and to so many others, for the wonderful book, *The Spirit of Community*, and for working on this as hard as you have."

What I heard next made me wonder why I had ever been as stupid as to leave my academic cubicle and where I had gotten the inane notion that I was cut out for any kind of public life. The president was talking about

Figure 11.1. With President Clinton, 1997

the reasons he had to order the closing of one block of Pennsylvania Avenue to traffic, the block in front of the White House. The president explained, in much detail, that he really did not wish to do so, but the Secret Service, a panel of public safety experts, and the FBI made him close the road to better protect the house of the people from terrorists. (The decision had been announced the day before our meeting and the president had come to our meeting directly from a press conference in which he justified the street closing.) As the president extended his explanation, I was desperately trying to figure out what I should tell the assembled educational leaders I had invited to come from all over the nation to hear the president's message on character education. But my mind was hysterically blank; nothing popped. As the president rambled on, I was growing angry and fantasized telling those in the room, "You see what happens when you do not have the needed self-discipline," one of our major character educational themes.

After twenty more minutes, in which the president continued to lay out the reasons others attributed to protecting the White House and the president and his family, just when I was about to crawl under the carpet, the president was suddenly done with his "here is why I was forced to close Pennsylvania Avenue" speech and delivered a sterling forty-minute dissertation on character education.

> Now, what's that got to do with what we're doing here today? Now, the question is, how can we preserve the traditional values and how can we find at least a measure of the fulfillment in doing right and good things in ordinary life that we find when disaster strikes? Is there something endemic to the modern world or human nature that says we can't do that? I don't think so.
>
> I also believe that the central insight of what Dr. Etzioni has done is important to emphasize here. Everyone has a role to play. And we can solve this in a free and open society, not by any governmental policy, but by government, like every other part of society, playing its own role.

The president continued to stress that "education is about more than intellect. Everybody knows, as my mother used to say, there's a lot of smart fools running around in this old world. And what we want to do is to build good citizens as well as intelligent people." He pointed to the roles communities and churches could play in character education. The close parallels between what the president was advocating and the positions we had spelled out made all the preparatory work (waiting included) very worthwhile indeed.

When Clinton had finished, everybody seemed to have forgotten about the inauspicious beginning; long applause was followed by a spontaneous standing ovation. We heard next from a panel of various members of the administration. The day closed with a reception in the elaborately elegant Indian Treaty Room, which never fails to impress people.

The conference was especially important for us because, by involving leaders from all over the country, we were able to get our message out much more effectively than if we had to visit with each group individually and repeat our spiel. The leaders, to the extent that they were persuaded, would take the word to their groups; thus, addressing them had a multiplying effect.

On the way out, many asked if and when we were going to meet again. Several educators congratulated us for bringing people of such diverse backgrounds together aside from a chance to listen to the president from close up. They particularly appreciated that we had provided a very unusual meeting ground for groups as different as the National Association of Evangelicals, the American Federation of Teachers, the relatively conservative PTA, and the liberal People for the American Way. It did not take much to conclude that the group ought to be reconvened annually in the following years.

Although ours was a White House conference, our nonpartisan status had to be maintained. Hence, I invited Bill Bennett to speak at the 1995 conference. As far I am concerned, there are two Bill Bennetts. One is a partisan pit bull who makes harsh, biting attacks on Democrats. The other is a moral voice who is relatively moderate compared to the leaders of the Moral Majority and who is more inclined to favor championing virtue than imposing it. Moreover, Bennett showed considerable political courage when he chided those on the religious right for being obsessed with gays and less vocal about divorce, a sin many of the Republican leaders were guilty of. (During the 1995 preparations for presidential election campaigns, I wrote an article for the *Wall Street Journal* arguing that Bennett should run on the GOP ticket because none of the other candidates represented the faith-in-faith position.)

In inviting Bennett, I told his staff openly, "We are inviting Bill Bennett the moral statesman, to a bipartisan event, and assume that the other Bill Bennett will stay at home." Bennett accepted the invitation and lived up to the implicit agreement: he delivered a powerful, evocative, very well received, and fully nonpartisan appeal for character education. The president publicly praised Bennett the next day for "his fine educational message." Thus, we helped create a bit of common ground on character education. (A few years later, during the Monica Lewinsky scandal, Bennett became one of Clinton's most outspoken critics. In sending a greeting for an issue of *The Responsive Community* dedicated to my work on the occasion of my seventieth birthday, Bennett remembered the bipartisan moment and complained teasingly, "You had me *praising* President Clinton.")

We had come a long way from a group of professors forming a "school." We had found ways to share our timely views with members of the public, community leaders, members of Congress, and the White House. Our message gained legitimacy by their participation in our teach-ins and conferences and ensured that we would not be seen as a one-sided, partisan group. For me it was a long way from building a case in opposition to a war that was not going away and from tilting at NASA, helping mobilize opposition, and bearing witness to immoral and dangerous policies. This time the message might do more than just be right on. This time there was hope for going all the way, of actually participating in the recasting of the social and moral foundations of society; a tall order at best.

CHAPTER TWELVE

---∞∞∞---

Getting the Word Out, Continued

Dole and the "Vision Thing"

For quite a while, our efforts to spread the communitarian message paid off among both our fellow citizens and public officials. In May 1995, the drive to share our message with both political parties landed me in a meeting with Senator Robert Dole, who was running against President Clinton, six days after I had attended a small dinner with the president in the White House. I was taken to see Dole through a circuitous route.

Paul Weyrich, a leading social conservative, suggested that he and I get together, as he saw an overlap between "my cultural conservatism and your communitarianism." Soon, we had an unusual conversation, in which we strongly agreed on some points and differed at least as strongly about others. This initial conversation was followed by an invitation to a meeting of social conservatives that Weyrich was convening. Its purpose was to formulate an agenda that Bob Dole would be lobbied to champion during the election campaign.

Soon, I found myself at a small gathering. The people around the table were all white males in dark suits. As they introduced themselves, it became clear that they were all affiliated with some conservative or right-wing group and were Republicans. I warned them that I was not a Republican, but they were riding so high on the wave of the 1994 elections, on what they perceived to be the conservative revolution, that they had no objection to including a nonpartisan type in their conclave.

The group batted around ideas about how to undo the government more quickly, more completely. The government programs to be slashed were not necessarily the biggest or most expensive, or the ones with the most onerous regulations, but those that promoted values the group found offensive.

Weyrich argued, "To undermine abortion we should get our newly elected friends in Congress (he was referring to the seventy-three conservative freshmen) to attach an amendment to each federal funding bill prohibiting the use of public funds, however indirectly, for abortions." Weyrich added, with a chuckle, that such a measure, among other things, would "block the flow of Medicare and Medicaid funds to numerous hospitals and clinics and get their attention."

Michael Schwartz (then working in Weyrich's office) enthusiastically agreed, adding, "Whatever we achieve, we must find ways to zero out *Roe v. Wade*."

Tom Jipping (vice president for legal policy at the Free Congress Foundation) explained that the best way "to stop the government from this diversity business" was to pass a law prohibiting the U.S. Department of Education from awarding grants to any institution that applies racial criteria in their admissions policies. He also favored banning federal funds from all colleges that have hate-speech codes.

Someone upped the ante: "We should simply close the place down," referring to a Republican plan to close the Department of Education.

Clinton Bolick (vice president and director of litigation, Institute for Justice) suggested "a comprehensive ban on all race preferences, from student loans to housing, from employment to contract placing."

Bill Myers (whose affiliation I could not make out) provided a long list of budget items he did not care for. He announced with visible delight, "We might not be able to cancel these programs outright, because they have been made into laws by liberals over the last decade, but we could get our friends in Congress to zero budget them!"

I was struck by the negativism of it all. The grab bag mixture of ideas all concerned undoing, banning, or slashing the government, or limiting people's choices. There was as much zeal in this group as I found when I was dealing with left-wing extremists during the campaign against the war in Vietnam. It was not their commitment to a cause that troubled me; I sort of respected it. But in this meeting there was no sign of their Christian spirit, that of reaching out and caring for vulnerable members of the community, which is so much a part of the values they were anxious to uphold. They had volumes to say about what to take away from the vulnerable members of society, but not a word about what should be done for them, on a voluntary basis if government help should be withdrawn. Indeed, one of the participants in the meeting argued that if churches picked up the slack, welfare clients would merely have substituted one dependency for another. Let them learn to swim by realizing that otherwise they would sink. The difference between the spirit of the meeting and that of communitarians could not be more striking.

My first instinct was to take to the door. But then I figured that I should try to redirect some of this dedication, alter its tenor, and stay with the group in case it did provide access for our message to Dole.

I spoke briefly about the need to change the moral culture of America by involving the people in a dialogue about America's core values, to convince Americans to spend more time with their children, and—once they had a decent standard of living—to refrain from frantically pursuing ever more consumer goods. The group listened politely, but there was no indication of interest. Those in attendance were mostly lobbyists for conservative groups and were very Washington-oriented. When I continued, I was interrupted by a question, "Do you have any specific measures to recommend?" Weyrich said something softly in my defense, but the original question hung in the air. I mumbled something about the importance of changing the habits of the heart, but awkwardly fell silent.

A few days later the same group was ushered into Dole's spacious office in the Capitol. I was especially anxious; the stakes were high, and I doubted that I could—in the minutes allotted to each of us—convey the communitarian message. Dole's aide introduced us to the senator, and other members of the group each proceeded to make a succinct case for the specific policy recasting they favored. Dole's reactions were quick and impressive. He listened attentively and then responded crisply. He promised to send one of the proposals to the chairman of a certain committee because, although the matter might be more in the turf of another chairman, the first one was more likely to be sympathetic. Another proposal Dole said he himself would push, but he noted that to do so he would have to find "a way around the objections of the parliamentarian of the Senate." Still another policy idea he instructed his senior staff to run with.

When my turn came, as the last one to speak, I explained that I did not have any specific policy proposals, but wanted to discuss the implications of the fact that "more than two-thirds of our fellow Americans believe that the country is in a moral crisis." I began to discuss the moral infrastructure when I lost eye contact with Dole, who was either staring out of the window or into his inner space. I made myself continue and discussed "the need to shore up the family, character education, and community without necessarily returning to the past." Dole looked at his senior aide, who nodded his head slightly. A minute later he reminded us that the time allotted to us was exhausted. Dole thanked us and we were out.

I was crestfallen. I kept asking myself how I could have made our case in a way that would have spoken more to the senator. Should I have started with a specific policy recommendation and then explained that it was but a lead for a much more encompassing agenda? Should I have asked to be one of the first to speak and not the last? I put down the meeting as probably my greatest missed opportunity of the communitarian drive to date. Luckily for my morale, I presented the communitarian case a bit better to President Clinton and company.

Bill, Al, Hillary, and Staff

Communitarianism Comes to Dinner

When a White House social secretary called to ask whether I could join the president for dinner, I was pleased, but also wary. On two other occasions, I ended up with several hundred others in White House receptions, one to mark the launching of one of the president's favorite communitarian programs, AmeriCorps; the other to see the president and the first lady handing out awards to numerous artists. These were pleasant occasions during which I had a chance to visit with old friends and meet new, interesting people. I consumed too many of the petits fours and went home disappointed that I had not had a chance to bend the president's ear for more than a glancing minute. Hence, when the call came this time, I asked for more information. The White House secretary assured me that it was going to be a very small dinner.

The evening started not unlike a dinner in an affluent private home. Waiters circulated with trays. A bartender supplied drinks. Music played in the background. Then the hosts, first the vice president and then the president, appeared from nowhere and mingled among us. After drinks, about half a dozen of us settled around a dining room table not much larger than in many upper middle class homes.

I should not make it sound as if this was one more social occasion. There is a special aura to the White House. It is hard to ignore that one is standing at the world's power apex. Words are more measured, as if each has a special weight. And every nod of the head, smile, and frown by the host—The President of The United States—registers.

Still, after another glass of wine, and an hour into the evening, we were engaged in an informal and lively conversation. It helped that both Clinton and Gore spent most of the time listening, unlike many public leaders I have met. Many politicians' eyes wander when a presentation runs longer than a minute and a half, or they cannot long resist injecting themselves into the conversation. Clinton and Gore cocked their ears for three hours. We talked about how communities might be mobilized to fight crime (which led to several "tell me more" requests by the president); the relative importance of providing jobs to the poor as compared to changing the culture that prevails in ghetto communities; the value of building up self-esteem as a way to empower people in inner cities; and the merit of V-chips as a way to protect children from violence on TV. On most issues, Gore carefully waited until the president had asked all he wanted to, but when it came to V-chips, Gore—who considers himself a tech maven—led the conversation.

When the president did speak briefly, he revealed a surprising command of public policy nuances. For example: he pointed out that in the past it had been conventional wisdom that when young offenders turned twenty-five or so, they tended to "graduate" from violent crime, often on their own. He asked, "Given the new wave of youth violence, can one assume that this trend will continue?" This question displayed a subtle understanding of social trends that escapes quite a few social scientists.

One mannerism of the president was somewhat unsettling. Often, after he did make a point, he would use his head like a radar dish, turning from left to right, scrutinizing the faces of those assembled. When, on one occasion, several of us expressed doubts about the relative importance of providing jobs as compared to changing the culture of dependency, the president repeated his previous position favoring jobs but this time added, "Of course, we all know that we must also be sure that people who can will take responsibility for themselves and their families." I had heard much about Clinton's strong need for approval, but I had never seen it in operation so close up. It left one uneasy, wondering if the man had a true north.

The only time the president's demeanor changed was when he talked about several measures he had sent to Congress that the Republicans were blocking. His face was angry, and he did not mince words. It was hard to tell whether he was only venting his frustration or also counting on us, despite the understanding that this was a private dinner, to leak the message to the press.

I spent most of the dinner worrying about what to say. I forgot that I had brought with me an index card with "talking points." Waiting for a lull in the conversation, I found an occasion to join in. I urged involving communities in fighting crime and drug abuse by allowing them to spend some of the substantial savings that would result from having to incarcerate fewer people and by allowing communities to participate in setting priorities for the police, say, in terms of which areas should be patrolled more often. I added that I realized that many people think that there are no communities in our major cities but that actually there are many, often organized along ethnic lines (such as Chinatown, Spanish Harlem, and so on), and that in areas in which communities died out, we can rejuvenate them by providing the neighborhoods with meaningful tasks they would have to undertake jointly. It was rewarding to see the president listen carefully and at one point actually state outright that he agreed with me. I realized that this did not mean that he was about to call aside his aides and instruct them to implement these ideas forthwith. But communitarian ideas were carried to the highest level of government that evening without any staff mediation, framing, or reformulation.

The next invitation to a small White House dinner was for the evening of January 7, 1996. The date matters because it was the night of one of the worst snowstorms Washington had experienced in many a year. The snow came down fast, as if each flake were rushing to catch up with the one that just dashed by. Cars and buses stopped running; even the Metro had trouble plowing through. Luckily, I could walk to the White House from my home.

The lineup for this dinner was even more august than the previous one. Aside from the president and the vice president, the first lady also joined us, as did several key staff members. The dinner was similar in format to the first one. The give-and-take was equally informal and lively, oscillating between liberal and communitarian thoughts on what the roots of our social problems were and what might be done about them. If you closed your eyes, this could have been a seminar on public policy at one of our better universities—other than that, it was hard to forget that one just might plant a seed that would sprout into a change in one of the administration's policies or, better yet, ways of thinking.

In the middle of it all, somewhere between the main dish and dessert, my mind wandered. Here I was, an immigrant with a foreign name and accent who had come to the United States but a few years back, spouting off to the president about what ought to be done. It was a shorter journey but still one that covered quite a bit of distance from the days when I used to demonstrate outside the White House fence, protesting—to dining in it, cheering its endeavors while trying to augment them. And although I did serve in the Carter White House, that was like serving on a slowly sinking ship. Clinton was flying high and there was no way of telling what communitarian policy idea he might take with him up, up, and away.

I directed myself back into the lively exchange of ideas. Outside the snow was coming down so heavily that the windows looked as if they were covered with puffy white blankets. At about 10:30 P.M., an aide came and whispered something in the first lady's ear. She gently knocked a knife against a water glass and informed us that unless we left for home, even the White House cars might not be able to take us through the snow. Bill Galston thanked the president for the evening, and we stood up. The president, though, wanted to continue to chat. We stood in a small circle around him. He put his arms around those closest to him, and we talked and talked until well past eleven. At this point, the first lady interrupted, assigned us to different cars according to our destination, and sent us on our way. One outgoing and effusive, one focused and organized, they made a remarkable couple.

Other Occasions

Over the eight years of his administration, I met one-on-one with President Clinton only once; on several occasions, we met in small groups. I also joined him at an annual get-together that has jokingly been called a meeting of his 1,200 "best friends"—the Renaissance weekends in Hilton Head. He changed a great deal over these years. Early in 1993, shortly after Clinton was elected president, he was exuberant, energetic, loaded with communitarian messages.

The December 1994 Renaissance weekend followed the GOP landslide victory in congressional elections, which was widely billed as the "conservative revolution" and viewed as a devastating rejection of the Clinton administration (including of its Third Way and communitarian tilt). The president came across as shell-shocked, disoriented, unsure of himself. He spoke in incomplete sentences. While on earlier occasions he would make and maintain direct eye contact with you, now his puffy eyes were aimed at some distant spot. One could not help but worry about him, simply as a person who has been hit over the head and boxed around the ears.

By the end of 1996, the president's ebullience was almost fully restored and so was his confidence in his Third Way/communitarian approach. In the Renaissance weekend tradition, as formulated over many years by the indefatigable organizers Phil and Linda Lader, there was a festive dinner to celebrate New Year's Eve, after which the Clintons got the floor for the last two hours of the year. Then, there were the usual midnight hugs and kisses, and the assembled gradually dispersed. The president, however, would hang around, in the middle of an ever smaller circle, often holding court until 2 A.M. or later.

During one of these chat-fests in the first hours of 1997, Clinton put his hand on his heart and, in the presence of some twenty others, intoned slowly to me with much studied affect: "You *are* my inspiration." I tried to tell myself that he was appreciating not me but the communitarian message. Still, it was my best New Year's Eve greeting ever.

In 1998, the president showed no sign of the scandal that was swirling around him when he met with a group of young people (about which I got a firsthand report from my son Oren) and then with the rest of the Renaissance crowd. It was an amazing performance; he seemed unaffected by the yearlong investigation and even by the fact that he had just become only the second president in American history to be impeached. He showed no sign of regret, repentance, bitterness, or anger, as if the whole mess had never happened.

Late at night, however, in a much smaller group, he was withdrawn, as if he were not all there. His responses were mechanical, lethargic, and his eyes drifted. "As if he is on Prozac," someone commented. This time I felt more sorry for the country than for the man.

The first lady and I make a shorter chapter. Our meetings were infrequent and brief: I ran into her in a corridor of the Hilton Head Hyatt, talking with Norman Ornstein (the most often cited political scientist), and joined the conversation. We had a meeting in which I briefed her on communitarian thinking in her office in the West Wing of the White House. There was another brief exchange at a dinner in Havel's castle in Prague. And she joined the 1996 national conference on character education, organized by the Communitarian Network (which I direct).

More often, I would drop a memo—followed by a visit—to Melanne Verveer, her chief of staff. (I admired Melanne before she joined the White

Figure 12.1. With Hillary Rodham Clinton, 1996

House; I even tried to hire her to direct the Communitarian Network just before she joined the first lady's staff.) Melanne pointed out candidly which ideas required more consideration (on my side) and which ones she held were ready to be passed on to Mrs. Clinton and, on some occasions, to the president. (I was far from the only one who benefited from this backdoor channel to the president.)

While the public's estimations of the first lady were more volatile than the stock market, the Hillary I knew barely changed. She was always focused, fully in control, and determined. Her style, which tended to the ironic, was markedly different from the president's. One afternoon when I ran into her in a corridor during one of the Renaissance year-end celebrations, she said, "You are in my book *It Takes a Village*; this may not be to your advantage . . . people may say 'if she says he is a good guy, he must be a bad guy,'" shaking her head in mock disapproval. I rushed to read the book and found it to be as good a communitarian text as they come. Several Republicans disparaged the ideas of the book, insisting that it was up to the family and not the village (which they equated with the government) to bring up children. But Hillary won this battle hands down when she pointed out, during the Democratic National Convention, as she does in the book, that bringing up children requires families, and schools, and places of worship, and businesses—a whole village. Hillary is often characterized as the more liberal of the two and for good reason. However, in her understanding of the importance of viable communities for human flourishing, she is second to none.

Having the more liberal of the two Clintons publicly and extensively embrace the core of communitarian thinking was one more sign, to put it grandly, that these ideas were in step with history and maybe egging it along some.

White House Character Education Conferences

I already mentioned that the White House conferences on character education (which I organized each year beginning in 1994) served as an excellent tool to disseminate our message. Approximately 300 educational leaders of a large variety of backgrounds participated in each conference. The meetings lasted between two and three days and provided ample opportunity to showcase our ideas.

A few examples of the presentations at the conference: Newt Minow commanded everyone's rapt attention when he showed a videotape on which he had collected what a child watching television is exposed to over a one-day period. It provided strong support for those of us who held that there was an intense need to enact various policies to protect children from violent and vile material in the media. Republican Senator Dan Coats put nearly everyone to sleep when he delivered in a dull monotone an excellent list of prescriptions of how the government might reactivate communities—so that the government could retreat and turn over some of its missions to communities. (When we published it in *The Responsive Community*, it read just fine.)

We received many compliments when we organized a very civil and productive dialogue between Deborah Haffner, head of the Sexuality Information and Education Council of the United States (SIECUS), a potent advocate of a very liberal approach to sex, and Don Browning, a soft-spoken communitarian professor from the University of Chicago Divinity School. (A sign of our ecumenical nature was that both became friends of mine in the years that followed.) It was later reflected in our position paper calling for what is called "abstinence plus"(strongly urging youngsters to defer sex, but also teaching them what to do if they engage in it).

The conference participants rose for a long, standing ovation for Kathleen Kennedy Townsend, the lieutenant governor of Maryland, after she delivered a heartfelt endorsement of character education and community service. Nancy Kassenbaum (a Republican senator from Kansas) addressed our conference in a soft voice from a podium that had to be specially lowered for her. But her communitarian message came across strong and clear.

After Clinton addressed the Character Education conference in 1995, the first lady was the star in 1996, and Gore in 1997. By 1998, the White House was mired knee-deep in the Monica Lewinsky scandal. Even by the president's own words, his conduct was reprehensible. And whatever one considered the relevance of his personal conduct to his ability to carry out his public duties, the 1998 White House was not the place to feature character education. Hence, we severed the association of our annual meeting with the White House and conducted it on the Hill and at The George Washington University.

One of our keynote speakers was Stephen Goldsmith, the Republican mayor of Indianapolis. He charmed the socks off everyone and regaled us with compelling accounts of how he tackled the various social problems of his city. His main device was to involve the communities, including faith-based groups, to improve the quality of life in the city in general and in poor neighborhoods especially. (He later described these endeavors in a book called *The Twenty-First Century City*.) He made one wonder why the Republicans were not nominating him for president.

Another keynote speaker was Senator Joseph Lieberman. He is not a towering figure, and he speaks softly and gently, in a more agonizing than preachy tone. But his presentation was pure communitarian gold. To provide but one quote:

Faith and the values that flow from it were central to the founding of this country. They have always shaped and stirred our national conscience. And now, at this moment of moral uncertainty, I believe our best hope for rekin-dling the American spirit and renewing our common values is to have faith again. Not just in our hearts, but in our communities. Not just in our private places of worship, but in our public spaces of conversation. And not just in our separate beliefs, but in our common commitment to our common purposes as Americans.

When he first addressed our group I introduced him as a *mensch*, which, if literally taken, means "man" in Yiddish, but actually means a good chap, a decent fellow, a fine person. When Lieberman joined us again, he extended the same compliment to me. It is a high one in my book.

Many others who addressed the conferences over the years included schol-ars (such as Professor James Comer and Edward Zigler from Yale, Tom Lick-ona from the State University of New York at Cortland, and Laurence Stein-berg from Temple), heads of educational organizations (such as those of the PTA, National Education Association [NEA], and American Federation of Teachers [AFT]), and education as well as community leaders (such as Mary Elayne Bennett and Linda Darling-Hammond).

While the White House Character Education conferences served mainly to "disseminate" our message, they also served to develop it. I formed half a dozen educational task forces that met at the annual conferences and were in touch between them. They produced an array of specific educational com-munitarian policy recommendations. Some covered our "basics," spelling out the need to teach self-discipline and empathy and how this might be done. Others zeroed in on specific issues, ranging from the role of sports in charac-ter building to the merit of keeping schools open more hours each day, more days each month, and more months each year.

When our position papers were issued, they contained notes alerting the readers that they spoke for only those who endorsed the particular position and not for all communitarians. However, by publishing these position pa-pers, we indicated that they fell somewhere within the admittedly broad and inclusive ballpark of communitarian philosophy. This procedure worked well—until Jennifer Howse chaired a task force called "New Americans."

Jennifer is one of my favorite public leaders. She succeeds in combining a very supportive, personally warm style with a highly organized and focused leadership. She has dedicated her life to public service (from serving as state commissioner for mental retardation in Pennsylvania to becoming the pres-ident of the March of Dimes). In the process of working together, we became friendly, often talking about communitarian as well as personal matters. A problem arose because Jennifer chose a number of left-liberals to serve on her task force. The group ended up composing a position paper that, in effect, called for separate but equal education—in direct contradiction to the Communitarian Platform and one of our most profoundly held beliefs!

To explain: the term *bilingual* or *bicultural education* is misleading because it encompasses two different ideas. According to one idea, best called transitional education, immigrant children are taught for a while in their native language as they learn English, but then are incorporated into regular classes. Critics argue that these children are better off if they are immediately immersed in English-only classes. The debate between these critics and the champions of *this kind* of bilingual education is not the issue.

The second kind of bilingual education, the one favored by Jennifer's task force, calls for *continuing* education, even K through 12, in the child's native language. It, in effect, seeks to keep immigrant children in a separate culture, without introducing them to mainstream American society and to learning in English. They are also socially segregated from other, "Anglo" children.

The Communitarian Platform opposes this second approach on the grounds that it would lead to excessive diversity, that it would undermine the community of communities essential for social peace and social stability. I carried this concern to Jennifer, and she, reluctantly, passed it on to her task force, which did not budge. Now what?

There was nothing in our very loose "network" procedures that anticipated or addressed this situation often dealt with by groups as different as the Democratic Party and the Committee for a Sane Nuclear Policy (SANE). We had faced no such difficulties with any of the other position papers. I sat on this one; I neglected to respond to phone calls on the matter and asked for permission to send the paper to be reviewed by respected authorities in the field. Finally, I encouraged the group to publish it elsewhere.

I still feel that I handled the matter poorly. I should have asked to meet with the task force and tried to convince its members of the merit of our position. Although I doubt that I could have swayed the group, I should have tried. Or, I should have told them outright that we could not live with their conclusions. Luckily, all the other task forces stayed within our expansive communitarian tent. Indeed, they generated a whole slew of papers that spelled out our basic position concerning character education and related matters.

Communitarians in the White House

To describe the ways communitarian ideas reached the seats of power (I am not saying pulled the levers) I must explain the finer points of what might be called "White House poker." I knew this "game" well because I played the White House side before I got to sit on the outsider side of the table. Basically, it begins with an outsider pleading for a cause (or special interest). The White House staffers being approached try to remain unresponsive so as not to show their hands. In contrast, outsiders try to find out what the staff, and more generally the White House, is up to, what the cards hold. (Bob Woodward, the *Washington Post* reporter, was a master of the game; he got the Clinton White House staff not only to show him the cards they were holding but also to spell out their game plans, which he included in his book *The Agenda: Inside the Clinton White House*.)

There are several reasons why White House staffers try to be poker-faced. Often, the White House has not yet made up its mind on an issue. If an outsider spreads the word that it is leaning in this or that direction, such a word can mobilize opposition, or the White House may seem to vacillate if it later moves otherwise or be locked into a position it was merely considering.

Also, outsiders use points gleaned during White House visits for their own gain. Michael Lerner (the editor of *Tikkun*), for instance, milked a ton of publicity when the impression was created that Hillary was taken by his ideas about the "politics of meaning." As a result, the first lady was subjected to a long round of ribbing in the press because of the New Age flavor of many of Lerner's views. Her staff may well have regretted that they had not held their cards closer to their vests. Instead, there were no more visits for Lerner.

To try to get the White House staffers to remove their poker faces, I stressed that I considered our conversations confidential. I stuck meticulously to this promise even if someone else who attended the same meeting did not. Getting the staff off poker was important because without some honest feedback it is difficult to discern which ideas are viewed favorably but require more elaboration and documentation versus those that are best parked until another day (or administration). Also, dealing with a nonresponsive staffer, or one who responds with a formulaic, "How good of you to come and share your views with us," is outright unpleasant. Fortunately, as I was making my rounds promoting communitarian ideas, only a few of the Clinton White House staff subjected me to poker for any length of time.

The White House staffer I saw most often was Bill Galston, who served for two and a half years as deputy assistant to the president for domestic policy. Both before and after these years, he was consulted often by the White House. Bill played a major role in drafting, negotiating, and steering through Congress the AmeriCorps program, a centerpiece of the Clinton administration and one of its most communitarian projects. (It brought many thousands of volunteers to community service and rewarded them with some college

tuition.) Bill Galston also helped to launch the drive to reduce teen pregnancies, which the White House favored but chose to support indirectly. (Isabel Sawhill headed it.) In addition, Bill had a hand in a dozen other White
House domestic policy projects.

Bill had an office the size of a broom closet in the coveted West Wing of
the White House, which he shared with Gene Sperling. During the numerous occasions when I dropped by, I made it a practice not to repeat to others
what was said nor to respond to queries by the press. Bill, though cautious,
knew me well enough to realize that he did not need to play White House
poker with me. While sometimes he would merely listen to my pitches,
adding my memos to a huge pile on the floor next to his small desk of material to be read, on other occasions he would promise to pass the ideas on to
the president and his staff, and, when we met again, hint at their fate. On
still other occasions, I would learn from him what the White House was up
to, which allowed me to make communitarian suggestions and to respond to
objections to communitarian points previously made.

Bill also advised me as to which other White House staffers had communitarian inclinations, of whom Bruce Reed was second to none. This information was especially welcome because Bruce himself was a master of White
House poker. He was known among the staff as Buddha, because he was so
good at keeping his reactions to himself. Although he always greeted me
warmly, and one could readily tell that he was one of the most naturally
communitarian members of the staff based on positions he took before joining the White House, I could only rarely tell which ideas he found compelling and which he deemed useless.

Other senior White House staff members varied greatly in their interest in
communitarian ideas—or in ideas of any kind. George Stephanopoulos, the
president's senior adviser whose office was right next to the Oval Office, had little interest in philosophical generalizations. He was, though, a keen listener for
specific ideas. I had a hard time remembering when addressing this very young
man, with his mop of hair and boyish smile, that he was not one of my younger
students. Although Stephanopoulos tried to be nonresponsive, lets say it's a
good thing he did not have to earn his living playing poker; it was written all
over his open face when he warmed up to an idea or when it left him cold.

Stephanopoulos seemed to favor several of our ideas, especially turning
schools into what we called "community schools," open many more days a
year and more hours a day and serving as community centers when not
needed for teaching. The only time I saw Stephanopoulos put on a strict "no
comment" face was when I suggested that the administration should favor
limiting gambling. I argued that there was growing evidence that gambling

was addicting a large number of people, especially those of few means; that it created fewer jobs and less urban renewal than its advocates claimed. No response. I asked that the administration at least should support the formation of a commission to study the matter, suggested by several religious and civic leaders. Nada. As if the man sitting across from me did not hear a thing. Shortly after that meeting, I read in the newspapers that the Democrats (like the Republicans) were filling their coffers with large campaign contributions from the gambling industry.

At first I berated myself for not doing my homework, for coming across as politically naive. Upon further consideration, I wondered: I was not a political adviser, nor did I aspire to become one; I was an outsider championing a broad social agenda that included—as a major plank—shoring up the moral foundation of the country. I realized, at the same time, that if I came up mainly with ideas that were politically unrealistic, I would soon lose whatever access I had. The trick was to find ideas that were both honestly communitarian and not impolitical.

I saw some of Rahm Emanuel while he served as special projects director, before he became senior adviser, a post he took over from Stephanopoulos. (In 2002, he was elected to Congress.) Rahm had a style I was familiar with from Israel and which I found easy to take. As far as I could tell, he played his cards face up. If he approved of your suggestions, he would let you know, and if he thought they were rubbish, he would make this at least as clear. He was straightforwardly pragmatic; if I ran through a list of suggested communitarian policies, Rahm would promise to look into some and would dismiss others without any particular principle behind his choices that I could discern. He was relatively tough on guns (not enough), troubled by immigration (too much), and OK with welfare reform (sorry to learn). A tough dude.

I had little direct contact with most members of Clinton's cabinet; however, I was especially interested when I learned that Donna Shalala, secretary of the Department of Health and Human Services (HHS), was drafting some 600 pages of privacy regulations. The relevance of these regs to our ideas deserves some elaboration. After my communitarian text *The New Golden Rule* was published in 1996, I was looking for more ways to help keep the communitarian dialogue going. I found that the tension between the right to privacy and the common good made for a good communitarian topic. I studied the issue at some length (regretting that I was not trained in constitutional law). In March 1999, I published my findings under the title *The Limits of Privacy*. (More about it later.)

Soon after my book was published, I learned that Shalala's staff was working with the White House on issuing regulations to protect medical privacy.

This was great news because the violations to the privacy of patients were particularly outrageous. Their records could be purchased on the Internet. Banks used them to call in loans of those who had heart attacks and employers used them to avoid hiring people who had "bad" genetic texts, among other abuses. The core of my recommendation was not to rely on individuals to protect themselves but on public systems put in place to protect privacy, especially from attacks by profiteers. I met repeatedly with some of those involved in drafting the new regs, but have no way of telling to what extent (if any) these meetings had an effect. (I was particularly fond of Peter Swire, who was appointed as the White House privacy "czar." I doubt that I convinced him of much of anything other than maybe to rewrite the regulation that would have allowed patients to insist that their physicians "correct" their medical records. I feared that the records would get dumbed down just as professors' letters of recommendations have been. I know even less about the results of my meeting with Gary Claxton, who was in charge of formulating policy regs in HHS and who had the demeanor of a consummate poker player of Las Vegas caliber.) Quite likely, my book did a better job than these face-to-face meetings, which is not saying much. Anyhow, the regulations that were issued just before the end of the Clinton administration, in December 2000, were very similar in spirit and in detail to those I considered communitarian. Shalala herself stated as much publicly.

I did meet with "A. G.," as staffers in the Department of Justice referred to the attorney general. When Janet Reno marched into her cavernous office, I was surprised to see how tall she was (and I am not exactly short at 5'10"). Reno listened patiently, responding little. The relations between her and the White House were tense, and she knew that I had friends in the White House and visited there often, which was reason enough for her to keep up her guard. She did point out that community policing, which I championed enthusiastically, was something Justice was already committed to. I had failed to explain the difference between the kind of community policing Justice supported and the "thick" kind that was called for.

Next, I rolled out for her my favorite idea, labeled "it takes a village to prevent a crime." The main idea is that if one could marshal the natural social processes of a community to help prevent crimes, public safety could be greatly improved. To energize these processes and to mobilize communities to fight crime, I suggested that communities that succeeded in reducing crimes be accorded half of the savings in public costs (police, court, jails) that their efforts engendered; the other half would serve to reduce government deficits or taxes. The communities would be required to employ these funds for communal purposes such as building swimming pools or fixing schools, rather than, say, sending refund checks to every member. Communities, however, would be free to choose which communal projects to spend the funds on.

The underlying reason for these requirements, I explained, was that the process of deciding which projects to favor would further strengthen the communities and thus enhance their ability to prevent crime. Reno wondered, "Do you expect that the police would agree to have their budget cut?" I responded that there was no harm in trying. After a few more questions, Reno allowed, "This seems like an interesting idea," which I translated to mean, "If I had nothing better to do, I might look into it." The same basic response greeted most of my other communitarian ideas, with one sharp exception.

Toward the end of my audience with Reno, I argued for a critical study of the ways courts often used the Fourth Amendment to rule in favor of civil libertarians. Several courts, I complained, considered as unreasonable searches the setting up of sobriety checkpoints, the erecting of barriers at entrances to areas known as open drug markets, and several other such public safety devices. I told Reno about what happened in Inkster, Michigan, a report I owed to Roger Connor. In Inkster, there was an open drug market serving many people from other communities. Various efforts to suppress it were unsuccessful. The sheriff set up roadblocks at the entrances to the area, asking drivers to show their licenses and ownership-of-car certificates. The drug market disappeared overnight. But the ACLU hauled the sheriff into court on the grounds that he violated the Fourth Amendment. The roadblocks were removed and the drug market was soon bustling again. "A study of such court cases might lead to a less liberal interpretation of the Fourth Amendment," I concluded.

After listening with visibly growing impatience, Reno responded, tartly, "I have no problem with the way courts interpret the Fourth Amendment." She looked at her watch and explained that it was time to go. Instead of returning to my office, I went for a long walk. I was cursing myself for not showing that the Fourth Amendment could be reinterpreted in ways that are more favorable to public safety without undermining its essential protection of individual rights and for not taking into account that Reno was a strong liberal.

In contrast to Justice, my communitarian pitching fared much better with the Department of Education, especially with Secretary Richard Riley. In our meetings in his office, during his participation in our Character Education conferences, and at the Renaissance retreats, I found him to be a natural communitarian. He showed keen interest and supported practically all of our ideas, from the need for schools to engage in character education (instead of merely focusing on academics), to the quest for ways to involve parents more in schools' work; from championing an educational role for sports, to promoting "community schools." He was especially supportive of community service by high school students and was fascinated by our ideas about changing sex education.

The significance of the fact that the head of a government department favored communitarian ideas should not be overestimated. Those unfamiliar with the ways of Washington may assume that once the head of a government department signs off on a policy, underlings will scurry to follow suit. Actually, both lower-ranking political appointees and civil servants often have views and agendas of their own. They do not necessarily openly challenge the heads of their departments, but they sidetrack, modify, or ignore their directions, often with considerable impunity. In our case, Marshall Smith (who served first as assistant secretary of education, then as deputy secretary) and the moderately feminist Madeleine Kunin, while personally friendly and interested in our messages, had their hearts in traditional liberal programs. Not surprisingly, the department ended up launching a mixture of both communitarian and liberal initiatives.

Communitarian ideas did best in helping to shape general themes that framed the underlying message of the Clinton administration. Various speechwriters often asked us for suggestions, especially when preparations for the annual State of the Union were underway. (The same was asked of many others.) More often than dealing directly with speechwriters, I shared ideas with Don Baer, who served as director of communications. Baer, a son of the South, was a natural communitarian and needed little convincing to value our basic tenets. His enthusiasm for his work and the administration and his continuous optimism, even when the White House was going through one of the numerous crises that plagued it, was infectious. And anybody who was as involved with his wife and two boys as Baer was appealed to something deep in me. I also appreciated that Baer did not play White House poker with me.

Anyhow, even someone much less anxious to get his message across might not be immune to the kind of letters he wrote; I certainly was not. For example, in 1995, Baer wrote:

> I am writing on behalf of the president to solicit your views about the upcoming State of the Union Address, which he is scheduled to deliver three weeks from today. Last year, you made an enormously important contribution to his Address to Congress when you provided written advice on what you then believed his speech should contain. I was hoping that you would be willing to do so again.

When Baer asked for suggestions, I made special efforts to respond in a timely fashion—even when I was out in the bush in Africa!

An invitation to join the president at Camp David arrived during the last days of 1994, shortly before I was about to take off with Pat and my five sons to Kenya for a camera safari. While my sons and I are spread around the world, from Seattle to Tel Aviv, we get together for a week at least once a year, often with spouses and grandchildren in tow. Kenya was our long-planned next family reunion. I was briefly tempted to try to reschedule the family trip, but soon realized it would mean delaying the opportunity for all of us to be together for at least six months. It did not take me long to decide; soon, I was learning about the communitarian habits of a Masai village and the rather uncommunitarian habits of many wild beasts. Often, one of the older males monopolize a whole herd of females, with the younger males hanging around the margins, trying to fight their way in.

While we were out on a safari tour, watching a lioness and her cute, cuddly cubs (from the safety of a car), an agitated tour staff member rushed up to us. "The White House wants you to call—right away! Now!" I was duly impressed that even the White House operators, known for their skill at locating people any place at any time, were able to track me down in a Kenyan game park. The call was placed by Don Baer, who was asking several people for points to include in the forthcoming State of the Union address. I composed some suggestions in a hurry. When I read the speech after my return, I was delighted to find it rich in communitarian ideas and expressions.

Clinton stated:

> Our civil life is suffering in America today. Citizens are working together less and shouting at each other more. The common bonds of community which have been the great strength of our country from its very beginning are badly frayed. . . . I call it the New Covenant but it's grounded in a very, very old idea that all Americans have not just a right but a solemn responsibility to rise as far as their God-given talents and determination can take them. And to give something back to their communities and their country in return. . . .
>
> We see our families and our communities all over this country coming apart. And we feel the common ground shifting from under us. The PTA, the town hall meeting, the ball park—it's hard for a lot of overworked parents to find the time and space for those things that strengthen the bonds of trust and cooperation.

When Baer left the White House in 1997, Ann Lewis was appointed as the communications director, which surprised me. I knew her as a very progressive and outspoken liberal, well to the left of the New Democrats and the communitarians. The fact that she was very bright and articulate only increased my concern. However, once in the White House, Lewis very rarely showed her previous ideological leanings and greatly moderated her tone. The fact that I'd known her previously, and we seemed to like one another, made conversations easy when we ran into one another. But soon after the Lewis appointment, the White House was engulfed in the Monica Lewinsky scandal, and I stopped visiting.

Even earlier, my White House contacts suffered when Bill Galston ended his White House service. Ezra, Bill and Miriam's only child, had written a very moving letter to Bill, which I would not quote had it not been published at least twice before. Ezra wrote: "Baseball's not fun when there's no one to applaud you when you hit a triple and a double and steal two bases including home. Baseball's not fun if there's no one there to congratulate you after the game. If all these were just the opposite baseball would be fun."

Bill, very dedicated to his family, resigned to be with his son. It made me respect Bill even more. In a farewell party in the Roosevelt Room, attended by the president, the first lady, many staffers, and Bill's family, Ezra spoke. He told the president that while he realized that the president was losing a valuable adviser, he, Ezra, needed his father more. By the time he finished, a lot of tissues were used up in the room.

Despite media reports that I had "contacts" in the Clinton White House, lobbies almost never approached me to help them plead their cases. One startling exception left me dumbfounded. Dick Morris called well after President Clinton terminated his role as the White House's Rasputin after Morris had an affair with a prostitute. Worse yet, Morris had allowed her to listen in on conversations he had with the president. Morris was trying to work his way back into the good graces of the White House and left no stone unturned. I, somehow, was to be turned.

First round, Morris visited my office. He has a mechanical, nervous smile and a soft and wet handshake. His flattery was so overblown that one would have to be a moron to be taken in by it. He suggested that we should work on a joint memo on how to introduce more communitarian ideas into the White House. "And then you could take it to Gore." Morris next let loose a rapid-fire barrage of specific suggestions, many off-the-wall. One moment he argued that corporations ought to be asked to provide to a national database the names and salaries of their employees, so that if people did not pay child support, the government could garnish their wages. Next, he argued that banks providing safety cameras for their automatic teller machines be given good citizen decals by Gore.

It was difficult to believe that this man had played a major role in the reelection of President Clinton. I was sure I was missing something. Intrigued, I agreed to stop by during an already-scheduled visit to New York City the next week and extend our "get to know each other" session. I found Morris in a bachelor pad next to the Coliseum, which was decorated in a garish purple with baroque mirrors in golden frames the way New Orleans bordellos are depicted in B-rated movies. He was sorry he had to keep me waiting for a moment; "I have to call my wife for a date; we are trying to work things out." I assumed this was a message I was supposed to carry someplace.

We had barely started when a Christian radio station called for a quick interview. Morris was full of repentance. "Yes, there was a spiritual vacuum in the White House. . . . I contributed to it. . . . I had an affair with a prostitute. . . . I am atoning now."

The interviewer asked, in line with what religion? Morris chuckled, "I work for both parties . . . would you expect me to sign up with one religion? . . . I atone in all of them." He then added, in what sounded like a well-rehearsed line: "Those who fear hell are religious; those who have been to hell are spiritual."

Interview over, Morris regaled me with the ways he was manipulating the elections in Honduras for a rich American guy from Rhode Island. Morris explained that he had to pull strings from his home in New York and from Miami because he was a persona non grata in Honduras.

I realized that I had been wrong. There was no more to Morris than what met the eye. I explained to him that the media vastly exaggerated my influence in Washington and elsewhere, made my excuses, and left.

My lesson for the day was to be reminded how blessed in some ways the life of a public intellectual is. I rarely had to deal with people who made me thoroughly uncomfortable. Opponents, plenty; people who vigorously defended their views, often; someone who angered me by resorting to personal attacks or derailing a project I was working to bring about, too frequently. But I encountered very few who made me ill at ease.

All said and done, communitarians had ready access to the Clinton White House; people with communitarian leanings served in various key positions. They had their own communitarian ideas, and we sent them some more suggestions both with regard to general themes and numerous specific public policies. Reviewing these contacts at the end of Clinton's administration, and the considerable efforts that nursing them entailed, I noted in my diary, "Lots of work. Some of it exhilarating; some tedious. Some stimulating; some frustrating. Results require detailed study, but it seems we did help make the Clinton administration more communitarian than it would have been otherwise."

The Scandal and Us

Early in 1998 when it became clear that the Monica Lewinsky matter was much more serious than it first seemed, I had a hard time making up my mind. I was convinced that President Clinton's policies did much good for the country; I found his personal conduct disgusting. I felt strongly that the president was not above the law—and that Kenneth Starr had conducted a highly inappropriate investigation. I did believe that a president's personal character was relevant to his public office, but also that he should be removed from office, violating the electorate's choice, only under extreme conditions.

I finally sorted out my views in the way I often do, by writing an article. The article reiterated the importance of the moral voice and argued that the press did its job by exposing Clinton. The moral voice can be raised only when it is informed about what was going on in the Oval Office. (I titled the article "It Takes a Village to Prevent an Indecent Act," a title the editors changed to "Gossip Keeps the Group in Bounds.") Moreover, the facts show such exposures often suffice to make people better than they would be otherwise. Hence, removal from office could not be justified on the grounds that it would deter future presidents from acting the way Clinton did. I further argued that the fact that the overwhelming majority of the American people did not find adultery, and lying about it under oath, sufficient cause for impeachment and conviction did not mean that they were morally indifferent.

The question still remained of how the scandal was going to affect the communitarian message. At first, I expected that it would intensify interest in communitarian ideas. After all, moral issues were now on all lips, and the subject of these moral dialogues was often appropriately much more general than the president's conduct: what do spouses owe one another? And what are the effects of immoral conduct and its exposure to one's children? And so on, all matters about which we had much to say.

Soon, I was forced to realize that much of the nation's attention was focused on minor points of the scandal and on legal rather than on the moral points. Most commentators in the media, especially on television, were lawyers or law professors and not ethicists, religious leaders, or public intellectuals. Following closely on the heels of the O. J. Simpson trial, which mesmerized the American people to the point that it interfered with their work and study, Americans in 1998 were immersed in legalistic questions such as what constitutes suborning, violation of grand jury secrecy, and contempt of court.

All this did not squash the moral dialogue (after all, there is a close connection between legal and ethical matters) nearly as much as the polarization that took place. On one side, most liberals, including many feminists, either avoided the issue altogether, refusing to chastise the president, or even coming to his defense. Betty Friedan, for instance, kept saying that he was being subjected to "sexual McCarthyism." On the other side, the right wing was self-righteous and zealous to the point that it undermined responsible moral considerations. Accusations that Clinton's people had murdered Vince Foster and calls to jail Clinton after his removal from office were flying high and furious. The fact that several conservative legislators, including Henry Hyde, Bob Livingston, Dan Burton, Newt Gingrich, and the most self-righteous of them all, Bob Barr, had had affairs and lied about them further fouled the moral dialogues. These affairs forced the conservative right to retreat to legalistic grounds, arguing that *their* sinners had not lied under oath, as if suddenly by their lights "mere" adultery and garden-variety lying were small potatoes.

Amid all of this, the communitarian message—strengthening marriages, educating people to control their impulses, chiding but not riding out of town those who violate moral tenets, and, above all, allowing for repentance (religious or otherwise)—was often lost. The media, in whose sun we basked for more years than I ever believed possible, continued to call on us, but much less often.

Once again I retreated into my academic self and worked more hours each day on explicating communitarian thinking in several essays. But I was also looking for new ways to revitalize the communitarian moral dialogue and new people to work with. It was not a long wait. In 1999, two major figures lined up to run for the presidency, and each had a communitarian twist of their own.

Gore and Bush, 2001

Among the candidates for the 2000 presidential election, Gore was the most familiar. He participated in our first teach-in and in several of our other events; we met during White House dinners and in his office; and he served as the keynote speaker of the last Character Education conference we conducted with the White House, in 1997.

People often considered Gore dull; indeed, he mocks himself about being stiff. Actually, he can be quite witty. One year, Newton Minow took me along to the Gridiron Club. There, Gore had himself delivered, like a heavy block of wood, on a dolly, and stood in front of the audience without moving a muscle, until the laughter subsided. He brought about the loudest and longest laugh of the evening, all of which was dedicated to satire, with the following line: "Senator Trent Lott (at the time, the Republican majority leader in the Senate), we shored up our standards of campaign financing; *up* yours!"

Figure 12.2. With Vice President Al Gore, 1997

Gore had the foresight to found a Congressional Clearing House on the Future, in which he conducted regular meetings with members of Congress, staffers, and select academics about future trends and their implications for the country. Serving as a speaker at one of those meetings, I was delighted to find a politician who showed a genuine interest in long-term trends and in threats that had not yet hit us on the head. Ever since, I have followed his public work with interest.

When Gore addressed our 1997 meeting, he referred to me as a "longtime friend" and other such things politicians say at the beginning of their speeches to people with whom they share a platform. I placed more value on what Gore stated next:

> I'd like to spend just a few minutes to talk about what this new idea that you are advancing means to me. We have had a philosophical debate in this century, and dating back longer than that, about the best ways to solve problems. I think that in the Communitarian movement . . . we see a rejection of the excesses of the state, a reaction against the mistakes and overindulgences of government-

sponsored solutions. And . . . the rejection of the opposite extreme, the overemphasis of individualism as the natural and best way to solve problems. And, of course, to use the old cliché, "they threw out the baby with the bath water."

Gore continued and showed that he was tuned in to the subtle points of communitarian thinking, often overlooked by those still caught in the debate between the statist left and the free-market right:

> They confused the State with the Community and they ignored the context in which individuals live their lives—they ignored the connection between individuals and their communities, their families, and their colleagues who live in the same community. Now, the communitarian idea moved into the vacuum left by this movement to the extreme and, I think, silly expression of ultra-individualism.

Gore's expressions of strong communitarian sentiments were welcome. Still, I continued to think of him as primarily a policy wonk and a technocrat, interested in matters such as space programs, the Internet, and improving the government's efficiency.

None of our themes played a significant role in his lackluster 2000 presidential campaign, nor did any other. True, he won the popular vote, but given the exceptionally strong state of the economy, a major factor in determining election outcomes, Gore should have garnered a much larger majority. The fact that he kept reinventing himself with every debate made one suspect that he did not have much of an inner core. I probably would have had more access to a Gore White House than to a Bush one, but I did not expect Gore to be a grand champion of the communitarian agenda, but to be pragmatic and detail-oriented.

Bush was reported to have been influenced by Marvin Olasky, an articulate social philosopher who came up with the phrase "compassionate conservatism." Bush made it a centerpiece of his 2000 election campaign.

Columnist Georgie Anne Geyer wrote:

> A lot of people like to make fun of his "compassionate conservatives," but this package of ideas is an eminently workable blend of a communitarianism that attracts elements of the right and of the left . . . and of a sense of the nation that shows Americans a way to have the renewed order and morality they seek, but with a compassion for the poor that knows and shows them how to rise in life.

Bush admired Myron Magnet's book *The Dream and Nightmare*. It stresses the role of *encouraging* good behavior and responsibility rather than legislating it and relying on not-for-profit organizations and churches in helping the disadvantaged instead of forcing them to behave by throwing them into the streets.

During the 2000 election campaign, Bush stuck most of the time to his communitarian theme of being a unifier, consensus builder, one able to work with Democrats. His tone and demeanor were often soft and conciliatory; that is, communitarian. After the divisive postelection fight, he took several measures to seek to unify the nation. He spoke eloquently about the need of the nation to be tied together by "bonds of friendship and community and solidarity." His inauguration speech was on the liberal end of a communitarian rainbow.

Equally important from a communitarian viewpoint was his repeated emphasis during the 2000 election campaign that, as far as moral social issues were concerned, he favored persuading people to adopt the values he championed instead of enacting laws to make them adhere to these values. Thus, he told Christian leaders that instead of trying to ban abortion he would seek to "change hearts." However, the appointment of John Ashcroft as attorney general did not fit this mold at all; Ashcroft openly called for "legislating morality" even before he was confirmed by the Senate.

Also communitarian was Bush's support for the three-legged approach, which was championed by Senator Bill Bradley, who bowed out of the 2000 campaign early. Bradley, writing in our communitarian quarterly *The Responsive Community*, and during our meetings, stressed that society was like a three-legged stool and not based merely on some combination of government and the market. Communities, not-for-profit corporations, and voluntary associations—many hundreds of thousands of them—had major societal roles. But, Bradley warned, society was unstable since the third-sector leg was short and those of the government and market were too long. In the early days of the Bush administration, the White House followed similar ideas, moving to shore up the third sector, although its efforts were highly controversial as it mainly sought to deal with faith-based institutions. (Bush initially appointed two communitarians to participate in dealing with this matter: Stephen Goldsmith and Don Eberly, both of whom were side-tracked later, as was this initiative.)

Also in these early days, the *Washington Post* wrote about Bush: "His actions have less to do with the left vs. right, they say, than with his embrace of many of the ideas contained in the movement known as 'communitarianism.' . . . Many of Bush's early proposals fit this approach." The reporter then specified:

This week, Bush moved to make it easier for the government to fund religious groups that cater to the poor and disadvantaged. He also gave a boost to AmeriCorps, the national service program that sends volunteers to help community initiatives. Last week, Bush rolled out an education plan that gave localities more authority over their schools. A week earlier, he spoke of the need for character education in schools. Even his tax plan, due next week, has what are touted as community-building elements: a new charitable tax credit, a charitable deduction for those who don't itemize, and a reduction of the marriage penalty.

Soon, there followed policies that were strongly conservative, including raining most benefits of the Bush tax cut on the rich, his pro-producers energy policies, and anti-environmental ones. But all this paled in comparison to the major changes in the balance between individual rights and the common good (especially public safety and public health) that Bush introduced following the assault on America in September of 2001. These are so pivotal to the communitarian agenda and the future of America that they deserve a separate treatment, to which I turn to later on these pages. From the viewpoint of January 2000, it seemed that a president who had some communitarian leanings had won. The main question for us was: how important a role would this play in his administration?

———⚬⚬⚬———

CHAPTER THIRTEEN

The Media and Us

Media as a Town Meeting

Rights and Responsibilities, Swiss Style

The snow was especially deep in Davos, Switzerland, during the 1999 meeting of the World Economic Forum. The temperature was about twenty below in the mornings. Hefty winds, drifting snow, and icy roads marred the day. None of these deterred demonstrators from seeking to express their opposition to "globalism," the theme of the annual meeting that year. The Swiss police, however, would have none of it. They canceled the trains and buses that the demonstrators, mainly young people with little means, needed to get to the exclusive ski resort from other parts of the country. Armored cars, police dogs, and machine guns already protected Davos—as part of the annual routine used to protect the many hundreds of assembled CEOs and national leaders who preside over about half of the world's GNP. Still, several SWAT teams were added.

When a few young people made it through all these obstacles, maybe to demonstrate or maybe to ski in the fresh snow, the police stopped them cold, demanding ID cards and detailed explanations of what they were doing on the main streets of Davos. The cops, usually three surrounding each youth, searched them intimately.

It is common knowledge that Europeans tend to be less respectful of individual rights and less tolerant of peaceful demonstrations than Americans. But it is one thing to read about it and another to see it with your own eyes. It drove a chill down my spine. I had not felt that way since my time in

Moscow when the Communists were still in full command. Communitarianism is too often misunderstood as favoring responsibilities over rights; we favor a carefully crafted balance between rights and responsibilities. I had no doubt in which direction the Swiss had lost their balance, if they ever had it.

Dialogues and Beyond

The rights of peaceful demonstrators were very much on my mind the following evening during my short presentation at a dinner session on the media, organized by the World Economic Forum at the elegant Fluela restaurant. Several speakers who preceded me competed in terms of who was more critical of the media than the other. (I participated in several Davos meetings—part of the intellectual fodder provided to those assembled. During the course of these meetings, listening to scores of CEOs from major corporations and national leaders at small dinners, over drinks, and in the corridors, I learned a great deal not found in books or even on the Internet.)

One argued that the media "trivializes, vulgarizes, and tabloidizes everything it touches; it is utterly irresponsible, making things up from the CIA selling drugs in inner cities to claiming that the U.S. used nerve gas in Iraq." Another bemoaned the "liberal bias of the press, especially the *New York Times* and network television, which in turn influences reporters everywhere." Still another one argued that Clinton's troubles (we were meeting as the Monica Lewinsky scandal was just beginning to wind down) were all due to a media that was hungry for scandal mongering and sales. Members of the audience heartily agreed, judging from the heads nodding with strong approval and the occasional "yeah!"

The group echoed the findings of a study Alan Wolfe did in the mid-1990s. When Wolfe interviewed people across the country for his groundbreaking book *One Nation After All*, there was no question about the media on his informal interview schedule. Yet, he reported, again and again people would bring the media up spontaneously and complain bitterly about them. Aside from complaining about the obsession with sex and scandals, negativity, and divisiveness, many also criticized the media for being dominated by liberals. I was surprised when Michael Elliott, at the time a *Newsweek* editor, spoke candidly to the group, adding his criticism of the media (of which he is a key part), saying that it was time for the media to cop a mea culpa for the way they had conducted themselves during the Clinton–Lewinsky scandal.

My turn came late in the evening, as waiters were filling wine glasses for the umpteenth time. I seriously doubted that those in attendance were ready for a real challenge—by that point, brandy and port were being passed around—but I could not stop myself. I told those assembled that I hoped that they would not mind hearing a different take. "First," I stated, with probably too much vigor in my voice, "there is no one media; there are media of all kinds. Some are tabloids, some have a tabloid streak in them; and some are carefully researched, written, and edited publications, although, like the rest of us, they occasionally err. For every *Hustler*, there is a *Partisan Review*."

Afraid that I would be interrupted, I hurried on: "True, some are liberal, but there are also numerous conservative publications, as well as radio and TV stations. For every *Nation* there is a *National Review*; for every *Dissent* there is a *Commentary* (and *The Public Interest* to boot). There is not only a *New York Review of Books* but also *Books and Culture*. And for every left *Pacifica* radio, there are Pat Robertsons, *700 Clubs*, and Rush Limbaughs.

"Even if one focuses only on the media with the widest circulation, the *New York Times* may be somewhat liberal, but the *Wall Street Journal's* editorial page is strongly conservative. The three major television networks have no clear political profile and they are losing much of their clout to smaller networks and local stations that tend to reflect local values."

By now waiters, dressed like penguins, solemnly passed around minted chocolates (a hint—time to let us go home) but—thanks be given—no cigars. I refused to be distracted.

"Most importantly, the media serve our society in two very significant ways, aside from being a major source of information and a major check on the government, as the Fourth Estate. The media are the place national town hall meetings take place, and the way we reach new shared understandings as to how we are to conduct ourselves. The media are a force we draw on heavily to change our direction as a society, to make our history.

"Many who examine the ways people come to share values see this as a matter in which small communities may readily engage, but assume that a society that encompasses many millions of people could not possibly participate in one moral dialogue. Actually, such dialogues about our moral condition and the direction we ought to move in occur often through the media. The media links millions of local conversations (between couples, in neighborhood bars or pubs, in coffee or tea houses, around water coolers at work) into national (sometimes cross-national) networks, creating what I call 'megalogue.'" By now, side conversations had ceased and the trickle out of the back door stopped.

"Every few months or so, the media zero in on a topic to dramatize, which in turn engages the national conversation. During the 1960s, the media put racial segregation on the American agenda by showing police dogs and fire hoses being turned on demonstrators, their being kicked out of segregated lunch counters, and much more. The media put the war in Vietnam on the agenda by showing pictures of tarmacs full of body bags and company Charlie slugging through the mud in Vietnam, raising the question of what our children were dying for. And pictures of the atrocities in Kosovo put our role in Yugoslavia on the table."

I continued: "The media do more than offer up topics for discussion (although the public can and does sometimes refuse to pick them up); the media report back what people are saying in various parts of the country and from various backgrounds. This feedback is based on personal interviews as well as public opinion polls."

I realized that people consider megalogues to be disorderly and hence added: "Megalogues are often extensive and meandering; they typically have no clear beginning or decisive conclusion. But as they mature, they often change the way most of us think, believe, and, most importantly, conduct ourselves."

This was getting too abstract. I rushed to add some examples. "Until 1968, a person was considered dead when the heart and lungs stopped functioning. As technology made extension of life that violated these criteria rather common—to well beyond the point where a person's chances of regaining a meaningful life were nil—a group of scientists and ethicists formulated a new definition of death: brain death. But community mores continued to demand that doctors do 'all that could be done for their loved ones.' At this point several scholars turned to the media, which primed a society-wide dialogue about the definition of death. The issue was dramatized by the Karen Ann Quinlan case in the 1970s; she survived for ten years in a vegetative state. The ensuing megalogue gradually led to a change in the public perception (and the movies' images) of death. Although the change is still not complete, it advanced sufficiently to establish new social mores, expectations, and behavior. In recent decades, there were similar dialogues about women's rights, our obligations to the environment, the deficit, welfare, and the role of the state—all leading to changes in our moral culture and in the ways we conduct ourselves."

The chair, Hilary Bowker, indicated that my time was more than up. She permitted just one question. "What about abortion?" someone asked in a challenging voice, as if saying, "Even you could not find consensus here." I responded, "I do not claim that every megalogue will result in consensus. But, if I were to push the point, Roger Rosenblatt has shown that most Americans even agree with one another on this issue. The vast majority of Americans favor granting women the right to an abortion, but the vast majority also have significant moral qualms about it." After the chair provided the usual "let's give the speaker a hand," there followed a nice round of applause.

Everyone rushed out to find their limo driver or shuttle van. It was well below freezing, but for once I did not feel the chill. I believed that even if no one truly heard me, my points were well taken. Whole societies can carry out moral dialogues, essential for their communitarian nature, and the media is the only place an entire nation can conduct its town meetings. The fact that the media are not merely crucial to keeping the government (legislature included) accountable and the country free, but also are the only place a society can conduct essential moral dialogues, did not blind me to their flaws, as I was shortly reminded.

The Media and the Argument Culture

I was too keyed up to turn in, so I stopped at the bar of the hotel and joined two friends, Deborah Tannen and her husband Michael Macovski for a drink. We often go out for dinner together in Washington. I enjoy their nonpretentious style and informal warmth. Michael might talk about Byron and other English writers he studies. Deborah almost never looks back to her previous work on the different ways men and women converse, which brought her worldwide recognition. Instead, her mind is working on her next book. While she is quite willing to converse about a movie worth seeing or a fine place to dine, her ears perk up when the conversation turns to intellectual or social matters. Recently, it has been her concern that the American media and culture promote conflicts and culture wars, not civil dialogues and reconciliation. (She published those ideas in a book, *The Argument Culture*.)

That evening Deborah was speaking of a recent TV interview during which she had met a guy who was friendly in the waiting room, but attacked her views viciously once on the air. He claimed that women exploit men, that they prevent men from seeing their children, and that they only want to use men for their money. Deborah reported, "Once he unleashed his barrage, the audience visibly grew much more hostile."

I related a similar experience. A television producer, Rita McWilliams, called to ask whether I would participate in a public television discussion of multiculturalism. The other participant was going to be Ronald Walters, a political scientist from Howard University. As Rita and I discussed the subject, I explained that if by *multiculturalism* one means that Americans should learn more about the many backgrounds of those who together make up America, it would enrich us all. In contrast, if one meant that there would be no shared heroes and symbols extolling the value of democracy and individual rights— which find little support in non-European cultures—multiculturalism might destroy our unity and thus our society. Ms. McWilliams was interested in my ideas, but then added somewhat uneasily: "But you *do* disagree with him?" I responded that Ron was a person I respected a great deal and had had over to my home, but that we did differ on *some* of these matters.

During the show that followed, Ron and I had a genuine dialogue, agreeing on some issues, clarifying some others, and differing on still others. When the show was over and the moderator, Morton Kondracke, and I were taking off our makeup in the men's room, I could see that Mort was visibly peeved. "You should have disagreed more with one another," he exclaimed. "We should have put Pat Buchanan on the show!" When the show was aired, the dialogue between Ron and myself was cut by half and the first half of the show was dedicated to a one-sided sharp critique of multiculturalism by Daniel Boorstin. The incident, we all agreed over one more glass of wine, sent the message that if you are keen to air your views, you'd better be polarizing and confrontational.

Maybe confrontations of the kind that make for good episodes of *Hardball* and *Crossfire* serve mainly to stimulate new dialogues. As these mature, there is more room for moderate voices and civil exchange of the kind that one finds during *The NewsHour with Jim Lehrer* and on the *Diane Rehm Show*. It was a comforting thought on which to turn in.

Being Put through the Paces

The next morning, I had no session to attend; people who entered the hotel lobby from the street were bundled up as if they had just returned from the North Pole. It was a good day to linger over another cup of coffee. With the discussions of the role of the media fresh in my mind from the preceding night, I decided to do what I had done hundreds of times before: take notes on what I learned from my experience, with an eye to turning it into an article or chapter of a book, hoping it would be of some value to others. It turned out to be a complex story. Basically, our relationship with the media—the only medium we had to engage millions of Americans (and people in other countries) in a dialogue—passed through four phases. Three of them, I believe, are phases all who venture into public life should expect; the fourth, they must work hard to have a chance at getting. First, we were highly welcomed as the carrier of a new way of thinking; next, our ideas (and we) were critically assessed; then, the klieg lights were turned off and we were largely ignored. After much effort, we reached the fourth phase, regaining a public voice and once again participating in the national (and cross-national) give-and-take on our kinds of issues. All this deserves considerable elaboration because, it is worth repeating, without the media granting us a free megaphone, our message would never have been heard by millions of our fellow citizens and those in other countries. Yes, we could have written a memo or bent the ear of this or that government official, but even they are properly reluctant to move too far from the public. In short, no media, no public, no really large-scale societal change. All those who constantly dump on the media, take note.

Phase I: Loud and Clear

As I have already laid out, in the first years, our message was warmly received by most of the media. The fact that the media, in their attempt to be (or appear) balanced, also carried some digs from outlier critics from the left or the right only added to our credibility. The amount of media attention we received, from high- to lower-brow media (even the *Reader's Digest*), and from all the various kinds, including cable TV and electronic publications, can be described only as stupendous. It belies those who claim that the media pays no mind to ideas.

Even in this golden period, some in the media ignored us, while others were quite critical; but they were more than compensated for by others. For instance, public television mostly ignored us, with the exception of a thoughtful, extensive interview by Charlayne Hunter-Gault.

Figure 13.1.   With Charlayne Hunter-Gault, public television

This, it seemed, was largely because, like several other TV news programs, *The NewsHour with Jim Lehrer* format calls for a dialogue between one liberal and one conservative commentator (for instance, Mark Shields and David Brooks). There is no room for a third voice, that of the center, of communitarians. But these were exceptions to the rule. For months on end, we seemed to be on the front of most everyone's Rolodex.

During this first, golden stretch, we found out which media best carried our message. Whenever we were covered by the *New York Times*, NPR, or C-SPAN, we received a larger volume of requests for information, invitations to speak, and messages from those who wanted to join the movement and even send donations.

The *New York Times* was second to none in terms of making our voice heard. I was introduced to its special standing while still a neophyte, in Israel. When I was working briefly for an Israeli newspaper after the War of Independence, the paper had a total of eight pages. One day, an editor pointed to a roll of printed pages thicker than my thigh, and asked me: "You know what this is?" When I was forced to admit that I did not have the faintest idea, he pronounced with great admiration, "This is a real newspaper! This is the Sunday *New York Times!*"

The *New York Times*'s treatment of us has been varied and nuanced. Steve Holmes, an African American reporter, angrily demanded to know what we were planning to do about the disadvantaged, the poor, the minorities, and "why do you believe that you can return to an Ozzie and Harriet kind of marriage?" In contrast, Peter Steinfels, who covers religion, was more sympathetic to what we had to offer. In one of the first stories about us, he provided a characterization of what we were doing that stuck. He wrote:

> Joan W. Konner, dean of the Columbia University Graduate School of Journalism, puzzled over communitarianism at a dinner preceding [one of our] teach-in[s]. It appeared to be one part church sermon, one part reassertion of old values, one part political campaign message and one part social movement, Dean Konner said. The implicit criticism left Dr. Etzioni unfazed. "I couldn't have said it better myself," he replied.

The *New York Times*'s op-ed editors, at the time, did not let any of us make a communitarian case on this important page, despite numerous attempts; but the editors of the Sunday economic section repeatedly found a place for our ideas. The book review section was much less kind to us than "The Week in Review." In short, not only did the various media outlets treat us differently, but some segments of the same paper afforded us much more voice than others.

NPR enabled us to share our views with key audiences. After a ten-minute interview on *All Things Considered* or *Weekend Edition*, the flagship news programs carried by most NPR radio stations, our phones rang off the hook. The same held for interviews on the *Diane Rehm Show*. She did her homework, fully grasped the difference between our moral agenda and that of the social conservatives, and raised thoughtful questions. Her extensive program allowed for half an hour to develop ideas, followed by another half hour of questions from callers. After an appearance with Diane Rehm, colleagues would stop me in the corridor, sharing their reactions. This hardly ever happened following an appearance on *Larry King* and surprisingly rarely happened when we were on TV network programs, except CNN, which had more of our kind of audience.

C-SPAN has been God's gift to the communitarian movement. By repeatedly broadcasting unedited records of our meetings, we could bring many thousands of people from across the country to our teach-ins and conferences.

The *Washington Post* played an especially valuable role during our introductory phase. I read somewhere that if you want to reach a few Congress members, heads of agencies, or White House staffers, write them a memo. However, if you are keen to speak to them all, and many more, write an article for the *Washington Post*. The paper covered our first teach-in and reported about some

Figure 13.2. With Daniel Schorr on CNN

of the specific ideas we were promoting. At the same time, op-ed page editor Meg Greenfield, who tightly controlled the page for twenty years, vetoed practically all of the pieces sent to her by any of the leading communitarians.

William Raspberry wrote highly favorable columns about some of our ideas. I especially cherished his strong endorsement of our position on diversity. A good part of the writing of E. J. Dionne Jr., whether in the *Washington Post*, *Commonweal*, or in his books, displayed a strongly communitarian voice all his own. Others, especially social conservatives, paid us no mind. Columnists George Will and Charles Krauthammer, who often wrote on virtues from a strongly conservative viewpoint (even calling for a strong national government to impose virtue on people), roundly ignored us. In contrast, the *Wall Street Journal*'s op-ed page, which is also strongly conservative (unlike its news pages), did allow us to share communitarian ideas with its readers.

Among regional newspapers, we received our best hearing in the pages of the *Philadelphia Inquirer*. Reporter David R. Boldt's headline read "An Ideology that Could Get This Country Moving Again." Not far behind were the *Los Angeles Times, Chicago Tribune, Boston Globe, Minnesota Star Tribune,* and *Miami Herald.* (One of the best columns about us appeared in the *Cincinnati Post,* by Byron P. White.) Other newspapers were less interested, but scores ran reports about our ideas during the first, golden years.

Time covered us extensively and early, as did *U.S. News & World Report. Newsweek* was one of the last to join the parade but more than made up for it with a five-page story by Michael Elliott, published in 1994, under the banner "What's Left?" In it, he shows that left ideologies were bankrupt and argues that we were a major candidate to replace them with a more centrist position. In the process, he praised me some, needled me some (about my academic style, of all things)—and gave still more voice to communitarianism. I could take quite a bit more of this.

Mixed among these major occasions to share our ideas were numerous interviews with reporters of smaller newspapers, ranging from the *Lincoln (Nebraska) Journal Star* to the *Buffalo Magazine*, scores of radio call-in shows, and appearances on cable TV.

I list all these sources because it is easy to suspect that one who was at the center of such media coverage believes it to be much more expansive than it was. In this case, the opposite is true. We have eight huge scrapbooks with press clippings and a cabinet crowded with audio and videotapes from many scores of radio and TV appearances. For a while, the interest in the communitarian message was simply insatiable.

Ten million pamphlets and hundreds of millions of dollars worth of advertising would not have given us even a small bit of the voice the media freely provided. Hence, I did my best to feed them, involving my fellow communitarians whenever I could. I learned from previous experience that sooner rather than later the window of opportunity would narrow, if not close. For years, to my mounting surprise, it did not. But I never lost the uneasy feeling that soon we would become yesterday's news, which would make it much more difficult for us to participate in the all important society-wide dialogues.

Matthew Melton, a reporter for *Focus* magazine, caught the challenge we were about to face when he wrote:

> If the communitarian trend continues, soon the issue of rights and responsibilities will no longer be a subject for esoteric debate. Individuals of both left and right will have to halt and take stock of the communitarian accomplishments and will have to decide whether to fight them or, as they said in the Civil War South, "jyne up."

The Dubious Pleasures of Popularity

What was it like, in this golden phase of our relationship with the media, to be at the center of all this attention? Although many academics say they deplore their colleagues who are in the media "all the time," quite a few also wish to find out "how one does it." If I had a dollar for every colleague who asked me how to get an op-ed published (or sent me an abstract and jargon-laced article, with a note saying, "Please help me get it into the *New York Times*"), I would be able to finance the communitarian project for years to come. I shall hence disclose that the glory is both limited and comes with strings attached.

Drawing on mass-circulation newspapers to disseminate one's message by writing op-eds and articles runs into the following roadblocks: thousands of people try to place their pieces in newspapers everyday; hence, editors are very picky. Some insist on pieces tied to current events (*USA Today* often does). Others want them to be "different," reflecting some peculiar, unique viewpoint, although, as a rule, they will not tell you what their criteria are. Some wait for whatever comes over the transom; some call their favorites du jour and discuss with them what they want covered and from which general slant. This puts you into the tricky position of finding ways to respond to what they want you to write, but of still saying what you believe ought to be stated.

And, although op-ed editors are not expected to be politically biased, in effect many are. Max Frankel, who ought to know having worked for the *New York Times* for a lifetime, including as an executive editor, reports:

> Punch [Sulzberger] accepted my judgment that our op-ed columns were already too liberal and insufficiently "op" to our own points of view. Accordingly, he

refused to give columns to two survivors of my purge, Leonard Silk and Roger Wilkins . . . [or] hire Robert Semple, Jr. . . . The hardest thing was to find writers who shared our centrist values and yet brought diverse viewpoints to our table.

In addition, there are personal "chemistries" when it comes time for the articles to be edited. I found it easy to work with Robert Semple at the *New York Times*, Glen Nishimura at *USA Today*, David Brooks and Max Boot at the *Wall Street Journal*, and Noel Epstein at *Outlook*. However, Howard Goldberg, at the *New York Times* drove me batty with his nitpicking. He was hardly the only one who made one pay one's due for the privilege of speaking from sought-after platforms.

At first, seeing your name in print and hearing it on the air provides a high. And it is flattering to hear your friends say, "You were great on NPR today," even if you believe you flubbed your lines. Also, your name in headlines gets you invited to meetings from which you otherwise may have been excluded. But friends soon get used to seeing you in print; indeed, after a while they turn the tables with: "I have not seen you in the *New York Times* lately."

What remain are long hours laced with petty frustrations. Few would enjoy rushing to New York to be on NBC at the end of a full day, only to discover that the interview has been canceled because Joe DiMaggio died. An interview on *Good Morning America*, as on all network TV news shows, is a great occasion to explain your message—until you discover that your four-minute interview about the merit of the two-parent family has been cut to three-and-a-quarter minutes because the host liked the antics of a clown that preceded you and your interview opens with: "Wasn't he great?" Granted, these are small prices to pay for an opportunity to inject your ideas into the national dialogue, but you should be ready to keep paying them if you plan to be a public intellectual. And steel yourself for what is sure to follow.

Phase II: Turning Critical

The bell did not ring to mark the start of a second round, but slowly the media's tone began to turn, as the communitarian drive entered its fourth year. Truth be told, given the affinity between our ideas and those of the Clinton administration, and the hunger for a new approach to social and moral issues in the 1990s, the media interest in us continued to be considerable. But by the late 1990s, there were more and more days, then weeks, when no one called. Invitations to speak and to attend conferences ceased to pose scheduling problems; there were no longer any who wanted me to be in two places at the same time.

A study conducted by Richard Coughlin showed that the communitarian subject came up only 108 times in 1988; however, by 1990, our first year of operation, the number nearly tripled (to 291), doubled one more time by the end of 1992 (to 585), and almost doubled again a year later (to 1,005). Citations peaked in the mid-1990s, settling to a range of 1,392 to 1,476 per year, and declined sharply thereafter.

While the media often continued to cast us (and me) in a favorable light, sniping did increase. From the left, the nastiest shot came when a staffer at WNYC radio station in New York City, who, having heard that communitarians were "authoritarians," played as introduction music to my interview the official Nazi anthem! As the first notes struck, I was sure I was mistaken. "Come on; no one is going to do this to a Jewish refugee from Nazi Germany, however much they oppose his view." But as the bloodcurdling music plagued on, there was no room for doubt. I faced a quick decision: storm out in protest or—stick around to do my job. Should I vent my anger at the smearing of our position or should I redouble my efforts to explain that supporting social responsibilities was not a Fascist position in any shape or form? I did both. I told the audience in no uncertain terms how I felt about the introduction our message received, but dedicated most of the time to spelling out its democratic, moral, noncoercive essence. If it were up to me, I would find a way to preserve the recognition of the unique evil that the Nazis were. Anyone who calls another person a Nazi (assuming that the person was not one) would be automatically deemed to have libeled that person and would be fined appropriately.

On reflection, two things come to mind. First, the general decline in the civility of discourse and the watering down of the term *Nazi* to the point that it is often used merely as one more cuss word. Also there seem to be no limits to what people are willing to say or do to others, if they hold it will serve their cause.

Others merely provided distorted summaries of our views, convenient for them to pounce on. Thus, Michael Taves suggested in *Telos* that the communitarian vision concerns itself mostly with "reclaiming a reliance on traditional values and all that entails with regard to the family, sexual relations, religion and the rejection of secularism."

Much more criticism came from the right: the press quoted right-wing sources as believing that while we occasionally sounded like conservatives we were actually a bunch of liberals. Moreover, our moral positions were suspect given that they were not drawn from the scriptures and did not rely on the words of the Lord.

The *Wall Street Journal* assigned my book *The Spirit of Community* to a right-wing reviewer, the hard-hitting, take no prisoners, head of the Bradley

Foundation, Michael Joyce. He found that "there is not a single mention of God, divine purpose, natural law or natural right. When religion is mentioned at all, it is to warn fellow communitarians of the threat posed by the Puritanism that afflicts the 'religiously committed.'" Gary Bauer (later to become a social conservative presidential candidate) stressed the importance of this litmus test when he stated that if Americans forget that this country "was built on God, nothing else will matter."

"Communitarianism is a movement still heady with the excitement of its sudden celebrity and influence," wrote Charles J. Sykes in a conservative publication, *The World and I*. He continued: "Indeed, as Etzioni's book makes clear, much of the attention is deserved. Communitarians profess themselves to be weary of the usual ideological categories of liberal and conservative, right and left; and their ambition is nothing less than the creation of a 'new social, philosophical, and political map.'"

So far, so good, but then Sykes showed his hand:

> In this respect, Etzioni is a proud heir of the Enlightenment project to fashion a new ethics without reference to God. . . . The Ten Commandments are out, but Etzioni's alternative of public opinion polls seems a weak substitute at best. . . . Ultimately societies need to be held together by something more substantial than geography, economic interests, and vague sentiment. . . . Faith is inextricably enmeshed with the ties that bind man to man.

Other conservative religious publications were more ambivalent about us. One pointed out that "the Christian Right can agree with communitarian goals only when they happen to square with the Christian Right's interpretation of Biblical principles." The author then continued to favor our position on the need for moral values and community and to criticize us for the pro-choice position (which she correctly attributed to me but which communitarians as a group have never taken). She cheered our pro-family position, but objected to our ideas that government should help parents (for instance, through paid leave when a new child is born, as is common in Europe) and especially opposed our support of gun control and national service.

Other religious media were more favorable. For example, a reporter for the *Catholic News Service* stated, "To Catholics who may fear being identified too closely with any one party, the communitarian movement could present an attractive alternative."

Keeping My Cool, Unless . . .

Occasionally, after particularly unfair criticisms, I thought of packing it in—"who needs it?"—and turning full-time to the safety of academic life.

These feelings lasted for about a day and a half. Then I would remind myself that I had not chosen the life of an activist professor to be loved and appreciated. I still would rather have been kissed on both cheeks and lionized but . . . I comforted myself with the thought that there was a job to be done. So, I strapped on my armor one more time and charged into the fray. Only, given the nature of my battle, I found that I was most effective when I turned the other cheek, either not responding to barbs, or using them as an occasion to restate our case in a carefully moderated tone. (Lesson: Never mail in the first draft of your reaction to anything and avoid e-mail, which has no recall key.)

One of the very few occasions when I did lose my cool, and which I do not regret, was when the openly libertarian *London Economist* published its second lengthy article on communitarianism, this time equating my way of thinking to that of Carl Schmitt, a Nazi. I wrote:

> Your article lumps those who wish to impose their values by use of force with those of us who seek to combine individual rights with moral order based on dialogue. This is an old trick: it has often been used to dismiss social democrats by calling them communist. Those you refer to as "high" communitarian are authoritarians, with whom we have precious little in common. Guilt by phoney association is not a valid argument.
>
> Your obsession with individual liberty serves only to undermine it. Liberties require order. If order is not formed by people coming together voluntarily, the resulting moral vacuum could bring about a police state.

It occurred to me that Benjamin Barber was right, that the choice of the term *communitarian* might have been a mistake, because it kept requiring us to explain that we had nothing to do with East Asian, authoritarian communitarians. Nor did the prefix *responsive* that we used help much. It seemed to be the same reason Taylor, Sandal, and Walzer avoided the term. But for us, it was too late to change. (I tried to use "new communitarians," and it worked better than *responsive*, but not by much.) Maybe Jonathan Rau's term "soft communitarianism" would have been best.

My First Master Demands . . .

Increased sniping by academics that spilled into the press further complicated the defense of the communitarian position. Much of it was based on the legitimate concerns of scholars that the public cannot tell a scholar's book from that of a public intellectual, and hence the latter's tendency to generalize, popularize, and be loaded with normative messages undermines the reputation of those in the ivory towers.

The tone of sniping from academia that was gradually picked up by some of the media was set by a most unexpected source—Daniel Bell, very much a public intellectual himself. His main influence was in the public domain, especially from his well-written volume *The Cultural Contradictions of Capitalism*. Even after he found his way into Harvard, his publications continued to be almost exclusively in nonacademic publications, especially the neoconservative *Public Interest* rather than in sociological flagship journals such as the *American Sociological Review* and the *American Journal of Sociology*.

I am not given to psychological explanations as to why Bell led the charge that we were popularizers. Maybe it was in response to an unfavorable book review I wrote of one of his books, in an academic journal, in which I pointed out that the book had little new to say, although it said it very well. Maybe Bell, who by his own account got his Ph.D. from a friend, without meeting the standard academic requirements, was trying to be holier than thou. Soon, other academics and some reporters picked up on the characterization, for instance, Steven Lukes, writing in *Dissent*.

Aside from the fact that such criticism hurt us in the public square, critics ignored that—aside from taking the communitarian message to the public—we did profoundly recast it. I leave for a later chapter spelling out how, but for now, we overcame the tendency of communitarians to focus almost exclusively on the common good, the social realm, on community, and its particular values. This often led communitarians before us to neglect the importance of individual rights, liberty, as well as that of self-evident truths that protect one from cultural relativism.

At the same time, I could not but acknowledge that Bell and company's complaints, aside from undermining our public voice, had a large grain of truth. While we did considerably recast the communitarian way of thinking when we took it public, at this stage we had not provided an academic account of our version of the communitarian position. It only made the barbs sting some more.

Phases III and IV: Fall and Rise

Being chided, even occasionally mocked in the press, was not the worst to come. As our position lost its novelty, and as society changed in directions we favored, what in 1990 was cutting edge became almost commonplace by 1999. David Blatz, from the *Philadelphia Inquirer*, asked me, "Are you not a victim of your own success?" Rapidly, the media—our main and best dissemination channel, our cost-free broadcasting system—treated us as old hat.

I retreated into academic research, only to seek new ways to restart the public communitarian dialogue. I finally decided that examining in some detail the relationships between one specific but significant individual right and the common good might serve. I chose privacy and its relationship to public safety (for instance, should public authorities be able to decipher encrypted messages as they are able to tap phone calls, if accorded a court order?) and public health (e.g., was saving the life of infants more important than protecting the privacy of their HIV-carrying mothers?).

One of the key examples I used to illustrate how the excessive privileging of privacy could undermine the common good was the way people who were suspected of being terrorists were treated; their privacy was guarded even if it meant that we could not stop them. (Thus, the CIA often did not provide information to the FBI, border patrol, and customs agents, not to mention local cops. Also, requests to search the computers of suspects were not even filed because it was known that courts would not grant such searches.) When I mentioned my concerns during a keynote address at the annual conference on Computers, Freedom, and Privacy held in Austin, Texas (in February 1998), which included many cyber-libertarians, most did not share my viewpoint. Indeed, Simson Garfinkel wrote, "Many civil libertarians believe that law enforcement organizations are using the threat of terrorism as a justification for power grabs and budget expansions, much as the threat of sabotage was used during the First and Second World Wars to justify attacks on civil liberties." Here I go again, claiming, "I told you so," which is annoying but a matter of record.

More generally, I argued that the right to privacy should not be treated as an absolute right, putting the onus of proving their case only on those who were concerned with the common good. Instead, I held that the right to privacy should be based squarely on the Fourth Amendment because it recognizes, on the face of it, a category of reasonable searches, those in the public interest. Moreover, it provides a specific mechanism for sorting out whether a given search is reasonable. Most important, I showed that the great danger to privacy in the United States these days was from select corporations—Big Bucks, and not Big Brother. Indeed, Big Brother had to be relied upon to safeguard privacy. It took me three years to complete the study. It was published in March 1999 under the title *The Limits of Privacy*.

One week after the book was published, the *New York Times* carried a front-page story by John Markoff showing that Microsoft had placed a secret window in its Windows 98 program. It allowed the company to determine which documents an individual fashioned and which messages the person sent. It seemed to me a fine confirmation of my Big Bucks thesis. If the FBI had done the same, the whole country would have been in an uproar.

In response to the book, I expected a huge outcry from civil libertarians and the left, who treated privacy as a "sacred" right, one to be revered and best left untouched. But maybe because of changes in the culture over the preceding increasingly communitarian decade, or because I did my best to give voice to those I disagreed with in the book, it was surprisingly well received. *Booklist* called it "valuable and informative." Jean Bethke Elshtain wrote in the *Times Literary Supplement:*

> Etzioni's treatment of these complex issues is unfailingly interesting, and, to his credit, he gives an ample and fair hearing to the privacy side—this by refreshing contrast to the manner in which strong privacy advocates tend to treat communitarianism—as if it were the opening salvo in an all-out war against modernity, progress and all that is benign.

Scott Sundby wrote in the *Annals of the American Academy of Political and Social Science*, "He canvasses privacy advocates' arguments against the various practices. As to this step of the analysis, I must admit initial skepticism over how fairly a critic would voice the opposing viewpoint, but Etzioni's articulation of the strong privacy position for each topic was fair and objective." A *Washington Post* article by John Schwartz was similarly favorable.

As a bonus, the book reopened access to the media, and thus to the national town meeting, for communitarian messages on my part (other communitarians did not necessarily agree with my position on privacy). In rapid succession, my op-eds on privacy appeared in major newspapers (including the *Boston Globe*, the *New York Times*, and *Financial Times*). I was back on the highly respected news programs, *All Things Considered* and the Diane Rehm Show. Others followed.

On book tour. Dinner at the home of Ellen Winner and Howard Gardner, a MacArthur genius. (Ellen wrote several definitive works on the psychology of art.) Joining us are Nate Glazer, a quintessential public intellectual, a man who lives for ideas and by ideas, and his wife Lochi, just back from India. Know them from Berkeley and Columbia days. Also, Gerald Holton, a grand philosopher of science, I have known almost as long, and a poet and a professor of medicine. Good to spend an evening with old friends and meeting new people. It is one of those evenings in which the dialogue and the wine all flow together easily and leave a warm afterglow.

One subject of conversation is the fate of public intellectuals. Howard, who straddles the academic and public realms with ease and confidence, says, "Look what they did to Jay Gould." Next, I am asked about what is first for tomorrow. A radio call-in show. Someone says, "You will love the 'Connection' host."

The next morning, before we go on the air, the host, Chris Lyden, and I chat briefly. He keeps rubbing his eyes and yawning politely. He bemoans the loss of privacy and points out that people have become shameless and expose themselves in the media in more ways than one. (I am thinking, "This is a new one on me; if people expose themselves, does this constitute a loss of privacy?") Lyden continues: "Let me give you an example. The other day Nicole Kidman, the wife of Tom Cruise, was on the cover of *Newsweek*, with her boobs practically hanging out. We should talk about this on air." (I say to myself, "I'll be damned," and tell him something like, "Well, hmm, maybe, but how about HIV testing of newborns or Megan's Laws?") During the show, I try to avoid the subject, but Lyden persists. We end up wasting precious time exploring a non-event. It's all part of participating in the national town hall meetings. If you want to be a piper, you pay a price.

After a dry spell, a variety of articles on other communitarian subjects found a home. *The Public Interest* published my essay on diversity, which I called "The Monochrome Society" (in it I argue that the predictions that by 2050 America would be dominated by a nonwhite majority hostile to white and "European" values were way off the mark, as most Americans of all social backgrounds share the same core of values—our current ideals).

I was especially delighted when my article on shaming as an expression of the community's moral voice and as preferable to other forms of punishment found its way into the prestigious *American Scholar*. It is a journal that publishes precious few articles, and most of them are by humanists. The editor, Anne Fadiman, wrote, "I apologize that getting into the *Scholar* these days appears to be as hard as scaling a fortress, and certainly takes much longer." It made reaching it only that much sweeter. It was also a fine antidote to those who argued that we had turned too popular. Whatever the *American Scholar* is, popular it is not.

All together, the media was annoying, frustrating, polarizing, mercurial, and absolutely essential. Those who feel misquoted, quoted not often enough, overlooked (most public intellectuals and many others) tend to lose sight of the fact that they would not have a voice at all (on the societal level) without the media—that it is the only way to conduct effective national (and even cross-national) moral dialogues. Without the media, communitarianism would be no more than an esoteric academic study.

PART FIVE

OVERSEAS

CHAPTER FOURTEEN

Communitarianism Goes Overseas

Blair, a Communitarian Champion

Can Communitarianism Travel?

Early in 1995, I was invited to fly to London, conduct two seminars on communitarian thinking at Demos (a small but influential think tank), deliver a public lecture on the same subject, meet with a dozen members of Parliament interested in our approach—and "maybe see Blair." The invitation was signed by Geoff Mulgan, a young public intellectual. (He ended up working as a key staffer at 10 Downing Street during the Blair administration that followed.) I did not give much weight to Geoff's intimations that I might meet with Tony Blair, who in mid-1994 had been elected as the leader of the Labour Party. This would hardly be the first time that someone dangled a promise in front of a lecturer to get him or her to dash across the ocean to deliver a talk, especially when the fee was a big fat zero. Anyhow, I was content to try to carry our message across the ocean, even if it meant "only" conducting a few seminars on communitarian thinking and presenting a lecture at Church Hall. (The hall is right next to the Parliament and a place where members of parliament [MPs], public intellectuals, opinionmakers, and the press often attend public lectures.)

Long before the invitation hit my desk in March 1995, I was curious as to whether our ideas might be of service to other societies. The academic sociologist in me could make the case either way: different societies have distinct cultures and conditions, ergo, no need or place for communitarianism. But, just as the ideal of liberty appeals to people all over the world, so might our ideas about the importance of shared values and community and the need to balance rights with responsibilities.

Moreover, I had an inkling that Britain might be fertile ground for our message. Geoff had previously contacted me to prepare a position paper for Demos on the decline of the two-parent family and its ill effects on children, which he published under the title "The Parenting Deficit." It generated a fair amount of public discussion in the United Kingdom, which suggested that other communitarian ideas might also travel well.

I was impressed by Geoff's drive, energy, and, above all, acumen. By issuing a slew of cutting-edge position papers, he quickly put Demos on the map as a center for new policy thinking in general, as well as one of special interest to the traditional and (at the time) moribund Labour Party. Geoff got the London *Times* to cosponsor my public lecture and to print both an op-ed by me on the same subject and an editorial supporting us. Quite a feat.

With such spirited and well-placed assistance, my trip promised to provide a chance to find out whether "the word" could be spread and whether I could bring it to a rising political star, Tony Blair. I was especially intrigued by the stories about him that characterized him so differently from the way Washington had Clinton. Whatever meeting I went to—left, right, or center—people used the same line about Blair: "He is a good husband, father, and Christian." His personal conduct was not an issue; the focus was on his political philosophy, policy positions as well as his leadership qualities and style, what a relief.

The suggestion that I might "see" Blair filled me with more misgivings than my usual anxiety. I had good reason to doubt that Blair would wish to lay eyes on me, and if he did, that his eyes would sparkle with pleasure.

"The Father of Blair's Ideas . . ."

Beginning in mid-1994, nine months earlier, the British press started to refer to me as someone whose ideas had influenced Blair. A headline in *The Observer* blatantly stated that I was the "Father of Tony Blair's Big Idea," with the subheading: "From Bill Clinton's White House to the new Labour leadership, the imprint of an American academic is being felt as politicians search for fresh policies. Melanie Phillips examines a philosophy that looks beyond the Welfare State."

What Phillips told her readers sets the context for much of what followed:

> Well before Labour's leadership campaign, Tony Blair had begun to set out a vision of community as a key feature of his redefinition of socialism. Now he is a leader, he has to say what he means. Hovering over this enterprise is the shadow of an American sociologist and a new philosophical movement.

Etzioni, professor of sociology at George Washington University, appears to advocate a new politics. State solutions, he says, have failed. The market has also failed. Our recoil from authoritarianism created instead a social wasteland of libertarian fragments.

The attractiveness of such thinking is all too plain for a Labour Party desperate for a high-minded vision that will distance it from the Tories while drawing a line under its past. But it is hard to exaggerate the challenge this poses for many Labour activists and all those who still believe the individual has rights which the State must provide.

So far, so good, but the story continued: "Etzioni started to influence thinking among Labour's modernisers around 1990, when his ideas struck a chord with Blair and Gordon Brown. The Scottish and Christian Socialist traditions to which they subscribed strongly emphasized the ethical basis for community."

The Guardian soon followed with a huge profile of this American who was said to influence Blair, accompanied by a sketch that made me look like a cross between a nut and a prophet: glistening eyes, standing tall above the crowd. A highly respected observer, Martin Walker (later a biographer of Bill Clinton), wrote: "The broad themes of his thought find so many echoes in the political philosophy of Tony Blair that the speech [my lecture to be] will be scoured for its clues to a future Labour government's social policy."

The London *Times* followed, telling its readers that before I carried the communitarian message to Britain, "much of Bill Clinton's election campaign was based on the 'communitarian' principles developed by Etzioni, who is professor of sociology at [George] Washington University. Vice-President Al Gore keeps in constant contact." Accompanying the story was a large picture of me, surrounded by several small pictures of heads of state and that of Tony Blair, out of whose mouth emerged bubbles containing my words!

The merit of these press reports was that they provided extensive and fairly accurate accounts of our basic ideas. Better yet, the press stressed the historical need for a communitarian kind of message, pointing out that if Labour was not going to embrace this timely message, the Tories might. And, the fact that communitarian ideas were gaining so much attention showed that they spoke not merely to Americans. At the same time, I was troubled by the credit I was accorded. I am not immune to flattery and love to be credited for my work as much as the next guy, but I feared that these stories might cost me much more than they delivered—that they might block my all-important opportunity to share our ideas with Blair.

If I learned anything in Washington it was that if you succeed in getting a politician to buy into your ideas, the last thing you want to happen is for the press to find out that you are the source. Politicians like to take credit for new ideas and dislike intensely for it to be said that they have been influenced by anybody, let alone a professor, not to mention a foreign one. (John Gardner put it well when he said, "You must say it over and over again until people think they knew it all the time—and then you do not get any credit for it.") True, none of the press reports suggested that I had made any such claims, because I had not. I was quoted in the *Sunday Times* with, "I see all over the place not my own influence, but an idea whose time has come. People have come to this in their own way and all we can do is hold each other's hands and cheer each other on," and the same was repeated on BBC radio. But Blair's staff would have to read the press clippings closely to notice my disclaimer.

I spent my first day in London at Demos's modest quarters. A seminar on communitarian ideas, in which several MPs and press people participated, was followed by another with community and Labour leaders. Gordon Brown, believed to be a major contender for the head of the Labour Party, stopped by, and we visited in the corridor for a while. (Brown was young and burly, quick-witted, and greatly enamored with economics and American capitalism.) Geoff called me aside and noted in his laconic way: "Blair will see you tomorrow at noon."

Blair All Ears

Aside from being concerned about Blair's reaction to press stories, I also worried whether I would truly have his ear. I've had my share of meetings with politicians whose attention spans were short, especially when it came to the "vision thing." Sitting on a long bench in the bowels of Parliament, waiting for the appointed hour, I kept editing down the mini presentation I had prepared, seeking to put across the communitarian points in a jiffy without doing them gross injustice.

With five minutes to go, a young man walked me through a series of long corridors. They were paneled in the same manner as fancy law firms in New York are: covered with aged wood, only here the panels were much more worn out and did not look as if they had been beaten with chains to look "historical." Up and down the corridors, guys in overalls were hard at work inserting cables behind the old panels. My guide shrugged his shoulders and explained, "We would like to enter the age of computers."

Jonathan Powell, Blair's chief of staff, whom I knew from Washington, did the introductions. Soon, Blair was slouching in a soft armchair too large for his boyish body. Powell parked himself to Blair's right and David Miliband, his policy chief, found a seat to the left. David was taking notes in longhand on a legal-size ledger that must have been left behind from Dickens's time. The office was small and modest by American standards.

Blair offered a wide, open-ended question: "It is good of you to visit. We are, of course, familiar with the essence of your work. Would you, though, lay out for us what you consider to be the essence of the communitarian message?"

I started by repeating the jury story about young Americans eager to have their rights but not to shoulder their responsibilities, which I knew worked best to highlight our main communitarian thesis when there was little time to lay out more detailed arguments. However, Blair seemed ready to hear more. I rolled out what I considered our most salient points, about the importance of realizing that rights and responsibilities go hand in hand, that we were seeking to leapfrog the old debate between left and right and focus on the role of the community, culture, and virtues rather than on either the private sector or the government. The three sectors ought to treat each other as partners and not adversaries, while at the same time keeping each partner in check. While a good society requires a lean state, such a society cannot do without the state playing a significant role, and that such a society must also allow the market sufficient room to provide for the needs of a growing economy.

I went on for a while. While speaking, I wondered if I was missing some kind of cue. Blair and his two associates continued to lean back and take in what I was laying out, as if they had all the time in the world. I laid out some of the implications of the communitarian approach (as I saw it) for fighting crime and drug abuse, dealing with dissolving families, and resolving tensions among people of different racial backgrounds.

Blair's eyes continued to focus on me. He occasionally nodded in agreement and smiled boyishly a good part of the time. When I had tried to run such ideas by Fritz Mondale in the White House, where he served as Carter's vice president, I lost him more quickly than you can say, "Third Sector." Bob Dole's attention span was shorter still. However, when I started to talk about a general vision of a better, nobler society, Blair said, "You mentioned the moral culture." My God, I thought, he has been listening for more than half an hour and is asking for more! I was not going to demure. I realized, however, that I was about to broach the most controversial part of our agenda.

I spelled out the importance of sharing basic notions of what is right and wrong, that community means much more than warm, fuzzy relationships. Communities can encourage people to be better than they would be otherwise by cherishing their pro-social conduct and gently chiding them when they stray. Much of the "social business" takes place this way. When one must rely largely on cops and inspectors and accountants to keep a society on the straight and narrow, much is already lost and must be retrieved, although not necessarily by returning to the old mores.

I could not read Blair's reaction. While he looked truly intrigued, I knew that you had to watch yourself with politicians. He asked whether there was a reason why any of these ideas could not work in Britain.

I responded, "I am, of course, quite unfamiliar with British society. However, from the little I know, there seems no apparent reason why this should be the case."

Then came a probing question for which I was quite unprepared. Blair wanted to know, "What do communitarians have to say about the concern with equality?" He added that inequality is of major concern to the Labour Party. In the seconds I had to ponder the matter, I realized that this was a subject we had not broached and that it was of special importance to Blair, given that he was trying to move his party from traditional socialism to some other way of thinking, one that nevertheless would not ignore this central socialist concern. All I could muster was, "This is a subject we need to think much more about. I would suggest that high inequality, and certainly growing inequality, is not compatible with maintaining a good community. One should aspire to ensure that all members of society gain at least a rich basic minimum, which can move to higher levels as the economy and politics allow. This is, though, quite different from seeking equality, which raises philosophical difficulties (how to square it with liberty) and political ones. Also, one should not ignore *social* inclusiveness, for instance, in matters such as admission to elite universities." Blair seemed less than enthusiastic. He said something that I did not capture, but that sounded like reserving judgment. "Well. . . ."

I mentioned to Blair, "I realize that you are strongly committed to joining the European community and respect you for it, and communitarians are sure to favor integrating nations into more encompassing communities. However, to convince your people of such a move would require a very difficult and prolonged moral dialogue."

Blair was not convinced. "I believe that the British people will see the need not to be left out of the important free market that is developing on the Continent." I tried to argue that one could not separate high-level economic integration from political community building and that the British people seemed (to me) far from ready to proceed, but Blair made it clear that he saw it as his duty to bring them along. A man of true north, with a real inner core.

We continued to explore the finer points of communitarian thinking as the time flew by. An hour was almost up. I did not wait for a secretary to buzz or for his chief of staff to nudge me out. I had made a promise to myself that there was one matter I was going to attend to before it was all over. After all, I was not going to see Blair again next week or next month: "I greatly appreciate the chance to share our ideas with you. Before my time is up, I want to explain: I *never* claimed to influence you." Blair's response made me blush (not a frequent condition) and feel as if I had been warmly embraced.

As we walked to the door, Blair waved aside my apology and said, "I am not at all embarrassed by being associated with you." Usually, I am leery when a public leader, even one known for his integrity, says flattering things; this one, however, made me glow. Over the years that followed, Blair never suggested or hinted that he in any way sought to distance himself from communitarian thinking. On the contrary; Blair himself declared that the "irreducible core" of his beliefs are "Christian, communitarian and thoroughly interventionist."

Most important, there was a major British leader who understood and cared about our message. As it turned out, communitarian ideas in Britain did even better, much better.

A Historical Turning Point

The timing of my visit turned out to be especially auspicious. Several months earlier, Blair was engaged in a fight over the soul of his party, which he was trying to change from a socialist party to a centrist, Third Way one. Blair had lost a major round of that battle in October 1994 when the party refused to drop its Clause IV, to which it stubbornly held for seventy-seven years. The clause stated:

> To secure for the workers by hand or by brain the full fruits of their industry, and the most equitable distribution thereof that may be possible upon the basis of the common ownership of the means of production, distribution and exchange and the best obtainable system of popular administration and control of each industry or service.

In plain English, it meant that Labour threatened (promised, if you prefer) that if it ever returned to power it would nationalize most anything that moves, at least most British industry, commerce, and financial institutions. Although this socialist idea had been long abandoned by all but the doctrinaire left, the Tories used the fact that it remained in the Labour Party platform to scare voters. It was one major reason Labour had lost the 1992 election. Still, in 1994, the old left dug in and refused to drop the obsolete and politically damaging clause. Removing Clause IV became the litmus test of New Labour for which Blair was fighting.

While I was still in London, Blair got another chance to do battle within his party over the Old Labour clause. Unless he could win this round, a victory over the Tories was considered at best unlikely. Some counseled Blair not to push the matter, arguing that if he lost this battle again, his ability to lead would be very much in question. He was also warned that many of the labor unions and left intellectuals were adamant about keeping the antiquated clause. (Indeed, one of the Labour Party leaders close to Blair, John Prescott, told him he was "mad" to take it on.)

Blair, whom Geoff characterized accurately as a "high-risk, high-gain" public leader, unlike his pollster-driven American counterparts, decided that he had to go for it. The outcome was by no means a foregone conclusion given the strength of the opposition and Blair's previous defeat. But this time Blair prevailed. The Labour Party dropped the old Clause IV and replaced it with a communitarian text he offered.

The phrase "defining moment" was often invoked in reference to that day. I found out about all of this when I joined Geoff, a few MPs, and a reporter for a meal in a modest restaurant not far from Church House. Someone brought an evening paper which carried the headline: "A New Approach. New Leader. New Labour Party. New Britain."

The new clause states: "The Labour Party . . . believe that by the strength of our common endeavour we achieve more than we achieve alone . . . the rights we enjoy reflect the duties we owe, and where we live together, freely, in a spirit of solidarity, tolerance and respect."

The newspaper called the clause a "communitarian document" and added: "The new clause 4, with its emphasis on rights and duties, sounds remarkably Etzioni-ite. . . . 'Community' has been talked about as the big idea for some time, since the end of the Reagan–Thatcher 'me-first' era."

The fact that communitarian ideas had played such a pivotal role was great news for our project. For me, it was a high point of my public endeavors. It was one thing to participate in formulating a message, spreading it, mobilizing opposition, bearing witness, but it was another for it to have a true, measurable, significant societal consequence. It was a sure sign that the communitarian message (and my messengership) was of service beyond the boundaries of my homeland. If I pretended that my cup did not flow over that day, you would not believe it. And you would be damn right not to.

A Nonpartisan Agenda: United Kingdom, 1995

Success gave birth to a new concern. The association of the communitarian message with Blair and his New Labour Party called for finding ways to establish our nonpartisan status on this side of the Atlantic as we had on the other.

As the total time scheduled for my visit in London was two-and-a-half days; fast footwork was necessary. Luckily, the voice of Trish Thomas, my secretary, charmed many of the people who called me. This time she employed it to convince my scheduler in London, part boasting, part landing a little dig: "He does not need a break, and he does not want one either."

No sooner had I left Blair than I was on to visit Paddy Ashdown, the head of the British Liberal Democratic Party. He was much keener to tell me about his thinking and achievements than to hear about communitarianism. I tried to share with him at least the essence of our position, but he instead demonstrated that he was a communitarian all on his own. He repeatedly referred to his book, *Citizen's Britain: A Radical Agenda for the 1990s*, and thrust a copy into my hands. I suppose a natural communitarian was as good as a new convert.

My next chance at nonpartisanship came when I met with an All Parliamentary Committee on Voluntary Participation, composed of members of all the political parties. The MPs asked what kind of missions I thought could be carried out by communities compared to what must be kept by the state or relegated to the market. I argued that one cannot turn over health, education, or welfare to the community, but that in each of these major areas of human services, communities could carry part of the load. Most members of the committee seemed to take to our message.

The last evening of my visit completed the roundup: a dinner with seven Tory MPs (Alan Howarth, George Walden, Nigel Forman, David Willetts, David Currie, Gyles Brandreth, and Richard Shepherd). When I tried to take notes at the end of the day, I was no longer sure who had said what, with one major exception: I believed that in Willetts I had found another natural communitarian, albeit of a different brand.

Although he was a Tory, Willetts's book *Modern Conservatism* stressed that one must and can find ways to reconcile capitalism with community—a caring capitalism, based more on Burke than on Thatcher. When I asked how this might be achieved, Willetts answered, "Two things have to happen: the government has to retreat from trying to micromanage our lives and we have to reassess the values we share." I found particularly intriguing his characterization of the City, the Wall Street of London. He was nostalgic for the days when deals were sealed with a handshake and a man's word was his bond. Willett observed wryly that once you had to rely on government regulators, much was already lost.

As we talked more, I realized that although on several issues our differences were mainly questions of emphasis, Willetts's hostility toward efforts to reduce inequality troubled me. It was not an issue communitarians had explored, but he made me revisit the question of whether one can sustain community when differences in wealth, status, and power are steadily becoming more pronounced.

Henceforth, maybe with a little assistance from my side, Willetts was considered a leading conservative communitarian. He shared his ideas with our summit in Geneva and here and there spoke in our defense. But I should have known from the mischievous glint in his eyes that sooner or later he would get into trouble. He lost much of his credibility when he was accused of "dissembling" before a Commons select committee and was forced to resign his position as junior whip. I continued to respect his views.

One reporter who joined a dinner after my public lecture at Church House did not waste her time. Writing for the London *Times*, she mocked me under the headline, "I Am the Way and I Am the Truth." She reported that having met with leaders of all three parties and MPs, I would have completed the "political equivalent of a grand slam" were it not for the bad luck that the head of the government, John Major, was out of the country visiting, of all places, Gaza. I was much too pleased with the fact that our nonpartisanship was to be recognized to allow her ribbing to get to me.

Later in the evening, I tried to unwind with a Scotch while flipping channels. On the BBC there was a half-hour debate between a New Labour MP and an Old Labour one about the merits of communitarian thinking. What an encore!

One last stop on the way to the airport: a visit to the home of the chief rabbi of Britain, Jonathan Sacks. Sacks had written several strongly communitarian books, drawing mainly on the Old Testament instead of modern social philosophers, although he was thoroughly familiar with them. He agreed to participate in our future events and has since been a major voice for communitarian values in the United Kingdom.

The Left Is Up in Arms

In the year that followed, the British media continued to report that Blair was (and to some extent a few Tories were) influenced by communitarian ideas and hence dedicated considerable space to explaining this new breed of thinking.

Shortly after my meeting with Blair, the highly influential *Economist* carried a long essay about communitarianism. Even a relatively brief quote from it captures how far we reached.

> Foreign sociologists who visit London are seldom feted so splendidly as was Amitai Etzioni, the founder of America's "communitarian" movement, this week. Tony Blair, the Labour leader, and Paddy Ashdown, his Liberal Democrat

counterpart, received Mr. Etzioni, a professor from George Washington University, while Conservative cabinet ministers attended a dinner in his honor. Tickets for Mr. Etzioni's public lecture on March 13th were sold out. . . . Mr. Blair, who has read Mr. Etzioni's books, is sympathetic. In his speech to last October's party conference, the Labour leader mentioned community 11 times and responsibility 14 times.

The *Guardian* published one of my essays on communitarianism; the *Independent* listed it among key "Ideas for Our Times" in one issue. In a press that knows no limits, a year-end issue of the *Independent* listed me as one of the "Prophets of the 21st Century."

A major drumbeat of criticisms rose from the left, first on the pages of the *New Statesman*. To its credit, it allowed me to respond extensively, only to hit me again—and thus granting more space to communitarianism. The *Fabian Review* chimed in with some more criticism, as did John Gray, a brilliant British professor at the London School of Economics. (Luckily for us, he published a pro-communitarian book two years later.)

Another barrage of criticism—and discussion of our ideas—was unleashed by British libertarians. Norman Stone argued that communitarianism was representing itself as a third way between capitalism and socialism, whose appeal was not surprising given that "until now the left-versus-right argument had been stuck in a boring terrain. It was obvious that both were badly in need of an idea." But Stone maintained that the ideas of communitarianism were similar to those of the Counter-Reformation, whose saints, such as St. Vincent de Paul, thought that community meant taxing the rich to pay the poor. Ergo, according to Mr. Stone, while communitarians claim that they want less government and more reliance on mutuality, "behind it all, however, lingers a sense there must be a less unforgiving mode of governance." Stone did not bother to give any evidence of this claim other than that our position reminded him of some people, hundreds of years ago, who sounded what were to his deaf ear similar notes. Well, not all of them were that far in the past. We also, Stone divulged, reminded him of *Rerum Novarum*, an encyclical by Leo XIII, which Stone claims attempts to replace capitalism and was implemented by none other than Mussolini. Anyone who could get from our brand of communitarianism to Italian fascism in three steps or four paragraphs could also make Mother Teresa into a slumlord.

I realized that to some extent such criticisms were unavoidable. (Irving Goffman once told me during our Berkeley days that I should remember that "a ship that moves forward makes counter-currents. If you cannot stand them, stop making progress." He then pointed to a much-loved colleague who did very little work.) However, I feared that people would remember us the way we appeared in these crooked mirrors. I found some comfort in what happened next.

Over the two years that followed Blair's 1995 victory inside the Labour Party, he gradually unfolded his campaign to unseat the Tories, building on communitarian themes. He stressed: "The rights we enjoy reflect the duties we owe" and "responsibility from all, responsibility for all." He wrote, "The founding principle, the guiding principle, of the Labour Party is the belief in community and society. It's the notion that for individuals to advance you need a strong community behind you."

Better yet: "Individual liberty is best secured through a strong and just community, where people recognize their interdependence as well as independence and where action by society as a whole is used to help fulfil the aspirations of the individuals within it."

There was much more in the same communitarian vein. Ultimately, Blair centered his campaign around three concepts—responsibility, community, and opportunity. (The same used by the New Democrats.) He stressed the role of communities as the partners of government and introduced numerous other openly communitarian themes.

Communitarian influence on Blair and the Labour Party has been widely reported, not merely in popular press. This influence is documented and analyzed at great length in Elizabeth Frazer's book *The Problems of Communitarian Politics*. Her numerous quotes of Blair include: "The founding principle, the guiding principle, of the Labour Party is the belief in community and society. It's the notion that for individuals to advance you need a strong and fair community behind you." Emma Heron and Peter Dwyer wrote:

> It has been argued that Labour embraces a distinctly communitarian agenda. Blair himself sees the positive potential for communitarianism to inform Labour's social policy; . . . "a communitarian philosophy . . . allow[s] us to move beyond the choice between narrow individualism and old-style socialism." Certainly many of the communitarians' concerns are echoed in New Labour's literature with the translation of communitarian language into a social policy reality looking set to equate responsibility with the work ethic and an increased emphasis on individual responsibility.

Blair's victory was more sweeping than almost anybody had predicted, larger than Labour had ever dreamed. The party gained 148 more seats, adding to the 271 it already held, for a total of 419 out of 659 seats in Parliament, which secured Blair a very solid base. Thus, by 1997, there were two heads of state that were committed, to varying degrees, to Third Way and communitarian ideas, wherever they got them from. Soon, there were more.

Germany, West and East, Fertile Ground

Kohl (Blue), Fisher (Green), Scharping (Red), and the Rest

When I was invited in 1992 to visit Germany as the personal guest of the chancellor, Helmut Kohl, I faced a dilemma. As a Jewish refugee from Nazi Germany, I did not want to go near Germans of the age who could have been members of the Gestapo, concentration camp guards, or just garden-variety Nazis. On previous visits to Germany, mainly for meetings that sought to promote nuclear disarmament (conducted by a German association of scientists for social responsibility), I tried to avoid older Germans. I did not trust their claims of "I knew nothing" and their all too facile protestations: "Weren't those awful times?" The very notion of ending up spending an evening chitchatting over beer with someone who might have been in charge of the ovens, who maybe shot members of my family—how is one to know?—made me leery of any German with gray hair.

A quick trip to the library eased my concerns. Kohl had been fifteen years old when World War II ended. Hence, there was no need to fear that he played a role in Hitler's regime. And he was already the head of state, not just an aspiring one (which Blair was when I met him). To turn Kohl, a conservative, onto communitarian ideas would lift the message to new heights and bring it to the leader of another important nation. Next, I was curious as to why Kohl had invited me and whether I could parlay whatever was on his mind into a hearing for our message. It turned out that once a year Kohl invited a group of American opinionmakers to spend a considerable amount of time with him to strengthen the bonds between Germany and the United States.

Our small group, met by a fleet of black cars at the Bonn railroad station, included James Wolfensohn (later the head of the Kennedy Center and then the World Bank), Strobe Talbott of *Time Magazine* (later deputy Secretary of State under Clinton), the CEOs of Boeing and Procter & Gamble, as well as a few others. There was going to be quite a bit of competition for Kohl's attention.

Instead of a hotel, we checked into the Petersberg, a modern-looking, cold building with polished marble floors and unadorned windows; Hitler was said to have frequented it. I did not expect a building to do what Kohl's invitation did not: give me a creepy feeling that I was listening to Hitler screeching one of his anti-Semitic tirades or hearing echoes of him ordering mass executions. I had an extra drink that evening, promising myself that I would not let these ghosts prevent me from what I had come to Germany to do.

Our small group was ushered into a modest room, which looked like a typical seminar room in a state university. Soon, Kohl waded in. After extensive greetings and rambling comments about NATO, Germany, France, and assorted other subjects, he invited our questions to which he responded with long monologues. Three hours later, we had heard nothing he had not repeatedly stated publicly.

Slowly, Kohl's purpose emerged. The chancellor spoke about "my two sons, who *both* have been educated in the United States, one at MIT and one at Harvard. Both speak with great admiration of your great country." Kohl faced the problem of all community builders: exclusion of others. The more he worked to strengthen the European community, the more he seemed to undermine Germany's special relationship with the United States—the Atlantic alliance. He tried to reassure us that his dedication to one community did not mean he loved the United States less. Obviously, we were supposed to take this message back home.

I tried to turn to communitarian topics during the Q&A period and asked a convoluted question that, by the time it was translated, lost whatever focus it had. Kohl responded by speaking both to my communitarian and Jewish heart. (Clearly, he had been carefully briefed about each of us.)

Kohl emphasized in his response the reasons he was pushing the development of the European community. "Germany must be protected from itself by being blended into a United Europe," he said. And, "In the future Germany will be held down by Europe." To avoid leaving the impression that his commitment to the European community diluted his alliance with the United States, he rushed to make some cracks about his main European partner. "The French," he said, "on V-day they march up and down the Champs-Elysées, waving flags, celebrating their victory over Germany. It's time to stop these parades. Anyhow, it is the Americans who won the war!"

Later that evening, we had dinner in his private residence.

In comparison to the White House, the place was much less security conscious; at least I did not see a lot of muscular types running around with "hearing aides" and curious bulges under their armpits. (When I asked the U.S. ambassador about it later, he explained: "Germans are still living with the memory of the Nazis. They are allergic to any measures that might smack of police excesses.")

I ended up at a table next to Mrs. Kohl. After a few toasts, the conversation turned to World War II. She complained about "indiscriminate" bomb-

Figure 14.1. With Chancellor Helmut Kohl at his home, 1992

ing by British and American forces of her city and how difficult it had been to get eggs. Moreover, "One day," she confided, "I had to run into the shelter with only one shoe on!"

I felt like telling her right there and then, in her own home, that her insensitivity was stupendous. I was tempted to say, "How dare you even mention such 'suffering' to a Jew, given what your people did to us?" To be fair, I thought, there is no denying that some of the bombing by the allied forces was aimed deliberately at starting firestorms in civilian areas of some German cities, especially Dresden, but—a shortage of eggs! Having to make it to a shelter without a shoe!

I did not say a word. Was it the notion that such a response was somehow "inappropriate" for a guest? Was I cowed by being in the home of a head of state? Should I have stormed out in protest? Was it really just a fear that a scene would prevent me from carrying out what I considered my mission? I am still not sure what I would do if the whole thing happened again. I am sure I did not handle it well.

The next day we visited with President Richard von Weizsäcker. German presidents are merely symbolic heads of state. Weizsäcker, however, chose to serve as the conscience of his country. The next stop was the German minister of foreign affairs, Klaus Kinkel, who was just six years younger than

Kohl. He did not speak of the indelible shame with which the Holocaust tarred Germany, nor did he speak of holding Germany down. On the contrary, he favored revising the international structure set up at the end of World War II "to adjust it to the new power realities. Japan should be given a seat on the powerful UN Security Council." He added: "Germany then should be accorded the same status." The time had come to regularize the place of Germany among the nations. Speaking about sending international peacekeeping forces to Bosnia, Kinkel declared: "I am tired of paying for the fire brigade, but not being on the ladder."

Strobe Talbott, a member of our group, asked whether ten years hence, as the European community built up its unity, Germany would have to consult with the secretaries of state of the other members of the European community before making such a statement. Kinkel did not dignify this possibility with a response. Indeed, he dismissed it with a swipe of his hand, the way one chases away a nettlesome fly. The contrast with Kohl's response stayed with me. Kinkel and other German leaders I met later were getting ready to put history aside, not to pretend it did not happen, but to not allow it to prevent Germany from being restored to what they considered a normal status among nations. Indeed, it looked as if Germany's restoring sense of independence was rising more quickly than its integration into the European community. The Kinkels were going to win over the Kohls; national self-awareness was going to win over community building.

The visit so far had not provided an occasion to share communitarian ideas. Our next stop: Leipzig, in eastern Germany. I asked myself what a communitarian could possibly tell people who moved from the Nazi regime directly to communist control, most of whom had never lived in a free society.

Eastern Germany: A Latent Communitarian Hunger

Our first stop was in a small church where the leaders of the uprising that toppled the Wall (and the communist regime in East Germany) in 1989 had assembled before demonstrating against the communist tyranny. A small man with warm, sad, puppy dog eyes named Friedrich Magirius, a clergyman who played a major role in keeping the uprising nonviolent, greeted us. The nonviolence made the uprising that ended the East German regime more difficult for the Stasi to suppress and thus greatly contributed to its success.

Far from gushing about the newly won liberty of his country, Magirius bemoaned the moral vacuum of his new world. During communism, the state was supposed to be worshiped. It told people what it considered right and wrong and took care of them, although on a meager level. Since the liberation from communism, the market, especially privatization, he said, had become the new gospel. But it left as many as 30 percent of his people unemployed. Child care centers, provided by workplaces under the communists, were closing as plants now focused on output and profit making. Above all, Magirius said that people lacked a source of moral guidance. He reported that eastern parts of Germany had been hit by a tidal wave of divorce that left in its wake lonely singles and abandoned children. He closed with a deep sigh. "Freedom casts a long shadow."

The next day we met with a number of local leaders, city officials, editors, and intellectuals. They all made basically the same point: first we worshiped the state; now we are told that the market is the savior. Something profound is missing. We are told that all we believed in for the last forty-five years is garbage or worse. What is supposed to fill the resulting vacuum?

Taking all this in, it dawned on me that not only was there a need for the communitarian message in eastern Germany and other former communist countries, but it might well be the place where such a message was most needed. The free-market ideology, whatever its merits, did not even seek to address the basic questions about the foundations of morality and the meaning of life. Without these, whether or not these societies became affluent, their members could not be truly content, let alone lead morally sound lives. Here was a whole new world to reach.

Soon, the official visit to Germany was over. A couple of young German friends took us to an outstanding performance of Verdi's *Requiem* in Berlin. During a quick dinner, we chatted about our children, other friends, and music. It was no different from an evening with friends in Washington.

On the flight back it was all too evident to me that while I had learned a lot, I had taught nothing. If Germany was going to be exposed to communitarian ideas, we had not yet even started.

Nine Forays

In the six years following my "official" visit to Germany in 1992, I returned nine times. By 1998, I could negotiate my way through the crowded Frankfurt airport with my eyes closed. Gradually, the communitarian message found its way into German politics, media, and intellectual life. *The Spirit of Community*, *The New Golden Rule*, and even *The Moral Dimension* were translated into German. More important, several German activists and scholars took the lead.

On one of those trips, I asked myself why I hit the road even one more time, a reflection prompted by a profile in the *Los Angeles Times* that depicted me as an indefatigable salesman. Many people, I realize, think that societies change in a dramatic manner. A prophet chides the king, the king's guilt is evoked, and, bingo, he marches the society to a new tune, in a new direction. This is, for instance, the way much of the media depicted the effect of Michael Harrington's book *The Other America:* he called attention to the poor, John F. Kennedy read a review of the book, and soon America was engaged in a full-scale war against poverty. If they only knew how much groundwork had preceded the book and the numerous steps that had to be taken after Kennedy heard about it—many of which fell to his successor, President Johnson, and none of which conquered poverty. Societal change is hard to come by, is drawn out at best, and almost always is annoyingly gradual. My assignment was to keep chipping away at the German objections, hoping to open ever more doors, minds, and hearts to the communitarian message.

The numerous trips blurred together as I made the same basic points to one audience after another in one German city after another and laid them out one more time before still another public leader. Back in Bonn, I attended a small meeting of Social Democrat leaders and intellectuals. They were still in the old socialist mode, much like the pre-Blair Old Labour. (They even addressed one another as "comrade," a form of salutation they shared with communists.) The group was torn between those keen to find a new message (the last Social Democratic chancellor was Helmut Schmidt, who had been defeated by Helmut Kohl in 1983) and those fiercely loyal to the obsolescent, socialist one. I spoke briefly and asked for them to support a dialogue on our message. (I knew better than to ask for more.) Thomas Meyer, a German Social Democrat and public intellectual, grasped our message in no time and tried to work with it. The older types were visibly angry at such heresy. "What is wrong with making the state the main agent of society?" they demanded to know. "True, it now seems hard to pay for the welfare state, but if the government would only get the economy to grow faster and reduce unemployment, the additional revenue and savings could pay for the existing welfare system and much more." And, "Let them cut the salaries of executives and dividends to the stockholders if the government needs cash." Their fury was aimed mainly at Meyer, who quickly fell mum. This was going to be uphill all the way.

On my next trip, I was invited to meet with Rudolf Scharping, who at the time was the head of the Social Democratic opposition in the German parliament. Scharping was reported to be dull and pedantic, more suited to being a schoolteacher than a party leader. (He was later unseated as the party leader. In 1999, he was appointed minister of defense in the Gerhard Schröder government, where he very much came into his own.) It was the end of the day as we sat down to talk communitarianism. Scharping was accompanied by an aide who subjected me to a cross-examination while Scharping listened like a patient judge.

The aide: "Will you admit that you are hostile to women, as one can see from your plan to resurrect the patriarchal family?"

Having learned not to respond as I wished ("Why start with such a loaded question instead of asking me what our position is?"), I explained, "We do not wish to return to the traditional family but favor one based on full equality between women and men. However, we do believe that children—and their parents—are better off if marriages work."

The aide was just warming up. "So, you are against single mothers?"

With some pain, I stuck to my best manners. "We are not against anyone. We recognize that there are some circumstances in which divorce is called for, and we do respect the difficult job single mothers have when they must earn a living and take care of their children on their own. However, the evidence shows that *on average* married mothers can do better."

The aide: "So, you favor measures that punish single women?"

I was not sure how much longer I could keep my cool, but I held on: "We favor policies that support families, several of which you already have but we do not, such as paid leave for new parents—fathers or mothers—as well as flex time, opportunities to work at home, and *pre*marital counseling."

We continued to slug it out for several more rounds. The visit ended when Scharping noted only that all this was new to him and he had to learn much more about it. He hoped that "we have another chance to see you." A for effort, F for outcome.

A year and a half later, the poor fortunes of the Social Democrats—who, like Old Labour in Britain, lost an election they seemed poised to win—whetted Scharping's interest in our message. He promised to address our first international summit, which was to take place in Geneva in July 1996. I was counting on finding some private time with him before or after the presentation. However, on the appointed date, he did not show up. A rush of phone calls established that he had been incapacitated when he fell off his bike. Fortunately, Scharping had sent the text of the speech he was going to deliver.

While looking for someone of stature to read the speech to our summit, no one better came to mind than Hans Joas. Joas is a sociologist who combines solid scholarship with dedication to social democracy. What especially struck me about him was the way he spoke with well-controlled passion. He would raise his voice only ever so much; but you could sense that he had the intensity of a true believer combined with the demeanor of a moderate Quaker. There was no other German I knew who was more troubled by the atrocities his forefathers had committed. Picking Joas turned out to be a sound choice. Joas read the valuable but far from captivating text with so much conviction that it gained the undivided attention of the jet-lagged audience. As a bonus, from then on, Joas's own ambivalence about us, as a Social Democrat, subsided. He often explained our cause to others while maintaining some distance.

In the speech, Scharping had celebrated several major communitarian tenets.

> Wherever the community is in a position to solve a given problem, it must take the lead. Wherever it needs state assistance, this must be provided. The state should watch over processes rather than encumber them with red tape. This is less a withdrawal of the state than a change in its role. It can restore to the welfare state the moral dimension that many people feel it lacks today.

He closed with the all-important note, recognizing our significance as co-equals: "I believe that we are working on the same project: freedom, solidarity, and individual responsibility. Beginning at different ends, we will meet in the middle." After the meeting, there was an excited buzz in the corridors. The communitarian message had found a German leader.

Figure 14.2.   With Rudolf Scharping, 1995, in Bonn

Following the summit, the press listed Scharping as one of our supporters. He wrote a highly favorable review of *The Spirit of Community* when it was published in German and chaired a meeting dedicated to its discussion. We continued to see each other in Bonn and in Washington.

One more invitation to Bonn, this time by the leader of the Green Party, Joschka Fischer (later the very popular secretary of state in the Schröder government). He invited some 250 intellectuals and public leaders to listen to our message. At the meeting, Fischer pointed to clear parallels between the concern for the common good, which is the heart of the environmental movement, and our concern for the well-being of society.

Fischer is easy to like. He is very informal and has a quick mind. Our conversation ranged from German politics to a communitarian form of child care, *kinder ladden*, which his children received when he had been part of the counterculture in Germany. (It requires parents to work at the center a certain number of hours each week.) However, he did not commit himself to our position.

To adhere to the nonpartisan agenda in Germany, having the support of a key Social Democrat and visible interest from a major Green leader, I tried to find a leading conservative supporter. I found him in Kurt Biedenkopf, an influential Christian Democratic Union (CDU) leader, governor of lower Saxony (nicknamed the King of Saxony), and a natural communitarian. He delivered ringing communitarian speeches to several of our meetings. Whenever he joined us, he instantly became the center of attention, especially among the young people. They liked the fact that he acted less like a politician and more like a professor. Wherever Biedenkopf rested, smoking his pipe, a small crowd would assemble around him and engage him in hourslong dialogues on communitarian issues and many other matters.

Gaining support from three German leaders, a red, a green, and a blue one, was a solid achievement. Still another opportunity to spread the word arose when I was invited to testify before a committee of the German parliament. Following Buber's emphasis on the importance of dialogue, I tried to keep my presentations short and to spend most of the time allotted to answering questions and criticisms. In this case, given a large room full of legislators from all parties and a two-hour window, I lectured even more briefly than usual and answered dozens of questions. As the hours passed, the mood in the room warmed up. When it was time to leave, the sound of applause suggested that I had not failed. Indeed, several of those present joined me on the way out to talk some more.

The German press put me through different paces than the American and British ones. At first, they referred to the communitarian position as authoritarian. Later stories depicted me as a doe-eyed visionary, well-meaning but naive; an improvement of sorts. At the same time, both small intellectual publications and mass-circulation ones as well as radio and television covered our ideas extensively.

The German press served the cause best when the libertarian but highly influential *Frankfurter Allgemeine Zeitung* published the full text of the communitarian platform in German. It was symptomatic that the term *member* was translated into German as *burger*, meaning citizen. The distinction is crucial, because you can be a good citizen if you obey the laws, pay your taxes, follow public affairs, and vote. Your responsibilities as a member of a community are much broader, less defined, voluntary, and informal. It turned out that there is no word in German that quite captures the notion of *member*; the closest word is *mitglider*, which evokes the much thinner image of the English term "dues payer." Germany is one of the many societies enamored with the state, that sometimes does not even see society as a distinct realm.

Another influential German newspaper, *Die Zeit*, also libertarian, published the text of a panel discussion it organized in Hamburg in which Hans Joas and I participated along with the paper's editor. Even the semi tabloids gave us a hand. Many Germans learned about us following a three-page interview in the popular *Der Spiegel*. A two-page spread in the much-respected *Die Woche* also helped. Gradually, our appeal to a wide range of the political spectrum was being recognized.

German scholars were among the last attracted to our cause. Hans Joas continued to lead the list, growing ever more in stature as he was courted by universities from Stockholm to Berkeley. (He ended up affiliating with the University of Chicago.) Eventually, he joined the board of our quarterly, *The Responsive Community*. As we saw each other more often, we became good friends, a bonus for those of us who spend too much of our lives zipping from one place to another.

Among other German scholars who took to us were a young scholar from East Germany, Walter Reese-Schäfer, and Hans Ulrich Nübel from Freiburg. Later, Warnfried Dettling became a friend and one who spoke about and for communitarian ideas. When I met Dettling, he was introduced as a "publicist," which I took to mean a PR guy. That made good sense because he was very personable, outgoing, and an enthusiastic and inspiring speaker. It turned out that in German the term means "public intellectual," which made his voice even more valuable than I first presumed.

Town Meetings

The increased interest in our message from German public leaders and the media led to numerous invitations to present our ideas in a curious variety of places. These ranged from a church group in Stuttgart to a group of members of the state assembly (called "parliament") of Mainz, and from the America House in Munich to dinner with then-President Roman Herzog, organized by a German foundation. The invitations also included presenting lectures in the formerly communist parts of Germany and a debate before a philosophical society in Bad Homburg.

Often, the line of questioning was the same: "You want us to return to oppressive villages, Soviet-style mandated 'volunteerism,' and Hitler's notion of a *volksgemeinschaft*?" (This was usually said more as an accusation than as a question.)

My response was: "We cannot junk a good idea because it has been abused. True, in earlier ages and under totalitarian regimes communities have been oppressive; today's problem in our kind of societies is excessive individualism. Moreover, people often choose in which community to live and are members of several communities, say, work- and church-based. Hence, none of them can gain a stranglehold on their lives."

I found that Germans, in effect many Europeans, have less difficulties with the Third Way (some kind of combination of statism with a strong private market) than with the communitarian notions of a third leg—communities as a major social partner. To illustrate this, I often drew on two illustrative examples.

The first example is my favorite anecdote, about the Seattle CPR program, which is about as communitarian as it gets. "To appreciate the importance of this program," I told my German audiences, "you must take into account that victims of heart failure have a much greater chance to survive if they are resuscitated, are given CPR, within four minutes. Indeed, the main result of having to wait for an ambulance crew for medical service to be initiated is often a dehumanizing and costly death. In contrast, victims who receive CPR on the spot from citizens, without waiting for an ambulance, are twice as likely to recover as those who had to wait for professional care.

"Given these facts, if you must have heart failure, try to have it in Seattle, Washington. Unlike residents of most cities, about 400,000 residents have been trained as volunteers in how to perform CPR, and as many as 40 percent of those suffering out-of-hospital heart failure in Seattle have their resuscitation begun by bystanders before they are moved to a hospital. Between them, the good citizens of Seattle have already saved hundreds of lives and sustained many others on a much more meaningful level.

"The civic program does much more than save large amounts of funds that would be needed if the same level of service were provided by having ambulances and crews spread around the city. It also brings citizens much closer to one another, at training and refresher courses, and, above all, in knowing that the next person you see may save your life—or you, his. We are not talking about charity or good deeds, like reading to the blind or opening a soup kitchen for the homeless, which have their own merit. Here, we are seeing mutuality, people helping one another, a major foundation of community." Many in my various German (and other) audiences found the Seattle story heartwarming and illuminating.

The second example I owed to a German health minister. When the German government realized that putting the elderly into nursing homes was very costly, it encouraged Germans to attend to their aging parents in their homes. However, instead of appealing to their sense of obligation to their parents, the authorities chose to pay those who took care of their elderly parents. "Economically," I told my audiences, "this makes eminently good sense. Socially and morally, it means undermining an obligation we have for one another, commodifying one more social relationship."

To further illustrate, I provided some details, courtesy of the same source: "An elderly father had a stroke. The state paid 1,100 marks a month to his son to take care of his father. However, the son was informed that once the father learned to wash himself, the fee would be cut to 800 marks. And if the father learned to talk, the fee would be only 400 marks. This policy puts children into a strong conflict between their moral sense, helping the parent to recover, and the well-being of their pocketbook."

A woman who translated my speech at Mainz was rushing home to be with her newborn son. I asked how long German hospitals allow women to stay after childbirth. She said that recently the time is being reduced to one or two days. I asked how she managed after she returned home, especially since she already had another young child. She explained that she was helped by a friend "who was paid for by the government."

After reciting these examples, I pointed out that these and other such policies concerned me. "Of course, one could have the state pay for more and more services previously provided by family members to one another, but there seems to be wide agreement that people are unwilling to pay still higher taxes. So, we must find some other ways to take care of *some* social needs." I added that turning ever more personal relationships into transactions was opposite from the direction we need to move in.

I found that these examples were well received and helped illuminate the general communitarian message. However, there was often one member of the audience who would state flatly: "This whole thing is an *American* idea; it will not work here."

I repeated the answer so many times that I sounded wooden: "American? Communitarian ideas are found in the Old and New Testaments, ancient Greek writings, Catholic social teachings, socialist concepts of solidarity, the Fabians. German sociologist Tönnies started the learning about *gemeinschaft*. My training was under the German-Jewish Martin Buber—in Asia."

Public lectures are like blind dates (unlike classrooms, which are more like developing a relationship). Over the years I've learned that the more I knew ahead of time about my audience, the better the chemistry. But under the best of circumstances, there is an initially awkward feeling; the audience is assessing the person who stands before them, while the presenter tries to read the audience. When the lecturer and the audience connect, delivering a lecture can be a fulfilling and enjoyable experience. When the chemistry is off, you cannot wait until it's over.

In Germany, as I learned more about the concerns Germans were bringing to our meetings and they knew more about our basic positions, spreading the word became less tedious. Often the meetings no longer started with curious hostility, but instead with fairly warm anticipation, and increasingly they ended with considerable excitement and warm applause. On several occasions people asked, "How can one join the Communitarian Network?" I explained that the Communitarian Network was not a membership organization, but an association of different groups and individuals who shared a communitarian perspective. Each country and community was free to form its own communitarian circles.

As the years turned, several initiatives along these lines were undertaken, first by Peter Werner, who soon moved on to become engaged in helping the people of Bosnia, then by a group calling itself the Kölner communitarians (from Köln) that slowly petered out. Hans Ulrich Nübel organized a more successful German communitarian network (for more information on his organization, see www.dekomnetz.de).

Somewhat similarly to the developments in Britain, once the German Social Democrats adopted a version of the Third Way (Neu Mitte, or New Middle) under the leadership of Gerhard Schröder, they won the elections in 1998 and formed a coalition government with the Greens in late 1998. (Scharping became the defense minister, and Fischer, the foreign minister.) In June 1999, Schröder issued a joint statement with Tony Blair about their agendas. It is a strongly communitarian text.

All said and done, in Germany, the 1990s opened with a conservative government that embraced a fairly moderate version of Thatcherist ideology; but by the end of the decade the country was governed by a Third Way government with some communitarian inclinations. The media and the educated public had acquired some familiarity with our ideas and had overcome some earlier misgivings. The fact that we reached a saturation point of sorts hit me when, following one more presentation, this one in Berlin, a reporter from Süddeutsche Zeitung complained: "We've heard all this before." I've heard worse complaints.

---∞∞∞---

CHAPTER FIFTEEN

Tomorrow, the World?

A wit suggested that it takes ideas seven years to cross the ocean in either direction. Even in the age of the Internet, books published in the United States often appear in Britain—in a separate British edition—a few years after they have been issued in the United States. And if they must be translated, they first see the light of day on the Continent years later still. Hence, it was not surprising that while our brand of communitarian seeds sprouted in the United States in the early nineties, they broke the ground in the United Kingdom only in the mid-1990s and saw dawn on the Continent (and other countries overseas) even later. But as the decade unfolded, there was a steady and growing stream of requests for interviews, articles, and lectures from all over the map.

Whether other societies would embrace our message was of great interest to both the sociologist and the activist in me. Sociologically, whether other societies would take to the communitarian message would test a theory I laid out in *The New Golden Rule*, which suggests that although different societies need to follow distinct courses—some making more room for individual rights and some for communal bonds and shared values—the characterization of a good, communitarian society is the same for all societies: a carefully crafted balance between liberty and social order. The activist in me was itching to find out whether the communitarian message had something to offer to people of different societies.

An academic could write a learned and lengthy tome about the differences among various societies, their own communitarian inclinations, and their responses to our ideas during the 1990s and beyond. To put it, instead, in a very few terse lines: by and large, the societies that have been the most resistant to communitarian ideas have been those continuing to hold that one should rely on the state as the provider of social services or as the promoter of moral and social virtues. These countries were the least ready to consider community a true partner, and they remain countries that the communitarian message still must reach the most. These include societies as different as Iran and Saudi Arabia are from Singapore and North Korea.

Following the end of the Cold War, the societies that ceased putting their faith in the state and realized that the welfare state could no longer shoulder an ever heavier load were much more willing to consider communitarianism's implications for their societies. The same was true for those that saw their moral order in disarray, but also feared the religious and ideological right and sought democratic, inclusive ways to formulate new shared understandings of the good.

France and Southern Europe: Terra Incognito

In France, a nation that is still deeply committed to relying on the government for most social services and cultural activities, the interest in communitarian thinking was limited to a few articles in the popular press and aca-

Figure 15.1. With Pat, Iran, 2002

demic journals. A French reporter who interviewed me suggested that the problem was that "France has no communities and no idea of community." I found the comment silly beyond belief and asked with some irritation: "Have you ever been in a French village?" and, "Are the French familiar with the concept of the 'commune'?" (The latter was a dig about communes that played an important role in the French Revolution.) He acknowledged that there may be some communitarian elements in French history and contemporary society—but continued to insist that we had nothing to say to France. I did not do much better with other French reporters. When a foundation offered to finance the translation into French of some communitarian books, it could not find a publishing house interested in issuing them. No French leader I know of expressed any interest in our ideas and I was invited only twice to give lectures in France. The audiences were modest, to put it charitably. In Italy, a country that is almost as statist as France, there has been only slightly more interest in communitarian thinking.

Spain has been much more hospitable. Spain is often unfairly listed as a country that has a very limited civic life because it has such a low level of participation in voluntary associations. It does, however, have strong family bonds and many of its communities are very much intact, even in cities. I got to see some of it firsthand following a lecture in February 1996. From then on, a fine Spanish scholar, José Pérez Adán, became our champion. He formed a Spanish communitarian network and has written extensively about communitarian ideas. A couple of communitarian books were also translated into Spanish. While Spanish society has strong communitarian elements and several of its scholars are open to communitarian thinking, it so far has not played an explicitly significant role in public discourse or politics.

I still believe that societies that are keen to provide a rich array of social services, from cradle to grave, will be unable to do so by loading ever more missions and costs on the state. They will have to make communities, existing and newly revived, a mainstay of their social fabric. Not to replace the welfare state, but to make it possible to keep it. And, in those matters communities take on, they will provide services that are much more humane and individually tailored than those any government delivers.

Not a Land of Milk and Honey

Israel is often considered a communitarian society. Actually, it is badly in need of our message. There is, of course, a savage, bloody, vicious conflict between the Israelis and the Palestinians, but one may construe this as a fight between two nations rather than within one society. However, internal divisions also plague Israel. A line Israeli newspapers have repeated from a variety of sources says it all: "I do not believe we will come to a civil war," referring to strife between the Orthodox and the civil libertarian Jewish Israelis. The fact that a war between religious and secular Jews can even be mentioned, in a country within missile range of Arab nations that consider Israel the devil incarnate, is a tragic indication of the weakness of the Israeli national community. In a country studded with numerous local and ethnic communities, including secular and religious ones, the community of communities—the Israeli society—is fragile indeed.

The tendency of Israelis to be in each other's faces only exacerbates the tension that emanates from divergent beliefs of the various camps (and divisions within each). The American press has made much of the fanatical religious groups that refuse burial in Jewish cemeteries to soldiers who died for Israel because their mothers were not properly converted to Judaism, pay young men much more for studying in the Yeshivas than young women, and make divorce much more difficult for women than men. The press has paid far less attention to the provocative acts of the civil libertarians, who have arranged caravans to drive on the Sabbath through religious neighborhoods to make the point that they have a right to free passage, have painted swastikas on synagogues, and defiled Torahs in their anger.

The conflict between secular and religious Israelis is closely tied to the horrible conflict between Israelis and Palestinians. Some of the most religious groups are also the ones most committed to blanketing the West Bank with Jewish settlements and opposed to most peace proposals. Finding common ground between these two groups is as urgent and tantalizing a communitarian mission as I can discern.

When I addressed an audience at the University of Tel Aviv, a civil libertarian center, about the community of communities, I knew better than to point to Israeli examples. Instead, I referred to an American minority, the supporters of the National Rifle Association (NRA). I argued that although they merely amount to an estimated 20 percent of the electorate, given the strong feelings these citizens have about guns, the American majority could not simply run roughshod over them. In a democracy, the intensity of commitments counts, not merely the number of votes. The first questioner wanted to be sure that he was reading me right: "So, you would say that the Israeli majority cannot simply overrule our religious zealots who also amount to about 20 percent?"

I allowed, "It would be much better to draw them into a dialogue and see if one could find common ground."

"You are condoning the killers of Yitzhak Rabin!" flew back the retort. It is hard to imagine a harsher condemnation. Most of the rest of the discussion had the same confrontational and uncommunitarian content and overtones.

I tried during several visits to find, in the Jewish religious tradition, sources of common ground between the two camps. It seemed to me that there was no hope of engaging even relatively moderate religious leaders in a conversation about Kant or the United Nations Universal Declaration of Human Rights. However, they could hardly refuse to engage in a dialogue if one pointed to longstanding Jewish tenets, such as the belief that saving a soul takes priority over all other dictates and that he who saves one soul is as if he saved a whole world—in short, ideas that reflect high respect for each individual. Others have tried to walk down similar alleys, but as far as I can tell, little, if any, ground has been gained. I certainly got nowhere.

One of my greatest disappointments continues to be my inability to find a way to be of more service to a society I care a great deal about and whose need to be healed, inside and out, cries out to the leaden heavens. Looking at the divided Israel at the end of the century was like looking at a wadi deeper than the Grand Canyon, with both sides much further apart; nobody seemed able to find a place to bridge it. Maybe what Israel needs first is a dialogue on how to talk, how to prevent differences of viewpoint from turning into culture wars and worse. (My primary schoolmate, Professor Shlomo Avineri, calls it the need to "learn to listen.")

Communitarian ideas other than building a community of communities were more readily received in Israel, especially the notion of the three-legged-stool (state, market, and community) approach that is so natural to Israel. Hence, as long as I stuck to these issues, the Israeli press, which tends to play up anyone who makes it "big" in the United States, would run a fair number of articles about these ideas and was relatively generous.

I found even less of a foothold in trying to do something about the horrible conflict between Israel and the Palestinians. My views are best quickly summarized in an op-ed jointly written by Shibley Telhami, an American Palestinian scholar, and myself, which follows. It was published in 2002 in the *Christian Science Monitor*.

As violence in the Middle East continues, hopes for a settlement have been further dimmed by an alarming polarization. Palestinians and Israelis have returned to the language of maximal demands, and to pointing fingers at all that has gone before. This trend can only make peace more elusive.

For now, we say, seek peace, not historical judgment. Far too much public discourse focuses on who is to blame—and by implication, who should carry the main burden of ending hostilities and settling the conflict.

Those who blame the intifada want the Palestinian Authority to suppress it. Those who blame Israeli occupation of the West Bank want Israeli troops withdrawn. One side points the finger at Israeli Prime Minister Ariel Sharon and seeks his removal, the other at Palestinian leader Yasser Arafat and seeks his.

Trying to sort out who has been most abusive, who has suffered more, and who has stronger claims will only extend the bloodshed. For now the focus should be on finding a formula that allows both sides to live together.

We say "for now," because once peace is firmly established, there will be time for a truth commission to look into matters of blame and justice. After all, even in other parts of the world, from South Africa to Argentina, such investigations took place after a new regime was established. Even there, the main purpose was reconciliation and healing rather than incrimination.

To envision peace, we must flesh out at the outset the "final status," the vision of what the world is going to look like—one in which a Palestinian state and Israel will live together, both not merely recognized by all governments but also enjoying normal relations with them.

To argue that political negotiations about the final status must await cessation of hostilities is to seek to prevent them from taking place. To hold that we can fight and talk is equally untenable. Clearly a significant scaling back, especially of attacks on civilians by Palestinians and military control of civilians by the Israeli army, must and can take place for a fleshing out of the final status to proceed.

We say fleshing out, because there is a surprising, widely shared informal understanding of what the outline of the final status is likely to be. It would entail a fully independent, viable, contiguous Palestinian state and a secure Israeli one. Their borders would be roughly along the 1967 lines, with some possible land swap between the two, based on mutual agreements.

Granted, this shared understanding seems not yet to extend to notions about Jerusalem, although even here there is much support on both sides for some kind of compromise.

It is precisely because "the basics" are in place that there is room for working them out in more detail. Without such a clear vision, it is hard to see people on either side putting new hope into what must be their shared future.

No settlement can be complete, or even merely reasonable, without attending to the refugees, including getting them out of camps. Ignoring their conditions, rights, and aspirations is not conducive to a lasting peace.

Two criteria must be met, beyond financial compensation: First, because a two-state solution is based on the notion of self-determination for two peoples, the Jewish character of Israel must be preserved through a robust Jewish majority. The second is that a solution must not be imposed on the refugees. They must be offered several options for permanent settlement, including in the Palestinian state.

Whatever final status agreements are made, the process must involve the people on the ground, not just diplomats. There has been too much death and destruction, too much hate and mistrust, and too much discourse of intransigence to overcome quickly.

Hence, while negotiations take place, we call for a process of cooling off, of preparing the public for compromise. Some unilateral gestures would help, such as under responding rather than overreacting to perceived transgressions; dismantling of some of the outlying Jewish settlements; and the arrest—and continued detention—of those who ignore the Palestinian Authority's ban on attacks on civilians.

A settlement of the Palestinian-Israeli conflict, or even the Arab-Israeli conflict, will neither end troubles in the region nor the challenges facing U.S. policy, but it is an important step toward tackling many of the region's ills. No issue is as critical to the political psychology in the region or to the perceptions of America as the Arab-Israeli conflict.

Clearly, the official positions of Israeli and Palestinian leaders are far from our outline of a settlement. Public support for tougher positions has also increased with every death, because people are losing faith in the possibility of peace—even as majorities continue to crave it. Among Americans who care about Arabs and Israelis, we find many who have been pained not only by the bloodshed, but also by the polarization of the past few months—but who refuse to be drawn into separate camps. Polls indicate they may even be a torn silent majority.

Now is the time to rally behind a vision of a fair, peaceful option that saves lives, and to postpone an accounting of history.

In the middle of 1999, my then ten-year-old granddaughter (who lives in Israel) called me, all excited: "Saba—your picture is in the newspaper!" Her mother explained that communitarian ideas were listed on that year's list of what is "hot." In Israel, I regret to note, that is about as far as we got.

A Former Communist Opposition

The hostile reception new communitarianism encountered from some of the Czech leaders mirrored concerns initially raised by leaders and intellectuals in other former communist countries when they were first exposed to our message. It also reflected the particular position of its prime minister, Václav Klaus. Klaus has been credited with the quick transition of the Czech Republic from a communist to a capitalist economy. He defines himself accurately as an extreme Milton Friedmanite and has taken great personal umbrage to my book *The Moral Dimension*, which challenges libertarian assumptions of Friedmanite economics. When Klaus ran into me during the World Economic Forum in Davos in 1997, he grabbed my lapel, waved his index finger in my face, and announced in a booming voice, "You are crippling my republic! You are undermining our efforts! You do not understand that egoism and the profit motive are the *best* part of human nature. You work for those who want to return my country to *communism!*"

Fortunately, I was aware before this encounter that understatements and mincing words were not Klaus's trademarks. Instead of punching back, I tried to calmly defend the communitarian position. My main argument was that by providing people with a strong but community-based social fabric, they would not react to rough-and-tumble capitalism by running back into the suffocating arms of a communist-ordered social life.

After the translation of my first communitarian book, *The Spirit of Community*, into German, Klaus joined a seminar I was conducting in Alpbach, Austria, for the European Forum in 1998. For a short while, he listened, but then he pulled out a prepared statement and read in a voice that vibrated down the corridors and up the Alps: "Communitarianism, in its aversion to individualism and its advocacy of coercive means of fostering human association, is another form of collectivism."

Klaus next voiced concern alluded to by other leaders of previously communist countries: "Communitarianism wants to socialize us by forcing us into artificial, not genuine, not spontaneously formed—groups or groupings. Communitarianism cannot win through preaching alone. . . . They try to reach the legislators and to legislate the world according to their dreams." By this time the seminar was familiar with our viewpoint. It seemed that most present considered Klaus's barrage to be way off the mark. It made it easier for me to respond gently one last time.

After the seminar, Klaus and I went for a long stroll and then joined a few others for a lunch that lasted nearly three hours. It soon became obvious that Klaus's bluster was skin deep. He rushed to emphasize that "there was nothing personal in my statements" and that "I just enjoy debating."

During lunch, he regaled us with stories about his boxing days, about testing a new racing car, and other daredevil acts he had undertaken. When others chimed in with their anecdotes, Klaus would soon work to recapture the center of attention. It did not take a psychologist to figure him out. Moderation, whether as a brand of communitarianism or lifestyle, did not suit Klaus's personality any more than a society could be based on his extreme libertarian principles. The fact that his government fell apart, despite his very considerable economic achievements, suggested that there might be more room for communitarianism in the Czech Republic than Klaus favored. (It would not take much.) Klaus tried again in June 2002 and was again defeated as Czech voters favored a less "contentious" candidate, as the *New York Times* put it.

The best evidence to that effect was the leadership of Václav Havel. When Klaus heard that Havel had invited me to participate in his Forum 2000, Klaus simply said, "He is not my kind of a guy!" and for once Klaus was very much on the money. Every bone in Havel's body—and more importantly, the depth of his soul—is dedicated to the civic society and, through it, to his version of communitarianism. Havel carried his vision not merely to his people but to large parts of the world, through speeches that have won him great acclaim and following.

I was very much looking forward to exchanging ideas with him. On arrival in the pompously elegant, baroque Prague Castle in which the forum took place, I found that Havel was surrounded by VIPs, including Hillary Clinton, Henry Kissinger, Adam Michnik (a flamboyant, well-known Polish dissident), Wei Jingsheng (a leading Chinese dissident), a bishop, a chief rabbi, and an Indian poet-philosopher who kept reciting the same poem about the inner beauty of lotus flowers. Moreover, Havel was absent from a good part of the proceedings; his staff explained that his health required that he rest frequently.

When I finally found myself alone with Havel, I found that his command of English was not much better than mine of Czech, in which I could not so much as buy a Pilsner Urquell. I did not leave Prague completely empty-handed though. I brought with me the text of a new address by Havel that we published in our quarterly *The Responsive Community*. In it, Havel predicted that in the next century the nation-state would cease to evoke the kind of emotional and irrational commitments it had in the past. Loyalty to the state would instead be divided among families, communities, and organizations of which we are members. Above all, he called for a commitment to principles higher than the particular interest of this or that nation, especially to human rights, freedom, and human dignity, which Havel suggested are a reflection of an "infinite" and "eternal" force.

I have no firsthand evidence to support my hunch that the Czech people's views lie somewhere between Klaus's hostility and Havel's communitarianism. Possibly, as the distance from the communist days increases, Czechs will find it less onerous to acknowledge their own communitarian bases and expand on them.

One thing I can conclude with much confidence: citizens of all former communist societies cannot go long without some new, shared moral understanding. Those in older capitalist nations need them, too, but their absence is merely more glaring in the vacuum left by the collapse of communism. Communitarianism has a lot to suggest to these people—especially if we are even better able to show that it has no affinity to communism.

Japan: Urgently Needed Rights

One of the prevailing stereotypes about communitarianism, which some communitarians have helped to perpetuate, is that we favor community while liberals favor liberty. I have argued, in all my writing on the subject, that the earmark of a good communitarian society is a balance between social order and liberty, between community and individualism.

From this viewpoint, East Asian societies are of special interest. I have pointed to them as the prime case of excessively communal societies, in which social pressures and conformity are high and individual rights are sorely neglected. The Japanese line "The nail that sticks out gets nailed down" has a scary ring of conformity to it. A Japanese student in one of my seminars deferred stating what his position was on an ethical issue we were discussing—until it became evident what the consensus of the class was. While conformity is powerful, the protection of individual rights, particularly those of women, minorities (mainly Koreans), and disabled persons is weak in Japan, to put it gently. Japanese society, though, it was repeatedly reported, has been changing. Hence, I was looking forward to returning to this part of the world some twenty-five years after my previous visit.

A particularly welcome occasion arose when Professor Yukimasa Nagayasu decided to translate *The New Golden Rule* into Japanese. He proceeded by assigning each chapter to a different colleague or student and then ironing out the differences in terminology used, which took a while. However, in 1999, as the publication date drew near, I found myself lecturing on communitarian thinking on his campus at Reitaku University and in a handful of other Japanese cities. I spoke unabashedly about the need for East Asian societies to build up the individual rights part of the communitarian formula.

The response was unanimous. In public meetings and in private conversations, intellectuals and editors, senior professors and young students were all occupied with an agenda *opposite* to what I held the communitarian diagnosis called for. Far from viewing extending individual rights as their number one priority—their prime concern was the fraying of the social fabric! Their rationale: crime had been rising in Japan (albeit from extremely low levels by U.S. standards to merely somewhat higher ones); there were a number of students, "even in primary schools!" who showed disrespect to their elders and a few who even assaulted some teachers; and there was some increase in the breakup of the family (especially middle-class women who, once their children were out of the nest, were divorcing their husbands who often had mistreated them for decades). In short, the Japanese feared, not without reason, that they were catching the American disease and centered their deliberations around finding ways to shore up their communal bonds and mores rather than granting first priority to strengthening individual rights.

I left torn. I was in Japan for a very short visit; I do not speak the language or understand the culture. How was I to form a reasoned judgment? Truth be told, though, I still hold that there must be a way to shore up the rights of women and minorities without giving up on community, even in Japan.

Beyond Germany: Communitarian Potential

German-speaking countries took to communitarianism much more slowly and to a lesser extent than Germany itself. (The same must be said of their dealing with their anti-Semitism.) The first to open up, just a crack, were the Swiss. I long had an image of Switzerland as a mosaic of German, French, and Italian cultures and social groupings. Actually, two-thirds of the Swiss are German-speaking, and they are more inclined to follow German trends than any other, but ploddingly and with a conservative bias.

The Swiss libertarian newspaper, *Neue Zuricher Zeitung*, sent an economist to interview me who was to the right of Milton Friedman, but who, after a few conversations, became somewhat less hostile. Stephan Wehowsky reviewed *The Spirit of Community* and greatly distorted what the book had to say. After we had a long dialogue, he published a lengthy article openly correcting the misimpression he had previously fashioned.

I lost my cool when a Swiss journalist, in the middle of a conversation about communitarian thinking, asked whether "the Jews were not embarrassed by being again associated with a frantic quest for gold?" He was referring to the demands of the Jewish community that the gold and other assets that belonged to the victims of the Holocaust, which the Swiss banks were concealing, be returned to their legal owners or their families. I responded with open anger that there was "nothing inappropriate in demanding the return of stolen property." And added, "I would find it very embarrassing if the only person that my government reprimanded—after systematic and prolonged looting by our banks—was the one you went after: the bank guard who refused to shred documents proving the banks' guilt." My comments surely were "off message," but then I am not merely a communitarian. On strict sociological grounds, one would expect communitarian thinking to flourish in a country like Switzerland which has a rich civic tradition and culture and strong local bonds. Not quite.

Many Austrians are candid about their tendency to follow German leads, albeit in their particular leisurely way. Three years after the communitarian message took off in Germany, and following several visits to Austria in 1997 and meetings with political leaders, scholars, and editors, the press gradually opened up to the communitarian message.

Of all the visits, one particularly sticks in my mind. I was delivering a lecture on Martin Buber as a communitarian at the Austrian National Academy. My friend Egon Matzner hosted the meeting. It was an unusually hot day for Vienna, and the old-fashioned building had never seen an air conditioner. The place was baking, but nobody got up and left as I laid out probably one of my densest lectures ever. Either Austrians are incredibly polite or their interest in Buber's communitarianism is staggering.

At the time, Austria seemed to be the model of a communitarian country, and hence one that would either take to our message like kibbutz members to a hora or—find it redundant. Not only was the Austrian moral infrastructure (families, schools, local communities) in good form, but the main political system was based on dialogues and shared understandings between the two major parties.

Unfortunately, Austria's consensus-based political system unraveled at the end of the 1990s, and the Austrian polity and electorate took a sharp turn to the right. It showed that if a communitarian society becomes too *gemütlich* and ignores new challenges (in this case, resulting from globalization, immigration, and European unification), its being communitarian per se will not save the day. Indeed, how to keep communitarian societies historically sensitive and dynamic rather than becoming comfortably complacent is a fine subject for a study of much public import. As far as I know, it remains to be carried out. Whoever does it may wish to start the investigation in Austria.

Going North

Nordic countries were historically not subject to either a church or a national government as hierarchical as those in southern Europe. Also, they had strong social democratic rather than communist or right-wing parties. Hence, they have what might be called great communitarian potential. This is especially true of Sweden, which suffered greatly from an overtaxing welfare state and was looking for ways to enhance the personal responsibility of its citizens and their mutual commitments. Visits and meetings with Swedish leaders and intellectuals at international meetings—ranging from the World

Economic Forum in Davos to a meeting of Christian Democratic Parties in Chile, of all places—triggered some good conversations and press stories, but to my regret that was about as far as we got.

I expected that the interest in communitarian ideas in Norway would be about the same as in Sweden, because of the similarities between these countries. It turned out to be much smaller, maybe because Norway in the 1990s relied on oil revenue to keep paying for extensive and encompassing social services provided by the state.

Danes are natural communitarians. During a visit, I picked up a communitarian idea the Danes were experimenting with. In the early nineties, the Danish government began allowing communities to introduce changes in school curricula and schedules, within nationally defined limits, if the communities were willing in the process to accept a somewhat lower budget. The result, I was told, was to energize the communities that were both accorded more autonomy and that had to reach shared decisions on how to live within a somewhat retrenched budget. It seemed a promising way for a government to foster the rejuvenation of communities.

In Finland, our approach was largely redundant. Whatever communitarian ideas I rolled out, the Finns responded with polite amusement, and with considerable justification—"been there, done that." While my visit (in August 1998) contributed little to communitarianism, it provided a personal high point when President Martti Ahtisaari invited me to his home. The conversation ranged from the Finns' success in weathering the restructuring of their economy after the collapse of communism in the Soviet Union to Ahtisaari's role as a mediator between the United States and the Soviet Union ("Kissinger was here!"). After more than an hour, during which I once more felt that there was little that communitarianism could bring to Finland but much we could learn from it, I was concerned about overstaying my welcome. I thanked the president for taking the time to speak with me. He responded by saying, "My wife is on vacation," and he proceeded to take me for a tour of his new presidential home.

The house, of which Finns speak with great pride, is made of solid granite and from the outside looks very spare. Its design evokes images of ice and snow. Its windows overlook a nearby gray sea. But inside, numerous striking art objects highlighting Finnish design are on display. For me, the high point of the visit was not being invited to examine the special Finnish wood of the president's hot tub, but in his dining room. Mounted on the wall were four vertical tapestries, each representing a different ethnic or racial group, but all of the same purple color. "Our differences are skin deep. We all have the same blood," the president explained.

There is little doubt in my mind that there is a lot of communitarian gold in Scandinavia. How one can mine it remains a nagging question that has yet to be answered.

Others

Other countries that share some sociological features with northern Europe also showed both considerable communitarian inclinations of their own and interest in the message. Dutch society functions as one large community, with a great deal of mutual consultation and consensus building. However, in contrast to Austria, where mutuality led to dangerous complacency and stagnation, the Dutch made deep and successful changes in their welfare state. They managed to respond to the pressures of globalism to stay competitive, reducing labor costs, but avoided the high level of unemployment that Germany and France experienced. They have become a model of communitarian polices, often referred to as the Dutch Miracle, the envy of many countries.

Among those who helped bring the word to Holland were Hans Joas, who was invited to explain communitarian ideas to leaders of the liberal party, and Philip Selznick, who had an especially dedicated following among Dutch legal scholars. Several Dutch scholars and public leaders developed communitarian positions of their own, including Ernst Hirsch Ballin and Paul van Seters. And I enjoyed leading a public dialogue in Amsterdam, organized at the intellectual coffee shop, De Balie.

Every trip to Holland is a special joy for me. Even the umpteenth visit still evokes memories of my family's past. My aunt and uncle were in Holland when the Nazis overran the country in 1940. The farmers around Zeist hid my family in the countryside during all the years of the Nazi occupation. The life of my cousin, Ruth, was spared when as a child she was hidden in a Catholic convent. After the war, when my cousin Rob had his bar mitzvah, practically the whole town joined the celebration. How could one not love such a people?

Closer to Home

Canada fascinates me as a country that, in several ways, is closer to the communitarian way of thinking than many and, in other ways, is among those societies that most need to adopt it. Canadians count "public order" among the values they cherish most; it is as much celebrated by Canadians as the pursuit of happiness is by Americans.

Moreover, Canada is the home of a communitarian giant—Charles Taylor, one of the leading academic communitarian scholars in the world, arguably the most outstanding of them all. He is widely respected in Canada not merely for his writings, but also for dedicating much of his energy to helping keep Quebec in Canada. (Ian Malcolm, a Canadian and editor at Princeton University Press, captured well Taylor's standing when he said, "Everybody respects Charles Taylor, even those who disagree with him. He is the closest thing Canada has to an academic saint.")

Our best event in Canada occurred when David Kilgour, then the deputy Speaker of the House of Commons, organized a nonpartisan meeting in Parliament dedicated to communitarian ideas. I was given the chance to extensively lay out the communitarian position. Taylor modestly agreed to serve as a commentator. (The day before Taylor was awarded the Order of Canada, the country's highest honor for lifetime achievement.) Taylor agreed to join the editorial board of *The Responsive Community*, further showing his support for our version of communitarian thinking which had begun to resonate north of the border.

The printed press and the CBC, the Canadian equivalent of the BBC, further gave us voice. To provide but one quote, Richard Gwyn wrote in the *Toronto Star:*

> Decency seems a soft, fuzzy idea. In fact, it has quite a sharp political edge. Decency, thus, should mean an end to "the premature sexualization of the child." Less commercialization of sex and more sex education that isn't just about the use of condoms but about "the stress(ing) of personal and social responsibility."
>
> It all adds up to an intriguing combination of the values of the 1950s— "two-parent families are better able to discharge their child-raising duties"— and of the politically correct values of the 1990s, as in, "We recognize the fundamental equality of fathers and mothers.". . .
>
> It's hard to doubt Etzioni is on to something when he says, "We have had, and still have and still need, an environmental movement. What we now need is a social environment movement, to heal society in the same way we're trying to heal nature.

Although the Canadian understanding of the need to balance individual rights with social responsibilities is well established, as is the need to shore up the moral infrastructure, sadly, the same cannot be said about the numerous efforts to make Canada into a solid community of communities. The fractious nature of Canada was driven home to me during a meeting in western Ontario of the "Victims of Canada," including Inuits, black Canadians, a few left-leaning, white, middle-class, aging activists, a representative of welfare mothers, and a large number of French Canadians.

They adopted a hip Marxist lingo, according to which they were the pro-
letariat who would inherit the earth as they organized their class, which
was the historically designated wave of the future. They would sweep away
the upper class, the Anglos.

During a break, I asked two French Canadians, "Given that the Anglo-
Canadians amount to 60 percent of the population of Canada, what do you
mean by 'overthrowing' them? Kill them all?" The two French Canadians responded without hesitation and only in part with mock glee, "Ya! Right on!"

Everything I have learned since that meeting about the tensions between
the French and Anglo-Canadians reinforced my sense that if one somehow
could convince Canadians to adopt the conception of a community of communities, or, as one of their own authors referred to it, the mosaic society,
they would be much better off (and even more solidly communitarian). I
tried to promote this idea, as have thousands of others, but so far to little
avail. Canada is far from being one society, let alone one community. But
each part of it is communitarian and open to further exploration of this way
of thinking.

When asked, "Has there ever been a communitarian society?" my stock
answer is that several societies have approximated this standing from various directions, but none has made it all the way. Statist societies were less
ready to embrace communitarianism than those that were breaking this formation. Those societies that had tried to build life around a Friedmanite
laissez-faire economy were particularly in need of communitarianism. All
societies that have strong communities—whether local, ethnic, religious, or
racial—face the danger of breaking up or turning into warring factions if
they do not form a communities of communities, evolve a core of shared
values and bonds that keep the diverse communities as autonomous, yet
parts of one whole.

Diversity within Unity

Finding ways to contain the rise of ethnic, intercommunity clashes that leave
in their wakes millions of victims and devastated societies from Kosovo to
East Timor, from Rwanda to Chechnya was just as important. We found that
the concept of a community of communities that would enable different
groups to maintain their culture, heritage, and pride and still live in peace
with others became a communitarian concept that still needed to be brought
to many people around the globe. This concept could also help deal with the
groundswell of hatred and xenophobia that was rising in many European nations as they had to contend with rising numbers of immigrants from cultures
different than their own. Every meeting I attended with European leaders

and intellectuals only convinced me how much work remained to be done here. A brief account of one will stand for all the others.

During a small private dinner at the Jefferson Hotel in Washington on April 24, 2001, with the head of the German CDU, Angela Merkel, the issue of the place of Turks in German society came up. I tried, poorly I grant, to briefly lay out the concept of a community of communities. Ms. Merkel sighed and then stated, "But these Turks do not want to become good Germans. You know what they do? They send their children to Turkey when they reach age twelve and bring them back when they are twenty!" It seemed that it never occurred to her that the Turks were merely trying to protect their kids from what they considered a youth culture ripe with sexual promiscuity and drug abuse. Or that maintaining a distinct subculture could be accommodated within a revising national culture and identity. She added that her party would seek to give voice to anti-immigrant feelings in the forthcoming election. Given the success of such tactics in electing right-wing leaders in Austria and Italy, one could not take lightly efforts to make political hay out of anti-immigrant feeling. The strong showing for Jean-Marie Le Pen in France and the rise of racist parties in Holland and Denmark followed.

There were interracial riots in Britain. Several Swiss cantons refused to grant citizenship to immigrant families despite the fact that they were second generation and completely acculturated. Most revealing, about 55 percent of Europeans openly told pollsters about their resentment of immigrants and minorities, suggesting that there were many more. It was time to do something about it.

The left reacted by labeling such feelings as racist and fascist, demanding the enactment of laws that would severely punish all those who expressed such hatred and requiring others to attend rehabilitation classes to develop the proper sensitivities. Furthermore, they angered majorities further by calling for the abolishment of any sense of shared values and identity to accommodate multiculturalism. Typically, a major report called for abolishing any notion of Britishness to make Pakistani, Indian, and West Indian immigrants feel more at home on the islands between Ireland and the Continent.

I held that it made no sense to throw these negative feelings into the faces of those that had them or to try to make them feel guilty about such feelings. One had to find a more constructive way to deal with their sense that their culture, history, identity, indeed, nation was under attack. I wanted to bring to bear the communitarian formula of diversity within unity. Its subtext was that people would be able to maintain their identity and culture and that immigrants would be expected to learn to speak the governing language (or languages), abide by the basic laws, and buy into the nation's core values—while the nation would allow for much more diversity in other matters, for instance, in religious expressions. Also, that which is unifying may be changed over time by responding to new memberships. I convinced colleagues from eleven European countries to join me in Brussels in 2001 to work out a joint statement along these lines. We had two days of thorough debates about the best approach to rising levels of minorities in Europe. Out of it came not merely a very sound communitarian statement, but also detailed suggestions of what its implications were for numerous specific policy issues.

One example will stand for all others. Assimilationists call for all children to attend the same schools, be taught the same material, period. Multiculturalists favor setting up separate schools for various groups, especially for Muslims. Our approach suggests that all children best attend the same schools so that children of different backgrounds will get to know one another. Also, we suggest that a great part of the curriculum be the same for all, but that parents could ask that their children be assigned to some elective classes, say, 15 percent of the curriculum, in which special attention is paid to their distinct culture, countries of origin, and traditions. Teachers from these groups may be drawn on to teach these classes (as long as they are not going to use them to preach hostility to the majority values and the democratic political system).

Our next step was to find academics and public intellectuals from all over to endorse this statement. Scores did. Next, the difficult part: finding elected officials to embrace our diversity within unity position.

A New Century

One could look back with some measure of satisfaction that all the efforts to spread the word across the seven seas did not amount to naught. (It would not have been the first time.) But looking back does not get you very far. As the century turned, I was more convinced than ever that too many academics, especially in political theory, were staring in the rearview mirror; they continued to support philosophies and social agendas that were preoccupied with ensuring that we never again experience the horrors of twentieth-century totalitarianism, of fascism and communism. I filed with those who held that the main challenge the world faced was religious fanaticism, which rushed to fill the moral vacuum left in the wake of modernism. The battle lines were most clearly drawn in numerous countries touched by extreme Islamic groups, which included not merely Afghanistan and Iran, but also played an increasingly important role in countries as different as Indonesia and Turkey, Algeria and Uzbekistan, and in the fight between the Palestinians and the Israelis. Within Israel, Jewish fundamentalism threatened the prospect of peace and, thus, the very future of Zion. And while religious fundamentalism has been moderate in the United States since the beginning of the communitarian project in 1990, the challenge of the remoralization of American society and the question on what terms—moderate or extreme—it is going to be carried out remained unanswered by the beginning of the twenty-first century. Filling the gnawing moral vacuum with moral dialogues and soft morality rather than state-driven, imposed values remains a major communitarian task.

And there was a whole new issue to tackle. When I was a student and later, a young professor and activist, any talk about a world government, not to mention global community, was met with derision. However, by the year 2000 it seemed increasingly evident—as global terrorism, economic forces, the Internet, crime cartels, pollution, trade in sex slaves, plagues, and many other issues ran circles around national borders—that there was a call for some form of political and social institutions that would parallel the reach of these forces. Finding and promoting some form of global governance posed a whole additional communitarian agenda.

I have a weakness for remembering proverbs and sayings—only not quite the way everyone else does. For years, I thought that the fisherman's prayer was "oh God, the sea is so large and my *oar* is so small." When I was told that the prayer speaks of a small boat, not an oar, I asked myself why I misremembered it in this particular way. The original text seems to concern someone who is cowed by the sea, who fears being overwhelmed by its mighty squalls. My fear was that I would not travel far enough, would not deliver what I was destined to deliver.

Oh, Lord, the sea is so large and my oar is so small.

PART SIX

IMPACT

CHAPTER SIXTEEN

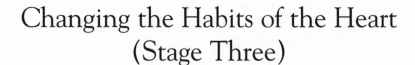

Changing the Habits of the Heart (Stage Three)

The Communitarian Nineties

Three Stages, Ten Years Later

Early in 1999, my wife Pat was preparing two parties to mark my seventieth birthday, when even one would have been plenty. One was small, limited to family and a few friends. It was a particularly glowing evening. My five sons flew in, from places as far as Tel Aviv and Seattle. My favorite extended family member, Ruth Vleeschhouwer, came from Jerusalem with her husband Joseph. Ruth is my cousin who started her life like Anne Frank, hiding in Holland from the Nazis for years during World War II. Unlike Anne, she was spared. Despite the trauma, she grew up to be a particularly loving person. There is no family funeral she will miss, no fight she will not try to work out. Joseph and her household is a welcoming home in which most days you'll find one or more lingering guests.

Pat's son Cliff Kellogg (who worked for the antipoverty bank Shout Shore) and his wife Betsy Cavendish (soon to become vice president of NARAL) joined us. She delighted me by reporting that I had succeeded in filling the role of "saba" for her and Cliff's daughter, as both her grandfathers had passed away. John Leo, columnist and author, recalled that I had attended his first marriage, which had not lasted nearly as long as our friendship. He added, "Maybe I should have married you," which had everybody in stitches. Others, too, avoided much of the roasting that has become fashionable on such occasions—often turning into rather uncommunitarian, mean-spirited digs—and instead found some heartwarming sentiments to express.

The evening ended with the assembled singing of a mixture of Hebrew, Jewish, and American melodies. It was already my best birthday since the one in Athens some sixty-five years earlier.

For an encore, Pat arranged another celebration the next day. This one was grafted onto the dinner that took place during the 1999 communitarian summit, which marked ten years of the communitarian project. Some 400 participants gathered, including full-time academics, community leaders, and those who had a foot in both camps.

The summit provided an occasion to review what we had achieved over the preceding decade—a true cause for celebration. I struggled mightily with preparing an extensive report, aiming to make one main point: during the 1990s, American society slowly became less individualistic and more communitarian. The decade served, to some extent, to correct the excesses of the period between 1960 and 1990, marked by a decline of values and social bonds. Communitarians had been on the side of history and the angels: we labored to move society in the right direction, in which history was ready to allow it to move. (To keep the report from growing unwieldy, I limited it to the United States.) This, of course, does not mean that I am such a poor sociologist or so much of a megalomaniac that I would argue that we made history turn. We were, however, part of the flow and did do some to redirect it. This is the claim I was reviewing.

In drafting my report, I returned to the three-stage idea, that for a social movement to take off it must first fashion a message, then disseminate it, and then be able to change people's hearts and behavior. We have been successful in fashioning a new communitarian message. After all, by 1999 we had a platform endorsed by a diverse group of leading Americans, essays explaining our position that appeared in magazines ranging from *Society* to the *National Review*, books, and a quarterly. Our task forces generated many position papers. I planned to close this part of the assessment with: "We might receive an A– for formulating the public communitarian message, and an incomplete for our academic work." I was hoping for a modest chuckle.

The second part of my report, covering dissemination, noted that by the year 2000 practically every form of media had carried our message repeatedly. Many gave voice to our basic ideas, such as the need to balance individual rights with the assumption of social responsibilities, the goal of making communities full partners of the social agenda rather than relying merely on the government or the market, and our notions of how to best cultivate the seedbeds of virtue. Several observers in the 1990s even referred to a third way of thinking, beyond liberal and conservative—a communitarian way. (When introduced to people, I was often greeted with, "Ah, you are the communitarian guru," replacing a previous line, "You must be the author of *Modern Organizations*; they made us read that when I was in college. I thought you were long dead.") Numerous opinionmakers and elected officials who had never heard the term "communitarian" (and who certainly didn't know me from Adam) were still increasingly familiar with the essence of our message.

Many of our ideas and ideals, which seemed novel or even controversial in 1990, had become clichés ten years later. In 1990, it was still common to extol rights, period. By the year 2000, more and more individuals, leaders, and even whole associations declared their commitments to advancing rights *and* responsibilities. Watching out for Numero Uno was replaced by extolling the spirit of community. In short, while communitarianism hardly became a household word, our basic message became fairly widely disseminated.

While drafting the report, I ran into my neighbor, Irving Kristol, who always greeted me with a great warm hello. I was delighted to learn that he had stopped smoking, both for his sake and because I hate having smoke blown in my face. We chatted about the travails of publishing journals (his neo-conservative *The Public Interest*, and my *The Responsive Community*). The encounter reminded me of a criterion to use in the assessment of the effect of communitarianism. Obviously, our thinking—merely ten years old—was much less well known than big "isms," such as socialism and liberalism. Compared to the changes achieved by movements such as the civil rights, women's, and environmental movements, ours has been puny indeed. However, it seemed to me, we measure much better when compared to the neo-conservatives, another school and movement started by a few professors. (Granted, their influence is easier to assess than ours because of their focus on deregulation and blocking legislation and cutting taxes, while ours is more cultural, institutional, and broadly gauged.)

Above all, our ideas provided a significant alternative to the religious right for those who were troubled by the moral decline of the last decades, but were opposed to returning to the values of the 1950s and to simple, predetermined answers. We opened an inclusive and democratic dialogue on moral virtues and the institutions that undergird them. We agreed that the time was overdue for moral and social reconstruction, but not by returning to authoritarian by-the-book traditionalistic answers.

My draft report ran into great difficulties when I turned to the most important and difficult stage—stage three: the role we played, if any, in changing the ways we behave both personally and as a community, the habits of our hearts and institutions. The academic sociologist in me resisted practically every statement that the activist in me thought we were entitled—and needed—to make in order to keep ourselves and the public mobilized. I kept slugging along, but it was one of the most difficult reports I have ever prepared, like writing in two languages at the same time. I started by reviewing changes in specific institutions and ended up by trying to get my arms around more general societal trends. (Of course, I focused on our kind of social indicators and not on statistics on economic growth, inflation, and interest rates.)

The Family Stabilizes and Changes
I started by noting that our core idea regarding the family gained some currency in the nineties. We favored a two-parent family, but one based on a peer marriage (in which husbands and wives—above all fathers and mothers—had the same rights and the same duties). This was an area in which many of us were particularly active, above all as members of other groups. These included the National Fatherhood Initiative (run by Wade Horn), the Institute for American Values (headed by David Blankenhorn), and the National Marriage Project (conducted by David Popenoe and Barbara Defoe Whitehead). Blankenhorn, Popenoe, and Whitehead were among those who endorsed the Communitarian Platform and participated in many of our events and publications. Don Browning, a professor of ethics and the social sciences at the University of Chicago Divinity School, added a particularly compelling voice. Linda Waite, also from Chicago, provided strong pro-family sociological findings.

In the 1980s there still was a strong tendency to view the two-parent family with children as one lifestyle choice among many. This attitude was paralleled by high divorce rates, increases in the number of single mothers, and high rates of teen pregnancy. Furthermore, mothers or fathers who stayed home to take care of their young children were looked down upon. "Finding yourself" was a much-advocated way of life. The way many viewed the family was modified by the end of the nineties toward a higher commitment to parenting and toward a peer marriage rather than a return to "wives submitting graciously to their husbands."

A turning point of sorts occurred in 1992, after Vice President Dan Quayle criticized the sitcom *Murphy Brown* for positively depicting a TV character having a child outside of wedlock. His remark triggered a storm of derision in the mass media. However, shortly thereafter, in 1993, Barbara Dafoe Whitehead wrote a cover article for the *Atlantic Monthly* entitled, "Dan Quayle Was Right." In it, she documents the continued pivotal role of the family in our society. The article is often credited with triggering an intense nationwide dialogue on the value of the family.

Over the years that followed, the divorce rate declined somewhat and the rate of teen pregnancy fell. One of our founding members, Isabel Sawhill, headed a major campaign to prevent teen pregnancies. One of her greatest successes, along the lines advocated by our task force on sex education, was that she was able to move beyond the opposition between those who felt that sex was basically natural and healthy and therefore merely sought to teach youngsters to have safer sex, and those who believed that sex before marriage was sinful and therefore sought to educate young people to wait. Her campaign settled on what is known as the abstinence-plus concept; teenagers should be encouraged to defer having sex, but also told what to do if they proceed.

We were among many others who championed a Family and Medical Leave Act, a modest version of which was enacted in 1993; called for repealing the marriage penalty in the tax code; and argued for more flex-time and part-time work and opportunities to work at home.

There is an underlying communitarian idea behind all of these: namely, that society should be more supportive of families rather than punitive of those who abandon them, for instance, by banning divorce.

Schools: The Rise of Character Education

Building on the White House conferences we conducted and related task forces we fielded, we ended up as a major player in this area. (Others included the Josephson Institute and the Character Education Partnership.)

In the 1980s, there was still widespread and strong resistance to character education in public schools; in the 1990s, this resistance abated and numerous schools in all states introduced character education programs, strengthened their disciplinary procedures, and introduced peer mentors into their corridors and playgrounds. Congress earmarked funds for grants for character education development programs in thirty-six states. Eleven states enacted legislation mandating character education, and another eight states called on their schools to incorporate it into their curricula.

Crime Declines

Everyone knows that crime rates of all kinds plunged in the 1990s. I used to live in New York; it is a different city now than it was then. More and more people feel free again to use Central Park and the subway and to venture out after dark.

Our analyses and policy recommendations—unlike those of the liberals and the right wing—were on target. Beginning with our early workshop in the White House on crime, we stressed that communities could serve as major resources for fighting crime if properly mobilized. And we emphasized that communities exist in public spaces, and that enhancing the safety of these areas is especially important for community building. We favored "thicker" community policing, reducing quality-of-life offenses to shore up community mores (especially as formulated by George Kelling), recapturing public parks and street corners from drug dealers, fostering neighborhood watch and anticrime patrols. Kelling shared the Broken Window theory with the police department in New York City. And once it was a smashing success there, it was copied in numerous places, to good effect. The idea is quintessentially communitarian: reinvigorating the mores and informal control of the community by curbing petty crime results in the prevention of major crimes.

We argued for numerous crime prevention measures, from roadblocks to curfews to DNA testing of criminals. In the 1990s, public policies and court cases moved in the direction of interpreting the Fourth Amendment (which protects Americans against *unreasonable* search and seizure) in ways that were more accommodating to the common good.

And I must mention our unique and strong (some called it radical) position on gun control. I scoffed at gun control and argued that only following British and Canadian policies, basically disarming the public (and eventually most of the police) will do.

During most of the decade, our ideas on this matter interested only a few law professors who wrote about our interpretation of the Second Amendment in law review articles. However, a few baby steps were taken in the right direction (the Brady Bill, for example), and attitudes toward gun control shifted in the right direction.

The Three-Legged Society

A major public policy change during the 1990s was an increase in acceptance of the "three legs" approach. Accordingly, the public policy debate moved beyond the question of what role the government should play versus the private sector. Increasingly, it also included the Third Sector, examining the role communities can and ought to assume in carrying the load of social programs.

There are several major communitarian programs that developed in the 1990s that follow this model. Charitable Choice is one that was introduced toward the end of the decade. In essence, it means that some social missions, such as administering to the poor, would be best served by providing public funds to faith-based groups. Other third-sector programs have been built around the idea that the government must provide communal efforts with some seed money, planning grants, leadership, and infrastructure, but then should gradually withdraw. Some of the most promising ones entail involving the ever larger and healthier senior citizen class in helping the young people.

I'll limit myself to pointing to two good sources. Lisbeth Schorr, whom I initially knew only as the wife of friend and much-admired public commentator Daniel Schorr, wrote a book that contains page after page of success stories of numerous community endeavors, entitled *Common Purpose: Strengthening Families and Neighborhoods to Rebuild America*. The second is Steve Goldsmith, a moderate Republican and one of the important speakers at our conferences, who introduced a whole slew of communitarian programs into a major American city. When Steve Goldsmith served as the mayor of Indianapolis, he formed the Front-Porch Alliance, which pulled together city agencies, religious and community leaders, and businesses and succeeded in revitalizing the inner-city communities.

And More

A few other changes occurred during the 1990s, heading in a communitarian direction.

- Our voice, joined with much stronger ones, resulted in somewhat greater willingness (even among some key gay leaders) to call for voluntary HIV testing and contact tracing.
- We were among those who championed "community schools," schools that are open longer days, more days a year, and, above all, that serve as a hub for community activities. A fair number of schools changed their calendar in the 1990s.
- We supported the V-chip, ratings of TV programs, and putting filters on computers in schools and libraries where children have access, but opposed censorship. All these were introduced in the 1990s with varying degrees of effectiveness. All were opposed by the ACLU and several libertarian groups.
- We were among the very first to advocate limitations on HMOs and more important, pointed to other ways to curtail health care costs.

In 1990, as Pat and I got to know each other, I listened to her experiences as a physician ever more beleaguered by HMOs. I drafted a position paper about other ways to cut health care costs (such as reducing paperwork, administrative costs, drug promotions, as well as many procedures that proved not to be effective) and on the danger that HMOs would break the delicate balance between profit and professional ethics in medicine. We convened a task force whose conclusions were strongly endorsed by a powerful association of heads of medical centers led by Dr. David Low, the president of the University of Texas Health Science Center at Houston, a leading communitarian.

Rights and Responsibilities

In the 1980s, the blame-the-other mentality was evident all over the place. Whether in courts of law or those of public opinion, a recurrent theme was, "I am a victim and hence need not take responsibility for my acts." Common pleas were, "My father was an alcoholic and abused me," "My mother neglected me," and "We were poor." Instead of recanting the old refrain, the devil made me do it, now it was: the "System" made me do it. Juries often accepted this line of reasoning.

A major turning point came during the Menendez brothers' trial, in which two brothers charged with gunning down both of their parents in cold blood blamed their vile crime on abuses they claimed were inflicted upon them by their father. The jury rejected this line of defense. Ever since, juries and the public have become less willing to accept the argument that if one suffered, one was no longer responsible for one's acts.

Without denying that personal and social circumstances affect a person's behavior, when public policies were reformed in the 1990s, especially those concerning crime and welfare, there was less willingness to accept that "conditions" exempt people from doing what is right. In this sense, increasing segments of the public adopted a communitarian position.

While in the 1980s it was common to speak of the importance of "our rights," in the 1990s more and more people started referring to our "rights *and* responsibilities." In the 1990s, the phrase appeared some 6,183 times in the top fifty newspapers alone. Some very divergent groups and organizations embraced our leading motto, which we flagged whenever we had a chance, from the back of envelopes to the subtitle of our quarterly. These included Cornell University's computer center, which provided its students with a manual on "Information Technology: Rights and Responsibilities," and the Learning Disabilities Association of America, which issued a statement on "Rights and Responsibilities of Parents of Children with Disabilities"; the American Psychological Association defined the rights and responsibilities of test takers. Candy Galyean pointed to our influence in the making of her video, "Bill of Rights, Bill of Responsibilities," for Cambridge Educational. College web pages cite the rights and responsibilities of students with regard to housing, use of the computer systems, and hazing, among thousands of others. It even made it into an editorial cartoon.

The most influential communitarian publication in this area, cited very often by public leaders and the media, was Mary Ann Glendon's book *Rights Talk*. She warned that rights talk ("I'll sue you") makes it more difficult to work out differences than recognizing that differing parties have different needs or interests.

Stressing that "strong rights presume the assumption of strong social responsibilities" is a central theme of our platform, of *The Spirit of Community*, and of our quarterly. No other group so much as claims to have made this change in culture the core of their agenda.

The period between 1990 and 2000 was rich in projects aiming to increase volunteerism, to strengthen communities, and to improve the civic quality of society. President Clinton made AmeriCorps a major element of his administration. Colin Powell launched a major drive to enhance volunteerism. Many schools introduced community service into their curricula.

Robert Putnam's thesis, first published in his 1995 article "Bowling Alone," that most, if not all, forms of social connectedness declined in the period between 1960 and 1990, has been widely contested. If there was no decline, there cannot be a post-1990 revival.

Francis Fukuyama's concluded that a period of "remoralization" started in the 1990s. And practically all the measurements used by Bill Bennett to show the deterioration of the moral order of American society have been moving up since 1990. The same holds true for the measurements used by the National Commission on Civic Renewal.

To sum up, I planned to tell the communitarian summit, our strongest suit is that we were on the side of history; next, that here and there we helped move it in the right direction, to some extent; and our greatest role was cultural and political, framing thoughts and ideas and making them available to public leaders.

Was Clinton a Communitarian?

Several observers pointed to the influence of communitarian thinking on Clinton. Alan Ehrenhalt, for instance, listed it among three influences on Clinton's 1991 election campaign: his experiences as a governor of Arkansas, ideas advanced by the New Democrats, and "the intellectual movement that has been gaining strength in a variety of places in the past several years, that goes by the name of communitarianism."

Ehrenhalt then added:

Clinton doesn't describe himself as a communitarian, or present himself as the candidate of any movement or alliance, for that matter. But the elements of his domestic program, as he unveils it, coincide remarkably closely with the planks of the communitarian "platform" that was published in Washington in November; with the views expressed in *The Responsive Community*, the movement's quarterly newsletter; and with the writing of Amitai Etzioni and William Galston.

Here come more quotes for evidence and "flavor." Robert Wright wrote in a *Time* magazine essay:

Something does seem to be amiss beyond the reach of government. Virtue does seem in need of restoring. What's a liberal to do? In recent years many have flirted with the bipartisan communitarian movement. Liberal Communitarians say they've amended traditional liberalism, which too often was morally neutral, confining its role in the realm of values to protecting rights such as free speech. The new liberal conception of citizenship stresses moral obligations.

Wright then introduced me as the main communitarian spokesman and noted what many others overlooked, that we did not simply side with community and responsibility, but merely sought to balance respect for individual rights with concerns for the common good. Wright wrote:

He codified this point with an emphasized conjunction in the subtitle of his journal, *The Responsive Community: Rights and Responsibilities.* Clinton has adopted this formula. In his acceptance speech [on the night of his election victory], he asked that "all Americans take personal responsibility" and endorsed "responsibility from all."

When Clinton left a copy of my book *The Spirit of Community* on his desk in the Oval Office when the press was invited in, this served as another minor signal to the same effect.

Others made similar observations. Charles J. Sykes wrote in *The World and I:* "As a candidate, Clinton's posturing as a 'New Democrat' drew heavily on communitarian themes (in one campaign speech he mentioned the word *responsibility* twenty-eight times). His inaugural address was virtually a communitarian anthem."

Joshua Abramowitz in *The Public Interest* wrote:

It's a good time to be a communitarian. Not only is the philosophy *au courant* in the press and in academia, but even our president got his job partially by invoking communitarian ideals (more responsibilities, fewer rights) and pushing for communitarian public policies (national service, campaign finance reform, welfare reform).

As I see it, Clinton's record is that of an inconsistent communitarian. In his public office, unlike in his personal life, he often acted like a communitarian. Being by nature a conciliator, a consensus builder, he was rarely confrontational and typically sought the middle or common ground.

Clinton, the community builder, served as the nation's number one healer. After the bombing of the Federal Building in Oklahoma City, which traumatized the nation, Clinton reached a communitarian high point when he called for hatemongers to tone down the venom that had produced the tense and violent atmosphere. After his speech, Rush Limbaugh and company had little choice but to moderate their rhetoric.

Rarely noted is that Clinton succeeded in largely defusing conflict between those who sought to introduce prayer in public schools and those who found such prayer a frontal assault on the separation of church and state. Clinton issued a series of guidelines that "clarified" the government's position on these matters. These guidelines provided some more legroom to the pro-religious groups without seriously offending liberals' concerns. Clinton's attempt to conduct a national dialogue among the races was far less successful, but was very much in the communitarian spirit.

While Clinton often followed a communitarian agenda, he veered off in several directions. His personal conduct was damaging to values and institutions that needed to be shored up. Clinton also zigged to the liberal side when he introduced what amounted to a new social entitlement, the Earned Income Tax Credit. And he zagged to the right when reforming welfare; he agreed to totally cut people off from any public support under some conditions. Worse, at the same time, he shied away from curtailing corporate welfare, the very large handouts the government dishes out to corporations.

All said and done, Clinton was like a football player who rarely runs forward in a straight line. By veering here to the left, then some to the right, and again the other way, he did make progress, often toward a communitarian goal. One naturally might favor a more straightforward approach and consistent performance. The fact that we had a small hand—OK, a finger— in his game plan was something any report on the communitarian movement in the 1990s had to note.

A Communitarian Majority

To round off our first decade review, I employed an academic tool. We believed that a good part of the American public shared our moral and policy concerns, but we had no evidence to this effect that a social scientist would consider reliable. To proceed, I commissioned a public opinion study that was conducted in 1996 by the University of Maryland and analyzed for us by a rising young sociologist, David Karp.

The study found that over half (58 percent) of all respondents agreed with the basic communitarian tenets, if one combined responses to numerous questions. The rest responded as social conservatives or neoconservatives. Few were liberals.

On specific issues, there was considerable difference of opinion, but still considerable support for communitarian positions. Thus, more than half (54 percent) agreed with our position that "we should carefully balance our individual rights and social responsibilities." One out of four (26 percent) supported the social conservative position that, "in an age of moral decay, Americans need most to live up to their social responsibilities." Only 15 percent supported the liberal position that limited itself to "we should vigilantly protect our rights against the intrusion of government."

Asked about character education, nearly two-thirds of the respondents (63 percent) selected the communitarian response that public schools should "teach only the values we all share." Twenty-two percent favored the conservative position that schools should "teach religious values." Only one out of 10 percent supported a liberal position, that schools should "not teach values at all."

In response to the question: "What kind of family structure do you think would be best for kids?" more than half of the respondents (58 percent) endorsed the communitarian position of "both parents sharing responsibility for chores and child-raising." Twenty-four percent supported the conservative position of having the "mother at home while the father works." And 17 percent backed a liberal position that "there is no one best structure."

When asked how closely the police need to be scrutinized, a hefty 62 percent seconded the communitarian position, "monitoring police closely, but giving them more leeway." Only 18 percent backed the conservative view of "giving police more leeway in catching criminals," and 17 percent picked the liberal position calling for "stricter rules to protect citizens from police abuse."

When asked, "regarding the government's role in influencing morality, do you think the government should . . ." our position scored less well. A plurality of Americans (45 percent) struck the liberal position that the government should "not get involved because morality is everyone's personal business." Thirty-five percent favored the communitarian response that the government should "discourage, but not prohibit immoral acts." Only 15 percent favored the social conservative response that the government should "prohibit immoral acts."

Regarding diversity, 38 percent envisioned America along communitarian lines, as a community of communities, agreeing that "people of different racial, ethnic, and other backgrounds should be encouraged to maintain separate identities, but also share a commitment to America as a nation." Ten percent endorsed a liberal position that encourages Americans to "maintain separate identities, that is, maintain diversity." The strongest support (50 percent) was for the social conservative position that Americans should "be Americans, period." This was an area in which we were especially called upon to work in the future, and not just in the United States.

Later public opinion polls, although not specifically focused on the communitarian agenda, provided additional evidence that while the American way of thinking about social-moral issues continued to be varied and complex, it contained strong communitarian elements.

And What I Did Not Report

Back to the 1999 communitarian summit which coincided with my seventieth birthday and the end of an intensive ten-year-long pursuit of the communitarian project. Two developments stood out for me personally. First, all my various lines of thought came together. My concern with human primacy, the quest for social formations that would minimize the chances of war and violence in general, acting out of conviction (following persuasion or the moral voice) rather than being coerced, the importance of shared values and bonds without suppressing liberty, the danger of allowing economic transactions to take precedence over human, social, and public considerations—all found a comfortable home in communitarian thinking. What seemed for a lifetime like projects that had little in common, turned out all to be roads leading to the same purpose, a good society based on communitarian principles. Second, on the public action front, I was not sure how well I did but felt confident that I had never done better. My ideas may have been just as on-target before, but never did they carry as far and have that much impact.

The managing editor of *The Responsive Community*, Dan Doherty, arranged in 1998 for a special issue reviewing my work. It opened with congratulatory letters from President Clinton, First Lady Hillary Clinton, Vice President Al Gore, and Bill Bennett. They all said the kinds of things people are wont to say on such occasions. I found Bennett's letter particularly flattering; it even invited a chuckle. He wrote:

> Happy birthday and congratulations. You have my respect for being a thoughtful, astute, and erudite observer of American culture and politics. More than that, you are a man of principle. You bring all of us together not just for the sake of bipartisanship but for good, constructive ideas.
>
> That leads to unfamiliar territory. I remember a few years ago you invited me to speak at one of your conferences at The George Washington University. You

had me praising President Clinton for that great speech he gave in Memphis in 1993. Your goodwill rubs off on all of us. We thank and honor you for it.

Benjamin Barber, who often was ambivalent about our communitarian endeavor and occasionally was quite critical, generously noted:

> Amitai Etzioni has been a communitarian pioneer, not simply because he has been a communitarian (many have preceded him) but because he has adapted communitarian ideas to the purposes of concrete and non-reactionary public policy, even as he has labored to harmonize a communitarian interest in civic responsibility with a liberal concern for individual rights. He has fostered a relatively progressive communitarian agenda and managed to wrest from the Right its sense of proprietorship over communitarian ideas.

The essays in the special issue were far from fawning. The authors engaged my work critically and showed no qualms about pointing out shortcomings next to those achievements they did credit to me. I greatly appreciated these essays.

It all raised the question, why did this project travel so much further than my others? The main answer that came to mind was that, this time, my analysis and prescription were not only valid, but these were ideas whose time had come. The best evidence that "history" made all the difference was that all the other measures taken also were pursued on previous projects: I did work to ensure that conceptions were fashioned in ways that spoke to people without graduate degrees in political theory or macrosociology. I took great pains to get the word out to both citizens and leaders. But this time, the issues that were tackled were still very much in flux rather than locked in, and there was a strong latent demand for the communitarian approach. Also, it might have helped that this time I stayed the course, overcoming my tendency to turn to some other cause when I sensed that I was banging my head against an unyielding wall. And I learned that to be an effective public intellectual, one cannot neglect the academic front, however well one may do off-campus.

How did I feel about it all? Like someone who decided to run marathons. The first time, he quit early. The second time, he did cover more miles but hit a wall. After considering quitting altogether, he tried three more times, making some progress here and there but never getting anywhere near the finish line. But the last time, huffing and puffing, he made it. True, once there, he discovered that this was but a beginning point of another, longer race, but there was some room for some satisfaction.

And, not to be too coy about it, I did not mind at all that this time my endeavors were widely recognized and credited. I cite but two examples. One comes from a scholar far away from American academic webs and known for his independence. Robert Goodin, a political and social philosopher at the Australian National University, wrote:

> Few people are privileged to launch their own "ism." Communitarianism in its contemporary academic form is arguably just warmed-over Hegelianism. But Amitai Etzioni's New Communitarianism is something genuinely new, or anyway certainly something that comes as news to contemporary social theorists.

The other was by a person who bridges the academic world (a professor at the University of Minnesota) and the public one (a legislator, member of the Minnesota Assembly), John Brandl. While we met several times, there was nothing personal about these encounters. I appreciated his kind words precisely because I knew they could not be tainted by feelings of friendship. John wrote:

> One contemporary form of communitarianism can be termed inclusive in two senses: it can be construed to contain the other forms, and it rests on the notion that the whole country is, or should be, a community. No American is more responsible for the recent renewed interest in community, so understood, than Amitai Etzioni. The prolific Etzioni has written a number of books on the subject as well as inspiring the formation of several journals of opinion, creating numerous discussion forums, convincing people coast to coast to sign a communitarian platform, and leading what he calls a communitarian movement.

Several more of these and still others were preserved in a book of clippings. (A copy of other documentation ended up in the Library of Congress at their request as part of a collection of material on social scientists the Library is forming.)

There also was a dramatic reminder how one really administers to people, at least when one seeks to save one life at a time rather than vaguely serve the whole world. We live next to the Kennedy Center, in The George Washington University's neighborhood. Hence, Pat and I sometimes wander over, to listen to free music played there before the official program starts. One evening a man standing right in front of us doubles up and falls to the ground in slow motion. Next, he is laying on the ground, as pale as I have ever seen a live person, only he is not breathing at all. A second later, Pat is leaning over him, holding her hand to his neck, to check his pulse. A man rushes to us, saying, "I am a doctor!" to which Pat calmly replies (she has been there before) "So am I," without stopping what she is doing by now: pumping the man's chest. By the time the ambulance arrives, the man is breathing heavily and his color is healthier. In my next incarnation, I might be a physician. They are blessed with being able to see, here and now, what good they do.

A Giant Communitarian Jolt

People sometimes ask me about my working habits. My secret is that on most mornings I avoid my office and its distracting phone, e-mail, and coworkers, and do my thing at home. Although my apartment overlooks the Potomac, the draperies are drawn to avoid the glare on the computer. One morning, September 11, 2001, to be exact, I was chatting with my son, who used to work in the World Trade Center but who now works—a source of great worry and some irony—in Tel Aviv. Suddenly, he interrupted the conversation to say, "You know that they bombed the Pentagon?" I rushed to the window to see heavy smoke emanating from across the river, then dashed to the TV, just in time to witness the horror of the first of the Twin Towers collapsing and then the never-to-be-forgotten sight of scores of people jumping from the windows of the other tower.

A year has passed since then. This book was primarily written before the 2001 attack. The account of the ways America has changed in the aftermath of the attack, and whatever role communitarianism has played in it, has to wait until we have a longer and deeper perspective than one year provides. Above all, much will depend on whether the predictions of more and heavier attacks come true. But a few preliminary notes can now be made.

The United States greatly changed the balance between freedom and the social order (above all, public safety) in the wake of 9/11. Numerous new safety measures have been introduced, many of which are justified, some of which are not. (Societies that have been tilting too far in one direction tend to overcorrect in the opposite one, which, in turn, in due time, invites some more reforms.) But basically, the changes were very much in line with what communitarianism advocates—and the society was tending toward—before the attack.

A New Balance

Confrontations between the champions of civil rights and those of public safety have prevented us from seeing numerous middle-of-the-road public policies. Both the Bush administration and its critics have been conducting themselves as if they were in one of our courts of law. Here, it is assumed that out of extreme advocacy by both sides, justice and truth will arise. It is considered proper for the defense to do "all it can" for its client, and similarly, district attorneys often pull out all the stops.

We hear civil libertarians claiming that the new public safety measures are "shredding the Constitution" (Senator Patrick Leahy) and "have undermined our most cherished rights" (the ACLU). The government responds that without these measures we shall be easy marks for terrorists carrying weapons of mass destruction and that critics "only aid terrorists" (Attorney General John Ashcroft). Both sides are pulling the courtroom trick of presenting highly emotive horror stories to sway the jury of public opinion. The ACLU recounts the story of Dr. Al Badr Al Hazimi, a Texas radiologist who was held—now hear this—for two and half hours before he could contact his lawyer and was investigated for two weeks before he was let go. The other side reminds us that we might well have avoided 9/11 if FBI agents had been granted permission to search the computer of Zacarias Moussaoui, believed to be the "twentieth hijacker," who did not make it because he was arrested before 9/11 on immigration charges. But the request to search never made it past the Justice Department, who found insufficient evidence to justify it.

If the advocates of civil rights and those of public safety would stop butting heads, we would see all kind of ways to advance our security while minimizing intrusions on our liberty. Take the relaxation of rules that allows the FBI to conduct surveillance on political and religious organizations. It is absurd to leave a situation in which terrorist cells can meet in a place of worship without any concern that their plotting might be overheard by public authorities. Or that if they call their cell a "political club," it will be hands-off until they strike. If you believe that I am being melodramatic, you might wish to note that in Britain (and elsewhere), mosques are a major ground for breeding and recruiting terrorists. Indeed, they were the source of some young men who left the United Kingdom to fight with the Taliban. But, you say, there is no evidence that this is happening in the United States. No wonder; until recently, the FBI was not allowed to cock an ear or take a look-see.

At the same time, no one wants to go back to the pre-1970s era, before the Church commission imposed strict limitations on the FBI's surveillance. In those days, the FBI infiltrated all kinds of civil rights and politically legitimate but dissenting groups (as I know from my own experience). But this was a very different FBI, one run by J. Edgar Hoover, accountable to no one, feared by presidents and Congress because of files he kept on their personal lives and because he succeeded in building a public myth around himself.

To ensure that the FBI will not slip back into its old habits, we need now a special oversight of its new surveillance powers. Whether this should be provided by the General Accounting Office, a subcommittee of the congressional intelligence committees, or some other body is a matter of small print. However, the public should get regular reports about the number of wiretaps granted and whether they were found to be legitimate by some outside body. In an imperfect world, this is about as close as we can get to enhancing safety and protecting rights.

The same holds for the trial of terrorists by military tribunals. There is a clear need to avoid disclosing in open court our sources and methods. Indeed, there have been several cases in which we let American spies bargain down their sentences only so that they would plead guilty and we would not have to take them to open court. Terrorists should not benefit from threatening us by demanding such trials. Otherwise, we may not even get to hang bin Laden. At the same time, there is no reason in the world why those tried in these tribunals should not be given a military advocate, cleared for classified material. And there is no reason I can find to refuse a terrorist convicted by a military tribunal the right to appeal his sentence to a supramilitary court.

More generally, we should stop pretending that any recalibration of our rights, in view of the changed world in which we must defend our homeland, amounts to an attack on the Constitution. If one refuses to treat the Constitution as a living document and insists on going by the text, one finds that non-Europeans are not counted as full persons and that privacy is not even so much as mentioned. Moreover, most rights were originally formulated in general terms in the Constitution. Their meanings have always been subject to interpretation and reinterpretation.

At the same time, mindlessly waving aside all claims that might go overboard for safety's sake is not warranted either. Societies have no precise control mechanisms; they tend to oversteer. Hence, all major corrections in the delicate balance between public safety and civil rights typically require corrections themselves. There was good reason in 2001 to rush the legislation expanding government authority, given the fear of more attacks. But since then there has been time to revise and fine-tune them, leading closer to the communitarian balance, although the fulcrum itself may need to be relocated.

Finally, far from retreating from the world into some kind of neoisolationism, the United States took it upon itself to advance a new world order, often to the great dismay of those who disagreed with the shape of that new formation. Whether what has been called an American "empire" will gradually lead to more conflicts or its transfiguration into some kind of world government and community remains to be seen. In any event, communitarianism now needs not merely a domestic and regional community-building agenda (as it has regarding bodies such as the European Union), but a global one.

More Communitarianism

Looking back at American society with one year's hindsight, we find that the terrorists gave us something to cheer about; they left deep marks on

American society, but hardly those they intended. Evidence shows that Americans have become better for it. They have become more public minded and less materialistic, more family- and community-oriented and less self-centered, even somewhat more spiritual. Although the effects of the 2001 attacks are receding, they have far from vanished, and some seem to have considerable staying power. No wonder; they are extending communitarian trends that were unfolding before September 11, 2001. All this deserves some elaboration.

Since the 2001 attacks, among the activities that have become more meaningful to Americans are "spending time with family" (77 percent), "helping others" (73 percent), and "serving the country" (67 percent). In contrast, only 30 percent said "getting ahead" means more. Similarly, "retiring young" and "making lots of money" only seemed more important to a minority (27 percent and 19 percent, respectively). Given that we were leaning heavily away from all these hard-core values, this change buys us at least one cheer.

Especially telling are the occupations that have gained in prestige in the wake of September 11. We now have new and true heroes: firefighters and police officers, whose star rose among three out of four Americans. The same holds for our fighting men and women. Less expected was that various professions that serve the public have gained in status, while those that do not have lost much of their luster. Thus, physicians and teachers are more admired than a year ago (respectively by 58 percent and 46 percent), while athletes and entertainers have lost prestige.

Americans not only say that they have "decided to spend more time with family," but also report that they have actually done so. In November 2001, over six in ten Americans (62 percent) felt a need to spend more time with family members as a result of the terrorist attacks. Far from falling as time lapsed, the proportion increased to seven out of ten Americans by May 2002. True, good intentions do not always lead to intended results; nevertheless, they often have an effect. One finds that about half of all Americans (46 percent) report that they actually have spent more time with family members.

Beyond one's immediate family, in-laws and relatives have also been newly embraced. One out of every two Americans planned to spend more time with their "extended family" during the holidays; 82 percent on Independence Day. By November 2001, many millions of Americans (30 percent) had reestablished contact with family members or friends with whom they had not spoken for a long time, and since 9/11 two-thirds have told a family member that they loved them. In short, people feel the need to be closer to their close ones, and they find family relations more important in the shadow of terrorism than before it was cast. One more cheer.

Although 38 percent of Americans tell pollsters that their spiritual and religious beliefs have been strengthened by the events of September 11, there has been no noticeable increase in traditional measures of religiosity. In October 2001, 57 percent of Americans said they had thought more about the spiritual parts of their lives since the attack, and 34 percent of those who planned to spend the holiday differently indicated that they planned to "put more emphasis on the religious aspects of the holiday." However, the percentage of those attending services "more than once a week," "once a week," "once or twice a month," "a few times a year," "seldom," or "never" has remained basically the same in recent years.

Here, the effect of 9/11 is not so much introducing a new trend as extending an existing one. Even before the 2001 attack only about one-quarter of Americans (24 percent) said that "doctrines and beliefs are the most important part of religion," compared to nearly seven out of ten (69 percent) who said that "an individual's spiritual experience is the most important part of religion." Indeed, to the extent that Americans experienced a religious revival, much of it was not institutionalized and found more charismatic expressions; sidewalk shrines, for instance.

While in the past, "government," "Washington," and "bureaucracy" were terms of derision and sources of mistrust, confidence in the government surged after September 11, has subsided a bit since, but still remains high. The percentage of those who have "great confidence" in the executive branch *more than tripled* after 9/11 (from 14 percent to 52 percent).

Increased trust in government is paralleled by higher trust in each other, making Americans more community-minded and secure, more communitarian. Before the attack, about half of all Americans (52 percent) thought that people were "fair," 46 percent thought they were helpful, and only a third (35 percent) found them "trustworthy." A few weeks after the attack, 63 percent thought people were fair, and 67 percent thought they were helpful, while 41 percent thought they were trustworthy. Equally telling, since the attacks Americans feel more closely aligned with the nation or their immediate community than with any other group. Asked to identify the group to which they feel most closely aligned, more than half of Americans (51 percent) replied "my fellow Americans." Thirty percent felt most closely aligned with "the people who live around me," and only 14 percent identified with "the people who share my faith," and 5 percent indicated "the people who share my political ideas." One nation, under attack, has become more indivisible. A third cheer.

This is not the whole picture. The terrorists left their toll; Americans continue to be more concerned about their security (e.g., they fly less), and we are forced to spend a lot of money on the military and homeland security. But in these clouds there is a silver lining: Americans have become closer to each other and more preoccupied with their Gods than with goods. The communitarian leanings of the 1990s were reinforced dramatically at the onset of the new century and age of insecurity.

—⚬⚬⚬—

CHAPTER SEVENTEEN

Going Academic

Nurturing the Academic Element

As our public following grew during the 1990s, communitarian writings—especially mine—took increasing flack from academic sources. Professors looked at these publications, aimed at the public at large, and complained about a lack of rigor. The paucity of documenting footnotes was bemoaned. Key terms (especially that of community) were said to be ill defined, undefined, or even indefinable. (Demanding crisp definitions of commonly understood terms is the number one academic calling card.) Little wonder, critics said, that you are popular, you are a popularizer, which is a sin akin to providing CliffsNotes to students instead of the original texts.

Worse, as there were no other texts to examine, some academic critics subjected our books meant for popular audiences to scholarly analysis and, surprise, surprise, found them lacking. An early, very influential communitarian book, *The Habits of the Heart*, by Robert Bellah and his associates, which has a stronger social science backing than our popular work, came under some such review. (Years later, Robert Putnam's work, *Bowling Alone*, was similarly criticized by academic colleagues.) I tried to make it clear that *The Spirit of Community* was addressing my fellow citizens and not my colleagues by avoiding technical terms, using no footnotes, even placing cartoons in it. Still, several academics criticized the book for its nonacademic nature. For example, I mentioned testifying before a congressional committee and being asked whether I believed that a single parent could not bring up a child properly. I responded that if it was up to me, "each child would have three parents." (I added that bringing up children is a very labor-intensive endeavor; that children do best when there is an extended family participating in bringing them up.) Well, one of my most distinguished colleagues found this a rather poorly thought out suggestion. (In a morose moment, I considered asking the publisher to put on the cover of the next edition: academics not allowed.) Similarly, other popular communitarian books, such as Henry Tam's *Communitarianism* and Dick Atkinson's *The Common Sense of Community*, were poorly received by academics.

Above all, academics were looking for a particular kind of presentation that for all too long we had not provided. The nature of what was missing deserves some explanation. Like other social movements, by the mid-1990s new communitarians had an elaborate conception of what had to be done to rebuild the moral and social foundations of society; a public voice (developed to the point that people kept sending us messages asking what our position was on this or that issue); a long list of public policies we favored, and numerous social science studies (most conducted independently from us) supported our key points. So, what was missing? New communitarians were speaking to the most profound questions of ethics, political theory, and social philosophy—without providing justification in terms these disciplines would recognize.

These disciplines tackle such questions as what gives meaning to life, what is virtuous, how to cultivate virtuous people, and what makes for a free and good society. One cannot join these academic dialogues by simply stating, say, that we hold that liberty must be balanced with concerns for the common good. To join an academic give-and-take, one must relate to what other scholars have stated before (say, that liberty is the one and true common good and hence should trump all other considerations). Because these are matters with which humanity has been struggling since the days of the Old Testament, the ancient Greeks, and Confucius, and there have been countless scholars who have written about them since (many of whom change their minds from one book to another), adding to these deliberations requires dealing with some very intricate and elaborate arguments. Mention liberty? But, pray tell, what kind of liberty are you writing about? The one Isaiah Berlin called positive or negative? You mentioned Adam Smith, but of course you know that he struck different positions in his *Wealth of Nations* and *Theory of Moral Sentiments*. And (here comes an arm's long string of names and references) have proposed bridging this gap differently by suggesting. . . . What say you to all that? And so on.

A nonacademic may consider all this nitpicking, but it is the way solid arguments are pieced together. One adds carefully chiseled building blocks to age-old pyramids rather than throwing up new constructions on vacant lots. And it was true that our popular works had not linked up in the established manner to the long chains of scholarship that preceded us.

In response, sometime in the mid-1990s, I devoted an increasing share of my time to trying to advance on this communitarian front. My first major chance came in 1995 when I was elected president of the American Sociological Association (indicating that perhaps my perception of collegial criticism was excessive). I used the customary presidential address to make the case to a ballroom full of sociologists. A year later, Basic Books published *The New Golden Rule*, in which I offered a scholarly case for new communitarian thinking.

Then I waited for the response. There are numerous movies that depict the struggle of a playwright: after months of rehearsal and rewriting, the dramatic opening night, waiting—typically at Sardi's—in the wee hours of the very next morning for the newspapers to come out, carrying the all-important, make-or-break reviews. Professors should be so lucky. It takes at least as long to write a book as a play; it gets rewritten at least as much if not more. Nine more months slowly pass while the manuscript is turned into a book. And then—there is no opening night. A year or so later, reviews in academic journals begin to dribble in, and gruelingly slowly, scholars begin to respond to the book in their own works. True, once in a while there is a rare book that captures the academic headlines, breaks away from the pack, and quickly becomes the talk of the campus. I was not sufficiently foolish enough to believe that *The New Golden Rule* would be one of those anymore than I expected to win the lottery, but I was anxious to see if it would do the job.

The New Golden Rule: A Sketch
What I am trying to do next is like squaring the circle, to describe the academic case I made—in nonacademic terms, in a tiny fraction of the 300 pages I needed the first time around, without jargon, and with a minimum of footnotes. Still, I hope that a reader who has other interests or specialization may be able to gain a feel for what the dialogue (to avoid the term debate, you see, here I go splitting concepts) was all about.

My focus is on *The New Golden Rule*, an academic book dedicated to making the new communitarian case. Other scholarly books published in the 1990s by academics, such as Taylor, Sandel, and Walzer, greatly enhanced the ideas these scholars were developing, but did not aim to speak for new communitarian thinking. Philip Selznick's seminal and scholarly outstanding 1992 book *The Moral Commonwealth* unfortunately received extremely little attention for reasons I cannot fathom. I have tried to correct this oversight by frequently calling attention to it, but to no avail. Daniel A. Bell's excellent book *Communitarianism and Its Critics* was well received, but is mainly an introductory text on communitarian thinking.

The New Golden Rule offers a synthesis of two antithetical schools of thought. One, in the Enlightenment tradition, draws on various liberal (in the political theory sense of the term) and libertarian philosophies that make liberty their core value. The other, in the neoromantic tradition, makes fostering virtues and promoting social order its cornerstone. Trying to combine these two major philosophical strands, *The New Golden Rule* argues that a good society must be based on a carefully crafted balance between liberty and social order. All societies can be assessed against this universal model. In turn, they are likely to deviate from it in different directions, which points to the directions toward which they need to move if they are to become good, communitarian societies. Thus, societies like Japan, where social order is very powerful but individual rights—especially those of women, minorities, and the disabled—are neglected, need to shore up rights to become balanced. In contrast, the American society of the 1980s, in which individualism was excessive, needed more social order to progress toward becoming a good society.

The book moves on to ask under what the conditions the tension between liberty and order can be significantly reduced. The answer is found in a social order that is recognized as truly legitimate in the eyes of the people involved, drawing on persuasion rather than coercion. (I drew on a study that showed that people pay taxes much more willingly if they believe that the burden is fairly shared and the funds are used for legitimate purposes.) The book highlights the importance of dialogues, rather than merely drawing on tradition, in sorting out on which values the social order should be based. The book next explores a distinct conception of human nature; namely, that people are born impulsive and irrational, necessitating social order, but human nature can be made better so that people are prepared for freer lives. It then turns to explore the relationships between communities and society at large (as a community of communities). It closes by trying to respond to what I have found the most challenging question: how is one to tell which values deserve our commitment? Are there universal values or merely those specific to one culture or another?

The first academic reaction to the book came when its "pub" date (the date it was officially issued) was marked by a full-day conclave at New York University. Among the participants were two highly regarded sociologists (Dennis Wrong and Craig Calhoun) and two fine political theorists (Ronald Beiner and R. Bruce Douglass). My colleagues approved of some of the points made in *The New Golden Rule* and raised critical questions about others, which led to a vivid dialogue that I joined with gusto. Two other participants delivered papers about their own ideas. All in all, a typical academic meeting—exactly what I had hoped for.

Over the years that have passed since that meeting, it gradually—very gradually—became evident how the academic case for new communitarian thinking (the way I made it) was going to be received. With few exceptions, my colleagues' responses were fair ones. The criticism for merely being popular has mostly ceased and it has been replaced by serious assessments of the academic work in both senses of the word: careful review and determination of academic merits and defects.

In the first years following its publication, well over a hundred scholars passed judgment on the arguments made in *The New Golden Rule*. Although none found the work fully compelling, some did find that it significantly advanced the philosophical discourse. To quote but one political philosopher, Robert Goodin:

> *The New Golden Rule* . . . usefully draws attention to a blind spot in liberal theory. From the Magna Carta forward, we have concentrated upon state authority as the primary threat. . . . Etzioni's aim in drawing attention to non-statist forms of community was of course to disrupt old discourses and reorient social theory. . . . But at the same time he has usefully reminded liberals of something else they should fear, too. Having spent a lot of time thinking of how to prevent abuses of state power, they need to give some thought to non-state power and its potential for abuse.

One political theory star (Nancy Rosenblum) and one rising star (Daniel A. Bell) responded in detail to the ideas involved during a plenary session at the 1999 communitarian summit. Edward W. Lehman edited a whole volume of papers critical of *The New Golden Rule* entitled *Autonomy and Order*. Elizabeth Frazer (political theory, Oxford) devoted a full-sized book to a critical examination of the new communitarian position.

Academic Responses

I provide here a few limited examples to illustrate the nature of the issues raised and the texture and tenor of the points made in response to *The New Golden Rule*.

Questioning the Balance
Several scholars raised questions about the core concept of a carefully crafted balance between liberty and social order. William R. Lund (political science,

University of Idaho) had no problem with the basic approach but was concerned that it does not sufficiently protect liberty because it treats liberty as useful (for instance, free societies are more supportive of innovation, which in turn benefits the economy). In this way, the justification of liberty becomes dependent on the value of something else (what it is used for), which in turn makes it circumstantial. If conditions change, the case for liberty might vanish. (While Lund acknowledges that *The New Golden Rule* treats liberty as a self-evident truth in addition to being utilitarian, the very introduction of utility left him uneasy.)

Otto Newman (sociology, San Diego State University) and Richard de Zoysa (politics, South Bank University) also approved of the basic concept of balance between liberty and social order, but asked if *The New Golden Rule* erred by suggesting that, up to a point, a society can enhance both liberty and the social order. They suggested, "In the harsh reality of today, they more closely resemble a zero-sum game."

Other scholars, however, made the opposite point, arguing that the suggested balance borrowed *too much* from liberalism in assuming a fundamental conflict between liberty and order. Paul Lichterman wrote that my "zero-sum view of community boundaries" had the unintentional effect of narrowing "the prospects for communitarian pluralism." The underlying assumption about conflict among greater and smaller communities (and presumably individuals) comes too close to liberal pluralism. Aneta Gawkowska (sociology, Kan University) made a similar point, noting that I need to recognize "an objective order of values, which presupposes the existence of a common human good, the realization of which can constitute a legitimate goal of political institutions without endangering the freedom of the individual."

Elias Khalil (American Institute for Economic Research) pointed out that to advance the analysis one would have to take into account that there are different kinds of liberty: ethical/political as developed by Friedrich von Hayek and economic as championed by Milton Friedman. *The New Golden Rule* focused on only the first kind. The most extensive and welcoming treatment of the balance issue as I see it is to be found in the book *Civic Librarianship*, written by Ronald B. McCabe.

The Noncoercive Foundations of Social Order

The New Golden Rule argues that the more people view their social responsibilities (e.g., taking care of their elders) as morally legitimate, the more the inevitable tension between liberty and order can be curtailed. Hence, *The New Golden Rule* suggests that imposing virtue by law (as the United States did during Prohibition) tends to fail, while laws following the formation of new shared moral understanding serve much better (e.g., the ban on public smoking).

Jeff Spinner-Halev (political science, University of Nebraska) captured the position succinctly and accurately:

> While many liberals may be suspicious of a call for more order in society, what Etzioni often means by order is more familiar and palatable. He wants people to curb their desire to act selfishly. He contends that people are born self-interested, but over time a set of values that recognize our social nature and the communities in which we live can be encouraged and instilled within us.

Everett Ladd Jr. (political science, University of Connecticut) tied the notion of balance to an old debate on whether the American nation was Lockeian, centered on rights and liberty, or sought to form a "more perfect union" by fostering virtues, a communitarian position. He suggested that the latter is the correct historical interpretation and linked my position to this history. He concluded that the concept of a good society advanced in *The New Golden Rule* "requires a large measure of individual autonomy and freedom of choice. But it also requires that individuals frequently make good choices, and accept some measure of personal responsibility for society's well-being. Like America's founders, Etzioni believes that an individualist democracy cannot realize its promise without a moral and virtuous citizenry."

Some took my position to mean that there was no room for law or coercion in the paradigm. Frazer described the new communitarian positions in terms that are appropriate for a Marxist end-of-history utopia, when the state is supposed to wither away. She wrote: "The state–society formation altogether should become a community; power and authority that has been accrued by individuals on the one hand, and the state and its bureaucratic agencies on the other, should be given back to the 'community.'" She then proceeded to argue that because it is very difficult to achieve community—and, if attained, to sustain it—the new communitarian paradigm pays insufficient attention to key elements of the social and political reality.

Linda E. Fisher (law, Seton Hall University) stated, "Most notably, Etzioni's theory fails to take sufficient account of the constructive role of law in a communitarian polity. In particular, Etzioni's excessive wariness about the coercive aspect of law blinds him to the central role that the law can and should play in resolving issues that are not amenable to resolution by moral dialogue."

Hillel Steiner (government, University of Manchester) observed that "political liberalism is perfectly receptive to most of what Etzioni details as 'the means of nurturing virtue that good societies chiefly rely upon,'" but went on to suggest that I underestimate the extent to which laws and the state are involved. For instance, marriage is supported by law and by benefits bestowed by the state on those who are married, in matters such as adoption and child custody.

Communities Defined, Criticized, and Defended

The New Golden Rule suggests that communities play a central role in new communitarian thinking, not only because they provide bonds of affection but also because they nurture a moral culture. They not only satisfy a basic human need for social attachments but also constitute the most effective social instrument for fostering voluntary adherence to shared moral understandings.

In reaction to the oft-repeated charge that "community" is a vague concept, The New Golden Rule provides a definition: "a web of affect-laden relationships among a group of individuals, relationships that often crisscross and reinforce one another (rather than merely one-on-one or chainlike individual relationships), and a measure of commitment to a set of shared values, norms, and meanings, and a shared history and identity—in short, to a particular culture."

In response to the argument that communities are oppressive, the observation is made that modern communities have much less power over their members than traditional ones. And in reply to the argument that communities were lost in modernity, The New Golden Rule points out that social entities meeting the defining criteria can be readily located in modern societies, indeed even in urban centers (often along ethnic lines).

Benjamin D. Zablocki (sociology, Rutgers) found the new definition of community satisfactory but raised doubts about whether communities could thrive in postmodern societies, a question that remains to be answered. Paul Lichterman (sociology, University of Wisconsin) showed that today people are often not members of one community but of several, which further supports the point that no one group can lord over people the way earlier ones did.

Steven Jones (political science, University of Charleston) approved of the book's emphasizing that communities are not necessarily good; there can be Nazi communities, for instance. He wondered, though, whether people who are members of several communities, but who are not strongly affiliated with any, would develop a clear moral voice. Zablocki concurred: postmodern communities would be either "toothless communities of discourse" or they would return to *enforcing* mores and thus become authoritarian.

Timothy L. Fort (University of Michigan Business School) put it all together:

> Unlike the civic republicans, Etzioni is concerned with constructing a com-
> munity whose common good is developed by all individuals in the society,
> not just the elites. . . . Perhaps his best insight, though, is that in a diverse
> society where individuals have many attachments, the risk of oppressive
> community structures is much less than was the case in past human history.
> The multiplicity of communities becomes a protection against communitar-
> ian excesses.

The Importance of Moral Dialogues

The New Golden Rule suggests that shared moral understandings are essential
for the good society but not stagnant, thus, need not be taken as given.
While tradition often provides a starting point, moral dialogues (even on a
national level, not just local ones) allow communities to change these understandings. Thus, moral reconstruction of American society does not require a return to the 1950s, as some social conservatives maintain, nor a reduction of all values to the status of "lifestyle options" up to each individual
to pick and choose as they deemed fit.

Francis Fukuyama (School of Advanced International Studies, Johns
Hopkins University) accepted this point but noted that "Etzioni rightly
criticizes calls for a stronger civil society that fail to define the moral rules
on which such a civil society can be built." But he then added, "The author maintains that such rules are to emerge only through an extended
moral dialogue."

Hans Joas was troubled by the sharp distinction *The New Golden Rule* drew
between Habermas's content-free proceduralism and moral dialogues, and he
suggested that they are not nearly as far apart as they seem. Academic work
often progresses by drawing such parallels and distinctions.

Marriage Model: Conflict within Unity

An often-stated criticism of the new communitarian paradigm is that it de-
picts society as one community in which people work out a value-based consensus rather than as an arena in which classes clash, a social world dominated by power relations and conflict. *The New Golden Rule* did little to
remedy this deficiency, which did not go unnoticed. Peter Seybold (professor
of labor studies, University of Indiana) wrote, "A critical gap in the book is
Etzioni's failure to integrate a discussion of the structure of power in capitalist society and its impact on morality."

Steven Lukes (sociology, NYU and the European University Institute) wrote, "What communitarians have systematically avoided is concern with uncovering relations of power and dependency that render individuals resistant—and often immune—to calls for moral reawakening and mutual concern."

I took these criticisms to heart and concluded that a future publication was needed to show that one can include considerations of power within the communitarian framework. To start, one might come to view community (and society) like marriage: in it, members act on the assumption that the union should be maintained, but it does not entail giving up their specific interests. They can learn to advance their causes by changing the structure of the relationship—the division of labor, power relations, distribution of assets, and so on—without terminating the relationship. This includes keeping conflict within limits, avoiding all-out warfare, but it does not require the suppression of either party's needs or interests. The fact that one seeks to refrain from engaging in all-out war need not prevent the exercise of power, as long as one keeps in mind that there must be some rules by which power is employed and limits to how far it reaches.

Empirically, it is easy to point to many such contained conflicts that both restructure and sustain community—from those that take place within numerous democratic legislatures and coalition governments, to those that take place between married couples, to those that parents have with their growing children. Because all-out conflicts over interests or values have a tendency to turn violent (from spousal abuse to civil war), within-the-union conflicts are to be preferred over union-wrecking conflicts, unless those in power resist the attempts to restructure the union.

Self-Evident Truths

Much less response was dedicated to what I consider the most distinct—and controversial—position taken in *The New Golden Rule*, one that concerns the toughest issue communitarians face: finding a way out of group (or cultural) relativism, from the notion that there are no moral standards that are not conditional or situational. Communitarians often fall into a relativist trap when they imply that a community is and ought to be the ultimate arbiter of that which is moral, of what is right and wrong for its members. All one has to do to realize the moral untenability of such a position is to think of a community in which all members heartily agree to lynch whomever they consider deviant or an outsider.

Criticizing relativism is easy; providing defensible criteria for judging the morality of other communities and cultures is a daunting challenge. The

Constitution provides a partial answer. If a community violates the Constitution, in which our society-wide key shared values are ensconced (for instance, if a community denies some of its members the right to free speech),
we can draw on the Constitution to justify our disapproval. Beyond any one
society or nation, for similar judgments we can draw on the United Nations
Universal Declaration of Human Rights. Beyond these, *The New Golden Rule*
suggests, if cross-cultural dialogues are extended and conducted openly, they
will lead to the development of a global core of shared values whose virtues
people of divergent backgrounds will recognize. (These shared values do not
reflect consensus but instead the rising to the surface of virtues all people will
come to consider as self-evident truths once they are allowed free examination of ideas—a deontological position.) These values, *The New Golden Rule*
holds, would be a carefully crafted balance of liberty and social order as the
foundation of a good society.

Among the few scholars who took on the response to relativism found in
the last chapter of my book was Daniel A. Bell. He favored criticizing other
cultures from the inside, so to speak. For instance, one might find elements
in other cultures that allow a Westerner to argue that respecting individual
rights (or other values one seeks to champion) is actually supported by that
culture. For instance, instead of condemning Islamic nations for chopping off
the right arm of thieves (*hudud*) because it offends human dignity, one should
stress that the Koran calls for meeting six conditions before such a punishment can be exacted—for example, the offender should not be poor—and
that these conditions are almost never met. (Amartya Sen, one of my heroes,
made a similar point in an extensive paper that showed that many Asian cultures had traditions of individual dignity and rights, some long before the
West.)

Shalom H. Schwartz (psychology, Hebrew University) and Anat Bardi
(postdoctoral fellow at UC Berkeley) reported that there is considerable
agreement on several important values across cultures, especially autonomy.
Social order scored less well, possibly because in the societies these two studied social order is high if not excessive, and hence not much valued. Still,
they argue that their data show a body of global values already growing.

Other scholars called for much more authoritative values than I suggested
and found these in religious traditions. J. Budziszewski (government, UT
Austin) wrote that Christians have no difficulties with the core communitarian concept of community, and he approved of the antirelativist position. But
shared values, according to him, were not to be found in shared human experiences but in Christianity. Thomas C. Kohler (Boston College Law School)
similarly looked for "more authoritative answers" than I offered and chastised

me for "palpable uneasiness about the topic of religion." Alan Deacon and Kirk Mann (University of Leeds) noted that my overall program shared many affinities with Christian socialism, and that my understanding of the moral voice comes "close to religious notions of personal conscience."

As I see it, deontologists (myself included), who recognize moral causes as given, are close to the basic religious position, because we in effect recognize a force beyond us and nature. (When I visited Father Richard Neuhaus in his office, he went on about the mental health benefits of being religious. I teased him a little and said: "You do not mean to say one should be religious because of some utilitarian benefits one gets out of it?" He responded instantly, "For those who do not have revelation, one gives reason." It was a profound observation.) Moreover, it is not merely a great mysterious X, but a force that guides us on the profoundest issues of life. The fact that some of us (like myself) have considerable trouble with the forms institutionalized religions have often taken does not mean we are deaf to authoritative answers. We just hear them spoken in a different way; more directly, if you wish.

Across Disciplines

One of the most curious phenomena that I repeatedly encountered working in the academic groves on communitarian thinking was the problem of exploring subjects across disciplines. Only someone who has ventured in this area can be fully aware of the oddities involved. Observations and insights most sociologists take for granted, the kind of stuff someone who completed Socio 101 as an undergraduate is assumed to know, are sharply contested in other disciplines. (For instance, the observation that individuals are "embedded" in social settings and the implications of being so situated.) At the same time, sociologists pay no mind to considerations that are pivotal to political theory and so on and on. Even the same terms have very different meanings even across sister disciplines (the term "liberal," for instance).

As a result, particularly when communitarian thinking is involved, scholars of different disciplines rarely—have a look at any index of their books—pay any mind to academic works on the same subject if written in another discipline. They may as well have been written in Sanskrit. Thus, even the best—Taylor, Sandel, and Walzer—almost never refer to Durkheim and Tönnies, let alone contemporary sociologists, who have written volumes about communitarianism. And sociologists such as Bellah and his coauthors in their major works, as well as Mark Granovetter who is credited with having introduced the term of embeddedness to sociology, often do not refer to political theory and philosophical writing on the same communitarian subjects. The same holds for other disciplines such as social psychology and economics.

More is involved than being unaware or estranged from the special vocabulary and assumptions of disciplines other than one's own. There is a strong sense that the members of other disciplines do not "get it"; they may have their own turf to play on, but nothing of any significance to bring to ours.

A bonus of the work of Philip Selznick, Hans Joas, and many others who wrote for our quarterly *The Responsive Community*, myself included, was that we took considerable pains to ensure that communitarian thinking turned into a subject in which colleagues from several disciplines learned about each other's works and took them into account. As the preceding comments about *The New Golden Rule* from colleagues from many disciplines suggest, we succeeded to some extent. To further highlight this fact, I cannot resist quoting one more, if only because he hails from still a different discipline (theological ethics) and his views are particularly dear to my heart. Don Browning (professor of ethics and social sciences at University of Chicago Divinity School) wrote: "By profession, Amitai Etzioni is a sociologist. . . . Because his thinking generally addresses particular issues in specific historic contexts, it is easy to miss the complexity—the thickness—of the underlying moral and political philosophy."

We did make the academic part of communitarianism much more cross-disciplinary than it was, though this is not to say that there were no longer bigwigs who continued to disregard contributions from disciplines other than their own.

In Toto

There were many more criticisms, challenges, and kudos that colleagues of various disciplines posed—all in the best academic tradition. Although critics pointed to several lacunas that needed to be filled, none claimed to have found a serious flaw in the basic arguments presented in *The New Golden Rule*. There was a growing recognition that there was now, following the work of Selznick and myself, a distinct position, reflected in the considerable number of scholars engaged in sorting out differences, finding points of convergence, and challenging the position we stated.

PART SEVEN

COMING TOGETHER

CHAPTER EIGHTEEN

At the End

Now our sands are almost run; More a little, and then dumb.

—Shakespeare, *Pericles, Prince of Tyre*, act V, scene 1

One Life to Live . . .

On the "Blessings" of the Golden Years

The hourglass is almost empty. Worse: it is opaque; one cannot see with any clarity how much is left. In one of my sociological science fiction fantasies, people will know precisely how much life is left in them. Thus equipped, they would be able to better employ their remaining days and schedule their farewells. They would not begin to draft a book that will never be of help to anyone, or slave over a lecture never to be heard by anybody. They would be able to look forward to dancing at their son's wedding next year without wondering whether they will live to see the day.

The conceit that old age is merely another stage of life with its own pluses and minuses—one more transition in a long series of passages, or, better yet, a fabulous golden age—is a damnable lie. The accumulating years are a curse that casts an ever heavier cloud over all that is yet to be done. By three o'clock in the afternoon I am slowing down; by five, my writing is not worth a damn, and my thinking is, well, exhausted. Ever more often I must check what I wrote three chapters back, so as not to repeat my points, and take careful lecture notes to avoid telling my students what they have already heard twice. That is, I am forgetful enough to repeat myself, but not forgetful enough not to notice. I still see much that cries out to be addressed, but increasingly the best I can do is pray that it will be taken on by others.

There are evenings, and some very early mornings, and weekend days, and some others in which a bitter image hangs over the road ahead. Good friends warned me not to include it here; "it's too macabre," they said. Hence, with due apologies, proceed with caution. Old age is like entering a jungle with a group. As the group slugs on, day in and day out, a monster grabs one or two members and slays or maims them. One day it is my good friend Jerry; next my mentor Marty. The lucky ones get chewed up right away; the others are eaten away slowly. You never know when your turn will come, but you know with full certainty that none of you will come out alive at the other end. March on and give a hand to the stragglers, but there is no sense in pretending that you are out on just one more hike.

There are nights that drag on in which Henry Wadsworth Longfellow's lines buzz in my head. They well capture the account due at the end of the day, as the pressing question increasingly becomes about what you have delivered rather than what it is you plan to bring about:

> The day is drawing to its close;
> And what good deeds, since it first rose,
> Have I presented, Lord, to thee,
> As offsprings of my ministry?
> What wrong repressed
> What right maintained,
> What struggle passed, what victory gained
> What good attempted and attained?
> Feeble, at best, is my endeavor!
> I see, but cannot reach, the height.

A Good Life But . . .

Mine was a good life. (I am told that this is too self-congratulatory a line, but only by those who have not yet read the next two.) To some this may mean fine wines, stupendous meals, traveling to exotic places, and climactic rolls in the hay. I did have more than my share of these. However, I rank among those for whom to have had a "good life" means to have had one with purpose, a life one can look back on with few gut-wrenching regrets. I do wish I had worked harder, understood the ways of the world earlier and more profoundly, served with more dispatch and dedication. But given a chance to rewind my life and roll it all out again, I would aim to run it in the same track. Nor is this an unexamined feeling. One reads so often about the virtue of being involved in matters greater than self, committing to transcendent causes, leading a life imbued with meanings that these notions have become clichés. Still, there is much truth here.

A Calling

In this book, I frequently refer to having to serve, a sense of calling. I am aware that people do not see themselves the way others do; there are several robust social science studies that document this fact. (Most Americans think that they are better providers, drivers, and lovers than the average American, which is not only far from the way they appear to the world, but also a mathematical impossibility.) I would not be surprised if more than one critic would chide me: "Come on, what is all this talk about serving; you wanted to rub shoulders with presidents and prime ministers, acquire influence and fame."

Moreover, I realize that many of my colleagues in neoclassical economics (as was driven home to me during my two years at the Harvard Business School) and more than a few psychologists maintain that there are no altruistic acts, that all such acts can be shown to actually be driven by selfish motives, whether or not the actors are conscious of their underlying intent.

I could not disagree more. There are numerous situations in which noble motives inspire good deeds. And aside from intent, consequences matter: there is a world of difference between running a soup kitchen and a sweatshop, between risking one's life for one's country versus risking one's wallet at a racetrack. Furthermore, in numerous other situations, people are propelled by a mixture of public-minded and self-oriented motives, which still render their acts morally superior to those of people who are merely selfish. Thus, even if it were true that I did some things to "get my name in the newspapers," this does not show that I was not also motivated by getting out the word about the evils of nuclear weapons, the debasing effects of the pseudoscience of economics, the dangers of religious fundamentalists, and so on. And it does not begin to show that such a life is not preferable to those that are consumed by self-aggrandizement. After all, you can get your picture on the front page merely by being the king of junk bonds or by showing up at a glitzy party with a stunning, high-priced call girl on your arm.

The life of a public intellectual is not without worldly rewards, but a good part of the satisfaction I reaped was of a different kind. I felt right most times about having tried to live up to my values. In this, of course, I was hardly unique or alone. There are many thousands of people who dedicate parts of their lives to serve in the Peace Corps, work with disabled children, nurse the sick, or counsel those who are in grief. They do not lead a life of sackcloth and ashes, of deprivation and altruism, but they do serve. I may not have measured up to their contributions, but in my own way I did pursue the calling I heard. The best I can say for myself is that I made up a bit for not saving anyone's life, or only too rarely helping others in their personal struggles, by attempting to render the world safer and better for the many. (As one wit put it, social workers are in retail; public intellectuals—in wholesale.)

But all said and nearly done, as it slowly sinks in that opportunities to balance the books with future deeds of merit, and to make up for past omissions and commissions with new entries, are closing up, there is not a lot I wish I could undo. If you hear a calling, trust me, following it will leave you at a good place when the curtain falls for the last time.

A Professor out of the Trenches

Public Intellectuals: Their Social Role

Public intellectuals are said to be dying out. Their demise is believed to reflect the increasing specialization of universities, the displacement of public intellectuals by handsome talking heads on television, and the general deterioration of public life. All this may be true, but it simply tells me that society's need for public intellectuals is not being provided for—not that public intellectuals have become superfluous. The mission of public intellectuals is to speak truth to power rather than to curry favor with the authorities or be held back by the reigning mores of the day. (Modern-day false prophets, who bless whatever those in power inflict on the world, are in ample supply. They are known as spin doctors.)

If our society is to avoid being trapped in obsolescent assumptions about the world and itself, about its natural and international environment, it must cultivate rather than ignore its public intellectuals. If we were not so long blinded by notions that may never have been true and that have become less realistic as the years ticked by, then the Cold War would have ended much earlier. We would not have waited until the mid-1990s to note that we can enjoy economic growth higher than 2.5 percent a year and unemployment rates lower than 6.5 percent without having to fear inflation, and we would have avoided much other grief. Society may be able to draw on experts to call attention to specific misguided policies; public intellectuals call into question whole ways of thinking.

Given that public intellectuals are required for the well-being of the realm and that they are in ever shorter supply, if you sense that this is your calling, do not be waylaid by barbs from academics, initially indifferent audiences, or policymakers' shut doors; taking these in stride is part of the job. Look at your brief from a vantage point more than four decades down the road. Neither should you expect to be right each time. But it is always right to get those who cling to old assumptions to reexamine them (yourself included).

To adhere to the course I just outlined requires a fair measure of pighead-edness. Without exception, when I wrote books addressing my fellow citizens, my spouse, a close friend, or young associate (occasionally all of the above) would exclaim, with much concern and alarm: "You'd better not say that!" or "This is not just going against the grain; it's going too far." This is what I was told when I criticized not merely NASA's vastly overblown military, economic, and scientific claims but also its repeated assertions that a trip to the moon would lift our spirits to new heights. This is what I was told when I wrote *The Spirit of Community* and suggested a *temporary* moratorium on the fashioning of *new* rights, after I showed that trivial rights were wantonly minted, undermining the currency of all rights. This is what I was warned when I argued in *The Limits of Privacy* that in the 1990s we were more concerned about violations of privacy than with finding terrorists. I said what I believed was true and had to be said. I may have been wrong, but I can tell you this much: if you are unwilling to call them the way you see them, to ignore well-meaning friends who counsel holding back or those who question your motives—find some other pursuit. But if you are ready, after due deliberation, to speak your piece, for the sake of king and country—Uncle Sam and the rest of us need you.

Dangerous Thoughts

Looking back, I sometimes wonder whether I would have done better if I had dedicated my life to one public project; say, to contributing to the drive to defuse nuclear weapons. For me, this is a strictly theoretical question. I was too keen to see progress. I did not have it in me to keep pulling weeds from the same field in the hope that one day—or one decade—flowers may eventually bloom but only to find it each time more overgrown than before.

In the end, many of the strands came together to make one whole, although I neither anticipated nor planned it that way. My interest in human primacy (the conditions under which ends would prevail and means would be limited to their proper, secondary, serving status), my aversion to violence and concern about social priorities, my quest for values that are compelling, and my concern for family and community all came together. They all found an ample home both in my public and academic communitarian project.

In addition, the issues I tackled had one common quality: I struggled to counter dangerous thoughts. Herman Kahn aimed to break the taboos against nuclear war (in his words "to make the unthinkable—thinkable"). Economic theory and libertarian philosophy have made people more selfish than they would otherwise be. Religious fundamentalists' ways of thinking have endangered liberty and human rights and have undermined people's support of moral virtues. The gun lobby maintains that guns don't kill, criminals do (and that the Second Amendment provides an individualized right to bear arms). I joined those who sought to counter these damaging ways of thinking by formulating and publicizing what immodestly may be termed "constructive thoughts."

One may object on the grounds that thoughts, per se, cannot be dangerous, arguing that they become so only once they are transformed into action. Yet to me, some bodies of belief are very disconcerting; others, outright alarming. Nothing makes people as nasty as when they hold that the brutality they inflict on others is justified by some higher cause. See the people who plant bombs in pubs in northern Ireland, burn trains full of people in India, attack each other with machetes in Rwanda, or engage in ethnic cleansing in Kosovo.

I would not ban such thinking, although, truth be told, I sometimes feel the urge. I just follow those who hold that the ideal of free speech presumes that dangerous thoughts will be corrected by more speech. Advocates of the First Amendment presume that the ill consequences of evil theories are worth absorbing because of our regard for freedom of expression, but they do not deny that there are bodies of thought that greatly harm the world. One unifying theme I see in my various endeavors is a quest for counterspeech to defang dangerous thinking.

Within History
Would one who paid more mind, much earlier than I did, to historical settings have better served? This question raises some complex deliberations. In the early days of the war in Vietnam, when opposition seemed premature, should I have kept mum and instead worked, say, in the civil rights movement because it was "too early" to protest the war? Or, is it precisely the job of the public intellectual to be among the first to point to dangers not yet widely perceived, challenges yet to be recognized?

Society, it seems, is served both by those who alert the community that hurricanes may be forming hundreds of miles away and those that rush about trying to batten down the hatches only as the storms close in. Hence, there is no need to bend one's personality to follow this or that course; there is plenty to do for both types. I tried my hand at both approaches, but often I yearned to be closer to the action and not merely to articulate ideas. I now believe that I might have accomplished more if I had stepped in later in the development of causes, when there was more room for effective action.

While it took me all too long to acquire a measure of historical sensibility, I do claim one credit: despite the considerable variety in the fronts in which I was engaged, my basic position has been consistent. A few of my most illustrious colleagues were Communists (or hailed from some other left fringe group) in the 1930s, turned liberal in the 1960s, and grew neoconservative in the 1970s and 1980s. (Some even advocated religious revival in the 1990s—without practicing what they preached.) Mine was consistently a communitarian position, long before I ever recognized this term. I never favored a command-and-control economy or cracking eggs to cook revolutions. I consistently saw the need for a vibrant market carefully contained by society and the state. I had no difficulties with a quest for a good—not just civil—society, one in which social virtues are celebrated and undergirded by strong social institutions, but not necessarily of the traditional kind. One may, of course, argue that I was consistently wrong, but I was no weathervane.

So, do I have no regrets, is there nothing I would do differently if I could relive my life? Hardly. While I am basically content with the double life I led, there are numerous secondary matters that I wish I could do over. I should have dedicated more of my youth to learning Arabic and joining those who tried to work things out with the Palestinians to avoid being forced to fight them. I should have skipped tackling NASA's lunacy; wasting billions that could be used for a better purpose is not only all too common but does not weigh in on the same scale as war, religious fanaticism, and large-scale systematic egotism. I should have found a way to work harder as well as a way to spend more time with my family (easier said than done). There are more such self-criticisms, but these missteps—some quite serious and prolonged—do not weigh sufficiently heavy on my dwindling days to lead me to conclude that my life was misdirected or poorly employed.

Given another chance, I would have better honed my skills. My refusal to submit to speech therapy, as good friends urged after they heard my first public speeches, stood in my way when I addressed audiences large and small. I am told that at best I still sound like Kissinger, which I do not mind too much until I am reminded that people cannot tell my *v*s from my *w*s and must listen extra hard to penetrate my still-German, mixed with Israeli, accent.

Writing fewer articles and books might have enabled me to better polish the remaining ones. Above all, being more patient with people I considered fools, being more tactful, more diplomatic, might have enhanced my ability to be heard. I did suffer bouts of foot-in-the-mouth disease. I wish I had put it in less often and taken it our more quickly. But I was not exactly refused a hearing or prevented from reaching out.

A Double Life Stitched

I have long wondered whether I would have delivered more if I had spent all of my time either sticking to my sociological knitting or to public work. In retrospect, I say to those who are inclined to follow a similar course that the price one pays for a double life is worth paying and that it throws off some handsome dividends, albeit not the kind you can cash in.

Did the long hours and days I spent in the public square undermine my academic work? At first, the answer seems obvious. There are only so many hours in the day. If you spend them on op-eds and radio call-in shows, you cannot dedicate them to digging in the stacks. If your day is consumed by dashing from one airport to another on the way to meeting this or that public leader, you do not invest it in trying to make sense out of regression analysis. Worse yet, public life is said to corrupt one's academic habits of thinking, leads one to yield to the twin temptation of overgeneralizing and underdocumenting.

To some extent, all this is true. However, there is no denying that many public intellectuals have learned to speak in two distinct voices. Just as a person can write, say, in French and in English, so a person can address his academic colleagues in one form and the public at large in another. The fact that one avoids footnotes and statistics, significance tests and technical vocabulary in one realm does not mean that one is a stranger to them in the other. True, those who speak only in one tongue may marshal it more perfectly than those who speak in two, but *it is also true that the two realms often enrich one another*. It is this point that the critics of public intellectuals too often overlook.

My public endeavors benefited from my social science training and lessons in social philosophy. For instance, the strategy of psychological disarmament was directly based on concepts and findings drawn from social psychology. And my recommendations to President Carter drew on studies in socioeconomics. At the same time, my academic work (like that of many other public intellectuals) gained from my public involvement. My public role reminded the scholar in me what was of significance and what was esoteric. Precisely because professors are basically not accountable to anyone once they gain tenure, and because there is a strongly held belief that one cannot foretell what is "productive," professors can get lost in prolonged bouts of trivial pursuit. Very trivial.

I am not saying that public needs should determine what academics study. Society—not merely scholarship—is served when academics can follow their own lead, even if it means that some spend their lives contemplating their navels and comparing the lint found in theirs to what they speculate might be found in those of others. But, I am confident that if more academics (voluntarily to be sure) also took into account social relevance when choosing the subjects of their study, both academia and society would be better for it.

Also, public involvement provides a reality test for ideas, a testing that does not come naturally to all academics. Thus, my theoretical notions of how government works were greatly revised after the year I spent in the White House. And hours of Q&A sessions after public lectures and participation in call-in shows enhanced my understanding of how the public thinks and—changes its thinking.

Most important, the cross-pollination between my public and academic lives affected my values. Social scientists often claim that their work is value-free, that their findings are neither liberal nor conservative, but evidence-driven. However, working in the public square serves as a constant reminder that academic findings and concepts have social consequences. Thus, the publication of a study that claims to have found that blacks are inherently inferior to whites, however tortured the evidence and rampant the speculation, such as *The Bell Curve* by Charles Murray, strengthens the hand of racists. Public intellectuals are more likely than pure academics to be aware of the social and moral consequences of such works. Hence, most will be more circumspect in the ways they report their findings. And those who disregard the public consequences of their publications, will do so with the malice of forethought rather than stumbling innocently into these thickets, as a pure academic might. (Years back, a young sociologist published a study that Jews are more sensitive to pain than other social groups; he was stunned by the anti-Semitic headlines and interpretations some of the press in mid-America gave his findings.) Although there is an academic presumption that you should publish whatever you discover, there is no rule that stops you from avoiding topics whose study you consider potentially harmful. In these cases, public sensibilities and moral values legitimately influence not the finding but the choice of topic of one's academic work. They often affected the choices of my academic work. When I come to the gates of heaven, if this confession is held against me and I am not allowed into the chambers where pure scientists rest, so be it.

All this is to say that I now realize that the two parts of my life have not been as irreconcilable as I originally thought. This book itself reflects my double life, the tax it imposes, and the benefits it reaps. Several friends who read previous drafts of this book offered one of two basic comments. One group urged me to cut out most discussions of what they called "abstract ideas" and tell more stories (especially those who knew that I left out quite a few, from the peculiar joys of serving under Margaret Mead on a committee that played a key role in preparing the 1976 bicentennial, to the fate of my report on peaceful demonstrations for the president's commission on the causes and prevention of violence). At the least, they wanted me to greatly shorten discussions of ideas and tell readers much more about what I felt at various twists and turns of my life. The other group prodded me in the opposite direction: to make this book much more analytic and, in this sense, academic. Several urged me to turn this volume into a social science study of the role, status, composition, and societal effects of public intellectuals.

Both groups warned that the book as written "falls between two chairs." For a while, I was tempted to yield and write it in one of the two voices, popular or academic. However, my pigheadedness prevailed one more time. This book reflects not merely who I am, but the sort of struggle in which other activist professors are engaged. It speaks—I hope—to both the minds and hearts of the readers on issues that are socially and morally significant, but in ways that benefit from my academic training. Maybe instead of falling between two chairs, it stands on both of them. Hope springs eternal.

When Self-Esteem and Status Clash

When one is in the public eye, it is especially important not to take one's self too seriously and to keep a sense of humor about one's self. I don't recall being offended when my accent is mimicked or the fact that I cannot spell if my life depends on it is recounted, and so on. That not everyone sees himself this way was driven home in my only direct encounter with Jürgen Habermas. It came about in a strange way. The *Frankfurter Allgemeine Zeitung* asked me to answer a twenty-question interview for a profile for their magazine. The questions included profundities such as which color do you prefer and what is your favorite flower. Asked to share a dream I had, I wrote "to talk with Immanuel Kant without Habermas in the room." (Habermas is considered a present-generation "cool Kant," and I do not quite agree with his moral proceduralism.) Habermas wrote me a hurt letter. He demanded to know why I wished to absent him. What possible reason could I have to dislike him? I responded that I believed his presence would be so overpowering Kant would pale in comparison, but that next time I would ask for "a conversation with you without Kant in the room." I never found out if Habermas was mollified. But I do credit myself with having been less quick to take umbrage.

In steeling myself to write this book, I read a fair number of autobiographies and memoirs. In all of them, the inevitable lines "I did this" and then "I did that" appear with considerable frequency, which sometimes leaves the reader wondering, "Are you quite sure this was really all your doing?" I tried my best to verify any claims I make on these pages, but I fear that despite my best efforts, I may have gotten carried away here and there and claimed more credit than was due, for which I apologize. But, in all candor, I should also note that, in writing about the communitarian project, I often wrote "we did" when I did much more than most, sometimes near all of what had to be done. Benjamin Barber wrote that I confused the achievements of the communitarian movement with mine; there are two ways to read this line. I leave it to others to sort out which is the more accurate one. At least I hope that these bouts of self-restraint will make up for whatever hubris is left in this text.

I've gotten into trouble more than once or twice, because I am painfully aware of my limitations, although others have viewed me as somewhat of a celebrity. Thus, I was taken aback during a meeting in Berlin organized by Werkstatt Deutschland, when a young man approached me and said, "Your writings not only changed my life, my values, but that of many others." I was lost for words, not a common condition. I was similarly unavailable when officials at my university were more than effusive about my being chosen to be one of ten intellectuals in the world to present a paper at the UN summit in Copenhagen in 1995. Frequently, at various receptions or book parties people come by and say, "My God, I had to read you in college!" or, "I saw you on TV the other day, for the second time in a week!" But I do not feel like a star or an important person. When I checked into the GWU hospital and "VIP" popped up on the computer screen, I assumed that they had pulled up the wrong file. And when a group of intellectuals issued a statement justifying the war against terrorism, in spring 2002, I was surprised to see my name featured among the handful the media highlighted from the list of sixty endorsers.

The trouble with disregarding such accolades is not so much my inability to deal with the halos people try to crown me with, but also forgetting about them while dealing with students and junior colleagues. When I was critical of a student's paper—a student I knew to be a mature person—I was astonished to see how crushed he was. Similarly, when I frowned about an article by one of my young colleagues, he reacted as if I'd told him that he was not cut out to be a scholar. I had to reassure him that he would do well if he merely improved his draft some. Slowly, I learned, but never quite enough, to tread very lightly. Others seem to think that I have a much heavier presence than I do.

On another occasion, after a particularly strident debate at the London School of Economics (reiterating one more time "no, we are not hostile to single parents, but data show on *average* two parents are better for the kids" and "we are for *rights* and responsibilities"), the assembled retreated to a pub. After one more beer than I should have had, a woman asked me, in an accusing tone, "Why can't you recognize that marriage is yesterday?" I simply walked away, definitely not the right thing to do. The last thing in the world I expected was that anyone would care enough about my uncouth behavior for it to be the subject of repeated commentary in the press—even years after the non-event.

The fact that usually my estimation of myself is well below that attributed to me by fans and detractors alike has one exception. When people introduce me during public lectures and read off (in deadly monotones, as if to say, "I wish I were somewhere else") the various books I have published, positions I've held, the honors I was awarded, and so on and on, I find these recitations embarrassing. But I do appreciate when they mention one prize about which I am unabashedly proud: the Simon Wiesenthal Center's Tolerance Book Award, given to *The New Golden Rule*. Frankly, I am not sure why I care more about this one than any of the others or why it lifts my spirit higher. Maybe it is my revenge on the Nazis who rattled my childhood and decimated my family. Maybe it is proof positive (for which I yearn) that my pigheadedness has not made me intolerant. Or simply that I appreciate that the *New Golden Rule* is singled out, an academic work that is my response to abuse from academics. I know not which.

One consequence of my particular sense of self that I do not regret is that I have been repeatedly ready to put my prestige (such as it is) on the line. Colleagues, and occasionally the media, chastise me for being "forward." Someone criticized me for suggesting to the editors of *Human Behavior* (a popular social science publication in its day) to write a monthly column, instead of demurely waiting for them to call on me. You bet I did. Forwardness for one's own gain may well be uncouth. However, to actively search for new outlets to express your ideas is no sin in my book. Similarly, a reporter who composed a profile of me wrote with a mixture of amusement and slight disbelief that I conscientiously returned phone calls from the press. Guilty as charged. A pure academic may well avoid the press. As I see it, what matters is not how to protect one's prestige, but how to find one more way of getting the word out. Prestige is not like a collection of gold coins to be polished and displayed; it's like political capital to be spent for a good purpose.

Thus, when I was exercised about the way the ACLU and the American Library Association have been fighting tooth and nail the devices that protected children from violent and vile material on computers and in the media, I did not sit back and wait until someone asked me to write about it. And when I was outraged that schools were teaching sex education as if it were merely a biological matter, reluctant to touch the moral issues involved, I did not wait to be asked by anyone to say my piece. If you have an idea to share with other members of the community, I hope you will not hesitate either.

My Love Life

My Country Right and Wrong

What is it like to be a public intellectual in America? I love my country despite all its flaws. I can match criticisms with most anybody who speaks about dark periods in our history, events that America's detractors are fond of bringing up as if they occurred last week (slavery, Haymarket, the detention of Japanese Americans, McCarthyism). I am painfully aware that even contemporary America is not free of racial discrimination, still lacks national health insurance, and much else. At the same time, I am too much of a sociologist not to realize that often those who catalogue these flaws are, in the backs of their minds, comparing America to some perfect never-never land. Or they hold the United States up to some small, homogeneous, middle-class society—one that never had to deal with millions of people long deprived or absorb millions of immigrants, especially of different social backgrounds. For instance, the "fabulous" social democracies of Scandinavia.

My admiration for a country that made liberty and government-by-law its cornerstones, and one that repeatedly put millions of its children in harm's way to bail out other free societies under siege on the other side of large oceans does not blind me to our faults. After all, I spent a good part of my life fighting against a war in which America should not have been entangled, trying to reverse the nuclear arms race, and seeking to end the indulgence in excessive individualism. But at the end of the day, one cannot but have an enormous respect for a society in which diverse people have learned to live together in peace and, as a rule, civilly. This fact alone is enough to make one proud to be an American. When I salute the flag and try to intone "America the Beautiful," my heart does strike an extra beat, and I am not ashamed to admit it.

There are few, if any, other countries (Canada and Australia maybe) in which an immigrant, with a considerable accent and a strange foreign name, could get the kind of hearing I was accorded in America year in, year out. Two of my colleagues at Columbia, who have had a much greater say than I, were, like me, immigrants. Henry Kissinger had a history and accent not that different from mine. Few minded that foreign-born Zbigniew Brzezinski (whose Polish name was misspelled even more often than mine) served as the national security adviser in the White House.

The same might be said about many others, from Hannah Arendt to Dinesh D'Souza to Fareed Zakaria. Time and time again, the United States has been extraordinarily open to voices likely to be ignored, if not silenced, in many other societies, from Switzerland to Japan (although there are some exceptions as with all such rules). I hence felt free to chastise my newly found home, sometimes quite relentlessly and in unmistakable terms, and still be proud of a nation that tolerates such people.

I had some run-ins with bigoted people, but they were surprisingly rare. Usually, they dared not speak up in public, sensing that the community would hiss them silent. They sent their missives as disembodied voices to call-in shows or as anonymous e-mail messages—which shows that they knew that their conduct would be considered inappropriate by their fellow citizens. For example, on a call-in show at Jeff Eisenberg's ultraconservative cable TV network, I shared a panel with Newt Gingrich. When I expressed concern about the decline of American morals, a caller demanded, "If you don't like it here, why don't you go back where you came from?" A number of the responses to one of my articles regarding gun control posted on IntellectualCapital.com were abusive and personal. Among the nicest names I was called were "commie bastard" and "fascist/Nazi." And it was suggested that I "should be deported for seditious propaganda." I should have answered as Nicholas D. Kristof did when he wrote on the same subject, anticipating the same "start packing" response. He wrote: "If you are so bothered by gun registration, and so convinced that guns don't kill people, then consider moving" to a place where guns are freely available, for instance, Yemen. He closed with, "You'll love the freedom!"

One blast deserves citing because it succeeded in rolling several prejudices into a few short lines about communitarianism, my influence on Clinton, my origin, and my profoundest beliefs:

> Etzioni is a Communitarian, in short individual rights are nothing, the COL-
> LECTIVE is everything. This Un-American was Clinton's mentor. Etzioni is
> one of the truly malignant forces at work in the world today. While the snooz-
> ing public thinks saddam [sic] or Slobodan are the villains the cognoscenti re-
> alize that Etzioni is the chief theoretician for totalitarianism.

The message was signed "Real American." But such hateful communications were rare; most messages I got were truly American—surprisingly open and tolerant.

Oddly, my name not only did not close any doors of which I am aware, but it opened some I did not expect to pass through. On quite a few occasions, my fellow Americans took it for granted that I was of Italian decent. The talented *Washington Post* correspondent T. R. Reid wrote about me in his book, *Confucius Lives Next Door*: "The scholar Amitai Etzioni, an American of Italian extraction and Roman Catholic upbringing." People were so sure about my (mistaken) ethnic background that they addressed me in Italian. But these misidentifications were merely a source of chuckles and were utterly harmless, at least for me. Indeed, they led me to be invited to places that otherwise might well have chosen to do without me. Thus, Frank Sinatra asked me to join an Italian antidefamation organization, which I reluctantly declined. However, I did not turn down a request to participate in a conference at Notre Dame on 150 Years of *Catholic* Social Thought. The invitation did not mention that the other invitees were Catholic scholars or that it was presumed that I was a Catholic, and the lineup was very impressive. I hope the Lord, whatever His (Her?) religious affiliation, will forgive me for accepting the invitation without warning my host, "By the way, do you realize . . . ?"

Indeed, in my case, American openness was carried to an extreme: I was elected to the National Board of *Americans* for Democratic Action in 1963 (and served until 1968)—before I became an American citizen! Only in America.

In March 2002, sixty intellectuals issued a statement justifying the war against terrorism. In the United States it was a one-day wonder; overseas it was greeted with a storm of controversy. The indefatigable Mary Schwartz, who works with David Blankenhorn (who played a key role in drafting the statement), called to see whether I could join a debate about the statement organized by the Aspen Institute in Berlin. When I asked about the date, it turned out to be a day I was going to be in Berlin anyhow for a meeting on the dialogue of civilizations. What happened next speaks for itself.

Early in the meeting, a voice from the audience startled me with the flat statement: "You are in Afghanistan for the oil." When I responded in shock, "Oil?" he corrected himself, "Well, for the pipeline." (He was referring to a pipeline some corporations are considering running from Turkmenistan through Afghanistan to a port on the Arabian Sea.) I had just repeated the criteria we have used to call the war against terrorism a just one: protecting innocents from harm (as distinct from sheer self-defense), a clear and present danger (not just a questionable threat), and that the situation cannot be plausibly mitigated through negotiations.

During the debate that followed, Ekkehart Krippendorff from the Free University, a well-known left-leaning professor, argued that it is wrong in principle for intellectuals to support a government. "They should be critical; you never know what a government will do with its power," he said.

During a dinner after the debate, Andrea Fischer, a member of the German parliament from the dovish Green Party, argued that any highfalutin moral blessing of a war was at best troublesome. "Just say it is in self-defense," she said.

At a meeting at the Center for Social Science in Berlin later the same day, a colleague quoted a counterstatement issued in the United States by the left that mocked ours, calling us "celebrants of war" and arguing that the United States had appropriated the right of self-defense.

I asked the audience in Berlin, "Fair enough, you are critical of what the United States is doing. If it is ever justified to go to war, what are your criteria for a call to arms?" When I found no takers, I asked if fighting Hitler was just. This got me a lot of positive nodding, but also a voice from the back of the room: "Saddam is no Hitler; Sharon comes close."

In Afghanistan, the United States caused some very regrettable collateral damage, I admitted. But, I held, there also was what might be called "collateral gain." While the United States did not set out merely to liberate women denied the right to work, to education, and to leaving their homes unescorted—or help all to enjoy some form of culture other than prayer—America did bring liberty to millions of Afghans. This, I said, brings up the question: if the United States should not fight terror aimed at Americans, how about terror that wipes out other people?

Half a million people were slaughtered in Rwanda in 1994. Should the United States intervene with force if another genocide looms? A woman from the audience argued that the UN should act, but it could not last time because the United States failed to pay its dues.

I asked why the European Union did not act on its own, if it was so critical of the way Americans do things? And whether the Europeans preferred the way Dutch peacekeepers acted in Srebrenica, Bosnia, where 7,000 Muslims were slaughtered by Serbs while the peacekeepers refused to fire a shot in their defense? I argued that the "collateral damage" of not acting was much higher than America's in Afghanistan and that the United States did its best to minimize it.

The response? I was told that the "official" number of civilian deaths in Afghanistan was 50,000 and that nobody knows what really happened because the United States did not allow the press in.

At this point I lost it. I allowed that they could afford to be de facto pacifists, as long as Americans were the bullies, on call to save them. Who kept West Berlin free? Our airlift. Who stopped Hitler? The Dutch? The French? Who stopped the military expansion of communism in Europe?

Renowned historian Jurgen Kocka responded, "You are . . . right. If it was not for the U.S., I would have grown up a Nazi. I am forever grateful."

When I returned home, I published my impressions from the debate, adding:

> I felt I had planted a seed, but many more need to be sown and nurtured if the American antiterrorism drive is to keep support overseas. It is time to reestablish the US Information Agency.
>
> The US needs to consult with its allies more about the next moves in the war on terrorism, although America must make clear that if all the allies do is

veto what the US considers must be done, without suggesting viable alternatives, America shall go it alone at the end of the day.

The US should also allow more press access during the next rounds of the war. But ultimately, I fear, Americans had better steel themselves to the fact that they shall have to carry much of the burden of defending the free world yet again, while critics crowd the coffee shops of Europe, trading paranoiac stories about US motives and second-guessing every move.

It's sniping we Americans would rather do without, but it is often the price of leadership.

The article generated some e-mail. One of them did me proud:

Professor, I read your column in *The Christian Science Monitor* this morning (in fact I read it to my troops). At last someone of intellect has had the spine to stand up for the truth! . . . I feels so good to now be receiving some gratitude for what we've been doing day in and day out for years, with nary a passing thought from most of the citizens that we do our best to protect from the barbarian horde. Personally I could care less if the European coffee shop dwellers like us or not. Who will they come crying to when they need protection? Of course we'll go and die by the thousands to protect their ability to criticize us.

Linda Feldman, an editor at the *Christian Science Monitor*, in response to the message, wrote, "I love the image of the Navy man reading the piece aloud to his marines!"

Fellow Communitarians

One of the joys of communitarianism is that the people I work with, even only tangentially, are exceptionally fine people. Not all, but I believe a disproportionate number. Many social scientists go berserk at the mere suggestion that there is a connection between the kind of views one holds and the inner makings of one's personality. For instance, studies that show that those with authoritarian personalities tend to be right-wingers have been largely discredited. Neither can I claim that I did some kind of psychological testing to prove that leading communitarians are good people. But Bill Galston, who anyone would agree has a most gentle soul and disposition, is a case in point. Phil Selznick turns passionate when he speaks about piety and community, family and virtue, but as a person, I doubt that he could step on a roach. My favorite image of Michael Sandel is a picture in the *New York Times*, showing him coaching his son's little league team. I have never heard him raise his voice or criticize anyone. Michael Walzer cuts a boyish figure; he has a joy of ideas that I associate with the best first-year students. Color him naive, but if he has a mean bone in his body, I have not seen it. Charles Taylor invites respect not by being stuffy or self-important, but by the depth of conviction in which he carefully lays out the strong commitments he holds on various moral and social issues. He somehow combines being compelling and temperate. Jean Bethke Elshtain is the kind of person everyone hopes to have as a friend. Ernst Hirsh-Ballin and Hans Joas are most atypical true believers: passionate yet moderate and modest. I have not listed others because I believe I've made my point and not because they are exceptions to the rule, although if forced, I might be able to come up with one or two communitarians that do not immediately invite affection.

My Greatest Love

There is little in this book about my family. Yet, my family has had an immense influence on my life. Not having done better by my sons and others I loved is the main source of those deep regrets I do harbor.

I believe that I did not miss any birthdays or graduations. When I smell chlorine, I cannot but help to recall the humid swimming pool halls in which I lasted through day-long swim meets. I stuck around for the awards after numerous running competitions, which, for some reason, were handed out at the end of the day even to those who completed their matches in the morning. When a medical need arose or a teacher called in the parents, trips got canceled, much to the justified annoyance of those who had expected a presentation at the other end. My sons and I talk often and I believe openly. In effect, they are now, by far, my best and closest young friends. (One of them complained about how difficult it was to rebel in our home.) But still, I wish I had dedicated more of my time and attention to my kids.

I have largely avoided exploring my relationships with my family in this book because it would not merely entail digging deeper into my psyche than I am prepared to do, but also would violate the privacy of those nearest and dearest to me. (My great respect for Betty Friedan rose even more when I learned that she refused to participate in a movie about her life in response to her kids' pleas, especially out of respect for their father.) On those few occasions that I do mention my children and Pat, it is only after they reviewed the text.

My family ties have been very strong indeed. My children and grandchildren are spread all over the world. Yet, with great effort by all of us, we get together for a week—twice most years—for a family reunion. Here, Eli (from Seattle) beams and shrieks with joy as he rushes to hug Shira (from Tel Aviv). Danielle flies into the arms of her four uncles. We play enough board games to drive new members of the family to distraction. We play sports, from group mountain biking to fielding an Etzioni water polo team. We have long one-on-one conversations and "family council" meetings. There is nothing like family in either the academic or the public realm.

One gathering especially deserves recounting. Here is the way I journaled it at the time: the family assembles in Amsterdam for a most unusual bar mitzvah, that of Daniel, the severely autistic son of my niece. We are delighted to find each other's arms and pleased that we made the trek to honor the Dutch branch of the family as well as the gargantuan efforts we hear were made to teach Daniel a few lines of the essential prayers for the occasion. Some of us doubt that even given these efforts Daniel will be able to meet the minimal requirements of ritual that turns youngsters into members of the Jewish community. My mother has no doubt. "No way, never, not in this life. I wonder why they are even trying? The poor boy."

The synagogue is packed. Daniel climbs on the *bima* with much effort, his parents supporting him on the left and right. On the *bima*, he is unstable on his feet, drooling on his suit. He smiles apologetically. I wish I could whisper into his ear, "Its OK; no matter."

The ritual is started by others, but when it is Daniel's turn to bless the reading of the Torah, he looks like someone who has a huge lump stuck in his throat, straining to get it out, but is able to cough up only a little. He

Figure 18.1. My sons, from left to right: Michael, Ethan, Benjamin, David, and Oren at Martha's Vineyard, 1999

flushes as he tries to speak, eking out one or two legible words. He becomes flustered, strains harder, but now only grunts can be heard. We all wish we could just go up there, hug him, say the prayer for him, ending this wrenching scene. Indeed, two members of the congregation who stand on his left and right, chime in. An embarrassed smile occupies Daniel's face. His body twitches. He is perspiring profusely; his mother keeps wiping it off, which seems to trouble him even more. I am searching desperately for what one could do to spare him even another minute of this very public ordeal.

Someone else reads the portion of this week's Torah the bar mitzvah boy is supposed to chant. During the following rounds of prayers, Daniel is a bit more relaxed, able to utter a few words he has rehearsed scores of time. The congregation joins in a song praising the Lord, and Daniel hums along; somehow he finds it easier to sing than speak.

Then there is a moment of silence. And Daniel suddenly recites in full, in a clear, though halting voice: "Sh'ma Israel, Adoni Elohenu, Adoni Echad" (Hear, O Israel, the Lord is God, the Lord is One). It is the line Jews who were given the option by the Inquisition to eat pork and convert to Christianity or be burned at the stake recited when they chose to jump into the fire; the line Jews repeated when they finally realized that they were being marched not into showers to be deloused but into gas chambers in the Nazi concentration camps; the line that more than any other captures the Jewish essence.

There is not a dry eye in the place. The community rises, without any signal from the Rabbi, and breaks with much gusto into a song of thanksgiving. Daniel's body stops twitching; he seems drained but beams widely. My mother whispers, "My God, he made it."

I don't know what made for the magical movement; did God interrupt all he is doing to intercede or—did the community's love carry Daniel over the threshold? I am not even sure what exact difference it makes. I am sure that there was a presence of a kind I never witnessed before. It was surely the most unique family get-together of them all.

The rest of the year, we stay in touch via a device on which we stumbled: a worldwide family conference call on the first Sunday of each month. While initially these calls were somewhat stiff, we have learned to conduct open and genuine conversations. One of us may seek advice as to whether to quit his job to try his hand at something else, another may wonder about continuing a long-term relationship with a girlfriend, and so on. We give a lot of asked-for (and some unasked-for) advice on bringing up children. If someone is not well, international phone lines buzz, and e-mail messages pile up one on top of the other.

Did my children ever give me heartache even after they supposedly came of age? You bet, but that, too, is family. There is not, nor ever was, a colleague or friend I feel closer to than my children.

Pat and I continue, after more than ten years of marriage, our almost daily routine of what might be called psychiatric first-aid. After work, we "debrief" each other on the events of the day. I typically feel better after such chats, and often the light goes on, illuminating approaches to problems that I did not see before. We have been and are good friends.

And Pat brought a bonus. Her children and grandchildren live close by, which bestows me with the blessing of an extended family. I still feel awkward when they introduce me as their stepfather (Pat's children are in their thirties), probably because the term reminds me of the bad witch in German fairy tales. But I am the great beneficiary of much love both given and taken. I melt when Margaret and Luci Kellogg rush toward me with the delighted cry of "Saba!"

Next . . .

Now my sands are almost run. There are daily reminders. Friends and colleagues my age—and younger!—whose funerals and memorial services I attend. Others who are too ill to continue their work, whether it is academic or public. I continue to be lucky for now, although my body is less and less responsive to commands that have not been properly scaled back.

But for now, maybe, there is time for one more project, or should I try for two? I would love to write a book about the role of rituals and holidays in undergirding our values, how we are losing such special days and what might be done to rejuvenate them in the age of 24/7 work. I am tempted to combine recent essays on the development of a global civil society into a book on world governance. Two recent books, one for my fellow citizens (*Next: The Road to the Good Society*) and one for my colleagues (*The Monochrome Society*), need to be nurtured. There are some invitations to speak at conferences on communitarian subjects, some academic papers to prepare for a political science meeting. I wish I could convince Karl Rove and his associates to lean further in the communitarian direction. And maybe I should also . . .

In any event, you can bet that when they carry me on my last journey they will find some unfinished manuscript in my desk drawers, some notes in my calendar about some public lectures I promised to deliver, and a bunch of notes about a project I hoped to launch. And then? The communitarian agenda is a communal one. Others will carry on; they have been partners from day one. I will be gone, but not the calling.

Acknowledgments

> You cannot fault the author of an autobiography for failing to be objective, or for substituting his story for the story of his subject. He is his subject.
>
> —Stanley Fish

A word or two about sources. This is a subjective account based on my memory and feelings. Obviously, my recall of events that occurred decades ago has been affected by the passage of time. In the few instances in which my notes or recollections differed from published sources, I relied on the published sources.

In writing these pages I benefited from a diary I started keeping when I was twelve years old, from notes I took over the years, from minutes to meetings, and from cabinets full of documents and correspondence and audio and videotapes. Of these, the ones I collected while serving in the White House turned out to be of special value. Visitors then and now are quite carefully screened when they enter the White House compound. Briefcases and people are x-rayed and sometimes searched and so on. Visitors are also supposed to be escorted at all times. However, when one leaves the White House, no searching of any kind takes place. Staff, too, leave without any examination of what they carry with them. Hence, on the last day of my work there, I parked my car next to the Situation Room in broad daylight, right next to the Secret Service sentry. He watched without the slightest interest or concern as I loaded two shopping carts full of documents into the trunk of my car and drove them out of the compound. (These documents came in handy once before. When I published some articles about my White House experience in *The Public Interest*, Victor

Palmieri challenged my version of events. In a later issue I was readily able to document my account.) The law making it illegal to remove one's papers from the White House was enacted after my service there.

Still, I fear that there was some detail, a conversation, a turn of events that was set down incorrectly—in part because, essentially, a memoir is about what I remember and experienced and in part because, despite my efforts, it is likely that some vetting fell through the cracks. I apologize to the readers for these lapses and, if they are called to my attention, will correct them in the next edition of this book.

The tense shifts occasionally in the book from past to present and back. I believe that in this way I can better capture what some books say (after all, they still say it) and the "atmosphere" in some situations.

I owe a very great debt of gratitude to Jennifer Ambrosino, who stayed with the book from conception to delivery. She came to work with me as an executive assistant for an unusual reason: she is a theater director and wanted to work in a place that would allow her to handle some of her artistic commitments during work hours. It turned out to be a fabulous bargain. Although she was sometimes on the phone, dealing with actors and designers, she is a very talented editor. Her comments and editing are reflected on every page of this book.

Joanna Cohn stayed with the book almost as long as Jennifer. She combined working with us with her studies at The George Washington University's School of Media and Public Affairs. There is no question in my mind that she will turn out to be a much sought after researcher and editor. There is little in this book that she did not help me to vet and say better than I would have otherwise.

I benefited enormously from my research assistants, who vetted details regarding events that took place long before they were born; indeed, in some cases, before their parents were born. They often acted as endlessly patient sounding boards and as literary critics. They include Natalie Klein, Deirdre Mead, Rachel Mears, Erin Riska, Wendy Rubin, and Mary Wilson. In addition, I benefited from numerous critical comments on previous drafts of the manuscript by Jason Marsh and Andrew Volmert.

Pat Kellogg-Etzioni patiently listened to my struggle with this new form of writing and doubts and misgivings about the book for several years, which is more than any spouse should have to put up with. Her support and suggestions are much appreciated. Katharine Bloeser, Elizabeth Tulis, and Dana Graber improved the final galleys.

Especially appreciated is the advice of editors/friends (not always two terms that live in harmony) Tim Bartlett, Steve Wrinn, and Paul Golob, as well as Sally Arteseros. I am also indebted to comments by Oren Etzioni, Carl Stern (on chapters 1 to 5), and Jessica Einhorn (the same first chapters).

---⊗⊗⊗---

Notes

Notes for Preface

xv *limited computer search* According to Lexis-Nexis, there were 115 documents mentioning *communitarian movement* in major newspapers between 1990 and April 2001. Major newspapers are those with the top fifty circulations. According to Lexis-Nexis, there were 41 documents mentioning *communitarian movement* in magazines and journals between 1990 and March 2001.

xv *"guru" and "godfather"* For instance, Tony Mauro, "'Communitarians' Want to Share the Stage," *USA Today*, November 18, 1992; and Martin Walker, "Community Spirit," *The Guardian*, March 13, 1995. James A. Barnes, "The New Guru of Communitarianism," *National Journal*, November 30, 1991, 2931. According to Lexis-Nexis, there were 89 newspaper articles and 26 magazine or journal articles between January 1990 and March 2001 mentioning *Etzioni* as the leader or founder or guru or head of the communitarian movement.

Notes for Chapter One

9 *"promotion to the next grade"* Date of note: 14 Tammuz 5701 (June 29, 1942).

11 *values of the institution in which they are formed* Chapter on cohesion in Amitai Etzioni, *A Comparative Analysis of Complex Organizations* (Glencoe, Ill.: Free Press, 1961).

11 *ringing in my ears* Author's diary, May 9, 1943.

13 *my school in Herzliya* Letter dated July 17, 1942.

16 *communities away from the coast* Author's diary, May 4, 1946. Report by Bezalel Herzog, in Hebrew, in *Our Village*, June 1978 (unpublished).

18 *"letter to my father"* Ba Ma'Aley, February 21, 1947.

19 *hush-hush location* Author's diary, June 30, 1946 about Black Saturday; June 1, 1946, about decision to join the Palmach; August 4, 1946, actually joined.

Notes for Chapter Two

34 *"tell it the way it was?"* Her name was Gila Ben Akiva (Drucker) according to Professor Nessia Shafransky. She was killed on the way to Petra, long after the war of independence.

35 *bestseller list* Ha'aretz bestseller list, November and December 1952.

36 *the war as just one* "What We're Fighting For: A Letter from America," *Responsive Community* 12, no. 4 (Fall 2002): 30–42.

43 *"societal rewards"* All in BeTerem, respectively, January 15, 1952, February 5, 1952, and March 27, 1953.

Notes for Chapter Three

49 *a choice lot* Including Robert Blauner, Fred Goldner, Juan Linz, David Matza, Guenther Roth, and Arthur Stinchcombe.

51 *to teach English* Rise B. Axelrod and Charles R. Cooper, *The St. Martin's Guide to Writing*, 4th ed. (New York: St. Martin's, 1994).

54 *recognized as a science* Dennis Wrong writes that the "Columbia department [was in a] period of strenuous discipline building." Dennis Wrong, "Imagining the Real," in *Authors of Their Own Lives*, ed. Bennett M. Berger (Berkeley: University of California Press, 1990), 13.

54 *imposed on me* Whether Mills was allowed or not allowed to teach graduate students or did not want to teach them has been a subject of considerable controversy. I report here the way things seemed to me at the time.

56 *he particularly cared for them* Si reviewed these lines in January 2001, and I made some additions and clarifications accordingly. Letter from Si and notes on the draft manuscript are dated January 10, 2001.

57 *office was but a building away* Others who commanded a public voice over the decades that followed included Daniel Bell, Peter Berkowitz, Alan Brinkley, Stephen Carter, Jean Bethke Elshtain, Francis Fukuyama, Henry Louis Gates Jr., Robert George, Todd Gitlin, Nathan Glazer, Mary Ann Glendon, Samuel Huntington, Leon Kass, Richard Rorty, Thomas Sowell, James Q. Wilson, and Alan Wolfe. Note that reference is to those public intellectuals who are professors and, hence, have academic lives and commitments. None of these criticisms should be applied to people who are full-time, off-campus public intellectuals, such as David Brooks, William Buckley Jr., E. J. Dionne Jr., Dinesh D'Souza, David Frum, Gertrude Himmelfarb, Michael Kelly, Irving Kristol, and Bill Moyers. The differences between the two types would make for a lovely academic piece of research someday.

57 *The Public Intellectual* I am not included in Posner's list of public intellectuals. According to Alan Wolfe, a public intellectual star, neither are any of the following: Fouad Ajami, Paul Berman, Robert Brustein, Ian Buruma, Frederick Crews, Robert Dallek, Andrew Delbanco, John Patrick Diggins, Maureen Dowd, Michael Eric Dyson, Gerald Early, Hans Magnus Enzensberger, Elizabeth Fox-Genovese, Jerome Groopman, Hendrik Hertzberg, Robert Hughes, Michael Ignatieff, Kathleen Hall Jamieson, Tony Judt, Wendy Kaminer, Robert Kuttner, Jonathan Lear, Jackson Lears, Adam Michnik, Sherwin B. Nuland, Kevin Phillips, Marge Piercy, Robert Pinsky, Katha Pollitt, John Rawls, David Remnick, David Rieff, Philip Rieff, Edward Rothstein, Alan Ryan, Juliet Schor, Simon Schama, Jim Sleeper, Peter Steinfels, Margaret Talbot, Sam Tanenhaus, Terry Teachout, Deborah Tannen, Tzvetan Todorov, James Traub, Geoffrey Wheatcroft, C. K. Williams, Ellen Willis, James Wood, and Fareed Zakaria. (Alan Wolfe, "The Fame Game," *New Republic*, December 31, 2001, and January 7, 2002, 34–38.) Possibly, I qualified in some periods of my life and not others. Being a public intellectual is not a title bestowed by the queen or a degree earned for perpetuity; it must be earned year in and year out.

57 *"gessellshaft"* Bennett M. Berger, ed., *Authors of Their Own Lives: Intellectual Autobiographies by Twenty American Sociologists* (Berkeley: University of California Press, 1990), 60.

57 *"worst of all, a 'journalist'"* John Cassidy, "Height of Eloquence," *The New Yorker*, November 30, 1998, 70–75.

57 *"compulsive popularizer"* Thomas Mallon, "Billions and Billions," *The New Yorker*, November 22, 1999, 196.

58 *"criticized as 'popularizers.'"* Howard S. Becker, "Professional Sociology: The Case of C. Wright Mills," at www.soc.ucsb.edu/faculty/hbecker/mills.html (accessed April 11, 2002).

62 *"serious organizational scholars"* James L. Price, "Review of 'A Comparative Analysis of Complex Organizations,'" *American Journal of Sociology* 83, no. 5 (March 1978): 1304–1305.

63 *various elements of it* For citations and overview, see Amitai Etzioni, *A Comparative Analysis of Complex Organizations*, rev. and enl. ed. (New York: Free Press, 1975).

63 *G. William Skinner* G. William Skinner and Edwin A. Winckler, "Compliance Succession in Rural Communist China: A Cyclical Theory," in *A Sociological Reader on Complex Organizations*, 3d ed., ed. Amitai Etzioni and Edward W. Lehman (New York: Holt, Rinehart and Winston, 1980), 401–423.

63 *the theory spawned* Etzioni, *Comparative Analysis*.

63 *Talcott Parsons* Eugene Garfield, "Current Contents," *Institute for Scientific Information*, August 7, 1978, 11.

63 *students of social systems* Peter Fricke, "Etzioni, 'A Comparative Analysis of Complex Organizations,' rev. ed. (Book Review)" *Political Science Quarterly* 91, no. 2 (Summer 1976): 341.

64 *implicit in the book*   Jerald Hage, "The Evolution of Compliance Structures: The Problem of Moral Progress," paper presented at the American Sociological Association Theory Day, Washington, D.C., August 18, 1995.

64 *privileged position*   Edward W. Lehman, "From Compliance to Community in the Works of Amitai Etzioni," *Responsive Community* 9, no. 1 (Winter 1998/99): 42.

67 *the Pope came to mind*   Stanley Newman, along with Gerard Piel, Leo Szilard, and Marc Raskin, attended the meeting regarding the Pope in 1962 and remembers it all. Told at lunch with David Anderson, November 14, 2000.

68 *"nobody can foresee"*   "Pope Bids Rulers Save the Peace," *New York Times*, October 26, 1962.

70 *under earlier conditions*   Gabriel A. Almond, *American People and Foreign Policy* (New York: Praeger, 1960), xvi.

70 *(the communist nations)*   Urie Bronfenbrenner, a psychologist, found that when American schoolchildren were asked why the Russians planted trees alongside a road, they responded that the trees blocked vision and "made work for the prisoners," whereas American trees were planted "for shade." *Saturday Review*, January 5, 1963, 96.

71 *analogous to "gradualism"*   Anatol Rapoport, "Getting Off the Limb," *The Nation*, March 30, 1963.

71 *Nagel (philosophy)*   February 26, 1962.

71 *Christian Science Monitor*   February 24, 1996.

71 *following my approach*   *The New Leader*, July 6, 1964. For an especially informative review of *Winning without War*, see Robert Strausz-Hupé, "How to Win without Really Trying," *Orbis* 8 (1964–1965): 449–459.

71 *Senate Foreign Relations Committee*   February 23, 1965.

73 *United States in 1962*   Richard D. Stebbins, *The United States in World Affairs 1963* (New York: Harper and Row for The Council on Foreign Relations, 1964), 84.

74 *shrewd new tactic*   *New York Times*, June 16, 1963.

74 *"Another Booby Trap"*   *New York Times*, July 7, 1963.

74 *interest in Moscow*   *New York Times*, June 16, 1963.

75 *to buy newspapers*   *New York Times*, June 16, 1963.

75 *by September 1963*   *Washington Post*, September 16, 1963.

75 *and the Soviet Union*   *New York Times*, August 4, 1963.

75 *(similar criticisms)*   Louis B. Sohn and David H. Frisch, "Arms Reduction in the Sixties," in *Arms Reduction: Programs and Issues*, ed. David H. Frisch (New York: Twentieth Century Fund, 1961), 24–34. Amry Vandenbosch, "Frisch, ed., 'Arms Reduction: Programs and Issues' (Book Review)," *Midwest Journal of Political Science* 6, no. 2 (May 1962): 221.

76 *And Gorbachev agreed!*   See Charles Krauthammer, "Arms Control: The End of an Illusion," *Weekly Standard*, November 1, 1999, 21.

78 *New York Times Magazine*   December 31, 1964.

79 *from Walewski*   Letter on file.

80 *Martin Luther King Jr. stayed* Senate Select Committee on Intelligence, "Political Abuses: Full Text of Official Report," *U.S. News & World Report*, December 15, 1975, 61.

Notes for Chapter Four

83 *"got along famously"* Joe Rosenbloom, "Peace Speakers Launch Vietnam Protest; Oratory Precedes White Plaza Camp-In," *Stanford Daily*, October 14, 1965; "Viet War Protest Launched," *Palo Alto Times*, October 14, 1965; "Sociologists Ask End of Viet War," *Palo Alto Times*, August 30, 1967.

84 *endear her to the audience* All quotes from Carleton Sterling, "Mme. Nhu Censures Press: Says Viet Cong Defeat Near," *Columbia Spectator*, October 14, 1963.

89 *not outer space* Amitai Etzioni, *The Moondoggle: Domestic and International Implications of the Space Race* (Garden City, N.Y.: Doubleday, 1964), 12–13.

89 *unmanned flights* Etzioni, *Moondoggle*, 14.

89 *"quest for political action"* Lloyd S. Swenson Jr., "The Moon-Doggle: The Images of Space," review of *The Moondoggle*, by Amitai Etzioni, *Technology and Culture* 9 (1968): 252–253.

89 *"should" and "ought"* "Briefer Notices," *Journal of Politics* 27, no. 1. (February 1965): 242.

90 *"instead of Columbus"* Richard Lewis, "Sociologist Takes Shot at the Moon Program," *Chicago Sun Times*, June 14, 1964.

90 *"other cave dwellers"* George W. Earley, "Space Waste?" *Hartford Courant Magazine*, March 7, 1965.

90 *"raise all the right questions"* Edward Edelson, "Genetic Fix" review, *Smithsonian* 4, no. 11 (February 1974).

91 *left by water* Warren E. Leary, "Evidence of Water Invigorates Study of Mars," *New York Times*, June 23, 2000; David Talbot, "Expert: Life, If Any, on Mars Would Be Primitive," *Boston Herald*, June 23, 2000.

91 *deeper in space* Homer H. Hickam, "We Must Go Back to the Moon—and Beyond," *Wall Street Journal*, July 20, 1999.

91 *"color enhanced"* Professor John Logsdon, director of The George Washington University's Space Policy Institute, private communication. Stories were also placed that claimed that NASA engineers invented Velcro, while actually Velcro was invented by George de Mestral of Switzerland—before NASA was even established. F. F. Scherer, "Letter to the Editor," *Business Week*, November 11, 1985, 15.

91 *spirit at home* Hedrick Smith, "Pride on the Mojave," *New York Times*, April 15, 1981.

92 *"This is cheap"*   Quotes from CBS News, "The Hubble," 60 *Minutes* transcript XXXV, no. 2 (October 6, 2002): 14, 15, 20.

92 *how prescient I had been*   David Streitfeld, "Footprints in the Cosmic Dust; Twenty Years Later, Six Voices on the Lost Promise of the Apollo Mission," *Washington Post*, July 20, 1989.

93 *(is taken into account)*   Amitai Etzioni and Laura Brodbeck, "The Intergenerational Covenant: Rights and Responsibilities," *Communitarian Working Paper* (Washington, D.C.: The Communitarian Network, 1995).

93 *health care*   Christine Cassel, Charles Dougherty, Amitai Etzioni, C. McCollister Everts, John Griffith, James L. Nelson, Marian Osterweis, and Daniel Wikler, "Core Values in Health-Care Reform: A Communitarian Approach," *Communitarian Position Paper* (Washington, D.C.: The Communitarian Network, 1993). Amitai Etzioni, "Spare the Old, Save the Young," *The Nation*, June 11, 1988, 818–822.

95 *three to five years*   James K. Glassman and Kevin A. Hassett, *Dow 36,000: The New Strategy for Profiting from the Coming Rise in the Stock Market* (New York: Times Business, 1999), 13.

96 *material in the environment*   Dinner on January 30, 1979.

97 *(called "mixed scanning")*   Amitai Etzioni, "Mixed Scanning: A 'Third' Approach to Decision-Making," *Public Administration Review* 27, no. 5 (December 1967): 385–392. This article received the William Mosher Award for the most distinguished academic article in the *Public Administration Review* in 1967.

100 *inner light*   Among those who attended the center in 1964–1965, my year, were Bruno Bethlehem, the authoritarian psychiatrist; Frederick Crews, a renowned English literature professor from Berkeley; John Higham, a distinguished historian from Johns Hopkins; Stanley Hoffman from Harvard who was fully aware of his importance; Joel Klein, who led the antitrust charge against Microsoft in 1999; and Nelson Polsby, a witty political science professor at UC Berkeley.

101 *values of its members?*   Robert L. Stewart, "Review of the Active Society," *Social Forces* 48, no. 2 (December 1969): 268–269.

102 *investigation in the future*   Peter Nettl, "Society's Last and Next Hundred Years," *Psychiatry and Social Science Review* (May 1969): 13–17.

102 *"social problems"*   Carl Dreher, "Review: The Active Society," *The Nation*, May 26, 1969.

102 *much more mixed*   See reviews in *Science*, October 10, 1969; *American Journal of Sociology*, January 1970; and letter July 1970. For an extensive and positive evaluation, see Margaret M. Poloma, "The Active Society: An Evaluative Synthesis of Naturalism and Humanism," in *Contemporary Sociological Theory* (New York: Macmillan, 1979), 227–240, and a book-length treatment by Warren Breed in *The Self-Guiding Society* (New York: Free Press, 1971).

102 *"macroscopic action"*   Hans Joas, "Macroscopic Action—On Amitai Etzioni's Contribution to Social Theory," *Responsive Community* 9, no. 1 (Winter 98/99): 23.

103 theoretical underpinning   Betty Friedan, *Responsive Community* 9, no. 1 (Winter 98/99): 8.

Notes for Chapter Five

110 *say "charisma"*   E-mail correspondence from Lois Grosse Tarter (lois@ infohouse.com) received January 7, 2000.

111 *several police headquarters*   August 24, 1970. A Weathermen bomb exploded in Sterling Hall on the main University of Wisconsin campus at Madison. Its purpose: "to strike a blow at the 'government war machine.'" The explosion destroyed work, caused $6 million in damages, injured three, and killed a thirty-three-year-old graduate student. Spencer C. Tucker, ed. "University of Wisconsin Bombing," in *Encyclopedia of the Vietnam War* (Denver: ABC-CLIO, 1998), 2: 745–746.

111 *"elder statesmen of the New Left"*   March 28, 1969.

111 *Vietcong everybody else*   "Clash Precedes Penn Debate on Student Power," *Washington Post*, March 30, 1969. James P. Sterba, "Student Unity Crumbles over Tactics," *New York Times*, March 31, 1969. Desmond Ryan, "Avoid Minor Battles, 'New Left' Bids Students," *Philadelphia Inquirer*, March 28, 1969.

112 *"justification for this"*   Brian Leary, *The Columbia Owl*, December 20, 1967.

112 *"Caught in a Revolution"*   Amitai Etzioni, "Confessions of a Professor Caught in a Revolution," *New York Times Magazine*, September 15, 1968, sec. 6, pp. 25, 27, 87–89, 92, 94, 97, 99, 100, 102, 104, 109.

113 *"happening right here!"*   *The Columbia Owl*, December 20, 1967.

116 *titled "Policy Research"*   Amitai Etzioni, "Policy Research," *American Sociologist* 6, supplementary issue (June 1971): 8–12.

116 *(directed ever since)*   Among the senior researchers who have worked at the center are Pamela Doty (sociology), Herbert Gans (sociology), Charles Kadushin (sociology), Steven Kelman (political science), Kurt Lang (sociology), Kenneth Louden (computer science), Matthew Miles (education), Murray Milner Jr. (sociology), Clyde Nunn (sociology), David and Sheila Rothman (history), Karolyn Siegel (sociology), Donald Treiman (sociology), Andrew von Hirsch (law), Benjamin Zablocki (sociology), and Margaret Zahn (sociology).

118 *"bureau's raw files"*   John Seigenthaler, "Publisher Finally Gets His FBI Files, or Some of Them," *The Tennessean*, July 10, 1977.

121 *landed me on a blacklist*   *New York Times*, March 15, 1984.

121 Stansfield Turner   *New York Times*, March 15, 1984.

122 *deep penetration*   Bob Zelnick, *Gore: A Political Life* (Washington, D.C.: Regnery, 1999), 127–129.

123 *boys over girls in the United States*   I determined this by relying not merely on surveys of what people said about the mixture of children they would prefer but on what people actually did. To the extent they engaged in family planning, people

differed systematically at what sex mix they would stop having children. They were somewhat more likely to stop after they had boys only or a preponderance of boys, than if they had girls.

124 *experimental gene therapy* Rick Weiss and Deborah Nelson, "Teen Dies Undergoing Experimental Gene Therapy," *Washington Post*, September 29, 1999.

124 *similar to leukemia* Sheryl Gay Stolberg, "Trials Are Halted on a Gene Therapy," *New York Times*, October 4, 2002.

126 Erschaffung des Menschen Amitai Etzioni, *Die Zweite Erschaffung des Menschen* (Opladen: Westdeutscher Verlag, 1977).

127 *"biomedical research"* Suzanne Fields, "Toward a Genetic Revolution," *Washington Post*, December 17, 1973.

127 *"an important message"* Larry Bush, "Are Superpeople in Your Future?" *Ann Arbor News*, April 7, 1974.

127 *social implications of amniocentesis* Amitai Etzioni, "Public Policy Issues Raised by a Medical Breakthrough," *Policy Analysis* 1, no. 1 (Winter 1975): 69–76; Amitai Etzioni, "Amniocentesis: A Case Study in the Management of Genetic Engineering," *Ethics in Science and Medicine* 2, no. 1 (May 1975): 13–24; Amitai Etzioni, "Amniocentesis: A Pandora's Box," *Medical Opinion* 5, no. 8 (August 1976): 53–54; Amitai Etzioni and Nancy Castleman, "Amniocentesis: A Forerunner of the Genetic Fix," *Connecticut Medicine* 38, no. 9 (September 1974): 487–488.

129 (*and* Science) Amitai Etzioni, "Interpersonal and Structural Factors in the Study of Mental Hospitals," *Psychiatry* 23, no. 1 (February 1960): 13–22; "The Dialectics of Supranational Unification," *American Political Science Review* LVI, no. 4 (December 1962): 927–935; "European Unification: A Strategy of Change," *World Politics* XVI, no. 1 (October 1963): 32–51; "On the National Guidance of Science," *Administrative Science Quarterly* 10, no. 4 (March 1966): 466–487; "Mixed Scanning: A 'Third' Approach to Decision-Making," *Public Administration Review* 27, no. 5 (December 1967): 385–392; "Agency for Technological Development for Domestic Programs," *Science* 164 (April 4, 1969): 43–50.

129 (*even a Bert*) Richard Coughlin, "Research Note: The Spreading of Communitarianism," *Responsive Community* 9, no.3 (Summer 1999): 91–92.

130 *"who is Amitai Etzioni?"* *National Observer*, published by Dow Jones, December 16, 1968.

131 *that politicians like* "The Everything Expert," *Time*, February 17, 1975, 68.

131 *Goddamn many of them* "Etzioni's Two Voices," *National Journal* 19, no. 17 (April 25, 1987): 997.

132 *antipoverty insurance* Amitai Etzioni, "Anti-Poverty Insurance," *Challenge* 20, no. 6 (January–February 1978): 57–58; "Nursing Homes: New Rules Are Not Enough," *Washington Post*, May 25, 1975; "Beware of Rain Dancers at the Fed," *New York Times*, Viewpoint, June 28, 1998.

132 *"between 1969–1980"* John S. Robey, "Major Contributors to Public Policy Analysis," *Policy Studies Journal* 10, no. 3 (March 1982): 442–447.

Notes for Chapter Six

139 *some other superpower* Ezra F. Vogel, *Japan as Number One: Lessons for America* (Cambridge, Mass.: Harvard University Press, 1979).

141 *each generation or so* George Thomas Kurian, *Datapedia of the United States 1790–2000* (Lanham, Md.: Bernan Press, 1994).

142 *lecture at Georgia State University* The main outline was later published as "Choose We Must," in Carl A. Bramlette Jr. and Michael H. Mescon, eds., *The Individual and the Future of Organizations* (Atlanta: Franklin Foundation Lecture Series, 1980), 25–40.

142 *"economist—Amitai Etzioni"* Richard J. Levine, "The Outlook: Review of Current Trends in Business and Finance," *Wall Street Journal*, June 25, 1979.

144 *my paper on reindustrialization* Herbert W. Cheshire, "The Industrial Aid Issue Heats Up," *Business Week*, June 2, 1980, 117.

144 *revitalizing the economy* "Industries in Trouble," *Washington Star*, June 2, 1980.

144 *special issue on reindustrialization* "Revitalizing the U.S. Economy," *Business Week*, June 30, 1980.

144 *summary of the thesis* *Business Week* started its special issue with a statement suggesting that its editors developed the idea. Following a discreet inquiry, *Business Week* later acknowledged my role. In an ad in the *New York Times* (January 12, 1981), *Business Week* pointed out that after it had promoted the idea, *Forbes* "apparently overcame its initial reservations and published an article by Dr. Amitai Etzioni, who first suggested the concept."

In March 1981, in its special "American Renewal" issue, *Fortune* recognized my contribution:

> Concern about America's competitive situation is much in evidence, but it remains free floating, not attached to any particular program. The talk of "reindustrialization" reflects awareness of a problem rather than focus on a remedy. Sociologist Amitai Etzioni, who put the word into circulation a few years back, had something sensible in mind. He perceived that the U.S. had let its industrial base deteriorate relative to those competing nations, and that rebuilding would require changes in attitudes and policies. But once in circulation the word lost specific content.

146 *but to no avail* "Reindustrialization: View from the Source," *New York Times*, June 29, 1980. "Riding a Whirlwind," *Society* 19, no. 3 (March–April 1982): 29–35. "The Father of Reindustrialization Speaks," *Christian Science Monitor*, October 7, 1980.

146 *late in the election campaign* Jimmy Carter, "Economic Renewal Program, Remarks Announcing the Program," speech delivered at the White House, August 28, 1980.

147 *"We Found It—In Us"* Amitai Etzioni, "The Lack of Leadership: We Found It—In Us," *National Journal* 12, no. 8 (February 23, 1980): 333–337.

148 *"stronger attention and attack"* On November 2, 1979, in a memorandum to Stuart Eizenstat (assistant to the president for domestic affairs and policy), Ellen Goldstein (assistant director of the domestic policy staff).

149 *over to the coalition* In a memorandum to Goldstein and White I argued for a basic decision, to move away from relying on the federal government.

> The main alternative is for the federal government to serve as a catalyst for voluntary, religious, community and other private agencies and foundations, expecting that a coalition of these agencies will lead, guide, coordinate, and finance the drive.
>
> The basic concept is of the government acting as a catalyst, an indirect provider of housing and jobs, and patron of last resort—but not the lead.

150 *in a major way* Document on file.

157 *"Thanks, Hamilton"* On file.

158 *favorite social programs* Jeff Bell made a similar point speaking about the Reagan era in a talk at the Hudson Institute, April 19, 2001. He said that it was easier to curtail government by cutting taxes than by cutting government programs.

160 *fined $200,000* U.S. attorney for the western district of Michigan and Sara Lee Corporation, "Press Release: Joint Statement Regarding the Bil Mar Settlement," June 22, 2001.

160 *over $17 billion* Sara Lee Corporation, *2001 Annual Report* (Chicago: Sara Lee Corporation, 2001). Available: saralee.com/investor_relations/annuals/annual01/32_FinSummary.pdf (accessed on March 1, 2002).

160 *was fined $100 million* Department of Justice, "Press Release: Archer Daniels Midland Co. to Plead Guilty and Pay $100 Million for Role in Two International Price-Fixing Conspiracies," October 15, 1996.

161 *in the same year* Archer Daniels Midland Company, *2001 Annual Report* (Decatur, Ill.: Archer Daniels Midland Company, 2001), 38–39. The ten-year summary is available at www.admworld.com/investor/pdf/ten_yr_sum.pdf (accessed February 5, 2002).

161 *"criminals of the 1990s"* Russell Mokhiber, "Crime Wave! The Top 100 Corporate Criminals of the 1990s," *Multinational Monitor* 20, no. 7–8 (July/August 1999).

161 *measures all together* Thomas Farragher, "Law and Politics Lax, Outdate System at the Root of INS Troubles," *Boston Globe*, September 30, 2001, p. A1. Jonathan Peterson, "US–Canada Border to be Scrutinized," *Los Angeles Times*, October 3, 2001, p. A10.

Notes for Chapter Seven

168 The Majority of One   Minerva M. Etzioni, *The Majority of One: Towards a Theory of Regional Compatibility* (Beverly Hills, Calif.: Sage, 1970).

171 *(and in a cookbook)*   Joan Nathan, *The Jewish Holiday Kitchen* (New York: Schocken Books, 1979). Recipe was reprinted in the *Washington Post*, April 21, 1989.

174 *(neoclassical)*   All references in this book to economics or economists are to neoclassical ones unless otherwise indicated. The prefix *socio–*, for example, in socio-economics, indicates these are not neoclassical ones.

174 *no data at all!*   Wassily Leontiel, "Interview: Why Economics Needs Input-Output Analysis," *Challenge* (March/April 1985): 27–35.

174 *cynical a manner*   Gerald Marwell and Ruth E. Ames, "Economists Free Ride, Does Anyone Else?" *Journal of Public Economists* 15 (1981): 295–310.

177 *arguments and manuscript*   Unfortunately, although the seminar had a rapporteur, the notes of the sessions are skimpy. Hence, I am forced to rely much more on my presentations, of which I have detailed records, than on the points made by others.

178 *(the opposite is true)*   Sherry L. Murphy, "Death: Final Data for 1998," *National Vital Statistics Report* 48, no. 11 (July 2000): 5; Centers for Disease Control and Prevention.

181 *called "Rational Fools"*   Amartya Sen, "Rational Fools: A Critique of the Behavioural Foundations of Economic Theory," *Philosophy and Public Affairs* 6, no. 4 (Summer 1977): 317–344.

181 *bridging economics and sociology*   Neil J. Smelser, *Sociology of Economic Life* (Englewood Cliffs, N.J.: Prentice Hall, 1963).

181 *learned to respect*   These included Mitchell Y. Abolafia from Cornell; Paul DiMaggio, Yale; Nancy DiTomaso, Rutgers; Mark Granovetter, Stony Brook; Leslie Hannah, London School of Economics; Arjo Klamer, Iowa; and David O. Sears, UCLA..

182 *first president*   The succeeding presidents of SASE include Nancy DiTomaso (Rutgers), Daniel Yankelovich (social philosopher and pollster), William Frederick (Pittsburgh), Rogers Hollingsworth (a powerhouse from the University of Wisconsin, Madison), and my students Jerald Hage (University of Maryland) and Wolfgang Streeck (Max-Planck Institute für Gesellschaftsforschung, Köln, Germany) followed by Robin Stryker (University of Minnesota).

182 *levels of analysis*   Society for the Advancement of Socio-Economics, 1990.

182 *series of books*   Studies in socio-economics, the books and editors are as follows: Amitai Etzioni and Paul R. Lawrence, eds., *Socio-economics: Toward a New Synthesis* (Armonk, N.Y.: M. E. Sharpe, 1991); Brian Forst, ed., *The Socio-economics of Crime and Justice* (Armonk, N.Y.: M. E. Sharpe, 1993); Lloyd J. Dumas, ed., *The Socio-economics of Conversion from War to Peace* (Armonk, N.Y.: M. E. Sharpe, 1995); Richard M. Coughlin, ed., *Morality, Rationality, and Efficiency: New Perspectives on*

Socio-economics (Armonk, N.Y.: M. E. Sharpe, 1991); Pierre Guillet de Monthoux, *The Moral Philosophy of Management: From Quesnay to Keynes* (Armonk, N.Y.: M. E. Sharpe, 1993); Sven-Erik Sjöstrand, ed., *Institutional Change: Theory and Empirical Findings* (Armonk, N.Y.: M. E. Sharpe, 1993); Beat Bürgenmeier, ed., *Economy, Environment, and Technology: A Socio-economic Approach* (Armonk, N.Y.: M. E. Sharpe, 1994).

184 *Marsden and Alexander Hicks* Amitai Etzioni, J. Rogers Hollingsworth, Michael Piore, Wolfgang Streeck, and Dennis Wrong, "Critical Forum: Towards a New Socio-Economic Paradigm," *Socio-Economic Review* 1, no. 1 (2003).

Notes for Chapter Eight

185 *the Braniff case* Braniff case: Kenneth Goodpaster and David Whiteside, "Braniff Inter-national: The Ethics of Bankruptcy" (a and b), Harvard Business School case 9-985-001.

186 *when people play poker* Harold A. Pollack and Arthur Applbaum, "Reflective Commitment and Professional Practice: The Ethics of Truthfulness in Management," *Report of the Faculty Seminar on Truthfulness in Management, Harvard University*, sponsored by HBS, JFK School of Government, and the Program in Ethics and the Professions, October 24, 1990, (draft), 6.

186 *"also through deceipt"* Sissela Bok, *Lying: Moral Choice in Public and Private Life* (New York: Vintage, 1979), and *Secrets: On the Ethics of Concealment and Revelations* (New York: Pantheon, 1982), 19.

187 *"through falsehood"* Bok, *Lying*, 19.

187 *"challenging ideas"* Pollack and Applebaum, "Reflective Commitment and Professional Practice."

188 *support ethics teaching* The gift was made in 1987.

190 *actually weakens it* The Aspen Institute, Initiative for Social Innovation through Business, *Where Will They Lead? MBA Student Attitudes About Business and Society* (New York: Aspen Institute, Initiative for Social Innovation through Business, January 2002).

192 *fame, and self-interest* Amitai Etzioni, "Money, Power and Fame," *Newsweek*, September 18, 1989, 10. Chosen to represent the My Turn column for 1989 for a thirty-year retrospective in *Newsweek*, 2002.

194 *headed by Robert Bellah* Robert N. Bella, Richard Madsen, William M. Sullivan, Ann Swidler, and Steven M. Tipton, *Habits of the Heart: Individualism and Commitment in American Life* (Berkeley: University of California Press, 1985).

195 *certain kinds of liberals* Liberals, as the term is used in political theory.

Notes for Chapter Nine

199 *sat in his lap* All students' names have been changed.

201 *roles the government could play* Irving Kristol, *Neoconservatism: The Autobiography of an Idea* (New York: Free Press, 1995); Brad Miner, *The Concise Conservative*

Encyclopedia (New York: Simon and Schuster, 1996), 173; Godfrey Hodgson, *The World Turned Right Side Up* (New York: Houghton Mifflin, 1996), 133; J. Richard Piper, *Ideologies and Institutions* (Oxford: Rowman & Littlefield, 1997), 209.

201 *annals of the communitarian movement* Sarah Fergusen, "The Communitarian Manifesto," *Village Voice*, August 18, 1992. Allan Winkler, "Centre of Attention," *The Times*, April 15, 1994.

203 *mensch* A Yiddish term meaning a person having admirable characteristics, such as fortitude and firmness of purpose.

204 *The George Washington University* The meeting took place on March 14 and 15, 1990.

205 *(peddled them maintained)* The American Bankers Association took out a full-page ad in the *Washington Post* (when Congress was considering putting a cap on interest banks may charge credit card holders) that read: "Will Congress Deny Millions the Right to Keep Their Credit Cards?"

206 *describe themselves as communitarians* Daniel A. Bell, *Communitarianism and Its Critics* (Oxford: Clarendon, 1993), 4. He expands this idea in a long footnote (note 4) on page 17. Alasdair MacIntyre is also often mentioned in this context, but he himself has stressed that he does not belong. Alasdair MacIntyre, "I'm Not a Communitarian, But . . ." *Responsive Community* 1, no. 3 (Summer 1991): 91–92.

207 *matters of public concern?* The discussion of the second meeting, which took place on October 11 and 12, 1990, at The George Washington University, is based on minutes, my personal notes, articles published by several participants, and interviews with them.

212 *service the government* Abigail Goldman, "Shrugging Off Community Service," *Los Angeles Times*, May 6, 1998.

212 *after compulsory service* Williamson M. Evers, ed., *National Service: Pro and Con* (Stanford, Calif.: Hoover Institution Press, 1990).

212 *Hitler Youth* Maralee Schwartz, "Economist Calls National Service Useless, Hitlerian," *Washington Post*, September 19, 1989.

214 *"The Responsive Communitarian Platform"* For the complete text, founding endorsers, and current endorsers, see our website: www.communitariannetwork.org.

215 *(themselves of this option)* They were Benjamin R. Barber (Rutgers University; signing with exception to moral education section), Janice M. Beyer (University of Texas, Austin; signing with exception to the family section), Harvey Cox (Harvard Divinity School; signing with exception to cleaning up the polity section), David Riesman (Harvard University; signing with exception to cleaning up the polity section).

Notes for Chapter Ten

220 *Randall Kennedy* His views are summarized in a book that was published later. See Randall Kennedy, *Race, Crime, and the Law* (New York: Pantheon, 1997).

220 *Stephen Carter* Stephen L. Carter, *Reflections of an Affirmative Action Baby* (New York: Basic, 1991).

220 *William Julius Wilson* William Julius Wilson, *The Declining Significance of Race: Blacks and Changing American Institutions* (Chicago: University of Chicago Press, 1980); William Julius Wilson, *The Truly Disadvantaged: The Inner City, the Underclass, and Public Policy* (Chicago: University of Chicago Press, Paperback Reprint edition, 1990).

220 *"literature, and art"* From the Cosmos Club homepage, www.cosmos-club. org (accessed April 5, 2002).

221 *"mere luncheon group"* Benjamin Weiser, "Proposal to Admit Women Is Agitating Cosmos Club," *Washington Post*, November 15, 1980.

221 *a "men's club"* "Clubs; Single Sex, Double Standard; American Survey," *The Economist*, April 6, 1985, 36.

221 "in the seventh century" "Cosmos Club Muzzles Members," *Washington Woman*, 9. Document on file.

225 *respective disciplines and beyond* These included, from economics, Albert O. Hirschman (Institute for Advanced Study at Princeton University) and Isabel Sawhill (the Urban Institute); from law, John C. Coffee (Columbia University), Carol Tucker Foreman (partner, Foreman & Heidepriem), and Elliot L. Richardson (former attorney general of the United States); from business schools, Thomas Donaldson (Georgetown University) and Thomas W. Dunfee (Wharton School); from divinity schools, Jean Bethke Elshtain (Vanderbilt University) and Harvey Cox (a liberal Protestant theologian from Harvard University); from sociology, David Riesman (Harvard); and two university presidents: George Rupp (at the time, president, Rice University; later Columbia University) and Joseph Duffey (then president of the American University, and later the head of the United States Information Agency). Affiliations are those at the time of signing.

228 *without misgivings* Richard Neuhaus, "The Communities Missing from 'Communitarianism,'" *First Things* (February 1994): 55–56.

228 *pattern in American life* Neuhaus, "Communities Missing from 'Communitarianism,'" 55–56.

230 *alarmed me* Daniel Kemmis, *Community and the Politics of Place* (Norman: University of Oklahoma Press, 1990).

232 *in the Washington Post* Raspberry was invited on May 16, 1990.

232 *first editorial board* The members of the first editorial board of *The Responsive Community* were Benjamin Barber, Robert Goodin, and Terry Pinkard, while some were new, including John Coffee, Anthony Cook, Jean Bethke Elshtain, John Gardner, Nathan Glazer, Jane Mansbridge, Irene Nagel, Martha Nussbaum, and Daniel Yankelovich.

233 *(of one of my books)* Amitai Etzioni, *The New Golden Rule: Community and Morality in a Democratic Society* (New York: Basic, 1997).

237 *"restored communities . . . "* Amitai Etzioni, *The Spirit of Community: Rights, Responsibilities and the Communitarian Agenda* (New York: Crown, 1993), 1–20.

238 *speak up at all* Amitai Etzioni, "Studying the Moral Voice," *Public Perspective* 8, no. 1 (December–January 1997): 67–68.

242 *be its victims*   Cited by Dorothy Rabinowitz at the Cato Institute, May 16, 2001. See also John Leo, *Incorrect Thoughts: Notes on Our Wayward Culture* (New Brunswick, N.J.: Transaction, 2000). On the rules, see especially Jeffrey Rosen, *The Unwanted Gaze: The Destruction of Privacy in America* (New York: Random House, 2000).

243 *issued over the years*   For a complete list, see our website: www.communitarian-network.org.

243 *consensus was formed*   Its members included Don Browning (University of Chicago), William D'Antonio (Catholic University), Margaret Pruitt Clark (Advocates for Youth), Neil Gilbert (UC Berkeley), Helen Leibowitz, Luigi Mastroianni (University of Pennsylvania Medical Center), David Meyers (Hope College), David Popenoe (Rutgers University), Isabel Sawhill (The Urban Institute) and myself.

244 *origins and links*   *Education for Interpersonal Relations, Family Life and Intimacy* (Washington, D.C.: The Communitarian Network), available at www.gwu.edu/~ccps/Intimacy.html (accessed October 10, 2002).

244 Tikkun, *among others*   Amitai Etzioni, "Education for Intimacy," *Tikkun* 12, no. 2 (March/April 1997): 38–42; Amitai Etzioni, "Education for Intimacy," *Educational Leadership* 54, no. 8 (May 1997): 20–23.

244 *lively dialogue*   Intellectual Capital went out of business; however, the article may still be accessed at speakout.com/activism/opinions/4301-1.html (accessed April 8, 2002).

244 *"our mature identity"*   William Raspberry, "Putting Families First," *Washington Post*, November 30, 1992.

244 *approaches to welfare reform*   Meeting on July 16, 1993. Letter from Sawhill on July 27, 1993.

Notes for Chapter Eleven

249 *carried a full-page story*   Elizabeth Ehrlich, "Your Rights vs. My Safety: Where Do We Draw the Line?" *Business Week*, September 3, 1990, 56.

250 *news stories*   Spencer Rich, "Balancing Community and Individual Rights: New Journal to Examine Ethical Issues," *Washington Post*, December 25, 1990. See also notes 8–12.

250 *restoring-the-moral-foundations theme*   John Leo, "The Lingo of Entitlement," *U.S. News & World Report*, October 14, 1991, 22.

250 *"laws based on connectedness"*   Leo, "Lingo of Entitlement," 22.

250 New York Magazine   John Taylor, "Don't Blame Me: The New Culture of Victimization," *New York Magazine*, June 3, 1991, 26–34.

250 *Michael Kramer*   Michael Kramer, "Who Owes What to Whom," *Time*, October 14, 1991, 32.

250 *Howard Fineman*   Howard Fineman, "Tough Love from the Democrats," *Newsweek*, December 23, 1991, 32.

250 National Journal   James A. Barnes, "The New Guru of Communitarianism," *National Journal*, November 30, 1991, 2931.

250 Star Tribune *of Minneapolis*   Cliff Haas, "New Political Group Asks: What's in It for the Community?" *Minneapolis Star Tribune*, November 19, 1991.

251 *oft-used one*   Richard Coughlin, "Research Note: The Spreading of Communitarianism," *Responsive Community* 9, no. 3 (Summer 1999): 91–92.

251 *third body of thought*   Robert Wright, "The False Politics of Values," *Time*, September 9, 1996, 42–45.

251 *"guru" of the new communitarian movement*   For instance, Tony Mauro, "'Communitarians' Want to Share the Stage," *USA Today*, November 18, 1992, A4; and Martin Walker, "Community Spirit," *The Guardian* (London), March 13, 1995, T10.

251 *"godfather" of the new communitarian movement*   Barnes, "New Guru," 2931.

251 Los Angeles Times   Michael D'Antonio, "Tough Medicine for a Sick America." *Los Angeles Times Magazine*, March 22, 1992, 32–35.

252 *"solve social problems"*   Elizabeth Ehrlich, "Your Rights vs. My Safety: Where Do We Draw the Line?" *Business Week*, September 3, 1990, 56.

252 Wall Street Journal   Amitai Etzioni, "A New Community of Thinkers, Both Liberal and Conservative," *Wall Street Journal*, October 8, 1991.

252 Washington Post   Amitai Etzioni, "The New Rugged Communitarianism: Maybe Americans Are Just Too Free," *Washington Post*, January 20, 1991.

252 *who needs it?*   Ira Glasser, "Mushy Thinking on Individual Rights," letter to the editor, *Wall Street Journal*, November 1, 1991.

253 *proper or abhorent*   Amitai Etzioni, *The Spirit of Community* (New York: Crown, 1993), 47.

253 *ACLU would protest*   For example, Ann Beeson and Chris Hansen, "Frontal Prudery in the Library," letter to the editor, *Wall Street Journal*, October 22, 1998.

254 *system to the core*   Amitai Etzioni, *Capital Corruption: The New Attack on American Democracy* (New York: Harcourt Brace Jovanovich, 1984).

254 *basic constitutional rights*   Show with Garrick Utley.

254 *"underlying structural problems"*   Sarah Ferguson, "The Communitarian Manifesto," *Village Voice*, August 15, 1992.

255 *New York Communists*   Amitai Etzioni, "Righting a Wrong," letter to *Village Voice*, September 22, 1992.

256 *"many of my views"*   Letter dated November 20, 1991.

256 *"to our countrymen"*   Letter dated August 5, 1993.

256 *"on to something"*   Thomas A. Shannon, "The Communitarian Network: A New Force in Character Education," *School Board News*, August 16, 1994, 2.

257 *responsibilities and obligations*   Paul Taylor, "An Agenda Focused Less on Rights, More on Responsibility" *Washington Post*, November 19, 1991.

260 *during the campaign*   Letter from Dave McCurdy, August 23, 1993.

260 *"credo of the Communitarians"*   Sarah Ferguson, "Communitarian Manifesto," *Village Voice*, August 15, 1992.

260 *similar reports*   Margaret Carlson and James Carney, "That's What Drives Me Nuts," *Time*, December 13, 1993. Kenneth T. Walsh, "Clinton's Journey Inward: He Seeks Answers to the Nation's Spiritual Crisis as Part of His Own Quest," *U.S. News*

& World Report, December 13, 1993, 40–41, 44. Martin Walker, "Community Spirit," *The Guardian,* March 13, 1995.

261 *mid-March 1994*   March 19, 1994.

267 *"intelligent people"*   Remarks by the president at Character Education Conference, May 20, 1995, released by the Office of the Press Secretary, the White House.

268 *(faith-in-faith position)*   Amitai Etzioni, "The Politics of Morality," *Wall Street Journal,* November 13, 1995.

268 *(praising President Clinton)*   William J. Bennett, *Responsive Community* 9, no. 1 (Winter 1998/99): 7.

Notes for Chapter Twelve

269 *Senator Robert Dole*   Meeting with Senator Dole, May 8, 1995.

272 *also wary*   Dinner, May 2, 1995.

274 *to the first one*   Participants included Ron Brown, George Stephanopoulos, Bruce Reed, Dan Baer, Michael Waldman, Benjamin Barber, Amy Gutmann, Robert Putnam, Randall Kennedy, William A. Galston, Jane Mansbridge, Henry Louis Gates Jr., Alan Ehrenhalt, and Elijah Anderson.

276 *(which I direct)*   "First Lady Speaks Out for Character Education at White House Conference," *Ethics Today* 1, no. 2 (Summer 1996): 1.

278 *(it read just fine)*   Dan Coats, "When Redistribution and Economic Growth Fail," *Responsive Community* 6, no. 1 (Winter 1995/96): 4–8.

279 *common purposes as Americans*   Joe Lieberman, "Vision for America: A Place for Faith," *Responsive Community* 11, no. 1 (Winter 2000/01): 41–48. Excerpt from a speech Lieberman delivered at Notre Dame University on October 24, 2000.

279 *months each year*   These include the following: Methods for Building Self-Discipline, chairs Shelley Berman and David Sluyter; Methods for Building Empathy, chair Diane Berreth; The Role of Civic Education, chair Charles Quigley; The Role of Family Involvement, chair Roberta Doering; Education for Human Relations, Family Life, and Intimacy, chair Amitai Etzioni; Building Character through Sports, chair Jeff Blatnick; Community Schools, chair Gaynor McCown; and New Americans— The Road to Citizenship, chair Jennifer Howse. See the Communitarian Network website: www.communitariannetwork.org.

284 *stated as much publicly*   Public speech, March 16, 1999.

286 *willing to do so again*   Letter from Donald Baer, director of speechwriting, to Amitai Etzioni, January 4, 1995.

287 *trust and cooperation*   William J. Clinton, "State of the Union: The President's Address: 'We Heard America Shouting,'" *New York Times,* January 25, 1995.

288 *"baseball would be fun"*   Ezra Moses Galston, *Responsive Community* 5, no. 3 (Summer 1995): 12.

289 *"get to know each other" session*   November 5, 1997.

290 *("Group in Bounds")*   Amitai Etzioni, "Gossip Keeps the Group in Bounds," *Newsday,* May 17, 1999.

291 *White House, in 1997* The *George Washington University, June 12, 1997*.

293 *ultra-individualism* Address of Vice President Albert Gore Jr. to the Communitarian Network's White House Conference on Character Education, June 12, 1997.

293 *how to rise in life* Georgie Anne Geyer, "George W. Bush: Media Attention Is Well Deserved," *Uexpress Online*, June 1999 (article no longer accessible online).

294 *"solidarity"* E. J. Dionne Jr., "A New Wind Blowing," *Washington Post*, August 3, 1999.

294 *"change hearts"* Hanna Rosin, "Wooing the Right with Personal Faith, Not Policy," *Washington Post*, June 2, 1999.

294 *confirmed by the Senate* Laurie Goodstein, "Ashcroft's Life and Judgments Are Steeped in Faith," *New York Times*, January 14, 2001.

294 *and the market* Bill Bradley, "Beyond the Economy: Cultural Priorities," *Responsive Community* 5, no. 2 (Spring 1995): 4–10. See also Bill Bradley, "Rebuilding Urban Communities," *Responsive Community* 3, no. 4 (Fall 1993): 12–21.

295 *marriage penalty* Dana Milbank, "Needed: Catchword for Bush Ideology," *Washington Post*, February 1, 2001.

Notes for Chapter Thirteen

298 *elegant Fluela restaurant* Dinner took place Monday, January 25, 1999.

298 *the occasional "yeah!"* Nametags in Davos are much smaller than those people hang around their collars during Renaissance Weekends. I had a hard time telling who was saying what. But those in attendance included Lawrence Minard, the editor of *Forbes*; William M. Drozdiak from the *Washington Post*; Michael Elliot from *Newsweek*; Richard Hornik of *Time* in the United Kingdom; and Hilary Bowker, a communications strategy adviser from the United Kingdom.

300 *expectations, and behavior* David Lamb, *Death, Brain Death, and Ethics* (London: Cromm Helm, 1985), 4.

300 *"moral qualms about it"* Roger Rosenblatt, *Life Itself: Abortion in the American Mind* (New York: Random House, 1992).

301 *"grew much more hostile"* E-mail from Deborah Tannen, December 12, 2000.

303 *(Reader's Digest)* Rachel Wildarsky, "What's Behind Success in School?" *Reader's Digest* 145, no. 870 (October 1994): 49.

304 *he replied* Peter Steinfels, "A Political Movement Blends Its Ideas from Left and Right," *New York Times*, May 24, 1992.

306 *position on diversity* William Raspberry, "Between Assimilation and Tribalism," *Washington Post*, December 8, 1995.

306 *"This Country Moving Again"* David R. Boldt, "An Ideology That Could Get This Country Moving Again," *Philadelphia Inquirer*, May 24, 1992.

306 *(Byron P. White)* Byron P. White, "Communitarians Are Middle-of-the-Road—and Proud of It," *Cincinnati Post*, May 29, 1992.

306 *"What's Left?"* Michael Elliott, "What's Left?" *Newsweek International*, October 10, 1994, 12–17.

307 *"jyne up"* Matthew Melton, "The Communitarians," *Focus* (Fall/Winter 1992): 20.

308 *viewpoints to our table* Max Frankel, *The Times of My Life and My Life with The Times* (Random House: New York, 1999), 386.

309 *(to 1,005)* Richard Coughlin, "Research Note: The Spreading of Communitarianism," *Responsive Community* 9, no. 3 (Summer 1999): 91–92.

309 *sharply thereafter* Coughlin, "Research Note," 91–92.

309 *"rejection of secularism"* Michael Taves, "Roundtable on Communitarianism," *Telos* 76 (Summer 1988): 7–8.

310 *"religiously committed"* Michael S. Joyce, "The New Impulse toward Self-Government," *Wall Street Journal*, April 19, 1993.

310 *"nothing else will matter"* Fred Barnes, "God, Gary and the GOP," *Weekly Standard*, May 24, 1999, 13ff. (Bauer and I had crossed swords when he was working for the U.S. Department of Education during the Reagan administration. Bauer had prepared a report that showed an enormous wave of violence in the public schools. I pointed out that he listed every item stolen *or* lost—valued at more than a dollar—as violent crimes and that such "crimes" made up for most of his statistics.) Report was completed in January 1984.

310 *man to man* Charles J. Sykes, "Liberal Angst," *World & I* (August 1993): 309–313.

310 *national service* Brandy Dutcher, "Communitarians and the Christian Right," *Focus* (Fall/Winter 1992): 20.

310 *"attractive alternative"* Mark Pattison, "A Secular Form of Catholic Social Teaching?" *Viewpoint*, May 13, 1993, 14.

311 *a Nazi* "Freedom and Community: The Politics of Restoration." *Economist*, December 24, 1994, 33.

311 *a police state* Amitai Etzioni, letter to the editor, *Economist*, January 21, 1995, 8.

312 *we were popularizers* Daniel Bell, "The Cultural Wars: American Intellectual Life, 1965–1992," *Wilson Quarterly* 16 (Summer 1992): 94.

312 *said it very well* Amitai Etzioni, "Review: Daniel Bell, 'The Coming of Post-Industrial Society: A Venture in Social Forecasting,'" *Contemporary Sociology* 3, no. 2 (March 1974): 105–107.

312 *holier than thou* Bell wrote on this point: "At one point, Jacques Barzun, then the provost, asked me if I had a Ph.D. I said no. He asked whether I had written any books. I said, three. In any event, I was *given* a Ph.D. for *The End of Ideology*" (letter, March 15, 2000; italics in original). The book is not an academic work and was not an original piece of research conducted for the degree, as Columbia University requires.

312 *writing in Dissent* Steven Lukes, "The Responsive Community," *Dissent* (Spring 1998): 87–89. Others include Stephen Gibb, "The Usefulness of Theory: A Case Study in Evaluating Formal Mentoring Schemes," *Human Relations* 52, no. 8 (August 1999): 1055–1075.

313 *"attacks on civil liberties"* Simson Garfinkel, *Database Nation* (Sebastopol, Calif.: O'Reilly, 2000), 239.

313 *the person sent* John Markoff, "Microsoft Will Alter Its Software in Response to Privacy Concerns," *New York Times*, March 7, 1999.

314 *surprisingly well received* Rita Thaemert, "The Limits of Privacy," *State Legislatures* (April 2000); Jonathan Kirsch, "Privacy as Privilege," *New York Review of Books*, June 10, 1999.

314 *"valuable and informative"* Vernon Ford, "The Limits of Privacy," *The Booklist*, March 1, 1999.

314 *all that is benign* Jean Bethke Elshtain, "When Privacy Goes Too Far;" *Times Literary Supplement*, September 24, 1999, 4.

314 *"fair and objective"* Scott Sundby, "The Limits of Privacy," *Annals of the American Academy of Political and Social Science* (July 2000): 202–203.

314 *similarly favorable* John Schwartz, "A Middle Ground in the Privacy War?" *Washington Post*, March 29, 1999.

314 Boston Globe Amitai Etzioni, "Privacy on the Internet? Don't Count on It," *Boston Globe*, March 29, 1999; New York Times Amitai Etzioni, "Privacy Isn't Dead Yet," *New York Times*, April 6, 1999; Financial Times Amitai Etzioni, "Protecting Privacy: Personal View of Amitai Etzioni," *Financial Times*, April 9, 1999, 18.

314 *Others followed* Amitai Etzioni, "Medical Records: Enhancing Privacy, Preserving the Common Good," *Hastings Center Report* (March/April 1999): 14–23; *Book and Culture* and even the *American Banker* ran page-long interviews about the book. *Governing* ran an editorial calling my position "courageous." C-SPAN taped my discussion of the book before the Divinity School of the University of Chicago. And there was a flurry of local press, radio, and TV interviews.

315 *(our current ideals)* Amitai Etzioni, "The Monochrome Society," *Public Interest*, no. 137 (Fall 1999): 42–55. It later became the lead essay of my collection of essays, *The Monochrome Society* (Princeton: Princeton University Press, 2001).

315 *"takes much longer"* Anne Fadiman, personal correspondence to Amitai Etzioni, April 8, 1999.

Notes for Chapter Fourteen

320 *Quite a feat* Amitai Etzioni, "Nation in Need of Community Values," *Times* (London), February 20, 1995; "High-Tech Bonds," *Times* (London), March 13, 1995; and "The High Ground," *Times* (London), March 15, 1995.

320 *"beyond the Welfare State"* Melanie Phillips, "Father of Tony Blair's Big Idea," *Observer* (London), July 24, 1994.

321 *"ethical basis for community"* Phillips, "Father of Tony Blair's Big Idea." See also, especially regarding Brown, Jonathan Steele, "Clinton Policies Are Caught in Communitarian Crossfire," *Guardian*, April 12, 1995.

321 *(biographer of Bill Clinton)* Martin Walker, *The President We Deserve: Bill Clinton; His Rise, Falls and Comebacks* (New York: Crown, 1996).

321 *"social policy"* Martin Walker, "Community Spirit," *Guardian*, March 13, 1995.

321 *"keeps in constant contact"* "The Man with the Big Idea," *Sunday Times*, October 9, 1994.

322 *"cheer each other on"* Sarah Baxter, "I Am the Way and I Am the Truth," *Sunday Times*, March 19, 1995.

325 *On the contrary* See, for instance, Martin Walker, "The Third Way," *Europe*, no. 400 (October 2000): 14–17; and Emma Heron, "Etzioni's Spirit of Communitarianism: Community Values and Welfare Realities in Blair's Britain," in *Social Policy Review 13: Developments and Debates: 2000–2001*, ed. Robert Sykes, Catherine Bochel, and Nick Ellison (Bristol: Policy Press, 2001).

325 *"thoroughly interventionist"* Marc Champion, "Tony Blair's Vision of the U.K.'s Role May Be Hard to Fill—Midsize Nation's Influence May Not Be Sufficient—and at Home, Hospitals and Railroads Crumble," *Wall Street Journal Europe*, January 9, 2002.

325 *industry or service* Stephen Castle and Paul Routledge, "Killing the Clause," *Independent*, October 9, 1994.

326 *("mad" to take it on)* Donald MacIntyre, "Prescott's Loyalty the Key to Leader's Decision; Prescott's Loyalty Key to Blair's Triumph; Defining Moment," *Independent*, March 14, 1995.

326 *"tolerance and respect"* "The Labour Party's New Aims and Values," *Times* (London), March 14, 1995.

326 *"'me-first' era"* Baxter, "I Am the Way."

328 *position as junior whip* Robert Shrimsley, "Members Emerge from Affair with Loss of Honour Willetts Resignation: MPs Will Be Forced to Give Evidence under Oath after Privileges Inquiry Disbelieves Minister," *Daily Telegraph*, December 12, 1996.

328 *familiar with them* Jonathan Sacks, *Crisis and Covenant: Jewish Thought after the Holocaust* (Manchester, N.Y.: Manchester University Press, 1992). Jonathan Sacks, *One People? Tradition, Modernity, and Jewish Unity* (London: Littman Library of Jewish Civilization, 1993).

329 *14 times* "Down with Rights," *Economist*, March 18, 1995, 59.

329 *essays on communitarianism* Amitai Etzioni, "Just a Social Crowd of Folk," *Guardian*, February 18, 1995.

329 *in one issue* Geoff Mulgan and Charles Leadbetter, "Ideas for Our Times," *Independent*, November 29, 1995.

329 *"Prophets of the 21st Century"* Matthew Sweet, "Prophets of the 21st Century," *Independent*, December 22, 1996.

329 *New Statesman* Paul Anderson and Kevin Davey, "Import Duties," *New Statesman & Society*, March 3, 1995, 18–20; Ray Pahl, "Friendly Society," *New Statesman & Society*, March 10, 1995, 20–22.

329 *respond extensively* Amitai Etzioni, "Common Values," *New Statesman & Society*, May 12, 1995, 24–25.

329 *space to communitarianism* Tony Wright, review of *The Spirit of Community*, by Amitai Etzioni, *New Statesman & Society*, November 3, 1995, 34–35.

329 *London School of Economics* John Gray, "Hollowing Out the Core," *Guardian*, March 8, 1995.

329 *(two years later)* John Gray, *Enlightenment's Wake: Politics and Culture at the Close of the Modern Age* (England: Methuen Drama, 1997).

329 *"in need of an idea"* Norman Stone, "A Mad Scramble for Centre," *Times* (London), October 9, 1994.

329 *"mode of governance"* Stone, "Mad Scramble."

329 *other than Mussolini* Stone, "Mad Scramble."

330 *"individuals within it"* Both statements are quoted in Elizabeth Frazer, *The Problems of Communitarian Politics: Unity and Conflict* (Oxford: Oxford University Press, 1999), 36, 41.

330 *openly communitarian themes* Frazer, *Problems of Communitarian Politics.*

330 *"community behind you"* Elizabeth Frazer, *The Problem of Communitarian Politics* (Oxford: Oxford University Press, 1999), 41.

330 *individual responsibility* Emma Heron and Peter Dwyer, "Doing the Right Thing: Labour's Attempt to Forge a New Welfare Deal between the Individual and the State," *Social Policy & Administration* 33, no. 1 (March 1999): 91–104. See also Mike Bottery, "Getting the Balance Right: Duty as a Core Ethic in the Life of the School," *Oxford Review of Education* 25, no. 3 (September 1999): 369–386.

331 *a dilemma* September 8–13, 1992.

335 *translated into German* The Spirit of Community: *Die Entdeckung des Gemein-Wesens* (Stuttgart, Germany: Schaffer Poeschel, 1995); paperback (Stuttgart, Germany: Schaffer Poeschel, 1998). The New Golden Rule: *Die Verantwortungsgesellschaft* (Frankfurt, Germany: Campus Verlag, 1997). The Moral Dimension: *Jenseits des Egoismus-Prinzips* (Stuttgart, Germany: Schaffer Poeschel, 1994).

337 *Geneva in July 1996* Took place July 12–14, 1996.

338 *"meet in the middle"* Rudolf Scharping, "Freedom, Solidarity, Individual Responsibility: Reflections on the Relationship between Politics, Money, and Morality," *Responsive Community* 6, no. 4 (Fall 1996): 51–58.

339 *dedicated to its discussion* Rudolf Scharping, "Von den Kommunitariern lernen," *Die Zeit*, September 22, 1995, 33.

339 *German parliament* Testimony before the German Bundestag on "A Communitarian Approach to the Welfare State," Bundeshaus, Bonn, Germany, October 7, 1996.

339 *position as authoritarian* Sibylle Tönnies, "Gemeinschaft von oben," *Frankfurter Allgemeine Zeitung*, December 30, 1994, 27.

340 *an improvement of sorts* Sebastian Berger, "Ein amerikanischer Traum," *Süddeutsche Zeitung*, January 4, 1999, 14.

340 *ideas extensively* Amitai Etzioni, "Kein besser Land," *Frankfurter Allgemeine Zeitung*, February 3, 1998; Hans Vorlander, "Dritter Weg und Kommunitarismus," *Aus Politik und Zeitgeschichte*, no. 16–17 (April 2001): 16–23.

340 *platform in German*   "Die Stimme der Gemeinschaft hörber machen," *Frankfurter Allgemeine Zeitung*, March 8, 1994, 37.

340 *Der Spiegel*   Michael Schmidt-Kligenberg and Sylvia Schreiber, "Hart im Sinkflug," *Der Spiegel* (October 1996): 88–92.

340 *Die Woche also helped*   Marion Rollin, "Mehr Mut zur Moral," *Die Woche*, September 12, 1997, 40–41.

340 *attracted to our cause*   For an essay explaining why German scholars were more reluctant than Americans to become communitarians, see Hans Joas, "Communitarianism in Germany," *Responsive Community* 5, no. 1 (Winter 1994/1995): 24–29.

343 *about their agendas*   Tony Blair and Gerhard Schröder, *Europe: The Third Way/ Die Neue Mitte*, Joint Declaration, London, June 8, 1999, at www.eurozoneadvisors. com/reports4/schroeder-blair0609.pdf (accessed April 12, 2002).

Notes for Chapter Fifteen

347 *academic journals*   Jean François Dortier and Martha Zuber, "Comment reconstruire la société?" *Sciences Humaines* (January 2001): 38–41. Gilles Delafon, "L'homme qui a inspiré Blair," *Le Journal du Dimanche*, May 11, 1997. Amitai Etzioni, "Faut-il réinventer le pilori?" *Courrier International*, August 21, 1997, 27. Jean-Francois Duval, "Les communautaristes partent en guerre a Geneve," *Construire*, June 5, 1996, 4–5. Jean Francois Duval, "Apres la gauche, la droite, le communautarisme/Amitai Etzioni, un gourou qui vous veut du bien," *Construire*, February 22, 1995, 36–40. Bruno Giussani, "Interview Exclusive D'Amitai Etzioni: 'Notre societe est devenue irresponsable,'" *L'Hebdo*, November 17, 1994, 13–15. François d'Alançon, "Les Nouveaux Pioniers de L'Esprit de Communauté," *La Croix Forum*, December 19, 1994.

347 *communitarian thinking*   "Solidarieta si, ideologie no," *Il messaggero Domenica*, February 20, 1994.

347 *lecture in February 1996*   Lecture, "The Responsive Community: Shared Values Balancing the Individual and the Common Good," Club de Debate, Complutense University, Madrid, Spain, February 1, 1996.

347 *became our champion*   José Pérez Adán, "A Spanish Perspective on Communitarianism," *Responsive Community* 9, no. 1 (Winter 1998/99): 83–86.

347 *Spanish communitarian network*   José Pérez Adán, "Comunitarismo, moralidad política y la crítica al neoaristotelismo emergente," *Sistema 142* (January 1998); José Pérez Adán, "El Communitarismo: Una Apuesta por la Esperanza Colectiva," *Temas Para El Debate*, October 9, 1995; José Pérez Adán, ed., *Las Terceras Vias* (Madrid: Ediciones Internacionales Universitarias, 2001). Includes a chapter by Adán, "Etzioni Y Giddens Frente A Frente," 235–264.

347 *translated into Spanish*   *The Spirit of Community* was reprinted in part in *Communitat i nacio*, chap. 2, "Nosaltres els communitaristes (Barcelona: Centre d'Estudis de Temes Contemporanis, 1995), 77–89. *The New Golden Rule* was translated as *La Nueva Regla De Oro: Comunidad Y Moralidad en una Sociedad Democrática*, trans.

Marco Aurelio Galmarini Rodríguez (Barcelona: Paidós, 1999). *The Active Society* was translated as *La Sociedad Activa*, trans. Eloy Fuente Herrero (Madrid: Aguilar, 1980).

349 *was relatively jealous* Ha'aretz, September 22, 1995; Ha'aretz, June 29, 1995; Jonathon Rosenblum, "With the Best of Intentions," *Jerusalem Post*, January 28, 2000.

351 *an accounting of history* Amitai Etzioni and Shibley Telhami, "Mideast: Focus on the Possible," *Christian Science Monitor*, June 17, 2002, 9.

351 *list of what is "hot"* Chaim Handorker, "Let Us Be Friends," *Ha'aretz*, September 22, 1995, 33 (in Hebrew). Akiva Eldar, "The Theory of Relativity by Amitai Etzioni," no source (in Hebrew).

352 *European Forum in 1998* Seminar given with Professor Dr. Viktor Vanberg of Universität Freiburg.

352 *"another form of collectivism"* Václav Klaus, "Communitarianism: A Medicine Worse Than the Disease?" *Responsive Community* 10, no. 2 (Spring 2000): 66–70.

352 *"according to their dreams"* Klaus, "Communitarianism," 69.

352 *New York Times put it* Ian Fisher, "Czech Voters Block Return of Center-Right Ex-Leader," *New York Times*, June 16, 2002.

352 *and "eternal" force* Václav Havel, "Beyond the Nation-State," *Responsive Community* 9, no. 3 (Summer 1999): 26–33.

352 *expand on them* We found some support in another former communist country, in Rumania. See Doina Balahur, "New International Political Trends. Communitarianism: A Self-Introduction," *Sociologie-Politologie* (1998–1999): Tomul II–III, 12–20.

355 *the Swiss* "Kommunitarismus—Antworten auf die Sinnkrise der neunziger Jahre?" *Tages-Anzeiger*, December 6, 1994; "Die Schalmeienklange des Kommunitarismus," *Neue Zurcher Zeitung*, April 15–16, 1995.

355 *what the book had to say* Stephan Wehowsky, "Kommunitaristisches Gleichgewicht," *Neue Züricher Zeitung*, October 14, 1997.

355 *had previously fashioned* Stephan Wehowsky, ". . . sich über Werte miteinander verbinden," *Neue Zürcher Zeitung*, November 23, 1997.

356 *opened up to the communitarian message* Babette Karner, "Eine Bewegung wider den Egoismus," *Die Presse*, October 31, 1997; Christoph Winder, "Klare Diagnosen, Unklare Therapie," *Der Standard*, November 14, 1997; Alfred Pfabigan, "Ich—und der Staat?" *Die Presse*, December 28, 1997; Klaus Taschwer, "Weniger Staat, weniger privat," *Falter* 47/97, 1997.

356 *densest lectures ever* The lecture was published in German as *Martin Buber und die kommunitarische Idee* (Vienna: Picus Verlag, 1999) and in English as "Communitarian Elements in Select Works of Martin Buber," *Journal of Value Inquiry* 33 (July 1999): 151–169.

357 *as far as we got* Goran Rosenberg, "Dygd i Historisk korsled," Swedish *Dagens Nyheter*, October 25, 1993; "Fran stat till samhalle," *Moderna Tider* (April 1995).

357 *natural communitarians* *Handelsblad*/Dutch newspaper, September 1995.

357 *"been there, done that"* Teksti Sirkku Hellsten and Nina Porra, "Amitai Etzioni: Kansalaishyveiden matkasaarnaaja," *Suomen Kuvalehti*, August 21, 1998, 33; Annikka Mutanen, "Vastalause yltioyksilollisyydelle," *Helsingin Sanomat*, August 25, 1998.

358 *leaders of the liberal party* The host was Fritz Bolkestein, later an EU commissioner. The moderator and organizer was a Dutch journalist, the editor of the journal *Ode*.

359 *("an academic saint")* Comments at Princeton's Nassau Inn, December 4, 2000.

359 *gave us voice* William Pol, "The Spirit of Community: The Reinvention of American Society," *Plan Canada* (January 1995): 44; Murray Campbell, "Movement Seeks Redefinition of Values," *Toronto Globe and Mail*, January 17, 1994; "Book Excerpt," *Ottawa Citizen*, October 2, 2000; Leonard Remis, "Spirit of Community Sought," *Winnipeg Free Press*, November 12, 1993; Thomas Scoville, "Q&A Cyberselfish Generation," *Ottawa Citizen*, October 2, 2000; Jeffrey Kuhner, "Simpson Seeks Lessons in Southward Migration," *(Montreal) Gazette*, August 26, 2000.

359 *trying to heal natural* Richard Gwyn, "'Value of the Family' a Fresh Slant on Morality," *Toronto Star*, December 13, 1992, p. B3.

360 *this way of thinking* Walter Goodman, "Review/Television; About Canada, 5 Programs' Worth," *New York Times*, January 22, 1992. Leonard Remis, "Spirit of Community Sought," *Winnipeg Free Press*, November 12, 1993, p. A7; Campbell, "Movement Seeks Redefinition," p. A1. "Communitarianism," *Politics Monitor* 1, no. 1 (November 1992): 11–13.

362 *along these lines* The meeting took place on November 1–2, 2001. Participants included, among others, Goran Bexell (Lund University, Sweden), Lord Bhiku Parekh (United Kingdom), Han Entzinger (University of Utrecht, the Netherlands), Silvio Ferrari (University of Milan, Italy), Noah Pickus (Institute for Emerging Issues, United States), Philip Selznick (University of California, Berkeley, United States), and Sophie van Bijsterveld (Catholic University Brabant, the Netherlands).

362 *unity position* To read the Diversity within Unity position paper and see the list of endorsers, see our website at www.gwu.edu/~ccps/diversity_within_unity.html (accessed December 18, 2002).

Notes for Chapter Sixteen

368 Society *to the* National Review Amitai Etzioni, "Lock Up Your TV Set," *National Review*, October 18, 1993, 50–54; Amitai Etzioni, "Some Diversity," *Society* (July/August 1998): 59–61.

368 *and a quarterly* Amitai Etzioni, *Rights and the Common Good: The Communitarian Perspective* (New York: St. Martin's, 1995); Amitai Etzioni, *New Communitarian Thinking: Persons, Virtues, Institutions and Communities* (Charlottesville: University of Virginia Press, 1995); and Amitai Etzioni, *The Essential Communitarian Reader* (Lanham, Md.: Rowman & Littlefield, 1998). *The Responsive Community: Rights and Responsibilities*, a communitarian quarterly.

368 *position papers* For a list of our position papers, see our website at www.gwu.edu/~ccps/catel.html (accessed October 16, 2002).

368 *carried our message repeatedly* Richard Coughlin, "Research Note: The Spreading of Communitarianism," *Responsive Community* 9, no. 3 (Summer 1999): 91–92.

368 *a communitarian way* See, for instance, Robert Wright, "The False Politics of Values," *Time*, September 9, 1996, 42–45.

371 *marriage penalty in the tax code* C. Eugene Steuerle, *A Comprehensive Approach to Removing Marriage Penalties* (Washington, D.C.: The Communitarian Network, 1999), at www.gwu.edu/~ccps/pop_marpen.html (accessed October 16, 2002).

372 *(George Kelling)* George Kelling, *Fixing Broken Windows: Restoring Order and Reducing Crime in Our Communities* (New York: Free Press, 1996); Suzanne Goldsmith, *The Takoma Orange Hats: Fighting Drugs and Building Community in Washington, D.C.* (Washington, D.C.: The Communitarian Network, 1994); Amitai Etzioni, "How Our Towns Fight Crime," *Wall Street Journal*, December 31, 1993.

372 *following British and Canadian policies* Amitai Etzioni and Steven Helland, *The Case for Domestic Disarmament* (Washington, D.C.: The Communitarian Network, 1992). Brannon P. Denning and Glenn Harlan Reynolds, "It Takes a Militia: A Communitarian Case for Compulsory Arms Bearing," *William and Mary Bill of Rights Journal* 5 (1996): 185–214. Mark Phillips wrote that Senator John Chafee (R-RI) had mailed him a copy of our position paper and that in 1993 he introduced a bill to "prohibit the manufacture, importation, exportation, sale, purchase, transfer, receipt, possession, or transportation of handguns or handgun ammunition with certain exceptions." It was comforting to learn that the senator was aware of and had further circulated our position paper on the subject. E-mail correspondence received August 13, 2000.

372 *law review articles* Linda McClain, "Rights and Irresponsibility," *Duke Law Journal* 43 (March 1994): 989; Andrew Jay McClurg, "The Rhetoric of Gun Control," *American University Law Review* 42 (Fall 1992); Don B. Kates Jr., "Gun Control: Separating Reality from Symbolism," *Journal of Contemporary Law* 20 (1994); David B. Kopel and Christopher C. Little, "Communitarians, Neorepublicans, and Guns: Assessing the Case for Firearms Prohibition," *Maryland Law Review* 56 (1997); Denning and Reynolds, "It Takes a Militia."

372 *"three legs" approach* Amitai Etzioni, *Next: The Road to the Good Society* (New York: Basic, 2001); Amitai Etzioni, *The Third Way to a Good Society*, pamphlet, 63 pp. (London: Demos, 2000).

373 *inner-city communities* Stephen Goldsmith, "The City and Civil Society," *Civil Society Project* 3, no.1 (June 1997): 1–11.

373 *hub for community activities* Carolyn Denham and Amitai Etzioni, *Community Schools* (Washington, D.C.: The Communitarian Network, 1997).

373 *opposed censorship* Amitai Etzioni, Joel Federman, and Stephanie Carbone, *Controlling Television: Parental Filters: A Communitarian Report* (Washington, D.C.:

The Communitarian Network, 1997), at www.gwu.edu/~ccps/tv.html (accessed April 12, 2002); Amitai Etzioni, "ACLU Favors Porn over Parents," *Wall Street Journal*, October 14, 1998; Amitai Etzioni, "Suffer the Children," *Good Society: A PEGS Journal* 10, no. 1 (2001): 67–71.

373 *ethics in medicine*   Christine Cassel, Charles Dougherty, Amitai Etzioni, C. McCollister Evarts, John Griffith, James L. Nelson, Marian Osterweis, and Daniel Wikler, *Core Values in Health-Care Reform: A Communitarian Approach* (Washington, D.C.: The Communitarian Network, 1993), at www.gwu.edu/~ccps/Health2.html (accessed April 12, 2002).

374 *top fifty newspapers alone*   Numbers from Lexis-Nexis search in November 2000.

374 *responsibilities of test takers*   Available at www.apa.org/science/ttrr.html (accessed April 12, 2002).

374 Cambridge Educational   Cambridge Educational, Bill of Rights, Bill of Responsibilities (Charleston, W.Va.: Cambridge Research Group, 1995), 28 min.

374 *among thousands of others*   See, for example, www.cit.cornell.edu/computer/responsible-use; www.housing.uci.edu/och/landlordt.htm; www-saris.admin.umass.edu/rights (accessed April 12, 2002).

374 *editorial cartoon*   Tom Toles, *Washington Post*, September 24, 2002.

375 *started in the 1990s*   Francis Fukuyama, *The Great Disruption: Human Nature and the Reconstitution of Social Order* (New York: Free Press, 1999), 7, 59.

375 *moving up since 1990*   William J. Bennett, *Broken Hearth: Reversing the Moral Collapse of the American Family* (New York: Doubleday, 2001).

375 *Commission on Civic Renewal*   The National Commission on Civic Renewal's website is www.puaf.umd.edu/Affiliates/CivicRenewal (accessed October 23, 2002).

375 *"by the name of communitarianism"*   Alan Ehrenhalt, "Bill Clinton and the Communitarian Idea," *Governing* (February 1992): 13.

375 *Ehrenhalt then added*   Ehrenhalt, "Bill Clinton," 13.

376 *stresses moral obligation*   Robert Wright, "The False Politics of Values," *Time*, September 9, 1996, 42–45.

376 *"responsibility from all"*   Wright, "False Politics," 42–45.

376 *to the same effect*   Margaret Carlson and James Carney, "That's What Drives Me Nuts," *Time*, December 13, 1993. Kenneth T. Walsh, "Clinton's Journey Inward: He Seeks Answers to the Nation's Spiritual Crisis as Part of His Own Quest," *U.S. News & World Report*, December 13, 1993, 40–41, 44.

376 *"communitarian anthem"*   Charles J. Sykes, "Liberal Angst," *The World & I* (August 1993): 309–313.

376 *(finance reform, welfare reform)*   Joshua Abramowitz, "The Tao of Community," *Public Interest*, no. 113 (Fall 1993): 119–121.

377 *David Karp*   David Karp, "Americans as Communitarians: An Empirical Study," *Responsive Community* 7, no. 1 (Winter 1996/97): 42–51.

379 *"be Americans, period"* Karp, "Americans as Communitarians," 42–51.

379 *strong communitarian elements* See our position paper, "American Society in the Age of Terrorism," available from our website: www.gwu.edu/~ccps/news_american_ society.htlm (accessed December 16, 2003).

380 *honor you for it* Letter from William J. Bennett, *Responsive Community* 9, no. 1 (Winter 1998/99): 7.

380 *over communitarian ideas* Benjamin R. Barber, "Tough Questions for Liberal Communitarians," *Responsive Community* 9, no.1 (Winter 1998/99): 99.

381 *social theorists* Robert E. Goodin, "Making Communities More Responsive," *Responsive Community* 9, no. 1 (Winter 1998/99): 87–92.

381 *what he calls a communitarian movement* John Brandl, *Money and Good Intentions Are Not Enough, or Why a Liberal Democrat Thinks States Need Both Competition and Community* (Washington, D.C.: Brookings Institution, 1998).

384 *a global one* For my own views on this, see Amitai Etzioni, "On Ending Nationalism," *International Politics and Society* 4, no. 2 (2001): 144–153; Amitai Etzioni, "Implications of the American Anti-Terrorism Coalition for Global Architectures," *European Journal of Political Thought* 1, no. 1 (July 2002): 9–30; and Amitai Etzioni, "Beyond Transnational Governance," *International Journal* LVI, no. 4 (Autumn 2001): 595–610.

385 *(67 percent)* All poll data cited in this section is from Amitai Etzioni, *American Society in the Age of Terrorism* (Washington, D.C.: The Communitarian Network, 2002), at www.gwu.edu/~ccps/news_american_society.html (accessed October 16, 2002).

Notes for Chapter Seventeen

389 *under some such review* Robert E. Goodin, review of *Habits of the Heart*, by Robert Bellah et al., *Ethics* 96, no. 2 (1986): 431–432. Joseph Gusfield, "I Gotta Be Me," review of *Habits of the Heart*, by Robert Bellah et al., *Contemporary Sociology* 15, no. 1 (1986): 7–9. Michael A. Weinstein, "Disconnected Moralizing," review of *Habits of the Heart*, by Robert Bellah et al., *Journal of Politics* 48, no. 3 (1986): 746–748.

390 *thought out suggestion* Elizabeth Frazer, *The Problems of Communitarian Politics* (Oxford: Oxford University Press, 1999), 177.

390 *Henry Tam's* Communitarianism Henry Tam, *Communitarianism: A New Agenda for Politics and Citizenship* (New York: New York University Press, 1998).

390 The Common Sense of Community Dick Atkinson, *The Common Sense of Community* (London: Demos, 1994).

392 *but to no avail* For one of the few extensive treatments, see David C. Williams, "Pragmatism and Faith: Selznick's Complex Commonwealth," *Law and Social Inquiry* 19, no. 3 (1994): 775–801. A special session dedicated to Phil's work was part of the Communitarian Summit I organized in 1999.

393 *potential for abuse* Robert E. Goodin, "Making Communities More Responsive," *Responsive Community* 9, no. 1 (Winter 1998/99): 91.

393 *1999 communitarian summit* Nancy Rosenblum's new book speaks particularly to this issue. See Nancy L. Rosenblum, *Membership and Morals: The Personal Uses of Pluralism in America* (Princeton, N.J.: Princeton University Press, 1998).

393 *new communitarian position* Frazer, *Problems of Communitarian Politics*.

394 *liberty might vanish* William R. Lund, "Autonomy, Functionalism, and the Common Good: Some Liberal Doubts about *The New Golden Rule*," in *Autonomy and Order: A Communitarian Anthology*, ed. Edward W. Lehman (Lanham, Md.: Rowman & Littlefield, 2000), 1–22.

394 *"zero-sum game"* Otto Newman and Richard de Zoysa, *The American Dream in the Information Age* (New York: St. Martin's, 1999), 145.

394 *liberal pluralism* Paul Lichter, "Integrating Diversity: Boundaries, Bonds, and the Greater Community in *The New Golden Rule*," *Autonomy and Order: A Communitarian Anthology*, ed. Edward W. Lehman (New York: Rowman & Littlefield, 2000), 128.

394 *"freedom of the individual"* Aneta Gawkowska, "Neutrality, Autonomy and Order: Amitai Etzioni's Communitarian Critique of Liberalism under Scrutiny," in *A Decade of Transformation*, IWM Junior Visiting Fellows Conferences, vol. 8: Vienna 1999, 5. Available at: www.iwm.at/publ-jvc/jc-08-04.pdf (accessed October 23, 2002).

394 *championed by Milton Friedman* Elias L. Khalil, "Commitment, the Multiple-Self Approach, and Communitarianism," *Responsive Community* 9, no.1 (Winter 1998/99): 117–118.

394 *Ronald B. McCabe* Ronald B. McCabe, *Civic Librarianship* (Lanham, Md.: Scarecrow, 2001).

395 *instilled within us* Jeff Spinner-Halev, "The New Golden Rule: Community and Morality in a Democratic Society," *American Political Science Review* (September 1998): 680.

395 *"virtuous citizenry"* Everett C. Ladd, "Amitai Etzioni: An American Individualist," *Responsive Community* 9, no. 1 (Winter 1998/99): 93.

395 *"given back to the 'community'"* Frazer, *Problems of Communitarian Politics*, 72.

395 *"resolution by moral dialogue"* Linda E. Fisher, "Alcohol, Tobacco, and Firearms: Autonomy, the Common Good, and the Courts," *Yale Law & Policy Review* 18 (2000): 353.

396 *"chiefly rely upon"* Hillel Steiner, "Debate: Permissiveness Pilloried: A Reply to Etzioni," *Journal of Political Philosophy* 7, no. 1 (1999): 106.

396 *"a particular culture"* Amitai Etzioni, *The New Golden Rule: Community and Morality in a Democratic Society* (New York: Basic, 1996), 127.

396 *in postmodern societies* Benjamin D. Zablocki, "What Can the Study of Communities Teach Us about Community," in *Autonomy and Order: A Communitarian Anthology*, ed. Edward W. Lehman (Lanham, Md.: Rowman & Littlefield, 2000), 71–88.

396 *the way earlier ones did* Paul Lichterman, "Integrating Diversity: Boundaries, Bonds, and the Greater Community in *The Golden Rule*," in *Autonomy and Order: A Communitarian Anthology*, ed. Edward W. Lehman (Lanham, Md.: Rowman & Littlefield, 2000), 125–141.

396 *Nazi communities, for instance*   Steven Jones, review of *The New Golden Rule: Community and Morality in a Democratic Society*, by Amitai Etzioni, *H-Teachpol*, *H-Net Reviews* (April 1999), atwww.h-net.msu.edu/reviews/showrev.cgi?path=2348925237422 (accessed April 12, 2002).

396 *become authoritarian*   Zablocki, "What Can the Study of Communities Teach Us?" 71–88.

397 *against communitarian excesses*   Timothy L. Fort, "The First Man and the Company Man: The Common Good, Transcendence, and Mediating Institutions," *American Business Law Journal* 36 (April 1999): 391–435. For someone who is comfortable with the definition of community, see William J. Doherty, "Family Science and Family Citizenship: Toward a Model of Community Partnership with Families," *Family Relations* 49, no. 3 (2000): 319–325.

397 *"society can be built"*   Francis Fukuyama, "The New Golden Rule," *Foreign Affairs*, May 15, 1997, 123.

397 *"extended dialogue"*   Fukuyama, "New Golden Rule," 123.

397 *as far apart as they seem*   Hans Joas, "Procedure and Conviction: On Moral Dialogues," in *Autonomy and Order: A Communitarian Anthology*, ed. Edward W. Lehman (Lanham, Md.: Rowman & Littlefield, 2000).

397 *"impact on morality"*   Peter Seybold, review of *The New Golden Rule: Community and Morality in a Democratic Society*, by Amitai Etzioni, *Choice* 34 (July 1997): 1879. Charles Derber et al., *What's Left? Radical Politics in the Postcommunist Era* (Amherst: University of Massachusetts Press, 1995); Otto Newman and Richard de Zoysa, "Communitarianism: The New Panacea?" *Sociological Perspectives* 40, no. 4: 630. See also Thomas S. Martin, "There Goes the Neighborhood: The Communitarians Move In," *The Progressive Review* (October 1996): 6–11:

> The moral lessons of The Spirit of Community have about as much depth as "early to bed, early to rise." . . . Etzioni wants to re-create an America that never was. . . . [The Nation reporter] Stiehm's innocent-looking poll revealed that most communitarian pace-setters send their children to private schools, rarely use public transport, donate blood, attend free public events or serve on juries. . . . [Communitarian] economic analysis is strictly corporate, capitalist and elitist. It discounts the significance of class and assumes that everyone wants to live like the Nelsons and the Cleavers. . . . The goal here is regimentation and control for the sake of greater profits, make no mistake about it. (6–7, 10)

398 *"mutual concern"*   Steven Lukes, "The Responsive Community," *Dissent* (Spring 1998): 87–89.

399 *justify our disapproval*   Sanford Levinson, *Constitutional Faith* (Princeton, N.J.: Princeton University Press, 1988).

399 *(deontological position)*   For more discussion on this topic, see chapter 8 of Amitai Etzioni, *New Golden Rule*. In a review of *Autonomy and Order*, Jonathan Marks noted that the book's most important contribution to the debate is to point to the importance of self-evident truths to the communitarian position, but also the

need for further elaboration and justification of the claim. Jonathan Marks, "Beyond the New Golden Rule," *Responsive Community* 12, no. 3 (Summer 2002): 81–85.

399 *(long before the West)* Amartya Sen, "Human Rights and Asian Values," *New Republic*, July 14 and 21, 1997, 33–40.

399 *antirelativist position* J. Budziszewski, "The Problem with Communitarianism," *First Things* 51 (March 1995): 22–26.

400 *"topic of religion"* Thomas C. Kohler, "The Integrity of Unrestricted Desire: Community, Values, and the Problem of Personhood," in *Autonomy and Order: A Communitarian Anthology*, ed. Edward W. Lehman (Lanham, Md.: Rowman & Littlefield, 2000), 61. See also Mac McCorkle and David E. Price, "Wilson Carey McWilliams and Communitarianism," in *Friends and Citizens: Essays in Honor of Wilson Carey McWilliams*, ed. Peter Dennis Bathory and Nancy L. Schwartz (Lanham, Md.: Rowman & Littlefield, 2000).

400 *"notions of personal conscience"* Alan Deacon and Kirk Mann, "Agency, Modernity and Social Policy," *Journal of Social Policy* 28, no. 3 (1999): 426–427.

401 *"moral and political philosophy"* Don Browning, "When Theory Meets Practice: Communitarian Ethics and the Family," in *Marriage in America*, ed. Martin King White (Lanham, Md.: Rowman & Littlefield, 2000), 293.

401 *best academic tradition* Linda C. McClain and James E. Fleming, "Some Questions for Civil Society-Revivalists," *Chicago Kent Law Review* 75, no. 2 (2000): 301–354; Mike Bottery, "Getting the Balance Right: Duty as a Core Ethic in the Life of the School," *Oxford Review of Education* 25, no. 3 (1999): 370–385; Dora Shu-fang Dien, "Worldviews and Morality: How Do They Intersect?" *Human Development* 40 (1997): 345–349; Emma Heron and Peter Dwyer, "Doing the Right Thing: Labour's Attempt to Forge a New Welfare Deal between the Individual and the State," *Social Policy & Administration* 33, no. 1 (1999): 91–104; Craig Calhoun, "Community without Propinquity Revisited: Communications Technology and the Transformation of the Urban Public Sphere," *Sociological Inquiry* 68, no. 3 (1998): 373–397. See also Mike Bottery, "Education under the New Modernisers: An Agenda for Centralisation, Illiberalism, and Inequality?" *Cambridge Journal of Education* 29, no. 1 (1999): 103–120, in which he argues that the United Kingdom is more suitable for communitarianism than the United States. David Miller discusses the relationship among various types of political and philosophical communitarianism and defends what he calls "left communitarianism" in *Citizenship and National Identity* (Malden, Mass.: Polity, 2002), 97 ff.

Notes for Chapter Eighteen

406 *"I see, but cannot reach, the height"* Henry Wadsworth Longfellow, "A Village Church," *Christus: A Mystery*, II, ii.

410 *(individualized right to bear arms)* Amitai Etzioni, "Are Liberal Scholars Acting Irresponsibly on Gun Control?" *Chronicle of Higher Education*, April 6, 2001, B14–15.

414 *(causes and prevention of violence)* Amitai Etzioni, *Demonstration Democracy* (New York: Gordon & Breach, 1971).

415 *Copenhagen in 1995* The summit had three parts: officials, NGOs, and presentations of papers.

416 *asked me to write about it* Amitai Etzioni, "Suffer the Children," *The Good Society: A PEGS Journal* 10, no. 1 (2001): 67–71.

418 *"You'll love the freedom!"* Nicholas D. Kristof, "Visiting N.R.A. Heaven," *New York Times*, March 19, 2002.

418 *theoritician for totalitarianism* E-mail, November 4, 1999.

418 *"Roman Catholic upbringing"* T. R. Reid, *Confucius Lives Next Door* (New York: Random House, 1999), 172.

421 *ability to criticize us* E-mail correspondence from CPO James W. Gagin, received May 1, 2002.

421 *his son's little league team* Sara Rimer, "Forget Fenway, Phillies Were Sweet This Night," *New York Times*, June 11, 1996.

Notes for the Acknowledgments

428 *(able to document my account)* Amitai Etzioni, "Refugee Resettlement: The Infighting in Washington," *Public Interest*, no. 65 (Fall 1981): 15–29. Victor H. Palmieri and Amitai Etzioni, "The Refugees Controversy," *Public Interest*, no. 68 (Summer 1982): 88–92.